CW01263156

THE CLERICS OF ISLAM

THE CLERICS OF ISLAM

Religious Authority and Political Power in Saudi Arabia

Nabil Mouline

Translated by Ethan S. Rundell

Yale
UNIVERSITY PRESS
New Haven & London

Cet ouvrage publié dans le cadre du programme d'aide à la publication bénéficie
du soutien de La Mission culturelle et universitaire française aux Etats-Unis.
This work received support from the French Mission for Culture and
Higher Education through its publishing assistance program.

English translation copyright © 2014 by Yale University.
Originally published as *Les Clercs de l'islam*.
Copyright © Presses Universitaires de France, 2011.
All rights reserved.

This book may not be reproduced, in whole or in part, including illustrations,
in any form (beyond that copying permitted by Sections 107 and 108 of the
U.S. Copyright Law and except by reviewers for the public press), without
written permission from the publishers.

Yale University Press books may be purchased in quantity for educational, business,
or promotional use. For information, please e-mail sales.press@yale.edu (U.S. office)
or sales@yaleup.co.uk (U.K. office).

Maps and figures 4 and 6 by Mapping Specialists, Ltd.

Set in Postscript Electra and Trajan types by Newgen North America.
Printed in the United States of America.

Library of Congress Cataloging-in-Publication Data

Mouline, Nabil.
[Clercs de l'islam. English]
The clerics of Islam : religious authority and political power
in Saudi Arabia / Nabil Mouline ; translated by Ethan S. Rundell.
pages cm
Includes bibliographical references and index.
Translated from French.
ISBN 978-0-300-17890-6 (hardback)
1. Ulama—Saudi Arabia—History.   2. Wahhabiyah—Saudi Arabia—
History.   3. Islam and state—Saudi Arabia—History.   4. Islam and politics—
Saudi Arabia—History.   I. Rundell, Ethan S.   II. Title.
BP63.S33M6813 2014
297.6'109538—dc23
2014007139

A catalogue record for this book is available from the British Library.

This paper meets the requirements of ANSI/NISO Z39.48-1992 (Permanence of Paper).

10 9 8 7 6 5 4 3 2 1

Contents

	Introduction: The Ulama, Clerics of Islam	1
1	The Birth of the Hanbali Tradition	17
2	Shedding New Light on the Life of Muhammad Ibn Abd Al-Wahhab	46
3	Hanbali-Wahhabism in the Nineteenth Century: Grandeur and Decadence	70
4	The Birth of a Kingdom and the Renaissance of a Tradition	94
5	Routinization and Institutionalization of Hanbali-Wahhabism	119
6	The Committee of Grand Ulama: An Organization in the Service of the Prince . . . and the Population	146
7	Raising the Veil on the Conditions of Access to the Religious Establishment	171
8	Religious Authority in Practice: The Promotion of Virtue and the Prevention of Vice	203
9	At the Crossroads: The Religious Establishment Put to the Test of the Saudi Politico-Religious Space	235
	Conclusion	257

Appendix: House of Saud and Map of Saudi Arabia, 265
Notes, 269
Bibliography, 311

INTRODUCTION
The Ulama, Clerics of Islam

"The ulama are the heirs of the prophets."[1] Attributed to the prophet Muhammad (d. 632), this tradition reflects the importance assigned to clerics in Arab-Muslim culture. Although in theory Islam gives all believers equal access to the sacred, in practice Muslims have found it necessary to create a group of "specialists" authorized to interpret the holy texts and oversee worship. In other words, the representation of the divine, the systematization of belief, and the regulation of social behavior to achieve salvation all require "an independent and professionally trained priesthood, permanently occupied with the cult and with the practical problems involved in the cure of souls."[2] For, as Émile Durkheim claimed, without the support of regular religious and cultural activity, the gods vanish.[3]

The term "ulama," which comes from the Arabic *'ulama'*, the plural of *'alim*, is derived from the *'-l-m* root. In the Qur'an, the various schemata issuing from this root generally designate knowledge and understanding.[4] It is thus not surprising that the action noun *'ilm* should have been chosen starting in the late seventh century to designate all transcendent knowledge of divine origin (specifically, knowledge based on the Qur'an and what gradually came to be known as the prophetic tradition).[5] According to the text of the Qur'an, however, such knowledge is available only to men who possess certain intellectual and spiritual qualities.[6] Under the Umayyad Caliphate (661–750), an identifiable group thus emerged that was more or less differentiated by its training and socialization. By the first century of the Abbasid Caliphate (750–1258), this group had established itself as the *al-'ulama'*.[7] Its rise went hand in hand with the consecration of the Law (*al-shari'a*) as the true mystical body of classical Islamic civilization.[8]

As the self-proclaimed guardians of this mystical body, the ulama—literally, "those who know" or "those who possess religious knowledge"—were quick to organize themselves into corporations (whatever their politico-religious allegiances). In doing so, they sought not only to protect themselves, but also to influence and even direct the worldly and otherworldly affairs of the Islamic city. By "corporation," I am referring to the principles of organization of this profession-vocation, principles requiring that most of its members participate in its regulation and perpetuation. The identity of a corporation depends not on its mode of organization, which can vary across space and time, but rather on an institutional order built upon feelings of collective belonging (shared knowledge, representations, references, rites of initiation, and so on). This means that, while they may have particular interests, members of a corporation must share common beliefs. As in all institutions responsible for managing meaning, conflicts of interpretation and interest cut across the corporation of the ulama.

Beginning in the second half of the ninth century, the term '*ulama*' came to refer to an identifiable socioreligious role—that of managing, promoting, and passing on the religious tradition. Because of the centrality of the Law in all areas of Islamic society and the ulama's near monopoly on reading, writing, and the transmission of knowledge, this group became a "collective actor," with specific attributes in several domains, a fact that was reflected in an ever larger array of duties.[9] While recognizing the diversity of historical trajectories and politico-religious beliefs at play, one can nonetheless sketch these duties in ideal-typical fashion.

Above all, the ulama were, to borrow an expression from Max Weber, "technicians of the routine cults" responsible for dispensing salvation goods. To that end, they performed cultural, missionary, legal, and theological duties. In the latter two domains, the ulama's work consisted of interpreting scriptural sources with a twofold objective: to determine beliefs, the geography of heaven, and the image of God (orthodoxy), and to define appropriate socioreligious behaviors and practices (orthopraxy). Once this work of systematization and rationalization had been carried out, the ulama used their almost daily contact with the population to propagate the faith through prayer, predication, instruction, sermons, ritual processions, legal and theological consultations, writings, and so on.

The ulama's efforts at centralization and cognitive codification gradually gave rise to cultural imperialism (due to the centrality of the Law)—that is, a desire for domination in all domains of knowledge. This only gradually came to an end with the second half of the nineteenth century. By virtue of their monopoly on '*ilm*—seen as the only exact science because directly inherited from the Prophet via an uninterrupted chain of transmission (*sanad* and/or *silsila*)— the ulama controlled the various channels by means of which knowledge was transmitted. In this way, they were able to impose their vision of the world on much of the population, particularly on the elites. This also gave them control over "high culture," then as now the path par excellence to social promotion and identity formation by way of literary, historic, and scientific production.[10] It thus may be argued that the ulama were the genuine guardians of what the ancient Greeks referred to as *klerôs*—that is, the patrimony and heritage, spiritual and profane, of classical Islam. They therefore can be described as clerics.

But in order to impose their vision of the world and disseminate it, the ulama needed order. For this, they mainly depended on the political authorities in the framework of what I will refer to as a symbiotic relationship, that is, one that, with the support of the population, secures the interests of two parties ensconced at the summit of the social pyramid.[11] In exchange for the ulama's ideological support—which took the form, variously, of a codified principle of obedience, the establishment of tax law, apologetic discourses and writings, and the (de)mobilization of the population—the political authorities gave them a monopoly on worship and instruction as well as control over part of the public sphere (the legal system). They sometimes even enjoyed the financing necessary to enforce orthodoxy, orthopraxy, and the political order. The clerics' social capital also gave them access to the higher reaches of the state, where they served as chancellors, ambassadors, viziers, advisors to princes, and so on. However, we should not allow these observations to mislead us. The ulama pursued religious interests above all else, in particular that of maximizing the chances for salvation. Their participation in or support for political power was generally confined to the maintenance of order, the condition sine qua non for imposing orthodoxy and orthopraxy. Throughout the present study, I endeavor to keep this essential factor in sight.

THE POWER OF THE WORD: THE AUTHORITY OF THE RELIGIOUS ELITE

The sociological characteristics of this group make it "the solid framework of a permanent government behind changing dynasties."[12] Indeed, ulama are considered members of the Muslim world's oldest and most stable elite. As I use it in the present study, the term "elite" refers to a minority that, in a given society at a given time, enjoys prestige, influence, and privilege.[13] These prerogatives derive from socially valued qualities that are either natural or acquired, or both. The elite thus consists of groups that are strongly stratified and differentiated from the disorganized, noncohesive mass of the population.[14]

The prestige, influence, and privilege of the elite confer authority, that is, the power to command and to be obeyed. Whatever its mode of legitimation (sacred, political, or martial, for example), the concept of *authority* is at the origin of the social order. According to Émile Benveniste, the term *auctoritas* comes from the Indo-European root *aug-*, designating "a power of a particular nature and effectiveness, an attribute of the gods."[15]

The text of the Qur'an also states that authority is an exclusively divine attribute.[16] Yet God can delegate this attribute to some elected men. With the support of divine evidence (scriptural testimony, miracles, and so on), the elected become mediators between God and humans.[17] Thanks to this type of "charismatic authority" (Weber), the Prophet Muhammad was able to establish a new social order and lay the foundations of an empire and civilization. But the death of this transcendent guarantor of truth raised the problem of how to routinize his charisma. Who, in other words, was to inherit his prerogatives?

Initially, it was the caliphs who did so, and for two reasons. First, they claimed to be the vicars of God on earth responsible for managing all affairs of the Islamic city. Second, the dedifferentiation of primitive Islamic society meant there was no body in charge of managing the goods of salvation. But the structural changes that occurred in the first century of the Hegira challenged the caliphs' theocratic pretensions.[18] Indeed, the rapid expansion of the Islamic empire required the establishment of stable organizational, legislative, and cultural frameworks for consolidating the structure of the state and strengthening the conquerors' sense of identity. This period was also characterized by politico-religious struggles within the *umma* (the Islamic community). These gradually undermined the legitimacy of the caliphs.

The concomitance of these factors favored the emergence of the corporation of the ulama, which, starting in the second half of the ninth century, recuperated a large portion of the caliphs' religious authority. Nevertheless, as leaders of their respective communities, the caliphs and their successors retained some of their duties in the religious domain (such as protection of the religious order, promotion of the faith, nomination of religious officers, and oversight of financial matters). This explains the influential place that politics has occupied in the religious domain through to the present. What, then, is the nature of the ulama's authority? Responding to this question requires us to call upon the tripartite typology of authority developed by Max Weber.[19]

Weber first identifies *traditional authority*, which is based on "customs sanctified by their immemorial validity and man's deep-rooted habit of respecting them."[20] Indeed, the ulama claimed to be the exclusive guardians of the tradition inherited from *al-salaf al-salih*—that is, the first generations of Muslims. The authenticity and power of this tradition were guaranteed by an uninterrupted chain of transmission (whether familial, esoteric, or exoteric in nature).

Second is *charismatic authority*, which is "based on the personal and extraordinary grace of an individual (charisma); it is characterized by the entirely personal devotion of subjects to the cause of a man and their confidence in his person alone, which is seen as distinguished by prodigious qualities."[21] Arab-Muslim history abounds with charismatic religious figures. These mainly fall within the scope of two ideal-typical dynamics: the messianism of the eschatological figures of the *al-Mahdi* (the Messiah) and the *Mujahid* (the combatant of the faith) on the one hand, and the religious reformism of the figures of the *al-Mujaddid* (the reformer of the century) and the *al-Mujtahid* (the independent jurist) on the other.

The third and last type of authority Weber identified is *legal-rational authority*, which "is necessary in virtue of 'legality,' in virtue of belief in the validity of a legal status and a positive 'competence' based on rationally established rules."[22] As experts of the scriptures and/or institutional agents (judges, muftis, *muhtasibs*, directors of madrasas, stewards of mortmain goods, members of a council of ulama, leaders of a brotherhood, and so on), certain ulama can command the population's obedience. In other words, they succeed in imposing their vision thanks to their learning and/or the charisma of their office.

While the ulama's authority does indeed reflect these three ideal-typical forms, which in practice intertwine and overlap one another, Weber's typology nevertheless fails to capture the real nature of that authority. This is because, as David E. Willer has shown, the typology is incomplete.[23] As we see in Table 1, Weber distinguishes among four types of social action and four types of social order legitimization, yet he identifies only three types of authority.[24]

In order to complete the Weberian schema, Willer proposes that we use the term "ideological" to refer to the ideal-type of authority that follows from action that is rational in value because it entails "belief in the absolute value of a rationalized structure of norms."[25] This type of authority, in other words, is based on the symbolic power of an *enunciator*—in general, a collective actor—to produce and transform beliefs inspired by a *first reference* (revelation, instruction, ideology, and so on). According to Roberta Lynn Satow, this type of authority allows those who hold it to meet a twofold challenge: to ensure the survival of an ideology promoted by a charismatic leader, and to allow it to be adapted to changing circumstances. To this end, those who hold ideological authority apply, not an *ethic of conviction*, but rather an *ethic of responsibility* implying a proper balance between moral demands and political and historical imperatives.[26] Moreover, ideological authority does not exclude recourse to legal-rational structures (systems

Table 1. Weber's Typology of Authority

Type of social action[a]	Instrumentally rational The activity is determined by expectations concerning the behavior of objects in the external world or that of other people, with these expectations used as "conditions" or "means" for rationally attaining the carefully considered aims one wishes to achieve.	Value rational The activity is determined by belief in the unconditional intrinsic value—whether ethical, aesthetic, religious, or other—of a given behavior that is valuable in itself and independently of its result.	Affectual The activity is determined by present feelings and sentiments.	Traditional The action is determined by well-established custom.
Type of social order legitimation[b]	Legal Positive disposition toward the legal order in which one believes.	Value rational Rational belief according to values: validity of that which one takes to be an absolute.	Affectual Belief in an affective (and, in particular, emotional) order; validity of the new revelation or of exemplarity.	Traditional Validity of what has always been.
Type of authority	Legal-rational	[Lacking in Weber]	Charismatic	Traditional

[a]Weber, *Economy and Society*, pp. 24–25.
[b]Ibid., p. 36.

and places of socialization, tools of ideological transmission, the administrative apparatus, financial resources, and so on) to realize its twofold objective.

Thanks to the information supplied by Willer and Satow, it can be said that the figure of the ʿalim is legitimated in ideal-typical manner by means of ideological authority. Indeed, the traditional, legal-rational, and charismatic authority of the clerics of Islam for the most part depends on the "proper" use of ideology.

Texts are never authorities in themselves. They must be gathered together, authenticated, linguistically and symbolically interpreted by authorized "readers" (the ulama), and legitimated in the context of a discursive and ideological system. It is only once this has taken place that texts acquire meaning and performative status. And while the ulama have always claimed that the fabrication of meaning was only the result of a humble attempt to comment upon the texts, "one must have no illusions concerning this pious under-statement: these are effective alterations, invisible rectifications, discrete nudges in the right direction."[27] The ulama, in other words, depend on revelation to elaborate a homogenous system of beliefs and representations regarding not only the afterlife, but also the sociopolitical organization of the city. Religion in this way acquires an ideological dimension.

It nevertheless must be noted that, to the degree that it is based on the interpretation of an absolute value, ideological authority can be debated, reinterpreted, and challenged in the name of that same value. Indeed, seen in an ideal-typical perspective, the corporation of the ulama is riven by ideological conflict (the result of dogmatic, methodological, political, and material divergences as well as the intervention of power). This gives rise to interpretive disagreement and, as a result, a multitude of paths to salvation and various ways of organizing the city. The emergence of subcorporations (legal and theological schools, mystical brotherhoods, politico-religious movements and parties, and so on) is a natural consequence of these disagreements. By adding the figure of an eponymous founder—the symbol of an orthodox interpretation of the texts and continuity with the golden age of Islam—these subcorporations almost fully reproduce the schema of the corporations from which they have broken.

The aim of the present book is to test this model of authority by applying it to the Saudi case. We thus examine the corporation of the ulama, which claims to represent the spiritual and temporal heritage of Muhammad ibn Abd al-Wahhab (d. 1792), himself a product of the Hanbali juridico-theological school. Before doing so, however, we must first define the nature and contours of this corporation, which dominates the socioreligious space of Saudi Arabia, as well as the sociopolitical framework in which it evolved.

WAHHABISM, HANBALISM, OR SALAFISM? THE CHOICE OF TERMINOLOGY

Since the second half of the eighteenth century, those who inherited the symbolic capital of Ibn Abd al-Wahhab in the central Arabian region of Najd have referred to themselves by several terms. These have included *al-Muwahhidun* or *Ahl al-Tawhid* (the people of the unity of God),[28] *'Ulama' al-Da'wa al-Islamiyya* (the ulama of Islamic predication),[29] and *A'immat al-Da'wa al-Najdiyya* (the guides of Najdi predication).[30] They have also referred to their doctrine as *al-da'wa al-islamiyya* (Islamic predication),[31] *al-tariqa al-Muhammadiyya* (the path of the Prophet Muhammad),[32] and *al-tariqa al-salafiyya* (the way of the pious ancestors).[33] And of course it should not be forgotten that they also claim to be followers of Hanbalism.[34] These various terms all reflect an obvious desire on the part of Najd ulama to identify themselves with the most orthodox Islamic tradition. Whereas the unity of God is at the very heart of the Muslim religion, the Prophet and the pious ancestors guarantee a direct line to the truth. The Hanbalis, for their part, see themselves as the heirs, guardians, and transmitters of orthodoxy and orthopraxy. Residing in the heart of the Arabian Peninsula, Najd ulama thus see themselves as the exclusive guardians of the "True Religion."

But this claim was contested even during Ibn Abd al-Wahhab's lifetime. Indeed, competing religious leaders and corporations described the followers of the Najdi preacher as *wahhabiyya*.[35] With the help of Ottoman propaganda, which was hostile to the movement, this pejorative designation spread like wildfire, reducing the new predication to little more than a marginal and extremist sect in thrall to a preacher who was as conceited as he was ignorant.

Though they initially rejected the word with all their strength, the ulama of the Najdi predication—an expression that I provisionally use to designate the corporation—seem to have eventually accepted it as a fait accompli, even referring to themselves with the term "wahhabiyya" from the turn of the twentieth century. In the absence of sources on this question, we do not know what caused this change of attitude or how it occurred. Whatever the case, Sulayman ibn Sahman (d. 1930), one of the most active *'alim* in the service of the Najdi predication, titled two of his most important works *The Sublime Present and the Najdi Wahhabi Jewel* and *Wahhabi Thunderbolts Launched against the Lying Syrian Assertions*.[36] In his other works, he abundantly used "Wahhabi" with approbation. A verse that appears in one of his poems nicely illustrates this process of appropriation: "Yes, we are Wahhabis, the true monotheists who make our enemies suffer."[37] The *'alim* Ahmad ibn Isa (d. 1911), for his part, titled one of his epistles *The Refutation of the Accusations Formulated by Dahlan against the Wahhabis in His History of Mecca and Its Emirs*.[38] Finally, it is claimed that other ulama used the term in a positive manner.[39] For example, Muhammad ibn Abd al-Latif (d. 1947), descendent of Ibn Abd al-Wahhab, often said that "people hear about us Wahhabis but no one knows the reality of our doctrine."[40] Up until the end of the 1920s, the official Saudi journal also used the term.[41]

In a similar vein, Arab supporters of the nascent, early-twentieth-century Saudi Kingdom adopted the word "wahhabiyya" in their apologetic works. Muhammad Rashid Rida (d. 1935) was the most influential reformer of his era, thanks to the large circulation of *Al-Manar* magazine. In 1904, he began to devote a large number of articles to the Najdi predication. Some of these were later republished in a collection titled *The Wahhabis and the Hejaz*.[42] In 1935, the reformer Muhammad Hamid al-Fiqi (d. 1959) published his book *The Influence of Wahhabi Predication on Religious and Social Reform in the Arab Peninsula and Elsewhere*.[43] One year later, *The Wahhabi Revolution* was published by Abd Allah al-Qasimi (d. 1996).[44]

These examples show that the term "wahhabiyya" was on its way to being normalized at the start of the twentieth century. For political reasons that we discuss below, however, King Abd al-Aziz (1902–1953) prohibited official use of it beginning in 1929, preferring the term *al-salafiyya*.[45] The latter enjoys a very positive connotation in Muslim circles thanks to the work of Arab-Muslim reformers since the end of the nineteenth century.[46] All of these terms nevertheless continue to be used in scholarly work, whether hostile or favorable to the Najdi predication, and reflect a genuine difficulty of identification and a source of confusion. This difficulty must be overcome before we move on to consider the structures and historical trajectory of the corporation of Najd ulama whose doctrines and practices dominate Saudi life.

It is first necessary to set aside the term *al-salafiyya*, a source of confusion that precludes proper understanding of the religious and political phenomena of contemporary Islam. Contrary to a widely held view, *al-salafiyya* is not a dogma (*'aqida*), legal school (*madhhab*), spiritual path (*tariqa* or *minhaj*), or political project. Like nearly all Islamic politico-religious movements since the High Middle Ages, it is simply a way to legitimate a political and/or religious approach and lend it historico-salvational depth. Islam is a justified religion; that is, all reforms must be perceived as returning to an original message. The referential framework for all of these movements thus becomes the "first century of the Hegira, this golden age that was the time of the Prophet and his Companions, and the first four centuries of the caliphs, the rightly guided (*rashidun*);

the kingdom of God on Earth, where the law of the Qur'an, the supreme seal of the Prophet, suffices to perfectly guide men in all the main lines of their temporal activities and toward the rewards of the other life."[47] Assigning the epithet *salafi* to an individual or group of individuals thus amounts to committing a twofold error: using a "catch-all" term to designate protean sociohistoric realities, and making a value judgment that legitimates a given individual or group of individuals to the detriment of others. In this way, we end up playing the actors' game, a pitfall that must be avoided at all costs. I thus propose to substitute an "objective" term drawn from the characteristics of the Najdi predication.

Like other corporations of ulama, followers of the Najdi predication seek to impose the "three O's": *orthodoxy, orthopraxy*, and political *order*. Orthodoxy, or the set of dogmas that are taken for norms of religious truth, supposes the existence of a theology. As we will see, the Najdis are in this respect Hanbalis: the writings of Ibn Abd al-Wahhab merely recapitulate and vulgarize a miniscule part of a thousand-year-old theological tradition. This is also the case in the domain of orthopraxy, or the set of behaviors that seek to literally reflect the original meaning of the scriptures in order to achieve salvation. Here, too, the Najdis are faithful followers of the Hanbali school. Without a doubt, the originality of Ibn Abd al-Wahhab's work resides in his effective and crucial participation in the foundation of a political order: the Saudi Emirate. At the start of the twentieth century, the emirate transformed itself into a kingdom, and to this day, it continues to dominate much of the Arab Peninsula. Since the second half of the eighteenth century, the ulama have contributed to the management and protection of this political entity at all levels.

"Hanbali-Wahhabism" is thus the term that most closely captures the doctrinal specificities, legal-political principles, and historical trajectory of the corporation of ulama who identify with the life and teachings of Muhammad ibn Abd al-Wahhab.

Throughout the present book, we consider Hanbali-Wahhabism as a tradition—that is, "a collection of ritual and symbolic practices that are normally governed by openly or tacitly accepted rules and seek to inculcate certain values and behavioral norms by repetition, something that automatically implies continuity with the past."[48] Tradition, of course, is a "conservative and protective power." But it is also "instructive and innovative. Turned lovingly toward the past where its treasure is located, it advances into the future, where its conquest and light are to be found. For it, even discovery involves the humble feeling of faithful rediscovery."[49] In other words, if tradition is to realize its ultimate objectives—the conservation and transmission of ancient statements and rituals capable of facilitating access to salvation—it must be discreetly adapted to the particularities of each period and population.

Moreover, as a device for legitimizing the power of the House of Saud, the Hanbali-Wahhabi tradition also contains an ideological dimension. The term "ideology" thus is used in the present book to refer to a coherent collection of concepts, images, symbols, and beliefs relating to the sociopolitical organization of the community.

POWER, RELIGION, KINSHIP, AND RENT: THE CHARACTERISTICS OF A PATRIMONIAL ROYALTY

In order to better understand the role played by the Hanbali-Wahhabi ulama in the various phases of the history of the Saudi political entity, some fundamental aspects of its political sociology must be taken into account. I do not intend to be exhaustive here; rather, I hope to present several salient facts that we consider later in greater detail.

The first of these concerns the alliance between the political and religious authorities. In addition to giving birth to the Saudi political entity, the symbiotic relationship that was established between Muhammad ibn Abd al-Wahhab and Muhammad ibn Saud (1744–1765) around 1744 also allowed each of the partners to consolidate their positions and extend their respective spheres of influence. Thanks to the unconditional support of the guardians of the Hanbali-Wahhabi tradition, Saudi sovereigns were able to adopt an imperial approach, conducting a hegemonic policy throughout the Arabian Peninsula and its surroundings. After many vicissitudes (about which more below), this dynamic led to the creation of the Kingdom of Saudi Arabia in 1932. Indeed, in the interest of establishing the new kingdom's religious legitimacy, historical rootedness, and place in salvation—a schema familiar in the Muslim world since the High Middle Ages—the ulama mobilized all available symbolic and ideological resources on behalf of the political authorities. The authorities, for their part, offered the ulama the resources necessary to promote and export Hanbali-Wahhabism. In short, the legitimacy of the political power is mainly based on this tradition while the authority and prestige of the ulama almost entirely depend on Saud support. Genuine elective affinity thus exists between the political power and the religious authority in Saudi Arabia. As Paul Veyne has written, "we all know that religious sincerity and the most worldly of interests can often make good bedfellows."[50] To this, it must be added that the kingdom contains the two holy sites of Islam (Mecca and Medina), which lend it a prestige, legitimacy, and responsibility that redound to the credit of the ruling family and the ulama.

The fact that Saudi territories were never colonized by Western powers should also be taken into account. Indeed, unlike the overwhelming majority of Arab-Islamic nation-states that arose in opposition to and/or with the help of Western powers, Saudi Arabia even succeeded in escaping Ottoman domination. To a large extent, the emergence of the Saudi state reflected a longer-term dynamic of Islamic history. While it required that a certain number of Western norms and institutions be introduced over the course of the twentieth century, it in no way diminished the belief in Islamic superiority. Also, the notion that the state was fundamentally Islamic in nature remained central to efforts to legitimate political power and continued to inflect processes of state and identity formation within the Saudi discursive system. As guardians of the religious tradition, the ulama were never marginalized in the manner of their counterparts elsewhere in the Arab-Muslim world. As we will see, however, they did lose a part of their prerogatives over the course of the twentieth century.

The third aspect of Saudi political sociology that needs to be recalled here is the patrimonial nature of the Saudi Kingdom. This type of exercise of power is characterized by confusion between public and private as well as between natural and legal personhood in the management of state affairs. It is also distinguished by the interpenetration of the political, economic, social, and domestic domains.[51] In short, the holder of patrimonial power "treats all political, administrative and judicial affairs as if they were personal matters, in the same way that he exploits his domain as if it were personal property."[52] According to Max Weber, patrimonialism gives rise to such phenomena as nepotism, clannishness, and clientelism, all of which are readily observable at all levels of the Saudi state, particularly within the corporation of the ulama.[53]

By treating the conquered territories as Saud family property, the very name chosen for the new kingdom nicely reflects this patrimonial conception of politics. In fact, the Sauds administer the country like a "house," in Claude Lévi-Strauss's sense of the term.[54] The cohesion of such a house is based mainly on personal ties that are generally expressed in the language of kinship (whether real or fictive, biological or spiritual). In the Saudi case, these ties appear to play a crucial role in social mobility to the degree that certain claims of law, status, and power depend, in Alfred Radcliffe-Brown's phrase, "on a network of genealogical relations."[55] Ibn Khaldun, for his part, used the term *'asabiyya*—that is, spirit of kinship in the family or tribe—to describe this phenomenon. In this country, the preeminence of personal ties at all levels of social interaction produces common interests and interdependence among the ruling elites, whatever their professional backgrounds. This dyadic relationship encourages us to adopt a monistic approach toward these elites.[56] The present book supplies empirical confirmation of this premise.

The fourth specificity worth underscoring here is the rentier nature of the Saudi state during the second half of the twentieth century.[57] The resilience, resonance, and expansion of the corporation of Hanbali-Wahhabi ulama cannot be properly appreciated if this characteristic is not taken into account. Indeed, the flow of petroleum revenue freed the monarchy from the need to draw upon other sources of legitimation, allowing it to strengthen its alliance with the ulama. As we will see below, the ulama used their access to political power to establish vast religious, educational, and charitable infrastructures far exceeding in scale those found in other Muslim countries. At the same time, the political authorities had to find openings for the thousands of graduates of religious institutions and maintain a very costly two-track legal system. This allowed the corporation to control a large part of Saudi social space and spread its beliefs and prestige across the planet, something that would have been unimaginable without its petroleum rent.

THE SAUDI ULAMA PUT TO THE TEST OF TIME AND SOCIAL SPACE: SOME INTERPRETIVE HYPOTHESES

These fundamental aspects of Saudi political sociology made the Hanbali-Wahhabi ulama key actors in the social space. It should be emphasized here that the present book considers only one category of cleric: the official ulama who form what I henceforth refer to as the "religious establishment." In discussing contemporary Saudi Arabia, I mainly study members of the Committee of Grand Ulama, the foremost body of the Saudi religious system.[58] When examining the preceding period, by contrast, I consider both the ulama and other religious agents who acted under the authority of the chief of the religious establishment.

Several considerations have determined this choice. They include Hanbali-Wahhabism's status as the dominant religious tradition and ideology in the service of the Saudi monarchy since the second half of the eighteenth century; the corporation's social and intellectual homogeneity, which allow one to easily test interpretive hypotheses; and finally, the paucity of works on this subject and their fragmentary character, which do not allow a general appreciation of the permanence and importance of the religious establishment.

It should be added that for some scholars and observers, the Saudi religious establishment is an opaque body that exists only to satisfy the desires of the ruling house, considerations that render it an unworthy subject of study in their eyes. The present book seeks to move beyond this view. Indeed, certain politico-religious phenomena—the hegemony of religious discourse in Saudi Arabia, the religious pretentions of the Saud, the Ikhwan, the Juhayman messianic group, and various Islamist factions and Jihadist groups—cannot be properly studied without prior knowledge of the history and sociology of the Hanbali-Wahhabi establishment.

The aim of this book is to reconstruct this history and sociology by attending to the particular challenge facing all corporations that depend on ideological authority for their legitimacy: managing change while remaining faithful to the original message of a charismatic leader. I seek to analyze the manner in which the ulama reacted to the issues of their times and, more particularly, how they assessed and attempted to formulate ideological and organizational responses to sociopolitical disruption and the emergence of new phenomena. In other words, I examine the manner in which they established and implemented an *ethic of responsibility* that evenly balanced spiritual obligations with temporal constraints and other, related difficulties. I consider the process by which Hanbali-Wahhabism was routinized and transformed from what Jan Assman calls a "counterreligion" into a state religion seeking not to integrate the family of "orthodox" Islamic traditions but to dominate it.[59] This central question is the corollary of equally important issues, including the processes by which the ulama are socialized, the conditions of access to the religious establishment, the nature and operation of ulama-led organizations, the theologico-religious leanings of the ulama, their political stance, their relations with society, and the manner in which they have responded to historical and social contingencies. In short, how has the Saudi religious establishment adapted to protect the three O's: orthodoxy, orthopraxy, and the political order?

My analysis is based on an historical sociology or sociological history type approach, with "sociology" understood in Max Weber's sense of the term as synonymous with political science. This sometimes involves explaining historical events in terms of such concepts as charisma and routinization (sociological history). At other times, it is a matter of fleshing out these concepts with the aid of historical examples (historical sociology). This approach attempts to set social phenomena in their historical *longue durée* in order to identify the contexts in which they emerged and developed. It reconciles the role played by structures and actors' strategies, respectively, by foregrounding analysis of their itineraries and interactions. It is for this reason that the various chapters of the present volume are organized around one or several central figures in the Hanbali-Wahhabi tradition. Finally, this approach encourages comparison wherever possible and relevant.

AVOIDING THE BIOGRAPHICAL ILLUSION: A WORD ABOUT SOURCES

The sociological history approach entails recourse to the methods of both disciplines. The better part of the resources upon which I draw in my discussion of contemporary Saudi Arabia are the product of fieldwork carried out in that country between April 2005 and March 2010. In the course of my visits, I was able to conduct about one hundred interviews with various actors (members of the Committee of Grand Ulama, highly placed religious officials, university professors, Islamist ulama, ulama representing other traditions, Islamist and liberal intellectuals, and observers of clerical circles). These were accompanied by dozens of informal interviews and participant observation sessions.

My interviews with members of the Committee of Grand Ulama and highly placed religious officials were organized around three main lines of inquiry. An initial series of questions allowed me to establish the origin, training, and professional trajectory of my interlocutors. Since the theologico-juridical positions of members of the religious establishment generally coincide with particular social and political leanings, a second set of questions raised various legal and theological problems—*al-fatwa* (the delivery of juridico-religious opinions), *al-nasiha* (advice), *waliyy al-amr* (the holder of legitimate power), *al-takfir* (excommunication), and so on. A third series of questions was devoted to my interlocutors' representations and sociopolitical roles, the body to which they belonged (the Committee of Grand Ulama, the Supreme Council of the Magistracy, the Ministry of Justice, the Ministry of Islamic Affairs, or the Committee for the Promotion of Virtue and the Prevention of Vice, and so on) and their positions vis-à-vis the other currents that have evolved in the Saudi politico-religious space. Finally, a last set of questions allowed me to collect information concerning poorly documented historical events in which some of the ulama with whom I spoke had participated.

In order to put the religious dignitaries at ease and collect as much information as possible, I attempted to proceed in what most of my interlocutors regarded as the "traditional" manner: *tarjama*. Indeed, the members of the establishment are familiar with this type of exercise. In their imaginary, the "laudatory biography" is reserved for the great men of Islam.[60] But the scholar must avoid the biographical illusion that confuses, in Pierre Bourdieu's expression, "history with the account of that history."[61] These *tarajim* (sing. *tarjama*), in other words, are a posteriori constructions that tend to idealize a career or life. Much of the information I received thus required verification, in particular via comparison with what other actors told me. In order to supplement, enrich, and give context to this data, I also systematically monitored "new media" sources (Internet and satellite networks). The use of the Internet as a research tool was of great assistance thanks to the vast trove of information available at Saudi websites, forums, and electronic libraries. Keeping abreast of the kingdom's socioreligious space via satellite television, in turn, allowed me to fully grasp the terms and evolution of discourse and debate in the country. I was also attentive to "classic" media outlets (newspapers and radio), which were important sources for this work. Official documents (such as royal decrees, regulations, circulars, communiqués, and decisions from the Committee of Grand Ulama) were also used.

Finally, systematic study and analysis of the principal historiographical, biographical, theological, and legal texts produced by Hanbali-Wahhabi ulama from Ibn Abd al-Wahhab (d. 1792) to Abd al-Aziz ibn Baz (d. 1999), together with that of their classical predecessors,[62] made it possible for me to locate this tradition in a diachronic and synchronic perspective through observation of its representatives and the concepts they wield.

1

THE BIRTH OF THE HANBALI TRADITION

THE EMERGENCE OF SCRIPTURAL SPECIALISTS

The political quarrels that followed the death of the Prophet Muhammad in 632 were driven by personal rivalry, factional conflict, and the question of how power was to be transmitted.[1] By contrast, the nature, legitimacy, and prerogatives of the institution of the Caliphate were almost never called into question. The first caliphs—or, as they were later known, the Rightly Guided Caliphs (*al-Khulafa' al-Rashidun*) (632–661)—inherited the religious authority and kingly prerogatives of the Prophet.

Though excluded from divine revelation, the first Muslim sovereigns enjoyed extensive prerogatives in the religious, legal, and political domains thanks to their messianic status. This status conferred a variety of titles, including God's Vicar on Earth (*khalifat Allah*), Commander of the Faithful Destined to Subjugate the World (*amir al-mu'minin*), and Inspired Guide (*imam*).[2] The caliph Umar ibn al-Khattab (634–644), for example, laid down new laws in all domains, from the establishment of the Hegira calendar to the institution of supererogatory prayers performed during the nights of the month of Ramadan (*al-tarawih*), a ban on temporary marriage (*zawaj al-mut'a*), and regulation of the status of non-Muslim populations (*ahl al-dhimma*).[3] It subsequently proved very difficult to conceal this historical reality, and the tradition was ultimately obliged to accept it, though it attempted to mitigate its effect by circulating hadith attributed to the Prophet. The most famous of these is, "If there were yet another prophet after me, it would surely be Umar [bin al-Khattab]."[4] In other words, the founder of Islam recognized and conferred a posteriori legitimacy upon the exceptional power of his first successors. These successors were vested with sacred status, and many of their deeds came to be seen as supplying nearly compulsory norms of behavior.

The political projects of the Umayyad (661–750) and early Abbasid (750–1258) caliphs were inspired by this foundational period. These sovereigns, whose approach in several ways resembled Byzantine caesaropapism, energetically intervened in the political, legal, and theological domains.[5] They believed that their status permitted them to govern relations between people as well as humanity's relationship to God.[6] Indeed, they claimed to be the true mystical body of the nascent Islamic community—that is, the at once symbolic and institutional link connecting the believer to the community's historico-salvational past and, through it, to God himself. The term *bay'a*, which refers to the oath of absolute allegiance sworn by believers to the caliphs, clearly expresses the caliphs' desire to establish themselves as a focal point and essential transcendental link on the path to salvation. This stance was inspired by a Qur'anic verse in which the Prophet is told that "those who swear an oath of allegiance to you are only swearing an oath to God."[7] As Patricia Crone and Martin Hinds have shown, the caliphs felt in no way inferior to Muhammad. They thus applied this verse to themselves: failure to obey their commands was seen as disobedience to God himself and was therefore punishable by immediate exclusion from the community of eternal salvation.[8] In practice, the sovereigns of the two dynasties continued to create legislation in various domains and even claimed to establish *sunna*, that is, normative rules covering issues not addressed in the Qur'an.[9] Considered to be one of the oldest and best known compilations of traditions, the *Muwatta'* of traditionalist Malik ibn Anas (d. 795) thus contains a large number of norms decreed by the Umayyad caliphs.[10] Later compilations followed the same route.

To summarize, the caliphs of the first century of the Hegira claimed and exercised theocratic power. As in all traditional monarchical systems, this power was based on the sovereign's privileged relationship with God. As *khalifat Allah*, the sovereign received superhuman inspiration (*al-ra'y*), making him the community's inspired and nearly infallible (*ma'sum*) guide (*al-imam*).

As Hamid Dabashi has pointed out, however, these theocratic pretensions were gradually called into question as a result of the major structural disruptions attendant upon the great conquests.[11] The politico-military expansion of the Islamic empire required that a large number of administrative, religious, and cultural structures be established in order to more effectively dominate the conquered territories and ensure the cohesion of the dominant group. To this must be added the emergence of politico-religious movements contesting the legitimacy of the power of the caliphs, whose lifestyle, which was worthy of the Byzantine and Sassanid courts, gradually distanced them from the primitive Islamic ideal.[12]

As a result of all these changes, a group of men interested by the *klerôs* gradually made their appearance over the course of the late seventh century. This group exhibited a threefold, ideal-typical dynamic. The first dynamic resulted from the caliphal authorities' need to rationalize the religious domain upon which they based their legitimacy. Their efforts focused on Qur'anic exegesis, the organization of worship, the apology of Islam vis-à-vis other religions, and above all the establishment of a legal norm for managing all aspects of community life. In pursuit of these efforts, the sovereigns gave pious individuals—of whom the most famous was Ibn Shihab al-Zuhri (d. 742)—responsibility for establishing an official religious system. The second dynamic was the work of the informal circles that had emerged around such pious figures as al-Hasan al-Basri (d. 728) and the Seven *Faqihs* (*al-Fuqaha' al-Sab'a*) of Medina. These began to discuss religious learning and established an embryonic methodology for interpreting the Qur'an and transmitting knowledge. The third dynamic resulted from the activities of politico-religious opposition groups. As part of their efforts to develop a powerful and legitimate counterdiscourse, these groups found themselves obliged to study and interpret the holy text.[13]

The interaction of these three ideal-typical environments gave rise to the figure of the *'alim*. Thanks to the establishment of an increasingly structured process of socialization and ever more sophisticated rules of interpretation, the figure of the *'alim* ultimately imposed himself as the authorized reader and interpreter of the holy text. The emergence of the prophetic hadith as a second scriptural source cemented the growing power of the ulama. Indeed, prophetic traditions began to acquire importance as performative and normative texts around the end of the seventh century, concomitant with the emergence of Muhammad as the central figure of Islam. This was due to two factors: on the one hand, the struggle against the Byzantine Empire obliged the caliphs to promote the figure of Muhammad to the status of Prophet of the Arabs, following the example of the biblical prophets; on the other, the politico-religious vicissitudes that roiled the *umma* throughout the first century of the Hegira established the Prophet as a common, abstract, and suprafactional reference. After all, did not the Qur'an inform the faithful that "in the messenger of Allah, you have an excellent model [to follow] for whoever hopes in Allah and the Last Day and invokes Allah frequently"?[14] As a result, the hadith became more than a political weapon legitimating this or that position; it was henceforth also a source of law and theology that completely escaped the caliphs' control.[15] The *sunna*, with a lowercase "s," which indiscriminately referred to the legal-religious maxims of the Prophet and those of the caliphs, gradually became the Sunna, with an uppercase "S"—that is, the collection of Muhammad's divinely inspired deeds and gestures. From that point on, the caliphs had to take this crucial change into account.

Around 750, the ulama succeeded in imposing themselves as authoritative actors in all domains of the Islamic social space thanks to their ever growing control over the tools of religious knowledge, particularly the Sunna. They were judges, imams in mosques, preachers, compilers of hadith, teachers, jurists, theologians, and so on. This phenomenon worried the empire's lay elites, who were suspicious of the autonomy of the religious sphere and looked askance upon the ulama's growing power. In a letter of admonishment, the secretary Ibn al-Muqaffa' (d. 757) advised Abbasid caliph Abu Ja'far al-Mansur (754–755) to issue instructions

> so that differing legal rulings and practices are submitted to him in the form of a register, accompanied by the corresponding hadith and solutions to which the ulama refer; if the Commander of the Faithful then examined these [documents] and expressed the judgment that God inspired in him [*ra'y*] for each case, if he firmly held to his opinion and forbade [the ulama] from straying from it, if, finally, he made an exhaustive corpus out of these [decisions], we might be able to hope that God would transform these judgments, in which error is mixed with truth, into a single and just code; we might hope for the unification of legal practices and their harmonization according to the inspired view of the Commander of the Faithful. Another inspired guide [imam] would then proceed in the same manner and so on until the end of time, God willing.[16]

This passage from Ibn al-Muqaffa' clearly shows that the ulama had already captured certain caliphal prerogatives in the religious and legal domains. This was mainly due to the density of their networks, their proximity to the population, and above all their mastery of the prophetic tradition. For the caliph, there was no longer any question of freely legislating, as had the first successors of Muhammad and the Umayyads; rather, he had simply to choose between norms already established by the ulama. In order to stop this drain on his power, a unified legal corpus had to be established that would allow the caliph to effectively control religious discourse and the representatives thereof. Ibn al-Muqaffa', in other words, already sensed that emergent sharia law threatened the caliph's status as mystical body.

Needing all the support he could get in his efforts to consolidate the nascent Abbasid Caliphate, al-Mansur reacted only halfheartedly to his secretary's recommendations, for fear of alienating the ulama: Abu Hanifa (d. 765), eponymous founder of the Hanafi school, and Malik (d. 795), eponymous founder of the Maliki school, supported the pretensions of Ali's descendants to the Caliphate. Nearly fifty years later, al-Mansur's grandson, Harun al-Rashid (786–809), tried to regain control of the situation. Drawing inspiration from the caesaropapist model of the Byzantine Empire, the caliph formed a commission of ulama to establish an imperial legal corpus after the example of the Justinian Code (527–565) and to appoint judges to administer it. His aim was to control the operation of the legal-religious space of the interior. But this tardy effort was short-lived.[17] Indeed, ulama of all legal, theological, and political stripes were socially and intellectually well-organized during this period. This fact, together with their close contact with the population, the result of near daily interaction, allowed them to construct a form of ideological authority that was completely independent of the power of the caliph, thanks to the promotion of sharia. They were thus able to acquire autonomy and visibility in the social space.

THE ORDEAL OF AHMAD IBN HANBAL AND THE EMERGENCE OF SUNNI ISLAM

The failure of Harun al-Rashid's effort led the authorities to adopt increasingly extreme positions. The caliph al-Ma'mun (813–833) sought to reestablish the theocratic power of the caliphal institution by all possible means.[18] Initially, he attempted to draw upon the proto-Shiite movement and its theocratic doctrine of the Caliphate, reintroducing (among others) the very religious title of imam (inspired guide) in support of his claims and naming Ali al-Rida (d. 818)—a descendant of 'Ali and future ninth imam of Twelver Shiism—as crown prince in order to win over his supporters. But this risky political and religious undertaking came to a sudden end: a rebellion fomented in Baghdad by the elites and members of the ruling house forced the caliph to abandon his "Shiite" ideas and rid himself of the crown prince and the prince's most prominent followers.

This first misadventure did not in the least prevent al-Ma'mun from continuing his quest for a form of legitimacy that would allow him to permanently consolidate his status as mystical body of the community. Toward the end of his reign, he opted for Mu'tazilism.[19] Thanks to the syncretic epistemological premise upon which it is based, the representatives of this doctrine were able to establish an original religious, legal, and social line of thought. However, specifically religious considerations aside, it seems that what most attracted al-Ma'mun to this current of thought was its stance in regards to the nature and status of the Qur'an. According to the Mu'tazilites, the Holy Book of Islam is a creation of God and is thus circumscribed in space and time. As a text, in other words, the Qur'an reflects a well-determined historical moment. It thus cannot respond to the needs of believers in different spatiotemporal realities. Only the person of the caliph qua inspired guide and practitioner of *ijtihad* (the activity of interpretation) can occupy the intermediary role between God and mankind.

According to Muʿtazili doctrine, the head of the community, who must answer to strict moral and intellectual requirements, may legislate in all domains in order to respond to the spiritual and temporal needs of his subjects.

Seen as the foundation of absolute monotheism, this principle was to be imposed on the entire community, if necessary by force. And who other than the inspired guide could perform such a task? Al-Maʾmun therefore set about imposing this new official dogma on the elites of the empire by subjecting them to a sort of inquisition. Referred to as the *mihna*, or the Ordeal, it sought to force ulama (in particular, judges and collectors of prophetic traditions) to affirm the truth of Muʿtazili theses.[20] The caliphal authorities in this way hoped to subjugate them and thereby permanently monopolize the juridico-religious domain and, through it, all paths to salvation.

But they underestimated the tenacity of the corporation of ulama, which was prepared to endure suffering and torture to defend its faith and the foundations of its ideological authority. The ulama believed that the community should be governed by sharia. This meant that norms should be deduced from the Qurʾan, understood as the eternal and immutable word of God. Therefore, no element could be added or subtracted by a human being. With the Prophet seen as the sole intermediary between believers and God, recourse to the prophetic tradition was the only way to explain and specify his designs for humanity. This was a fatal challenge to the theocratic pretensions of the Caliphate. A clash between these two mystical bodies was therefore inevitable.

While the final months of al-Maʾmun's reign were marked by a vigorous inquisitorial campaign (interrogations, dismissals, imprisonment, torture, public humiliation, and so on), his successors, al-Muʿtasim (833–842) and al-Wathiq (842–847), only occasionally resorted to these methods. Indeed, for both politico-military and social reasons, the Ordeal, which began in 833 and gradually ceased after 847, was not always pursued in an energetic manner: first, these two caliphs were far from sharing their predecessor's religious and intellectual preoccupations; second, the foundation in 836 of a new capital, Samaraʾ, took the caliph away from his court in Baghdad and that city's increasingly hostile population; third, the resumption of the secular struggle with the Byzantine Empire and the outbreak of several socioreligious rebellions in the eastern provinces turned the caliphs' attention away from the religious domain; and fourth, the caliphs gradually realized that the empire could not continue to exist without the aid of the ulama and the population that supported them. Indeed, thanks to a clear and powerful argument—the eternal Qurʾan and the Sunna of the Prophet—an increasingly vast and well-structured network of knowledge, and intense socioreligious activity, the religious elite were able to create privileged relationships with the population. It was quite the contrary for the caliphal authorities, who depended on an elitist doctrine characterized by a degree of intellectual refinement and an argument from authority, both of which were difficult to popularize. To this must be added the "oriental" lifestyle of these sovereigns, which ran contrary to the concepts, symbols, and ideals of the Rightly Guided Caliphate that the ulama had been promoting for several decades.

In 847, the failure of this policy of coercion, which neither the population at large nor a significant portion of the elites had supported, resulted in structural change: sharia was permanently enshrined as the mystical body of Islam and became the essential, nearly unique source of and support for any religious, political, or cultural undertaking. Islam consequently became a nomocentric religion and civilization. The caliphs and their successors were no longer able to intervene in the process of defining dogma and law in Islam. From that point on, they ceased to be sovereign legislators and became mere protectors of the faith responsible for overseeing the temporal affairs of the community (at least in the religious domain properly so called). Thanks to their mastery of networks of knowledge and monopoly over the transmission of tradition, only the ulama were authorized to interpret the holy texts and deduce norms from them. It is thus not surprising that the tradition according to which the ulama were the sole "heirs of the prophets" should have first appeared in the ninth century.[21] Nor is it surprising that the anecdote according to which Abu Bakr (632–634), the first caliph of Islam, chose the relatively modest title of "Lieutenant of the Prophet" (*khalifat rasul Allah*)[22] in place of "Vicar of God" (*khalifat Allah*)—indicating that he was only a protector and advocate of the prophetic tradition rather than a theocratic leader and legislator—also entered into circulation at this time. In this regard, it is to be noted that the meaning of several concepts and notions shifted, a reflection of the representational changes then taking place. While expressions such as *sallallahu 'alayhi* and *'alayhi al-salam* ("God pray for him and greet him") had been used interchangeably to designate the Prophet and the caliphs, they were now exclusively reserved for the Prophet. The title of imam, which initially designated the inspired guide, henceforth designated only the guide or model that people could imitate to reach terrestrial and eternal salvation. As a consequence, all pious Muslims who devoted their lives to worship and knowledge had the possibility of becoming imam. And what other category has a greater claim to this title than the ulama? The most influential among them were awarded it beginning in the second half of the ninth century, a practice that continues today. Even the title "Commander of the Believers" (*amir al-mu'minin*)—the caliphal title par excellence—was conferred upon ulama such as al-Bukhari (d. 870) to symbolize the end of the caliphal monopoly and the emergence of a new authority.

The routinization of prophetic charisma thus resulted in a genuine division of labor between the political power and the religious authority in the framework of a symbiotic relationship. Given the tendency on the part of each party to interfere in the other's domain throughout Islamic history, however, this division was in practice always less than clear-cut. The emergence of a two-tiered legislative system was the most palpable result of this interaction, with one tier founded on the interpretation of scriptural sources (*al-shari'a*) and the other on the public interest and political considerations (*al-siyasa*).

While historical accounts mention the names of several ulama and pious figures who refused to recognize the new caliphal orthodoxy, Islamic memory has retained only one of them: Ahmad ibn Hanbal (d. 855).[23] This was due not only to the major role he played in the events under discussion, but also to the fact that he was at the origin of a legal and theological school that played and continues to play a leading role in the Islamic space. His work and actions were at the origin of Sunni Islam. A brief survey of his career will allow us to see how he deployed an ethic of responsibility to preserve orthodoxy, orthopraxy, and the political order.

Born in Baghdad around 780, Ahmad ibn Hanbal belonged to an Arab lineage of which some members served the Abbasid Caliphate. He began his initiatory journey in his native town, where he frequented various teaching circles (*halaqat al-'ilm*). His desire to acquire as much knowledge as possible and collect a large number of prophetic traditions encouraged him to undertake a long voyage to southern Iraq, Syria, Yemen, and the Hijaz. Heavily influenced by the traditionist ulama (*ahl al-hadith* or *ahl al-sunna*) of the Hijaz, he returned home and launched a career as a teacher and mufti. Nothing therefore distinguished him from the dozens of other traditionists who taught in and traveled back and forth between the great cities of Islam. It was the Ordeal that made him "the most remarkable figure in the camp of Muslim orthodoxy."[24] Indeed, he figured among the rare individuals who refused to accept the doctrines promoted by the Caliphate (in particular, the dogma of the Qur'an's creation).

Ibn Hanbal was summoned by al-Ma'mun, who had just returned from the Anatolian region of Tarsus, where he led a military campaign against the Byzantine Empire in 833. Ibn Hanbal had already reached the town of Raqqa when news of the caliph's death reached him. He was thus sent back to Baghdad, where he was interrogated in the name of the new caliph by the military governor before being imprisoned. Ibn Hanbal's obstinacy led Caliph al-Mu'tasim

(833–842) to condemn him to flagellation in 834. But his unshakeable faith obliged al-Mu'tasim to ultimately liberate him on condition that he no longer teach. Ibn Hanbal is said to have spent a total of twenty-eight months in prison. He briefly attempted to resume his pedagogical activities at the beginning of the reign of al-Wathiq (842–847) but was immediately forced to abandon them. This religious conflict did not prevent him from remaining faithful to the Caliphate. Even during the darkest moments of the Ordeal, he refused to call for the overthrow of the authorities, preferring divine invocation, exemplary behavior, and the work of inculcation to bring the caliphs back to reason.[25]

Beginning in 847, the Ordeal gradually drew to a close. The ulama, with Ibn Hanbal at their head, were able to accumulate power as guardians of the Sunna. Even Caliph al-Mutawakkil (847–861) tried to co-opt Ibn Hanbal, asking him to become his children's tutor, naming members of his family to important posts, and showering him with gifts, in a vain effort to legitimate his power and win popular support. This victory allowed Ibn Hanbal and his counterparts—what the sources call the *ahl al-hadith* or *ahl al-sunna*—to continue working toward the consolidation and perpetuation of what I henceforth refer to as Sunnism.

Ibn Hanbal pursued purely religious designs. In his view, the essence and objective of human action is to achieve salvation by means of submission to divine precepts.[26] In order to do this, one must rely on the Qur'an, interpreted nonfiguratively, and the Sunna, that is, the collection of words and deeds that may be attributed to the Prophet after critical examination. His principal work was thus *al-Musnad*, a collection of what were considered authentic prophetic traditions in the ninth century. This system was supplemented by the maxims and judgments of the companions, which were organized according to proximity to the Prophet. His disciples and followers later appealed to other sources to deduce the norm. In particular, they drew upon deduction by analogy (*al-qiyas*) and the general interest (*al-maslaha*) in the framework of their efforts to establish a coherent theologico-juridical system. Far from being theoretical speculation, the objective of Ibn Hanbal's work, like that of the first ulama, was to respond to the practical issues and concerns of his contemporaries.

Access to salvation presupposes the existence of a strong and cohesive community (*al-jama'a*) that avoids all forms of discord (*al-fitna*). This premise encourages the adoption of a very open position concerning excommunication (*al-takfir*), which can be pronounced only in three cases: the abandonment of prayer, the consumption of fermented liquor, and the spreading of heretical doctrines. Moreover, those who introduce blameworthy innovations (*al-bida'*) must be systematically placed in "quarantine" to prevent them from contaminating the community.[27]

In order to ensure community order and cohesion, the Muslim community must be led by caliphs drawn from the Prophet's tribe, the Quraysh, and "no one may contest this right, revolt against them or grant it to others until the day of resurrection."[28] Ibn Hanbal also claimed that believers owe fidelity and obedience to their sovereign in all circumstances, whatever his moral qualities might be. He categorically condemned calls to revolt, even in the event that the sovereign attempts to impose a norm or practice that is contrary to the precepts of the Law. All that the believer can do is peacefully resist while lavishing the caliph with advice (al-nasiha) in the hopes that he will renounce these innovations. In other words: "jihad must be accomplished with all of the imams, whether they are men of good or men of evil. The injustice of the tyrant or the fairness of the just matter little. Friday prayer, the pilgrimage, the two annual festivals must be celebrated with the holders of power even if they are not pious individuals. We owe the rulers legal alms, the tithe, property taxes, and the fifth of plunder, whether they use it well or not."[29]

In order to preserve and maximize the interests of the community (al-maslaha), Ibn Hanbal believed that the sovereign had to enjoy broad prerogatives in carrying out his duties. These duties must nevertheless be in keeping with the precepts of the Qur'an and the tradition. This was the origin of al-siyasa al-shar'iyya (governance in accordance with the sharia), which was theorized by Ibn Taymiyya (d. 1328) and is recognized by all contemporary Hanbali-Wahhabi ulama.

While Ibn Hanbal considered the practices of certain mystics, including al-Muhasibi (d. 857), Sari al-Saqati (d. 867), and Dhu al-Nun al-Misri (d. 859), to be contrary to the Law, his hostility did not reflect an ipso facto rejection of nascent Sufism.[30] In addition to his eulogy for Bishr ibn al-Harith (d. 841), a mystic known in the tradition for his scrupulous observance of the precepts of sharia, Ibn Hanbal compiled *Kitab al-Wara'*, an anthology of hadith concerning the spirit of devotion and asceticism.[31] This work was later extensively cited by leading mystics, such as Abu Talib al-Makki (d. 996) and Abu Hamid al-Ghazali (d. 1111). Similarly, most of the Hanbali ulama of the medieval period were also leading Sufis.

Finally, depending on their knowledge and social position, believers were to apply the Law in the familial and public spheres, in keeping with the duty to promote virtue and prevent vice (*al-amr bil-ma'ruf wa nahy 'an al-munkar*) while simultaneously respecting the prerogatives of the political authorities (who must never be publicly challenged or criticized). More than any other social category, the ulama were thus called upon to fulfill this religious duty.[32]

The key concepts that would be developed, systematized, and defended by his disciples as they set about constructing the theologico-juridical school that bears his name were thus found in germinal form in the positions and recommendations of Ahmad ibn Hanbal, seen as the ideal-typical actor and representative for an entire current of thought. But his influence goes beyond this. With sharia firmly established as the mystical body of the Islamic community, Ibn Hanbal's stance became "one of the most specifically constitutive elements of Muslim culture."[33] This decisive contribution was mainly due to his exemplary predication, that is, his ability to show the way to salvation through personal example and an ethic of responsibility.[34] The ethic of responsibility led him to opt for political quietism, religious activism, and a submissive—rather than confrontational—attitude to power. In this way, he secured victory for orthodoxy and orthopraxy while maintaining the political order that is required if the rituals and cultural practices essential to salvation are to be observed. While no less virtuous according to the criteria of the tradition, other actors and groups, such as Ahmad al-Khuza'i (d. 846) and the *mutatawwi'a* (the volunteers), opted for an ethic of conviction that led to destructive confrontation with the authorities.[35]

HANBALISM IN THE SERVICE OF THE BAGHDAD CALIPHATE[36]

"There exist three categories of Hanbalis: those who spend their time praying and fasting, those who collect hadith and study jurisprudence, and those who brutalize people who do not respect orthopraxy."[37] This polemical observation on the part of a tenth-century adversary suggests that three ideal-typical currents emerged within the corporation between the death of Ibn Hanbal in 855 and the fall of the Abbasid Caliphate in 1258. In reality, the leading figures of Baghdad Hanbalism generally fell under all three categories simultaneously. The corporation's authority rested entirely on the triptych of orthodox asceticism, scrupulous application of the Law, and religious activism in the social space. Without being exhaustive, I will try to sketch the most prominent traits of this corporation under the Abbasid Caliphate. In this way, we will be in a better position to assess continuity and rupture vis-à-vis contemporary Hanbali-Wahhabism.

Hanbalism was the only corporation of ulama in Islam to produce a theological and legal school, which lent it power and cohesiveness. Though Hanbalism played only a limited role in the legal domain up until the appearance of Saudi Arabia and the reformist movements of the contemporary era, it has always occupied a central place in the theological domain. From the eleventh to the thirteenth centuries, Hanbalism was the official creed (*al-'aqida*) of the Abbasid Caliphate. Over the course of Islamic history, many Maliki, Shafi'i, and Hanafi ulama adopted the Hanbali creed. It suffices to note that two of the most famous Hanbali professions of faith, which remain in use to this day, were written by Ibn Khuzayma (d. 869) and al-Tahawi (d. 935), whose legal views were Shafi'i and Hanafi, respectively.[38] Nor should one forget such great authorities of Sunni Islam as al-Bukhari (d. 870), Muslim (d. 875), Ibn 'Abd al-Barr (d. 1071), al-Dhahabi (d. 1348), and Ibn Kathir (d. 1373).[39] Despite its small following, Hanbalism was thus never a marginal phenomenon in the Islamic religious and intellectual space of the classical period. Its numerical inferiority was due to a simple but decisive factor: in contrast to other schools, it was never supported by the dominant power (the Abbasids, Hanbalism's only supporters, lost most of their power in the tenth century). But whenever the political situation allowed, its followers showed themselves capable of the same missionary dynamism as the other corporations. That was the case in the eleventh, the twelfth, and above all the eighteenth centuries, when the Saudi state emerged.

Moreover, Hanbalism never evolved in isolation. Like any corporation that observes an ethic of responsibility to protect its beliefs, the disciples and followers of Ibn Hanbal had to adopt some of the epistemological and methodological assets of other currents of Islam and adapt them to their own ends. This was particularly the case for Mu'tazilism and Ash'arism, even though the Hanbalis were struggling against both.[40]

Last, the ideological authority upon which the corporation depends presupposes, as we have already seen, differences of opinion and analysis not only between ulama, but even in regards to the legal and dogmatic positions occupied by a single *'alim* over the course of his life. This explains the differences of opinion that to this day characterize the corporation.

Like any ideological corporation, Hanbalism is a collective creation based on the more or less clear teachings of its founder. Indeed, the period from 855 to 945 was characterized by the assembly, classification, and commentary of *fatawa* (juridico-religious opinions, sing. *fatwa*) and the writings of Ibn Hanbal. This led to the creation of a genuine corpus, the main architects of which were Ibn Hanbal's own sons, Abd Allah (d. 903), Abu Bakr al-Khallal (d. 923), Muhammad al-Razi (d. 939), al-Khiraqi (d. 945), and 'Abd al-'Aziz Ghulam al-Khallal (d. 948).[41] Collections of traditions, legal manuals, and biographical dictionaries circulated. Yet "professions of faith" continued to constitute the most highly prized literary genre among the Hanbali. Generally short and axiomatic, these (*'aqida, kitab al-tawhid,* and *kitab al-sunna*) enumerated the main dogma of

Islam: divine omnipotence in matters of good and evil, the affirmation of divine attributes, the preeminence of the prophetic figure as mediator between God and mankind, the defense of the uncreated character of the Qur'an (and thus its universal and eternal validity), the predetermination of human acts and the negation of free will, the affirmation of the unity of the community, and unconditional obedience to the rulers, even in the case of impiety.[42]

This period was also marked by energetic Hanbali action in the public sphere under the leadership of al-Barbahari (d. 941), who played an important role in defending Sunnism and the Caliphate.[43] Noting a clear decline in the three O's and a rise in blameworthy innovations, he called for a return to the True Religion through imitation of the Prophet and the pious ancestors. Yet he did not condemn reason. Rather, he affirmed that it had to be put to good use, particularly in what concerns the question of divine attributes, where one must make do with the information supplied by the Qur'an and the tradition. For al-Barbahari, combatting innovation implied continuous action on the ground in the framework of the commandment to promote virtue and prevent vice (*al-amr bi al-ma'ruf wa nahy 'an al-munkar*), predication (*al-da'wa*), and good advice (*al-nasiha*).

These principles were not just pious wishes; they served as a road map that he sought to apply throughout his career. Drawing on his personal charisma and ideological authority, between 921 and 941 al-Barbahari led a series of demonstrations aiming to ensure respect for orthodoxy and orthopraxy (such as imposing the Law in commercial transactions, censoring "heretical" readings of the Qur'an, forbidding visits to the tombs of certain religious figures, combatting all forms of Shiism, struggling against Mu'tazili ideas, prohibiting the sale of wine, and destroying musical instruments). Moreover, in the political domain, al-Barbahari adopted the legitimist positions of Ibn Hanbal, who condemned all acts of disobedience. This led him to become a staunch defender of the caliphal authorities throughout his career.[44]

The first century of Hanbali history was therefore centered on the elaboration of a collective identity. While some ulama applied themselves to establishing a coherent intellectual system, others worked to put the principles of the corporation into practice and clearly delimit the frontiers of its identity vis-à-vis the opposing religious forces.

This strong collective identity allowed the corporation of Hanbali ulama to become, in the words of Henri Laoust, "the avant-garde of the resistance to Shiism and all other sects regarded as suspect."[45] The division of the Caliphate in the tenth century was marked by a significant reduction in Sunni political power to the profit of Shia dynasties, in particular the Fatimids (909–1171), the Hamdanids (905–1004), and the Buyids (945–1055). The latter even seized Baghdad in 945 and imposed their power on the Abbasid caliphs. The Buyids' desire to favor Shiite practices ran afoul of the Hanbali ulama, whose ideological authority influenced most of the city's population.[46]

In order to defend their beliefs and positions, the ulama deployed their entire network of sermon writers, preachers, and imams—the most famous of whom was Ibn Samʿum (d. 997)—to defend the Caliphate and protect orthodoxy and orthopraxy in the framework of the promotion of virtue and the prevention of vice.[47] The work of Ibn Batta (d. 997) was part of this activist dynamic. His main work, *al-Ibana al-sughra*, is a simplified profession of faith mainly intended for the community's most underprivileged members: young people and non-Arabs. In a simple and direct style, the author explains that the only way to combat blameworthy innovations, maintain the unity of the community, and save one's soul is to imitate the Prophet and the pious ancestors in the areas of belief and behavior. He particularly objected to the intellectual and cultural innovations of the various sects (Shiites, Muʿtazilites, Qadarites, Murjiʾites, and so on) and called upon the faithful to abandon them, for "opposing them is to follow the Sunna and perfect one's faith . . . and move closer to God."[48] On other points, he hardly departed from the positions developed by his Hanbali counterparts and predecessors. His work would later be systematically adopted, in particular by Ibn Taymiyya (d. 1328) and his disciples.

The efforts of the Hanbali ulama proved decisive. The Shiite onslaught was not only halted, but a restoration movement, taking advantage of the weakening of the Buyids, was launched under the Caliphate of al-Qadir (991–1031). In a text published in 1017, al-Qadir even recognized the Hanbali *ʿaqida* as the Caliphate's only official creed.[49] This document, which adopted all of the dogmas mentioned above, firmly condemned Shiism, Muʿtazilism, and above all Ashʿarism.[50]

In addition to helping propagate the Hanbali creed in several provinces under the nominal authority of Baghdad via a process of "curialization"—that is, the extension of court practices to all of society through mimicry—this development allowed representatives of the tradition to attain ever more important official posts in the eleventh, twelfth, and thirteenth centuries.[51] The Hanbali ulama reinforced their ideological authority by means of charisma of office.

At first glance, this attitude would appear to contradict the position of Ibn Hanbal himself, who refused all official honors and posts and is even said to have shed tears when one of his sons agreed to become a judge.[52] This is once again an example of how an ethic of responsibility encourages representatives of a tradition to adapt to their milieu and sociohistoric context. The relationship with the Caliphate became so close that a Hanbali *'alim* is reputed to have said "the Caliphate is like an egg that the Hanbalis protect. Without the latter, the egg will break. The Caliphate is like a tent and the Hanbalis are like the pole that holds it up. If this pole were to fall, the tent would collapse."[53]

The career of Abu Ya'la ibn al-Farra' (d. 1066) nicely reflects this new situation. After receiving a classic Hanbali education, he became a witness to deeds (*shahid*) in Baghdad. Thanks to his master, Ibn Hamid (d. 1013), who was close to Caliph al-Qadir, Abu Ya'la was introduced to the court. Like the famous *'alim* al-Mawardi (d. 1058), he became a protégé of the vizier Ibn al-Muslima (d. 1058). That earned him the title of grand judge. Abu Ya'la devoted all of his energy to defending the rights of the Caliphate and spreading the Hanbali tradition. His book *al-Ahkam al-Sultaniyya* was a treatise of public law, the first of its type in the lands of Islam. In this book, he vigorously defended the rights of the Abbasid Caliphate against the provincial emirates and tried to submit all governmental acts to the precepts of sharia. In his other work, *al-Mu'tamad*, he once again defended the Caliphate and the theological positions of the Hanbali. But the work was original in two respects: its design was inspired by Mu'tazili and Ash'ari treatises of speculative theology, and its introduction sketched a theory of knowledge. While the first Hanbalis were fundamentally opposed to speculative theology, Abu Ya'la no doubt believed that the best way to win victory for the truth was to appropriate the arms of his adversaries. His approach very rapidly gained widespread acceptance, and Ibn Taymiyya was its main heir. These appropriations, however, had to be brought into conformity with scriptural norms. Transgressions were severely punished by the guardians of the *klerôs*, as in the case of Ibn 'Aqil (d. 1120).[54]

The other, more classic works of Abu Ya'la were devoted to the apology of Hanbalism, the refutation of opposing doctrines, and jurisprudence. On the ground, the "judge," as he would subsequently be known, established a network that not only helped strengthen the corporation, but also contributed to spreading the tradition to other provinces, particularly to Syria-Palestine, where it was to enjoy great success.[55] In parallel with these efforts, the Hanbalis pursued their promotion of virtue and prevention of vice campaigns in the public sphere in order to combat enemy sects and what they considered deviant behavior. In this, they were facilitated by the fact that a member of the caliph's family—al-Sharif Abu Ja'far (d. 1077)—was himself a member of the corporation.

Over the course of the eleventh century, the energetic action of the Hanbalis gave new religious and political impetus to the entire Sunni world and resulted in a great victory. While the Sunni authorities gradually reestablished themselves in the formerly lost territories, the ulama and the Hanbali tradition experienced a veritable golden age that ended only with the Mongol conquest of 1258. The careers of three of the corporation's major figures—the vizier Ibn Hubayra (d. 1165), the mystic Abd al-Qadir al-Jilani (d. 1166), and the sermon writer Ibn al-Jawzi (d.1200)—reflect the situation and tendencies of this tradition.

Trained by the best-known Hanbali ulama of his time, Ibn Hubayra entered into the Caliphate's service and climbed all of the rungs of the administrative hierarchy, finally achieving the position of grand vizier. From that point on, he devoted all of his energy to consolidating Sunnism and reaffirming the authority of the Caliphate. In pursuit of the first part of his project, he endeavored to unite all Sunni schools around the Hanbali *'aqida*. To that end, he attempted to strengthen the Hanbali presence in Baghdad by founding a madrasa to train the growing number of Hanbali officials. In the political domain, he did all that he could to free the Abbasid Caliphate from the Saljuq yoke and encourage Emir Nur al-Din Zangi (1146–1174) to conquer Egypt with a view to putting an end to the Fatimids' Shia Caliphate. Ibn Hubayra's efforts came to fruition just a few years after his death: the Hanbalis achieved full domination over Baghdad; Fatimid Egypt was reconquered by the Sunnis in 1171; and the Abbasid Caliphate, freed from Saljuq tutelage, once again became the only nominal leader of the Muslim community.

It was in this context that the traditionalist, jurist, and preacher Abd al-Qadir al-Jilani came of age. The main contribution of this figure was the foundation of Islam's first great Sufi order. Contrary to what is often thought, Hanbalism was never hostile to the principle of mysticism.[56] As we will see below, it condemned only those practices that challenged orthodoxy and orthopraxy. Indeed, most of the Hanbalis I have mentioned—particularly al-Barbahari—had affinities with mysticism. For example, Ibn Rajab draws attention to no less than one hundred Hanbali mystics in the classical period.[57] Similarly, one of the most famous works of Muslim mysticism, *Manazil al-Sa'irin* (*The Spiritual Steps [for Reaching God]*), was written by al-Harawi al-Ansari (d. 1089), who loudly and openly proclaimed, "I will be Hanbali until my death and I advise all to do likewise."[58] Al-Jilani was thus merely the heir of a long tradition that sought to reconcile the intellectual, formal, and emotional aspects of the religion. His main work, *al-Ghunya li-Talibi Tariq al-Haqq* (*What Is Necessary in the Path of Truth*), clearly reflects this concern.[59] The mystical teaching of al-Jilani "is closely inspired by the Qur'an and traditions and the religious exercises it recommends are irreproachable," for his only objective was to wage internal jihad in order to recognize the uniqueness of God and his will, in keeping with the Hanbali vision.[60] It was only later that his disciples and descendants "deformed" the founder's biography and teachings to serve the interests of adaptation and expansion.

The influence of Sufism made itself felt in the figure of Ibn al-Jawzi, the most prolific recorder of Hanbali tradition. Introduced at the court by Vizier Ibn Hubayra, he very rapidly became one of the most influential ulama in Baghdad. Known for his great energy, Ibn al-Jawzi was at once an effective madrasa supervisor, a brilliant preacher, and a formidable polemicist. Charged by several Abbasid caliphs to enforce respect for orthodoxy and orthopraxy, he was endowed with a genuine power of inquisition. This power allowed him not only to combat "heresies" and "blameworthy innovations," but also to favor members of his corporation. His influence has been perpetuated through the ages thanks to the roughly 250 texts he produced. In addition to a well-documented history of the Caliphate, he prepared a biographical dictionary of the holy figures of Islam that was intended to sketch the ideal contours of orthodox Sufism.[61] This was complemented on the one hand by a series of hagiographical sketches of the pious figures of early Islam presented as models to be emulated,[62] and on the other by a treatise condemning all of the deviant practices and doctrines of his time that had been introduced by the followers of popular Islam, philosophers, sects, and sometimes even thoughtless ulama.[63] The actions and intellectual project of Ibn al-Jawzi clearly incarnate the central preoccupation of the Hanbali corporation: to preserve orthodoxy, orthopraxy, and the political order.[64]

The fifty years following his death were marked by the growth of Hanbalism, the representatives of which controlled the highest juridico-religious offices under the protection of the Abbasid Caliphates. While the son of Ibn al-Jawzi became the *muhtasib* of Baghdad—that is, the highest ranking officer responsible for, among other things, enforcing orthodoxy and orthopraxy in the public sphere—one of Abd al-Qadir al-Jilani's grandsons was appointed grand judge. Yet this privileged position was swept away with the Mongol invasion of 1258, which destroyed the entire socioreligious edifice that the Hanbalis had spent four centuries constructing.

Far from disappearing, however, the Hanbali tradition found fertile new ground, particularly in Upper Mesopotamia, Egypt, Palestine, and Syria. But it was in the capital of Syria that the guardians of this corporation won renown, and for several centuries, Damascus became its new center. We will examine how the tradition adapted to its new sociohistoric environment and how its representatives once again gave voice to an ethic of responsibility.

IBN TAYMIYYA AND SYRO-PALESTINIAN HANBALISM[65]

Hanbalism first gained a foothold in Damascus in the early tenth century thanks to the efforts of Abu Salih Muflih (d. 941), who founded a mosque that was to become the school's first center of training and socialization in the region. Hanbalism nevertheless remained a marginal phenomenon there. It would be another one hundred years before the tradition solidly established itself and slowly spread to Syria and Palestine after successfully installing itself in Baghdad. This missionary work was carried out by a disciple of the judge Abu Ya'la, Abu al-Faraj al-Shirazi (d. 1093). The first official madrasa was built, and a stable relationship was established with Baghdad. Sunnism's twelfth-century comeback in the region under the Zand and Ayyubid dynasties allowed the Hanbalis to consolidate their positions and strengthen their institutional network via the creation of several madrasas and sites of worship. During the twelfth and thirteenth centuries, the Hanbali community of Syria-Palestine was overseen by two "houses" of ulama: the Banu al-Munajjah and the Banu Qudama (some members of which also bore the al-Maqdisi patronym).

As members of a minority group in Damascus, the leaders of this community, unlike their coreligionists in Baghdad, did little to draw attention to themselves in the public sphere. Their activities were confined to further exploration through teaching and writing of the theological, legal, and moral aspects of their tradition. It seems that the aim of the ulama during this period was to strengthen collective identity around an elite and a group of texts in order to avoid diluting their tradition. It must not be forgotten that the Shafi'i school, which had been promoted to the rank of official school by the Ayyubids (1174–1250), dominated the socioreligious space and tended to smother all others. The case of Muwaffaq al-Din ibn Qudama (d. 1223) illustrates this phenomenon. Most of his efforts were devoted to drawing out and systematizing the Hanbali legal tradition.[66] His voluminous *al-Mughni*, which is considered the most important survey of Hanbali jurisprudence, still constitutes an important reference for Hanbali-Wahhabi ulama and the Saudi legal system. Only the 'alim 'Abd al-Ghani al-Maqdisi (d. 1203), first cousin of Ibn Qudama, distinguished himself through his energetic efforts to enforce orthodoxy and orthopraxy in the public sphere. Offended by the rulers' lack of respect for Islamic norms, al-Maqdisi had several run-ins with the Ayyubid sultan al-'Adil (1200–1218).[67]

Yet the Damascene period of the Hanbali tradition was dominated by a single great figure whose thought and action were to have an impact for centuries to come. This was Ahmad ibn Taymiyya (d. 1328).[68] His doctrines are a fundamental part of the religious and political culture of many modern and contemporary Islamic groups, movements, and communities—in particular, the state that emerged from the preaching of Muhammad ibn Abd al-Wahhab.

The second half of the thirteenth century was characterized by a major event: the struggle against the Mongol invasion. After the fall of Baghdad, the Mamluk sultanate (1250–1517) became the last great bastion of Islam, with Damascus the new capital of Hanbalism. In order to strengthen his position, legitimate his power, and win popular support, Sultan Baybars (1260–1277) promoted Sunni Islam as a matter of policy. In addition to restoring the Caliphate in 1261, he endeavored to give equal standing to the four legal schools. To this end, he appointed for the first time four grand judges in Egypt and Syria, facilitated the activities of the mystical brotherhoods, restored the two holy places of Islam, funded the construction of pious foundations, and waged war against the Franks, Mongols, and various Shia sects. This policy redounded to the advantage of all clerical corporations, particularly the Hanbalis, who were able to establish a number of pious foundations and madrasas, the most important of which was the al-Salihiyya.

It was into this socioreligious context that Ibn Taymiyya was born in 1263 in the town of Harran, the center of Upper Mesopotamian Hanbalism. As the Mongols advanced, his family, which was known for having produced several ulama, fled its native land and took refuge in Damascus. The Mamluk's installation in the metropolis offered young Ahmad, whose father became supervisor of a madrasa, the opportunity to frequent the best-known ulama of his time. In 1284, having received a solid training in all domains of Islamic knowledge, Ibn Taymiyya began teaching in the family madrasa before moving on to the mosque of the Umayyad. In 1291, the year the Crusades ended, he received official authorization to issue fatawa.

Ibn Taymiyya's first intervention in the public sphere took place during his pilgrimage to Mecca in 1292: he denounced suspect rituals and popular practices and called for orthodoxy and orthopraxy to be respected. The following year, he had the occasion to express this opinion publicly and vigorously when the authorities refused to apply the legal punishment against a Christian accused of having insulted the Prophet. This stance led him to be beaten and imprisoned by the governor of Damascus. Far from resigning himself, Ibn Taymiyya continued his peaceful activism by writing a work titled *al-Sarim al-Maslul 'ala Shatim al-Rasul (The Saber Drawn against He Who Insults the Prophet)* in which he mobilized all available scriptural and historical data to demand that the Law be applied in the same way independently of the individuals or circumstances involved. Throughout his life, this legal and theological intransigence created trouble for him. In order to affirm the superiority of his own tradition, Ibn Taymiyya was naturally obliged to condemn the other religious doctrines and traditions present in the Islamic space of the era. While his condemnations of the Mahdism of Ibn Tumart (d. 1130), founder of the Almohad movement in Morocco, and of Shia philosophers caused little disturbance, least of all among the ruling elites, his condemnations (which did not include excommunication) of Ashʿarism, monism, and popular religious practices provoked a sharp reaction. The representatives of the latter two traditions, who at the time occupied the leading offices in the religious and legal domains, were obliged to defend their ideological authority and the beliefs upon which it was based. They thus used all of their influence with the political power to neutralize Ibn Taymiyya, who as a result was condemned to spend many months in prison in 1306, 1321, and 1326.[69]

Yet these condemnations hardly prevented him from pursuing his efforts as an activist. In the religious domain, he was involved in several punitive expeditions against the Shia sects of Mount Lebanon in 1300 and 1305 and participated in the destruction of popular religious sites. In 1305, he also obliged several figures he considered heretics to do penitence (*al-tawba*). At the political level, he was one of the most fervent defenders of the Mamluk sultanate. During the siege of Damascus by the Mongols in 1300, he was at the head of the town's defenders. The political authorities subsequently gave him and several other ulama the task of ideologically mobilizing the population and inciting jihad. He even took part in the military campaign that brought decisive victory in 1303. After the end of military operations, Ibn Taymiyya developed privileged relations with Sultan al-Nasir (1309–1341) and some of his collaborators,[70] who he supplied with extensive advice (*nasiha*), the substance of which can be found in his *al-Siyasa al-sharʿiyya*. He even inspired the Mamluk sovereign to carry out several reforms in keeping with the Law: the abrogation of illegal taxes, the application of the law of the talion, and so on. Through his close relations with the political authorities, Ibn Taymiyya no doubt hoped to contribute to "the reform of the ruler and those ruled" (the title of his most famous work, *al-Siyasa al-sharʿiyya fi islah al-raʿi wa al-raʿiyya*) in the aim of enforcing sharia.

His actions were simply the reflection of a conceptual and empirical undertaking, the originality and scale of which have yet to be surpassed in Hanbalism. His work can be considered this tradition's outcome and crowning achievement. While the main themes developed by his predecessors—in particular, Ibn Batta, Abu Yaʿla, and Ibn Qudama—can be clearly discerned in his work, he nevertheless treats them with greater methodological sophistication.

Advocating moderation (*al-wasatiyya*), Ibn Taymiyya aspired to construct a system that would reconcile the three ideal-typical paths to truth and salvation: tradition (*al-naql*), reason (*al-ʿaql*), and mysticism (*al-irada*).[71] Attaining a better understanding and full application of the Law was the sole objective of this desire for synthesis. For Ibn Taymiyya, the Law was more than ever the genuine mystical body of the Islamic community.

To properly grasp the thought of Ibn Taymiyya and its influence in the modern and contemporary period, we give particular attention to the following themes: orthodoxy, the promotion of virtue and prevention of vice, and power.

While he advocated a literalist, "Hanbali" reading of the dogma of divine unity—describing God as he described himself in the Qur'an and as the Prophet did in the Sunna—Ibn Taymiyya was far from being exclusivist. In a fatwa titled *The Destruction of Logic*, he held that the various traditions, doctrines, and sects of Islam constitute concentric spheres, with the Qur'an and the Sunna at their epicenter. The less one respects these two sources in theology, law, and politics (that is, orthodoxy, orthopraxy, and the political order), the farther one moves away from the center. This yields the following ranking: (1) the pious ancestors (*al-salaf al-salih*), (2) the Hanbalis, (3) the mystics (*al-sufiyya*), (4) the theologian-philosophers (*ahl al-kalam*), (5) the philosophers, (6) the Kharijites, and (7) the moderate Shiites. Only a few marginal sects, like the Nusayri, or ones that no longer existed in his time were excluded from the *umma*. The Hanbalis are not the exclusive representatives of the True Religion, in his view, but thanks to their scrupulous observance of scriptural rule and imitation of the pious ancestors, they are the purest.[72] Ibn Taymiyya thus recognized the Islamic character of all traditions and doctrines that admitted the centrality of the Qur'an and the Sunna as guides to all aspects of life. Nevertheless, their adoption of inappropriate methods, conceptual frameworks, or political ideologies distanced them from the mystical body and led them to introduce blameworthy innovations. They thus had to be combatted. God would be the judge in the afterlife.[73]

In his view, moreover, this debate over inclusion and exclusion concerned and should only concern the religious elites. Ignorant of the finer points of theology and legal details, the masses must never take part in them. Excommunicating them is thus out of the question.[74]

Contrary to a very widespread opinion, Ibn Taymiyya was never an enemy of Sufism, which he assigned to third place in his concentric vision of the *umma*. He had himself received a good mystical training and liked to say, "I dressed in the holy robe of mystical initiation [*al-khirqa*] of several shaykhs belonging to various mystical paths [*tariqa*, pl. *turuq*], among them 'Abd al-Qadir al-Jilani, whose path is the most important."[75]

It is thus not surprising to see certain mystics and their work praised here and there in his writings. They include Sahl al-Tustari (d. 896), al-Junayd (d. 910), and Abu Talib al-Makki (d. 996), all known for their strict observance of orthodoxy and orthopraxy in accordance with the Hanbali vision.[76] In keeping with

Hanbali tradition, however, Ibn Taymiyya firmly condemned the dogmatic excesses and suspect practices of certain confraternities that he regarded as "innovating sects and free thinkers who claim to be affiliated with Sufism. But in the opinion of true sufis, they do not belong to it."[77] Apart from his furious opposition to the pantheism of followers of Ibn al-'Arabi (d. 1248), he condemned a number of popular practices encouraged by mystical currents, the most important of which were the cult of the saints, the consumption of drugs in order to intensify religious experience, extracanonical cultural rituals, invented or reinvented religious formulas and expressions, and so on.[78]

We saw above that Ibn Taymiyya, like his predecessors, actively militated for the imposition of orthodoxy and orthopraxy in the social space and found himself in serious trouble as a result.[79] This action was part of the Islamic tradition of the promotion of virtue and the prevention of vice. Ibn Taymiyya's vision of this religious obligation was both elitist and pragmatic. While he saw it as a collective duty (*fard kifaya*), he nevertheless advocated Draconian restrictions. This was for two reasons. First,

> the interest it brings must prevail over the damage it brings about. It is the objective of the prophetic mission and the revelation of the Books. God does not love disorder [*al-fasad*]. The aim of everything he commands is order and prosperity [*al-salah*]. God has praised pious men, those who put things in order, those whose beliefs and actions are right. In many passages of the Qur'an, he blamed those who cause disorder.[80]

And second,

> [the men of the masses] command and forbid, by believing they obey God and his Prophet while in reality they cross the limits traced for them by the Law. Such is the error committed by those who indulge in blameworthy innovations or give themselves over to their passions like the Kharijites, the Mu'tazilites, and the Rafidites. In this way, they caused much more evil than good.[81]

To keep the order necessary to carrying out religious duties,[82] Ibn Taymiyya held that only the emirs (holders of coercive power) and the ulama (representatives of ideological authority) could accomplish this religious obligation.[83]

Regarding the issue of how to efficiently maintain order, Ibn Taymiyya addressed the form and prerogatives of the Islamic state. In keeping with a conception that is widespread in traditional societies, religion and the state are in his view inseparable because "the fact of being invested with a power over men constitutes one of the most significant duties of religion. We would even say that it is the fundamental condition if a religion is to survive."[84] Without the state's coercive power, religion declines. Similarly, without religion, the state is only an illegitimate and despotic form of domination.

This is why Ibn Taymiyya composed *al-Siyasa al-shar'iyya*. The main objective of this work is to show the importance of the interaction between political practice (*al-siyasa*) and the Law (*al-shari'a*). He therefore recommended genuine cooperation among the community's two main social categories: the emirs and the ulama. Indeed, "when these two categories are healthy," Ibn Taymiyya wrote, "everything is healthy in the community. Their corruption entails that of the entire social body."[85] This cooperation should result in a genuine division of labor between them,[86] according to which the ulama will look after the religious and legislative domains while the emirs will look after the political, economic, and military domains. The emirs will even dispose of regulatory power, though it may be used only in accordance with the spirit of the Law. It is a genuine symbiotic relationship.

As a cleric who pursued religious objectives, Ibn Taymiyya conceived of the state as a practical functional tool for imposing order and justice and thereby facilitating the advent of a united society fully devoted to God. Consequently, the Law—and not some sort of political entity—must be the only point of reference for the believer's identity. It is for this reason that he never advocated restoring the power of the Caliphate. On the contrary, he was the first medieval ulama to explicitly recognize the propriety of the political division of *dar al-islam* (the land of Islam). Each Muslim sovereign was henceforth considered a genuine imam in his own territories. The author of *al-Siyasa al-shar'iyya* merely recommended close cooperation between Muslim states whose populations were united by ties of faith and high culture: a form of Islamic society *avant la lettre*.

Like his predecessors, Ibn Taymiyya demanded absolute obedience from the population to stabilize the edifice and allow the three O's to be realized. This was so even in the case of grave sin or ignorance on the part of the sovereign, provided that he did not transgress the Law in public.[87] The people were obliged to cooperate with and support him. Above all, they were expected to give him good advice in the hope that he would return to the straight and narrow. Any act of violence aiming to overturn an established authority, whatever its claims to legitimacy, was definitively condemned on the grounds that it could only give rise to discord (*al-fitna*) and disturb religious affairs.[88]

The career of Ahmad ibn Taymiyya can for the most part be situated in the *longue durée* of Hanbali history. An important variation can nevertheless be identified. Deprived of even the weakest political support, the Hanbali tradition tended no longer to impose its vision but solely to defend its identity and even its existence. Having opted for silence for several decades, the tradition ran the risk of losing ideological authority and being marginalized. In keeping with the ethic of responsibility, Ibn Taymiyya was, consciously or not, obliged to act to remedy the situation. He must have realized or at least felt that the existence in the public sphere of a corporation founded on ideological authority mainly depends on taking clear and well-defined positions on issues of concern to society (without, of course, forgetting that conviction in the validity of its beliefs and the quest for salvation for oneself and others also constitute a fundamental factor). Like Ibn Hanbal and other figures of Islam, Ibn Taymiyya thus adopted an exemplary predication that joined theologico-juridical firmness with unwavering political loyalty. This permitted him to give new impetus to the Hanbali tradition, the second golden age of which precisely corresponded to his career and that of his leading disciples.

His most important disciple was no doubt Ibn Qayyim al-Jawziyya (d. 1350). Thanks to his encyclopedic knowledge, Ibn al-Qayyim succeeded not only in spreading his master's ideas, but also in producing an original body of work that remains very popular to this day. Less of an activist than his mentor, Ibn al-Qayyim preferred to avoid conflict with the ulama of other corporations, particularly the Shafi'ite-Asharites, who controlled the main religious and legal offices of society and sought to monopolize the socioreligious space. They therefore seized upon every occasion to neutralize their adversaries, in particular, the Hanbalis. This explains Ibn al-Qayyim's modest institutional career, a fact that encouraged him to devote himself entirely to intellectual pursuits.

Heavily influenced by Sufism in accordance with Hanbali requirements, he wrote a commentary on *Manazil al-Salikin* (*The Stations of the Travelers*) by al-Harawi (d. 1089). This work, which very quickly established itself as a masterpiece of Hanbali mysticism, claimed that complete adoration and love of God should necessarily lead to scrupulous observance of scriptural precepts in the area of dogma and socioreligious practice. This led Ibn al-Qayyim to once again condemn the practices of popular Islam and the monist ideas of Ibn al-'Arabi's disciples.

The idea that scriptural precepts should be respected in all aspects of life was systematically reiterated in all of his other works. While he presented the prophetic gesture as the model par excellence of human behavior in *Zad al-Ma'ad* (*Viaticum for Reaching Salvation*), in *I'lam al-muwaqqi'in* (*The Perfect Mufti's Guide*) he endeavored to guide future ulama (by means of a history of Muslim law, a clear methodology, and case studies) to a better understanding of the aims of sharia. In this way, he believed, they would be able to deduce a norm that was consistent with the texts and the interests of believers. This was also the case of his work on public law, *al-Turuq al-Hukmiyya* (*Political Practice in Keeping with the Law*), in which he devotes less attention to the nature of the Islamic state and the unity of the Caliphate than to the order that is necessary for the application of the Law. This system was complemented by a long profession of faith in verse, *al-Nuniyya*, which reiterated the main themes of Hanbali dogma.[89]

The work and career of Ibn Taymiyya and his disciple Ibn al-Qayyim exercised a fascination over several Shafi'ite ulama who rejected Asharite theology and suspect mystical practices in favor of the Hanbali credo. These "conversions" provoked a temporary schism within the corporation. This partly explains the Shafi'ite and Asharite hatred of Hanbalism, as demonstrated by their actions and intellectual production. Nevertheless, like al-Dhahabi (d. 1348) and Ibn Kathir (d. 1373) before them, the Shafi'ite-Hanbalis very rapidly established themselves as authorities on Sunni Islam in such important domains as commentary on the prophetic traditions, history, and Qur'anic exegesis.

At the turn of the fifteenth century, the Hanbali tradition gradually went into hibernation. This phenomenon was mainly due to a lack of leadership and politico-financial support. Indeed, for purely political reasons, the Mamluk authorities preferred to support the Hanbalis' adversaries, who were vastly more numerous and influential. The arrival of the Ottomans at the beginning of the sixteenth century only exacerbated this situation. In the interest of imposing their domination over the juridico-religious space of the conquered territories, the Ottomans encouraged expansion of the Hanafi-Maturidi tradition, which they promoted to the rank of official school of the empire. While several Hanbali ulama produced reference works in Islamic law between the fifteenth and eighteenth centuries—al-Mardawi (d. 1480), al-Hajjawi (d. 1560), al-Karami (d. 1624), and al-Buhuti (d. 1641)—Hanbali tradition crucially lacked figures whose charisma and ideological authority were capable of causing a stir or leaving an impression. By abandoning the ethic of responsibility, the Hanbali ulama brought about the decline and marginalization of their tradition. Symbolic action and a spectacular and well-funded undertaking with strong political backing was thus necessary if the Hanbali tradition was to rise from the ashes. This took place in Najd, located at the center of the Arabian Peninsula, in the middle of the eighteenth century.

THE NAJDIS: IN SEARCH OF KNOWLEDGE AND A LINK TO THE PAST

According to the meager information that is available, the Hanbali tradition has been present in Najd since the fifteenth century.[90] One can nevertheless suppose that it established itself there much earlier. Several complementary pieces of evidence can be called upon in support of this hypothesis: located on the route of the pilgrimage, the oases of Najd were at one time influenced by the Hanbali ulama of Baghdad; several Najdis doubtless traveled to that town for trade or education; after the fall of Baghdad, ulama or individual Hanbali must have taken refuge in Najd; and the Najdis' privileged relations with Damascus and all of Syria-Palestine encouraged the interaction and adoption of Hanbalism. To this must be added the pilgrimage and occasional trips to Cairo.

Whatever the case, it seems that Hanbalism consolidated its presence in the region during the sixteenth century. Thanks to cultural exchanges with Damascus and Cairo, a small center for teaching the Hanbali tradition was created in the oasis of Ushayqir.[91] Between the sixteenth and eighteenth centuries, around half of Najd's known ulama came from this oasis. Most of the clerics born elsewhere were at one point or another obliged to set down their pilgrim's staff there in order to complete their training or at least strengthen their network and legitimacy. It seems that the Hanbali tradition achieved majority status in Najd during the eighteenth century. There are nevertheless very few firsthand accounts of the period, and they do not allow us to trace a clear and direct line from medieval Hanbalism.

What needs to be underscored here is that the Najdi Hanbali tradition did not have one or several identifiable figures who served as "bridges" between Baghdadi and Damascene Hanbalism, on the one hand, and that of Najd, on the other. When one considers that the legitimacy of the Islamic sciences is entirely based on *al-sanad*—that is, an uninterrupted chain of identifiable guarantors—this fact represents a genuine epistemological problem.

It seems that Muhammad ibn Abd al-Wahhab, who, as we will see, precisely wanted to break with his socioreligious milieu and immediate history, was not in the least interested in establishing a direct line of descent from classical Hanbalism. On the contrary, the rare indications available to us suggest that he fully accepted the idea that the only ties attaching him to this golden age were assiduous reading and the scrupulous application of the precepts of such Hanbali authors as Ibn Taymiyya and Ibn al-Qayyim. He never sought—at least not according to his official biographers—to go beyond the accumulation of *ijazat* (authorizations) and/or the search for manuscripts. What's more, Michael Cook has shown that his references to Hanbali literature were late and rare.[92] Like the majority of his contemporaries, he was a man of few books.

Thanks to the symbolic capital he accumulated throughout his career, Ibn Abd al-Wahhab became the central figure upon whom his descendants and disciples drew to legitimate their ideological authority. While there were a few attempts at relative openness over the course of the nineteenth century, the system of self-legitimation employed by the ulama of Najd functioned so well that they hardly felt obliged to prove their filiation with medieval Hanbalism. Some—in particular, the descendants of Ibn Abd al-Wahhab—accumulated a number of *ijazat* from the Hanbali ulama of Egypt in the course of their involuntary stays in Cairo during the nineteenth century and were thus able to link themselves with the classical tradition. But this link was belated and exogenous.[93]

Things began to change gradually during the twentieth century. Promoted to the rank of state religion, Hanbali-Wahhabism had to legitimate its position and emphasize its pedigree vis-à-vis other Islamic traditions, which saw it as a form of religious social climbing. This meant that the Hanbali-Wahhabis were obliged to establish a system of legitimization beyond simple religious conviction to prove their direct filiation with medieval Hanbalism and, through it, the generation of pious ancestors from whom they drew inspiration. This process involved two concomitant procedures: the (re)invention of the tradition, and the (re)appropriation of the intellectual heritage of classical Hanbalism. As Eric Hobsbawm has noted, at some point in their existence, all political or religious traditions similarly attempt to "establish continuity with an appropriate historical past."[94]

The biographical dictionary of Najd ulama compiled by the *'alim* historiographer Abd Allah al-Bassam (d. 2003) is an excellent example of this (re)invention of tradition. The first edition of the dictionary was titled *The Ulama of Najd during Six Centuries* (*'Ulama' najd khilal sittat qurun*). Although most of its entries concern only Ibn Abd al-Wahhab and his descendants and disciples, al-Bassam attempts for the first time to establish a direct and clear line of descent from classical Hanbalism via three sixteenth-century figures: Ahmad ibn Atwa, Ahmad ibn Abi Humaydan, and Abu Numayy al-Tamimi.[95]

After having ended the first leg of their initiatory voyage in Najd, these three figures traveled to neighboring countries in search of science (*al-rihla fi talab al-'ilm*), as the expression goes. While the first two left for Damascus, the third traveled to Cairo. During his stay in the Syrian capital, Ibn Atwa frequented several Hanbali ulama, the most important of whom was al-Mardawi, the author of *al-Insaf*. Ibn Abi Humaydan was for his part the disciple of al-Buhuti, the author of *al-Iqna'*. Al-Tamimi assiduously followed the courses of al-Makrami, author of *Dalil al-Talib*. The three Najdi ulama were thus disciples of the heirs of the classical Hanbali tradition, whose legal writings still constitute major references in the Saudi religious and judicial systems. To this, al-Bassam adds a further claim, though here he breaks with habit and cites no sources: to wit, that upon returning home, the three ulama actively participated in spreading Hanbalism throughout Najd. While the substance of this account is true, al-Bassam exaggerated its contours and significance in order to fill in the "missing link" that would connect the Hanbali tradition of Central Arabia with the Syro-Egyptian tradition and, by extension, the classical period.

In the second edition of his dictionary, the *'alim*-historiographer went even further. First, he changed the title to *The Ulama of Najd during Eight Centuries*. The Hanbali presence in Najd thus found itself extended by two centuries. Al-Bassam managed this by simply adding the biography of an *'alim* who was said to have lived at the beginning of the fourteenth century: *al-hajj* Subayh.[96] While the existence of this person is attested to in a document relating to the establishment of a pious foundation (*waqf*) dating from the year 1346, no other historic document, ancient or modern, mentions him. This explains the author's recourse to popular tales that present the following, idealized portrait: Subayh was a devoted and very pious slave, traits that earned him freedom and holiness. Thanks to miraculous powers associated with his spiritual status (*karamat*, sing. *karama*), he was able to carry out "night voyages" to the great cities of Islam: Mecca, Medina, Jerusalem, and Damascus. In Damascus, he is said to have regularly frequented the teaching circle of Ibn Taymiyya. Although al-Bassam claims to give no credence to the fabrications of popular tales, the temptation to assert a direct link with medieval Hanbalism by way of its most famous representative was simply too great. The *'alim*-historiographer thus chose not only to retain the text, but also to give it the appearance of an historical account in order to lend it more credibility. He cites an *'alim*-magistrate who claims to be a descendant of Subayh and observes that the pious foundation he created still exists and is run by the descendants of its ancient master. We are here confronted with a typical case of invented tradition.

Without going as far as his colleague, the *'alim* Bakr Abu Zayd (d. 2008) cultivated the same ambition in his revealingly titled bio-bibliographical survey *The Hanbali Ulama from Imam Ahmad to 1999* (*'Ulama' al-hanabila min al-imam Ahmad al-mutawaffâ sanat 241 ila wafiyyat 'am 1420*).[97] By organizing his work chronologically, Abu Zayd encouraged uninformed readers to conclude that there was a natural continuity among the periods, regions, and individuals under discussion. Indeed, he draws up an exhaustive list of nearly all known Hanbali clerics, from Ahmad ibn Hanbal (d. 855) to Abd al-Aziz ibn Baz (d. 1999), mufti of Saudi Arabia. The author invents no tradition and does not go to the trouble of justifying this claim of continuity. Instead, he merely imposes this fait accompli on the reader. But this assumption of continuity comes at a price. Abu Zayd was obliged, on the one hand, to use all available Hanbali biographical collections, some of which contain what are considered heretical ideas from a Hanbali-Wahhabi perspective and, on the other hand, to mention heretical Hanbali ulama or those hostile to Ibn Abd al-Wahhab and his predication. The biographical dictionary *al-Suhub al-Wabila fi Dara'ih al-Hanabila* (by Ibn Humayd), for example, is interesting for two reasons: it contains "heretical" ideas, and its author is hostile to Hanbali-Wahhabism. Yet, as it is one of the most important Hanbali historical sources permitting one to draw a line from the Middle Ages to the modern era, it was very carefully reedited and its author rehabilitated.

Until the beginning of the twentieth century, the ulama of the Hanbali-Wahhabi establishment, like most Muslim ulama, drew on only a very limited theologico-legal corpus for reasons relating to the economic, cultural, and political constraints documented by Guido Steinberg.[98] While some figures from the Syro-Egyptian reformist movement tried to publish classical Hanbali works in the 1920s, it seems to have had little effect on the ulama of Najd, who continued to rely on the same sources.[99] For example, according to a Royal Order put about by the ulama, judges were authorized to refer to only four works of Hanbali law in handing down their sentences.[100]

It was only in the late 1950s that things gradually began to change. As we will see in greater detail, growth in petroleum revenue and Saudi Arabia's rise to power allowed the establishment to develop an educational infrastructure, send its children to the great Islamic universities of the region, and import religious personnel. A new awareness of the extent of the medieval Hanbali cultural heritage was the result. In order to establish themselves as the heirs of this tradition, the ulama had to establish a clear line of descent from it and also appropriate it. Between 1960 and 2000, more than three hundred classic Hanbali works were edited and published. Hundreds of master's theses and doctoral dissertations addressing the most varied aspects of medieval Hanbalism were defended in the country's various Islamic universities, to say nothing of the vast number of monographs, specialist articles, booklets, and popular brochures that were published. This attempt to appropriate the tradition concerned not only what are regarded as its more orthodox works, but also works that conflict with the doctrines of modern Hanbali-Wahhabism. These latter have been either faithfully edited, with footnotes and critical introductions correcting what are seen as their more "unorthodox" aspects, or simply republished absent the objectionable content.

We see here how the ethic of responsibility led the representatives of ideological authority to act in a pragmatic manner. In order to win an advantage for the corporation and the tradition upon which it is based, the agent may set aside one or more "eternal" values.

2

SHEDDING NEW LIGHT ON THE LIFE OF MUHAMMAD IBN ABD AL-WAHHAB

MEMORY VERSUS HISTORY: NAJD BEFORE IBN ABD AL-WAHHAB'S PREDICATION

The historiographer of the Saudi Emirate, Ibn Ghannam (d. 1810), presented a dark picture of the religious situation of Arabia and its surroundings at the beginning of the eighteenth century when he wrote:

> most Muslims had returned to the pre-Islamic darkness. Ignorant, at the mercy of potentates gone astray, deprived of the light of good guidance, they turned their backs on the book of God, thus imitating the custom of their ancestors. So they worshipped *marabouts*, living and dead, they venerated trees and substituted new idols for God.... Such was the situation in Najd..., in the holy places... in Yemen..., in Egypt... and in Iraq.[1]

It is clear that his objective was not to inform his readers of the real situation in the region, but rather to construct a history of alterity—that is, of change through difference and exclusion. This passage, which is typical of the first paragraphs of the majority of Saudi chronicles and annals,[2] defined everything that was external or prior to the advent of the Saudi Emirate as an anti-model. Doing this served to underscore the benefits conferred by Muhammad ibn Abd al-Wahhab's predication and helped impose a collective memory that marked a break with the past and the immediate environment.

In this type of undertaking, the historic event—the past—is merely a tool for constructing an identity. Revised, altered, or even invented, it is put to the service of creating a grand narrative. There is thus nothing surprising in the fact that official Saudi compendia mention only external or antecedent events—generally presented in stereotyped form—in order to flatter the claims of Ibn Abd al-Wahhab and his allies and followers. Yet it remains the case that most grand narratives are based on a more or less real event around which meaning is created. Also, history reasserts its rights over memory. In the case under consideration, the value judgment pronounced by Ibn Ghannam and his colleagues was inspired by Ibn Abd al-Wahhab's vision of his contemporaries and of the history of the region in the eighteenth century. Before we examine this image more closely, however, some words must be said regarding the principal social, political, and religious characteristics of the region at the dawn of the Hanbali-Wahhabi predication.[3]

Starting in the early sixteenth century, the Ottoman Empire gradually asserted dominion over "the useful Arabia"—that is, the Hijaz (in order to control the two holy cities as symbolic resources), the northwestern portion of Yemen (in order to control the Bab el-Mandab straits and protect the Red Sea from European incursions), and Al-Ahsa', the coastal band of eastern Arabia (in order to protect the empire's southern flank from Persian and European attack). These symbolic and military concerns went hand in hand with the empire's economic interests. Toward the end of the seventeenth century, however, the empire showed the first signs of weakness, and its political and religious troubles increased. Shiism consolidated its position in Iraq and Persia, and European interference began to make itself felt in the Arab East, in particular along the southern and southeastern coasts of the Arabian Peninsula. With setbacks in Europe, the Mediterranean, and Persia obliging the empire to redeploy its forces, the Sublime Porte retained only weak control over the region, which was largely abandoned to local powers.

Lacking any strategic interest, the central Arabian region of Najd was somewhat removed from these macro-political disturbances. Having almost no experience of direct political control by a centralized power, the region was no more than a vast desert plateau juxtaposing oases, pastureland, and water points held by Bedouin (*badw*) and sedentary (*hadar*) populations. Although it was Muslim, the socioreligious system of Najd nevertheless depended almost entirely on real or fictitious ties of kinship. Traditional authority was the only possible mode of ideal-typical authority in the region. While some lineages dominated the oases, more or less extended tribal confederations dominated the water places and pastures. This political configuration favored not only conflicts between Bedouins and sedentary groups, but also conflicts within each group. The result was significant political instability and major economic problems.

The economy and prestige of the Bedouin tribal confederations depended on the number of water places and the extent of the pastures the confederations controlled. The only way to increase their symbolic and material capital was recourse to force by way of hit-and-run raids (*ghazw*). Apart from the loot they amassed and the territory they conquered, the victors demanded that

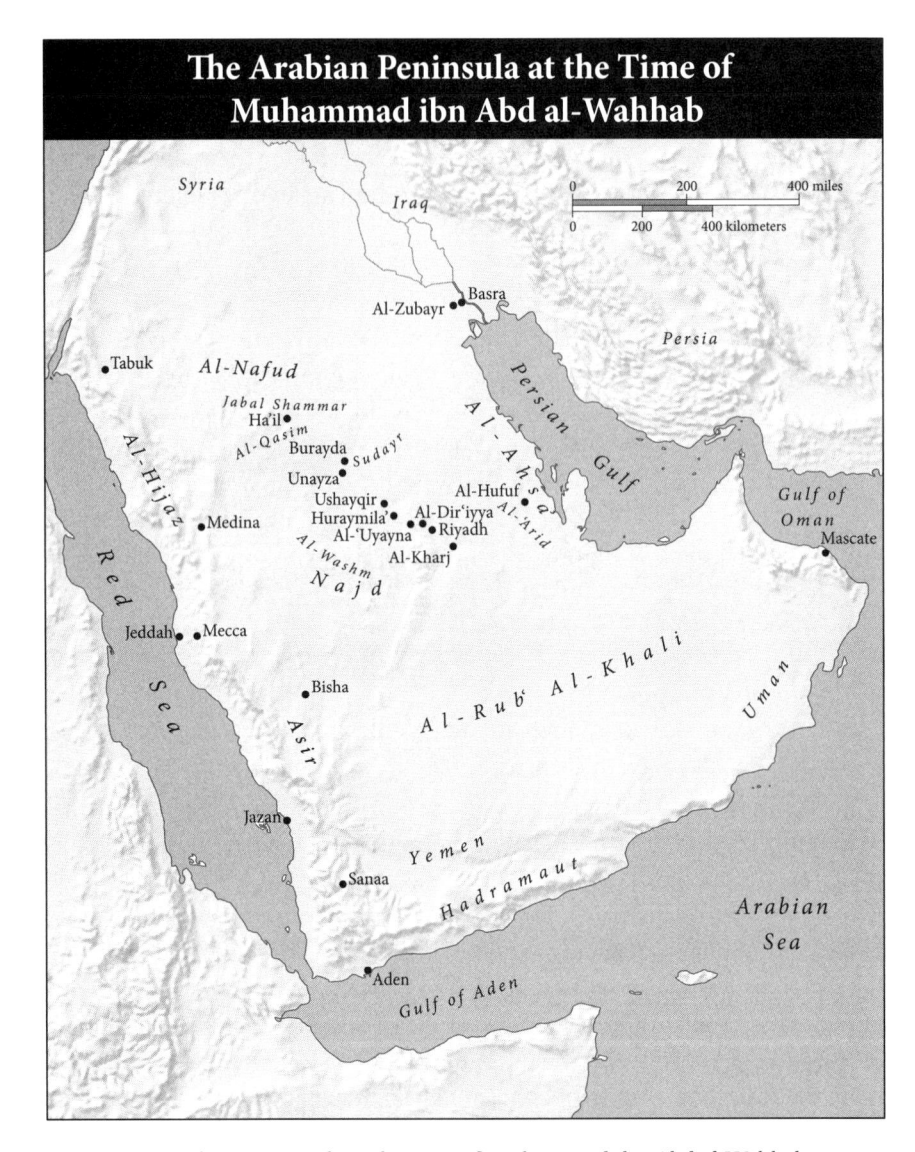

Map 1. The Arabian Peninsula at the time of Muhammad ibn Abd al-Wahhab (eighteenth century).

subjugated tribes pay tribute (*khuwa*). Far from resigning themselves to this, however, the latter only waited for the right moment to revolt, giving rise to a vicious circle of vendetta.

Sedentaries, whose economy was based on subsistence agriculture and the caravan trade, suffered from what may be called the "Bedouin problem" for two reasons: on the one hand, they had to pay a protection tax to the tribes on whose territories (*al-dira*) they resided, and on the other hand, they were exposed to the effects of the tribal conflicts that disrupted the caravan routes (banditry, kidnapping, cut roads, and so on). Lacking *'asabiyya* (spirit of kinship) and/or a mobilizing ideology, the sedentaries were incapable of creating a stable military structure for defending themselves. What's more, persistent rivalry between the sedentaries themselves did nothing to help the situation. In these populations, feelings of humiliation and resentment toward the Bedouins ran high. Their rancor was just as great in regards to their eastern and western neighbors, the emirs of Mecca and the Banu Khalid of Al-Ahsa', who conducted very lucrative raids on the oases of Najd and forced their populations to pay tribute.

Bedouins and sedentaries both suffered from problems of internal governance; the most important of these was related to the adelphic form of succession in Najd. According to this mode of horizontal succession, commonly found in traditional societies, all men belonging to the dominant lineage have equal power, and only providence or fortune is capable of deciding between them. The accession to power of the most powerful member of the lineage—in general, a brother, nephew, or cousin who is more or less closely tied to the deceased or deposed chief—is favored, even though primogeniture is not ruled out. This conception of the transmission of power implies that each offspring of the dominant line is authorized to see himself as the rightful heir of the family's possessions. In these conditions, more or less long phases of political transition—above all, in the event of generational change—are necessarily periods of crisis, conflict, and violence. Each branch of the dominant lineage in effect tries to exclude the others or minimize their role in the political space. Successive periods of crisis weaken the dominant group or even the political structure itself, encourage direct or indirect foreign intervention, and eventually bring about the dominant group's collapse.

Aside from the problems mentioned above, the political fragmentation of Najd was due to the absence of two factors that Ibn Khaldun (d. 1406) saw as indispensable to any political enterprise: ideology (*da'wa*) and spirit of kinship (*'asabiyya*). Since the end of the Middle Ages, several tribal confederations had tried to control Najd, but they did not have the human or symbolic resources necessary to succeed.[4] In other words, no local *'asabiyya* was powerful enough to impose absolute domination over the territory and its population. As I have observed in the case of sixteenth century Morocco, only an ideologically based, supratribal force was capable of achieving such an objective.[5] The age of the *'asabiyya* had come to an end.

None of the Sunni powers of the Arabian Peninsula laid claim to religious legitimacy and this for a simple reason: recognition of the suzerainty of the Ottomans, whose sovereign saw himself as the caliph of the Muslims, deprived them of ideological support.[6] Also, no religious tradition was sufficiently powerful in numerical and intellectual terms to impose itself on the others.

Like the political field, the religious space was fragmented. All of the religious traditions of Islam were represented in eighteenth-century Arabia: the four legal schools and the various theological currents of Sunni Islam, Twelver Shiism, Zaydism, Isma'ilism, Kharijism, and a number of mystical brotherhoods. Even if, over the course of several centuries, Hanbalism had spread throughout Najd, the other Sunni schools and the various Sufi brotherhoods were also present.[7] Moreover, as elsewhere in the lands of Islam, "popular" religious practices were commonplace, and ancestral customs were often applied, in certain tribes, in place of sharia to resolve disputes. The meager information available to us as well as the fact that Hanbali-Wahhabism encountered resistance in several regions of Arabia, including Najd, from the second half of the eighteenth century through the end of the nineteenth century are suggestive of firmly rooted traditions and well-organized corporations of ulama.

There was nothing "abnormal" about the political and religious situation of Najd and its environs during the first half of the eighteenth century. It was of a piece with the *longue durée* of local history and seemed to suit a large portion of the elite, who were content with the traditional authority they enjoyed.

Nevertheless, certain political and religious actors seem to have been shocked by the situation of the various Muslim countries in this period for different reasons. Indeed, some raised their voices to denounce socioreligious practices that failed to respect orthodoxy and orthopraxy and to criticize political divisions. According to them, the original message needed to be reestablished and sharia rehabilitated. In keeping with a schema familiar to the Muslim world and elsewhere since the High Middle Ages, such a return might be brought about in two ways: reformism or messianism. Whereas reformism advocates a reform of the socioreligious system by means of inculcation and interaction, messianism recommends breaking with it more or less violently in order to construct a new social system modeled upon the ideal city of Medina at the time of the Prophet.

Between 1740 and 1860, several charismatic figures thus took the initiative to make changes: Shah Waliyy Allah (d. 1762) in India, Sultan Muhammad ibn Abd Allah (d. 1790) in Morocco, Ibn Fudi (d. 1817) in West Africa, Muhammad al-Sanusi (d. 1859) in Cyrenaica, and Muhammad ibn Abd al-Wahhab in Najd (d. 1792). Yet, as Ahmad Dallal has so convincingly argued, the simultaneity of their actions must not be mistaken for an indication of a structured movement or as evidence of a direct link between them.[8] Evolving in different socioreligious contexts, these men shared only one point: the firm belief that they had been invested with an exceptional mission to rehabilitate the mystical body of Islam. To that end, each employed a specific method and strategy in keeping with his particular convictions.

In regards to Ibn Abd al-Wahhab, I do not think that his actions were a response to the ostensibly "chaotic" sociopolitical situation of Najd, as certain teleological readings of Saudi history would have it. Of course, the region suffered from several problems, but everyone more or less benefited from them. It suffices to recall that local forces and populations systematically exploited every moment of weakness on the part of the Saudi Emirate to return to the situation that had prevailed before its emergence. This was to be the case up until the start of the twentieth century.

Without excluding the influence of the sociopolitical context, I nevertheless believe that, like other reformers, Ibn Abd al-Wahhab was convinced that he had a role in the economy of salvation of his time. For him, things were simple: the mystical body of Islam had to be rehabilitated via the reestablishment of the three O's, which he believed had been flouted. Like Paul Veyne and Roland Mousnier, one must thus resign oneself to admitting, on the one hand, that "not everything in history is explained by the state of society," and on the other, that "there are men for whom relations with God are an important matter, the most important matter of their lives."[9]

Before I present and examine the career of Ibn Abd al-Wahhab, it is worth underscoring that he was neither an *'alim* in the service of a tradition nor the agent of a corporation. He was rather "a bearer of personal charisma who, by virtue of his mission, proclaimed a religious doctrine or a divine commandment."[10] In other words, his mission of imposing orthodoxy and orthopraxy was based on personal vocation and a belief in the intrinsic and unconditional value of an idea or behavior, independently of its effects. In order to succeed in this, he opted for the messianic path, for which personal charisma is the appropriate type of authority and uncompromising ideology is the medium. Without ever admitting it—no doubt because of his strict religious beliefs—he adopted the habitus of the *mujaddid* (the reformer of the century), who aspires to break with the past and the immediate environment in order to create a new social order—a counterreligion.

THE BANALITY OF THE EXCEPTIONAL: A PREACHER'S CAREER

Contrary to a commonly held view, Ibn Abd al-Wahhab was not a self-made man who wandered out of the desert. He was from the Al Musharraf, one of the most prestigious sedentary kindreds of Najd and the source of most of the province's religious personnel. Indeed, an inventory of the available biographical collections shows that more than 25 percent of Najd ulama between the sixteenth and eighteenth centuries belonged to this kindred, which was originally from the oasis of Ushayqir, the center of Najdi Hanbalism. The grandfather and father of Ibn Abd al-Wahhab were thus highly respected ulama and performed the duties of judge in various oases in the region and in particular, Al-'Uyayna, where Muhammad ibn Abd al-Wahhab was born in 1703.[11]

Like the offspring of ulama households (*buyutat 'ilm*) throughout the Muslim world, Muhammad probably had no choice but to carry on the family tradition. When he was very young, his basic education began under the direction of his father. Given the limited intellectual resources of Najd, however, he decided to follow the example of many ulama of the classical period, and in 1715, he set off on a long series of peregrinations in search of religious knowledge.[12] His travels took him to Mecca, Medina, Al-Ahsa', Basra, and no doubt elsewhere. Unfortunately, the chronology of these voyages is impossible to reconstruct because of a lack of sources.

These initiatory journeys were essential, not just to the education of the young Najdi, but also to shaping his religious vision of the world. During his stay in Medina and Basra, three ulama seem to have left a lasting mark on him: Muhammad Hayya al-Sindi (d. 1750), Abd Allah ibn Sayf al-Shammari (d. ?), and Muhammad al-Majmu'i (d. ?). Through his contact with them, Ibn Abd Al-Wahhab discovered the classical Hanbali creed, the writings of Ibn Taymiyya and Ibn al-Qayyim, and the need to move beyond the sterile prescriptions that featured in legal scholium and glosses to draw directly on the sources of the Law.

In parallel with these three fundamental intellectual discoveries, Ibn Abd al-Wahhab witnessed firsthand the practices of popular Islam—Sunni and Shia alike—so condemned by the Hanbali tradition as well as the neglect of basic religious duties. The conjunction of these two factors in all likelihood led him to act. It is in Basra that he is said to have begun preaching the obligation to respect orthodoxy and orthopraxy. According to one of his descendants, he even wrote his first and most famous work, *The Book of the Unity of God* (*Kitab al-tawhid*), there.[13] But his predication seems to have very rapidly come to the attention of the local religious elite, who persuaded the political authorities to expel him from the capital of southern Iraq.

Ibn Abd al-Wahhab subsequently reappeared in Al-Ahsa', where he is said to have been disappointed by the poor quality of instruction supplied by local ulama. Once there, however, this did not prevent him from reading and recopying the works of Ibn Taymiyya and Ibn al-Qayyim, henceforth his favorite readings and main sources of inspiration. Moreover, it should be emphasized that no source indicates that Ibn Abd al-Wahhab was involved in activism in this cosmopolitan region, where the same popular Islamic practices were to be observed as in Medina and Basra. This silence calls into question the truth of the account of his activity in Basra. Whatever the case, Ibn Abd al-Wahhab, wiser for his intellectual baggage and religious convictions, returned to his native Najd and installed himself in the oasis of Huraymila', the very town in which his father had served as a judge since 1727.

It was in this oasis that he began to agitate for orthodoxy and orthopraxy. While his actions initially seem to have been limited, he profited from the death of his father in 1740 to intensify them. Although he succeeded in attracting followers, Ibn Abd al-Wahhab was unable to persuade the local authorities to support his "salvational" approach. He was thus summarily expelled from Huraymila' just a few months after his father's death. He then found refuge in Al-'Uyayna, the oasis of his birth.

This is the way that the oldest sources recount the initiatory journey of Muhammad ibn Abd al-Wahhab and the start of his predication. Nothing could be more banal: this itinerary hardly differs from that of other activist ulama mentioned throughout Muslim history, particularly in the medieval Hanbali tradition. The success of his mission, however, brought about a change of scale, with the establishment of the Saudi Emirate and the creation of a new tradition. In order to touch minds and stir the imagination, the path followed by the charismatic leader now had to live up to his status as the founder of a tradition. His followers thus proceeded to reconstruct his life to present it as a foundational moment, edifying example, and source of authority. To that end, they mainly insisted on three points: the founder's predestination for this noble task, the similarities between his path and that of the Prophet, and his break with the immediate environment. The fundamental objectives of this revision were to demonstrate the founder's privileged relationship with God and the Prophet—the two ultimate sources of all legitimacy in Islam—and to prove his distance from the corrupt world.

A survey of some key episodes from the first part of Ibn Abd al-Wahhab's life allows us a closer look at how his followers went about bestowing a symbolic dimension upon his person and historic depth to his actions. This was nothing more or less than a process of discursive construction aiming to legitimate a nascent tradition and the claims of its guardians through the use (conscious or not) of homily—that is, stories and accounts that would be well-known to contemporaries. It should be pointed out that most of the processes to be discussed in this connection had been used in nearly identical manner by several Muslim dynasties and movements since the High Middle Age. This was particularly the case of the messianic movements that emerged with the Abbasids (750–1258), the Almohads (1130–1269), and the Zaydanids (1510–1658).

The French consul in Aleppo and Baghdad, Louis de Corancez (d. 1832), reported that Sulayman, the grandfather of Ibn Abd al-Wahhab,

> one night dreamed that a flame he saw leave his body spread far across the countryside and consumed in passing the tents of the desert and the habitations of towns. Sulayman, frightened by this dream, asked the shaykhs of his tribe to interpret it, and they explained it as a good omen. They announced to him that his son would be chief of a new religion that would convert the Arabs of the desert and subjugate townspeople. And indeed, the dream was realized, not in the person of Abd al-Wahhab, son of Sulayman, but in that of his grandson, shaykh Muhammad.[14]

This anecdote, which seems to have spread throughout the region within just a few years of Ibn Abd al-Wahhab's death, shows that his followers were quick to circulate a number of his "prophesies." Their objective was clear: to demonstrate that the founder of the new tradition was predestined to carry out his mission. In order to render this claim more credible, they drew upon the example of the Prophet. Indeed, the account cited above is just a modified version of a premonitory dream credited to the Prophet's mother, who is said to have seen in her sleep a light flow out of her and shine forth up to the stars and as far as the land of Syria.[15] In addition to drawing a parallel with the Prophet of Islam, the supporters of Ibn Abd al-Wahhab wished to profit from the symbolic reach of this dream: the flame represents the light of divine truth, which burns away all illusions and heresies and ushers in a new era, a new order, one that is pure and governed by the most orthodox religious precepts. The message glorified a break with the immediate past and the restoration of truth.[16]

As a child, the Prophet of Islam was precocious, serious, and showed no interest in the amusements of those his age, preferring meditation. The tradition also insists that he never prostrated himself before an idol. Here, too, those who sang the praises of Ibn Abd al-Wahhab drew upon the model of the Prophet to idealize the image of their charismatic leader. Firsthand accounts claim that the founder of Hanbali-Wahhabism did not play with the children of his age and preferred to study the Qur'an. Similarly precocious, he is said to have finished learning the Qur'an by heart before the age of ten. Two years later, he is said to have married, begun leading prayers in the Grand Mosque of Al-'Uyayna, and even gone on pilgrimage to Mecca.[17] These accounts also insist that Ibn Abd al-Wahhab realized very early on the need to return to orthodoxy and orthopraxy.[18]

After these "telltale signs" of the predestination of the new tradition's central figure—which were indispensable to erecting an idealized image—had been put into circulation, a detailed reconstruction of the founder's initiatory voyage was required. In order to legitimate their position and strengthen their ideological authority, the ulama had to study under the direction of as many recognized authorities as possible. Their aim was to acquire knowledge, create an extended network, and establish an uninterrupted chain of descent from the Prophet by way of the founders of traditions. Against all expectations, however, the biographers of Ibn Abd al-Wahhab are far removed from this model. Altogether, they mention the names of only three of the above-cited ulama. By contrast, the ulama of Al-Ahsa' were mentioned only to demonstrate the lamentable state of knowledge during that epoch. This amounted to another classic procedure for legitimating charismatic authority: deliberately choosing to hide the founder's relations with the best-known religious authorities of his time in order to underscore the break with the past. In the same spirit, primacy is instead accorded to peripheral figures, the "visionaries" who ensured continuity with the glorious past and recognized the founder's future as a great man. This strategy is reminiscent of the relations between John the Baptist and Jesus, for example, or those between Waraqa ibn Nawfal and the Prophet of Islam. Muhammad Hayya al-Sindi, Abd Allah ibn Sayf al-Shammari, and Muhammad al-Majmu'i play the same role vis-à-vis Ibn Abd al-Wahhab. While these three figures all recognized the latter to be an exceptional man, each of them supplied him with a distinct link to the golden age of Islam. The first bestowed upon him the treasures of the prophetic tradition, thereby allowing him to establish a link with the pious ancestors (al-salaf al-salih);[19] the second commented for him on the works of Ibn Taymiyya and Ibn al-Qayyim, opening the doors to Damascene Hanbalism; and the third taught him theology so that he could develop relations with Iraqi Hanbalism.

This is why Ibn Abd al-Wahhab's sycophants limit his movements to these three regions while other ancient sources claim that he traveled to Baghdad, Damascus, Kurdistan, and Persia.[20] Whatever the truth of his peregrinations, they did not feature in the official biographies of Ibn Abd al-Wahhab. These sought not to faithfully recount the preacher's career, but rather to erect a model, mark a break with the past, and herald the regeneration of Islam.

As I have already indicated, several episodes from the first stage of Ibn Abd al-Wahhab's life bear a striking resemblance to the prophetic model. I now present two elegantly symbolic examples of this. The first event took place in

Basra, where Ibn Abd al-Wahhab is said to have begun preaching against what he considered to be heterodox beliefs and practices. Far from persuading the people of this town, he provoked an angry response from the elite, who turned the authorities and population against him. Struck and stoned by the crowd, he ultimately fled.[21] Eleven centuries earlier, the Prophet of Islam had been subjected to exactly the same treatment after traveling to the town of Al-Ta'if to spread his message.[22]

The second event took place in the context of the oasis of Huraymila', where Ibn Abd al-Wahhab began delivering fiery sermons in 1740. Weary of his "moralizing" sermons, the elites of the oasis decided to rid themselves of him by arranging his assassination. Warned of the plot in time, Ibn Abd al-Wahhab took flight, finding refuge in the oasis of Al-'Uyayna. Once again, the event bears an evident parallel with a foundational moment of Islam: the Hegira. In 622, the inhabitants of Mecca, wishing to once and for all silence the Prophet of Islam, decided to execute him; but, hearing word of the conspiracy, the Prophet fled Mecca and took refuge in Medina.[23]

THE EMIRATE: AN EMERGENT EFFECT OF IBN ABD AL-WAHHAB'S PREDICATION

Whereas the Prophet of Islam pursued intense religious and political activities in Medina, Ibn Abd al-Wahhab contented himself with exclusively religious activity during his stay in Al-'Uyayna between 1740 and 1744. His main objective was purely religious: to reestablish orthodoxy and orthopraxy. His letters dating from this period, for example, were all addressed to religious actors, whom he sought to convince of the truth and cogency of his ideas.[24] In one of his fatawa from this period, Ibn Abd al-Wahhab went so far as to claim that the application of legal penalties hardly required the existence of a political authority.[25] As a consequence—and contrary to a widely held view—he was not at this time considering the idea of establishing a political entity. To all appearances, the emir of Al-'Uyayna, Uthman ibn Mu'ammar, had adopted the ideas of the shaykh while the latter was still preaching in Huraymila'.[26] On this basis, he offered Ibn Abd al-Wahhab asylum and allowed him to freely exercise his predication. The matrimonial alliance contracted between the two men seems to have been purely personal in nature[27] and was in no way the consecration of a symbiotic relationship between them.[28] Apart from the fact that both were issued from the two most prestigious clans of the Banu Tamim confederation—in a society in which endogamy was commonplace, this would have entailed frequent matrimonial exchanges—Emir Uthman ibn Mu'ammar played no significant role during this period and hastened to rid himself of his guest at the first sign of trouble. Moreover, the followers of Ibn Abd al-Wahhab who came to live in Al-'Uyayna swore allegiance (*al-bay'a*) to him rather than to the emir.[29]

Ibn Abd al-Wahhab devoted his first two years in Al-'Uyayna to inculcating and applying his ideas. Apart from teaching, he sent several disciples to the various oases of the region in order to spread his doctrine.[30] Only after this preliminary step did he begin his efforts, around 1742, to see to it that orthodoxy and orthopraxy were respected in the public sphere: he destroyed popular places of worship, which he judged centered on polytheism; obliged people to observe collective prayer; and enforced legal punishments (most famously, the stoning of a woman accused of adultery).[31] For the first time in his writing, he explicitly attacked the cult of saints, mystical brotherhoods, popular practices, and the corruption of the spiritual elites. He even claimed that those who followed this path immediately fell into heresy and even impiety.[32]

At the start of his career—particularly in *The Book of the Unity of God*—he condemned the practices of popular Islam on theoretical grounds, without really seeking to enforce his views in practical terms. It was only beginning in 1742 that he brought an activist approach to bear on his intellectual activities. But the most important consideration is elsewhere. In his writings and actions, he made a genuine distinction between true and false religion: for him, the sole path to salvation was to follow and apply his teachings. In other words, Ibn Abd al-Wahhab claimed that only the religion he proclaimed was the true Islam. This claim represented an indisputable break with his background and the recent past. In such cases, exclusion is the golden rule and interaction with other groups is possible only in the framework of conversion or confrontation. In other words, the position he adopted had all of the characteristics of a counterreligion.

The year 1742 was a decisive turning point in his career. While his activity had up until then gone unremarked and was limited to a local framework, his practices, uncompromising writings, and the growing number of followers he attracted began to cause a stir at the regional level.[33] The ulama and leaders of the mystical brotherhoods of Najd realized the danger that his ideas could represent, not just to their beliefs, but also to their social status and economic privileges.[34] For "the charisma of office, when taken to its logical conclusion, irremediably becomes the sworn enemy of all authentically personal charisma, which, attaching to the individual as such, encourages and teaches an autonomous path to God."[35] Some of them thus decided to mobilize all of the region's clerical corporations in order to prevent future "evil": they sent letters to Mecca, Basra, and Al-Ahsa' to encourage local ulama to write refutations (*rudud*) and promulgate fatawa against the heresy of Ibn Abd al-Wahhab.[36] Between 1742 and 1744, several refutations were put into circulation, and several ulama affiliated with religious brotherhoods and the cult of the saints excommunicated him and put a price on his head.[37]

These mainly violent condemnations succeeded in destabilizing some of the shaykh's supporters, who suggested he moderate his stance in order to win acceptance.[38] But, like any religious actor whose thoughts and actions are based on reason, Ibn Abd al-Wahhab believed in their absolute validity and therefore refused to give way to pressure. Counterreligions that claim to have a monopoly on truth refuse all compromise and are persistent in maintaining that only their followers will achieve eternal salvation. Indeed, according to a saying attributed to the Prophet, "'what happened to the sons of Israel will happen to my community. They divided themselves into seventy-two sects. My community will for its part divide itself into seventy-three factions. All will go to hell, with one exception.' Upon which the Prophet was asked: 'Which is this faction that is confident of salvation?' and he then answered: 'it is the one to which myself and my companions belong.'"[39] Ibn Abd al-Wahhab was intimately convinced that he belonged to this latter category. He therefore pursued his mission, which he thought led to salvation, with the same zeal.[40]

Noting the failure of all intellectual efforts to put an end to Ibn Abd al-Wahhab's activities, the region's religious actors decided to ask for help from the authorities. Over the course of 1744, they succeeded in convincing the emir of the Banu Khalid tribal confederation, which controlled the region of Al-Ahsa' and a part of Najd, of the threat posed to the region's political order by the shaykh's intrigues. The emir in question immediately reacted. He contacted the emir of Al-'Uyayna and ordered him, under threat of military and economic sanctions, to expel the preacher from his territory. Panicking at the thought of coming under devastating attack from the region's most powerful tribal confederation, Ibn Mu'ammar quickly gave way to pressure and informed Ibn Abd al-Wahhab that he was henceforth persona non grata in the oasis.[41] In vain, Ibn Abd al-Wahhab tried to persuade the emir to change his mind, promising to organize the territory's defense in the event of military attack. For the first time, Ibn Abd al-Wahhab referred to the notion of jihad, though in this case it was jihad of a strictly defensive nature.[42]

Obliged to leave his native oasis, toward the end of 1744 the shaykh moved to the oasis of Al-Dir'iyya.[43] Three considerations dictated this choice, in my view: first, Mishari, Thunayyan, and Abd al-Aziz—the brothers and eldest son, respectively, of the oasis's emir, Muhammad ibn Saud (d. 1765)—were among his oldest and most prominent followers.[44] Second, the Al Suʿud kindred,[45] which we will henceforth refer to as the Sauds, had governed the oasis for about two centuries and had no close ties of kinship or economic interest with the region's large tribal confederations. Third, the oasis possessed fortifications capable of protecting its inhabitants in the event of attack.[46]

After several weeks of discussion and negotiation, Ibn Abd al-Wahhab succeeded in convincing Ibn Saud of the legitimacy of his claims. According to the available sources, the head of the Saud family is said to have even entered into a symbiotic relationship with him in 1744, which was later to become one of the most famous and lasting alliances in Muslim history.[47] But the romantic image of it that is supplied by these sources leads one to doubt the truth of the event. The structure of the account and the formula it uses, which once again draw upon an episode from the Prophet's life—to wit, the agreement reached between Muhammad and the inhabitants of Medina before the Hegira—lead me to believe that it is a reflection of subsequent attempts to construct an identity that would justify the establishment of the Saudi Emirate. It cannot be a faithful account of events. What's more, the account's references to the notions of jihad and plunder strengthen these doubts. As we will see, the concept of conquest, which implies jihad and plunder, was at this time and for several years to come absent from the writings and actions of Ibn Abd al-Wahhab. In light of the above, it can be concluded that the basic agreement reached between Ibn Abd al-Wahhab and Ibn Saud covered only the religious domain, that is, the application of orthodoxy and orthopraxy.

Between 1744 and 1747, the preacher pursued his work undisturbed in the religious domain—destroying sites of popular worship, teaching, drafting minor tracts for the general public, organizing obligatory group prayers, sending preachers to the oases of the region, and so on.[48] In the same vein, he continued to send epistles to the religious leaders of the region in the hope of "converting" them.[49] And although he failed to persuade the latter, he succeeded in acculturating the inhabitants of Al-Dirʿiyya and winning over hundreds of people throughout the region, swelling the ranks of his followers. Better yet, several oases—including the large oases of Huraymila' and Thirmida'—"converted."

The rapid spread of Ibn Abd al-Wahhab's ideas disturbed the region's religious elites, who sought to rid themselves of him once and for all in order to preserve their beliefs and privileges. The ulama of Riyadh, who had always been his staunchest enemies, had to face the facts: only force would be able to put an end to this threat. To that end, they succeeded in persuading their emir, Dahham ibn Dawwas, to attack the shaykh's supporters. In 1747, Ibn Dawwas attacked the oasis of Manfuha.[50] Contrary to a widely held view, then, it was not Ibn Abd al-Wahhab and his followers who struck the first blow in the framework of a jihad of conquest.

Far from achieving its goal, the emir of Riyadh's campaign on the contrary provoked an emergent effect: the gradual creation of a political entity equipped with a small army and a public treasury to defend the ideas of Ibn Abd al-Wahhab. Between 1747 and 1758, the shaykh's supporters, led by Ibn Saud and his son, Abd al-Aziz, faced off against the troops of Ibn Dawwas no fewer than seventeen times. In the oases that had rallied to their side, they also had to confront several rebellions led by opposing ulama.[51] The victories won by the Hanbali-Wahhabis during this period only increased the fears of the region's elites, particularly those of the Banu Khalid, who decided to go on the offensive.[52] In less than a year, they attacked Al-Dir'iyya twice, though without success.[53] Despite defeat at the hands of the Isma'ilis of Najran, the supporters of Ibn Abd al-Wahhab gained confidence in themselves, and their political entity slowly grew strong thanks to a genuine division of labor between Ibn Abd al-Wahhab and Ibn Saud. While the former controlled the religious and financial spheres, the latter oversaw military operations. From that moment on, the shaykh no longer strived exclusively to apply orthodoxy and orthopraxy but also to defend the political order he had established.

The advent of the political entity, which was an emergent effect of Ibn Abd al-Wahhab's predication, gave his ideas a genuine territorial base and helped them to spread more rapidly. Between 1758 and 1774, the Hanbali-Wahhabis took the military initiative in the context of an increasingly offensive jihad. This allowed them to effectively control several districts of Najd, in particular, Al-Washm and Al-'Arid. They were also able to successfully repulse new attacks by the Banu Khalid and the Isma'ilis of Najran. Together with these military efforts, Ibn Abd al-Wahhab continued to send letters, books, and emissaries to the various regions of Arabia in the hope of winning religious dignitaries over to his ideas. In 1771, for example, he sent one of his leading disciples to Mecca to debate the central foundations of Islamic Law and dogma with the holy city's most prominent ulama.[54] As before, the three O's were inseparably linked to one another.

The capture of Riyadh in 1773 represented another turning point in the career of Ibn Abd al-Wahhab. Throughout the preceding period, the charismatic founder of Hanbali-Wahhabism seemed to dominate the nascent politico-religious entity. Indeed, Ibn Saud, who is considered the first Saudi sovereign, appears to have been no more than the secular arm of the nascent tradition. One may suppose that Ibn Abd al-Wahhab was in a position to permanently control both the political and religious domains had he wished to do so. But one must always keep in mind the fact that he was first and foremost a religious actor pursuing purely religious goals on the path to eternal salvation. As with many reformers, the state was not for him an objective in itself but rather a means to realizing the three O's. Having concluded that the political entity was strong enough to protect the nascent religious tradition, in the last twenty years of his life he withdrew from all temporal affairs in order to devote himself to worship, writing, and teaching.[55] He thus handed all of his duties (in particular, that of treasurer) over to his faithful ally and follower, one of the first to rally to his cause, Abd al-Aziz ibn Muhammad ibn Saud (d. 1803)—who may be considered the first genuine Saudi sovereign. Abd al-Aziz ibn Muhammad ibn Saud soon proved himself to be worthy of the shaykh's trust. In fewer than twenty years, he succeeded in unifying Najd for the first time under a single authority. Indeed, he was preparing for the final assault on Al-Ahsa' when, in 1792, Ibn Abd al-Wahhab died in Al-Dir'iyya.[56]

Before we return to the doctrine of Ibn Abd al-Wahhab, a last point should be emphasized. Nascent Hanbali-Wahhabism and the passions to which it gave rise were purely local phenomena. They hardly exceeded the framework of the Arabian Peninsula and its immediate environs (in particular, Basra and Damascus). The action of the shaykh hardly aroused the interest of the Ottoman authorities, whose documents only mention Ibn Abd al-Wahhab—and then only in passing—in 1749.[57] In response to a missive from the emir of Mecca concerning the measures to be taken against this emergent tradition, which was seen as a heretical sect, the Ottoman Porte simply ordered the emir to personally handle this "provincial" and "unimportant" problem.[58] The authorities in Istanbul no doubt felt they had more important business in the Balkans, the Caucasus, and along the frontiers with Persia.

Similarly, the intellectual and military struggles mentioned above only rarely exceeded the local Sunni framework. Ibn Abd al-Wahhab's most determined detractors belonged to the four schools of Sunni Islam. And, for the most part, the struggle took place within Hanbalism. The majority of the shaykh's letters were addressed to Hanbali dignitaries, and most of the nascent Saudi entity's military campaigns were directed against oases and tribes of Najd whose populations were mainly Hanbali. Contemporaneous annalists, such as Ibn Yusuf and Ibn Abbad, saw nothing exceptional in the military campaigns carried out by Ibn Abd al-Wahhab's supporters. On the contrary, such combat was, in their view, a "routine" part of the struggles between kindreds and oases that had for several centuries punctuated the history of the region.[59] This observation reflects a reality on the ground: it took the shaykh and his supporters no fewer than thirty-three years of intellectual and military struggle to politically dominate nearly all of Najd. The job was complex and victory was less clearly preordained than some teleological readings of Saudi history would lead one to believe.

THE KEY WORDS OF IBN ABD AL-WAHHAB'S DOCTRINE

Far from being an innovator, Muhammad ibn Abd al-Wahhab only adapted and simplified classic Hanbali doctrines in the service of his religious ideal. He was not a great intellectual like Ibn Qudama, Ibn Taymiyya, or Ibn al-Qayyim but rather an activist who shied away from nothing to impose his ideas.[60] Adopting a "messianic" approach, he claimed that the True Religion had been perverted by the heterodox beliefs and practices of his contemporaries. Energetic action was thus necessary to reform and restore it. Like any self-respecting founder of a counterreligion, Ibn Abd al-Wahhab claimed to possess the truth and, in that measure, access to the path of eternal salvation. This premise marks a break with classic Hanbalism: while it claimed preeminence vis-à-vis all other currents of Islam, as we saw above, it never pretended to hold a monopoly on the truth.

All of the shaykh's work and action tended to establish a distinction between true and false, between two antagonistic worlds: the world of Islam and the world of ignorance of the True Religion (*al-jahiliyya*).[61] While the inhabitants of the first sphere scrupulously observed orthodoxy and orthopraxy, those of the second worshipped the *taghut* (the idol) and found themselves in "the state of whoever oversteps the proper limits of worshipping God, the obligation to follow the Sunna of the Prophet, and the obedience due the authorities."[62]

For Ibn Abd al-Wahhab, the Muslim world, understood as Najd and its environs—the only regions he knew—had fallen into *jahiliyya* because of the neglect of orthodoxy and orthopraxy and the adoption of superstitious practices. He rose up against precisely these practices, which he saw as a form of idolatry amounting to *jahiliyya*. His first objective was to purify Islamic Law and dogma of all blameworthy innovations and return to a "pure" religion, that of the time of the Prophet and the pious ancestors (*al-salaf al-salih*). In order to do this, he thought it necessary to redefine the concept of divine unity (*tawhid*) as the foundation for the Muslim religion's "revival." According to Ibn Abd al-Wahhab, *tawhid* had three components: *tawhid al-rububiyya* (the sovereign unity of divine power), which consists of the objective recognition of divine unity and omnipotence; *tawhid al-uluhiyya* (unity of worship), or the subjective fact of recognizing God alone as one's master; and finally, *tawhid al-asma' wa al-sifat* (the affirmation of the unity of divine names and attributes)[63] as they were set out by Ibn Sahman: "We describe God as Himself and his Prophet did. We do not transform the terms of the Qur'an and the Sunna . . . God is not comparable to anything."[64] The concept of *tawhid*, in other words, does not uniquely consist of the recognition of a single, incomparable, sovereign, and all-powerful God. It also presupposes that the individual and collective serve him since obedience to him is the aim of everything. To that end, one should employ the "means" that God himself recommended.[65] This amounts to nothing more or less than strict observance of orthodoxy and orthopraxy in conformity with Hanbali doctrine.[66]

Ibn Abd al-Wahhab held that the only true creed was the Hanbali creed, the very same as that professed by the first three generations of Muslims (*'aqidat al-salaf*).[67] In addition to movements that had disappeared several centuries earlier, such as the Jahmites and the Mu'tazilites, he firmly but summarily condemned the speculative theology of the Ash'arites and the Shiites for its failure to observe *tawhid al-asma' wa al-sifat* (the affirmation of the unity of divine names and attributes).[68]

But the shaykh's denunciations were mainly directed against Sufism and the practices of popular Islam, which in his view violated the very essence of *tawhid al-rububiyya* and *tawhid al-uluhiyya*. Indeed, he held that extracanonical pilgrimages; the cult of the saints, places, and objects; the cenobitic life; religious brotherhoods; divinatory practices; and so on were forms of associationism (*al-shirk*) and idolatry (*al-wathaniyya*).[69] In keeping with a fundamental rule of Muslim law, which stipulates that one must prepare to defend oneself against evil before attending to the good (*dar' al-mafasid muqaddam 'ala jalb al-masalih*), he roundly condemned Sufism as it was practiced by his contemporaries.[70]

Ibn Abd al-Wahhab's hatred of idolatry even led him to forbid all forms of worship devoted to the Prophet. For in his view, "[Loving the Prophet] is to take him for one's guide and love and respect him without fear, demonstrate active submission to the Sunna, stop where it stops, finish where it finishes, in the principles of the religion and the domain of their application alike, in the external meaning of the Law and its deeper meaning alike."[71]

While he authorized believers to visit the Prophet's tomb and pray for him, he forbade them from considering their visits or prayers as constituting a form of a pilgrimage. He even more strongly rejected the idea that they should be used as an occasion for soliciting miraculous intervention on the part of the Prophet. In his eyes, even the Prophet's intercession on behalf of believers on the last day of judgment could not take place without divine authorization. In the same vein, he claimed that with the exception of the rights recognized by sharia, the descendants of the Prophet could lay claim to no particular temporal or religious status.[72] In order to discourage idolatrous practices, Ibn Abd al-Wahhab temporarily prohibited this group from wearing distinctive clothing (usually green in color). Similarly, he forbade believers from prostrating before the Prophet's descendants or kissing their hands, feet, or clothes. Finally, he condemned the endogamy practiced by Sharifian families and called upon them to open up to outsiders. As a consequence, he proclaimed that the clause of equivalence was not required in a marriage between Arabs.[73]

These drastic measures to counter associationism do not mean that Ibn Abd al-Wahhab did not recognize saintliness (*al-wilaya*). On the contrary, he admitted the existence from time immemorial of devout people who, thanks to their scrupulous observance of orthodoxy and orthopraxy, were able to achieve saintliness and even succeeded in producing miracles (*al-karamat*). Such miracles, however, were in his view more a matter of divine potency than of any supernatural power on the part of the saint, who, alone, could not cure the sick or fulfill wishes or intercede with God.[74]

This fear of falling into associationism and idolatry is at the very core of Ibn Abd al-Wahhab's doctrine and raises the question of exclusivism. All counter-religions are in effect based on the exclusion of other forms of religiosity, which are seen as abnormal. But exclusivism is expressed in various ways, particularly in the case of emergent traditions in which the vision of "the Other" remains unstable and incomplete.

Far from departing from this rule, Ibn Abd al-Wahhab's shifting views on the matter were confirmation of it—more a reflection of circumstantial and emotional responses than of scholastic positions that had been arrived at after sober reflection.[75] While he had no doubt that the religious precepts he advocated represented true Islam, he always hesitated when describing his rivals and enemies, as the terminology employed in his writings shows. These included such terms as *kufr* (unbelief), *shirk* (associationism), *din al-jahiliyya* (pre-Islamic religion), *nifaq* (hypocrisy), *ridda* (apostasy), *fisq* (impiety), *dalal* (deviation), *al-'isyan* (disobedience), and so on.[76] He used certain of these terms interchangeably and without hierarchization to designate a single person or phenomenon.[77]

Because of the absence of a performative body equivalent to the ecumenical councils of the Catholic Church, these various notions had never been defined in a normative manner. There is thus nothing surprising in the fact that the frontiers between them should be shifting or their use confused. What's more, Ibn Abd al-Wahhab distinguished between the three forms of *tawhid* mentioned above. Each is as much a matter of orthodoxy as of orthopraxy, a fact that rendered any infraction, however minor, punishable by exclusion. If the shaykh had systematically delivered the maximum punishment—that is, excommunication (*al-takfir*)—the Muslim community as he defined it would have been no more than a small sect of the elected.[78] That, however, was not his objective at all. In practice, he employed the various notions of exclusion (no doubt in an unconscious manner) in such a way as to leave the door open to a possible return to the "straight and narrow path."[79] Many more examples could be cited here. Two, in particular, reflect the terminological confusion mentioned above as well as the desire for a return to the "straight and narrow path." While Ibn Abd al-Wahhab did indeed excommunicate several groups and individuals on the grounds that they were incapable of achieving salvation, he elsewhere declared that no one could possess knowledge of the individual's ultimate fate since the human mind is incapable of divining the reality of the heart.[80] Similarly, he excluded the Ash'arites from Sunnism because of their use of speculative theology.[81] Yet he elsewhere claimed to accept, after examination, a large part of the work of al-Ghazali (d. 1111), one of the most important leaders of the Ash'arite school.[82]

In order to better apply divine prescription, Ibn Abd al-Wahhab called upon believers to free themselves from latter-day glosses and manuals. He also encouraged the practice of *ijtihad* (the activity of interpretation).[83] Only the Qur'an, the Sunna, and the consensus of the first three generations of Muslims were thus considered legitimate sources of Muslim Law. However, there was nothing revolutionary about his calls for *ijtihad*: Ibn Abd al-Wahhab simply wished to base every legal norm on evidence (*adilla*, sing. *dalil*) directly drawn from the Qur'an, the Sunna, or the consensus. In other respects, he was a "classic" Hanbali who, apart from the works of Ibn Taymiyya and Ibn al-Qayyim, relied mainly on the very latter-day glosses and manuals he otherwise vigorously denounced. In order to better understand the text of the Qur'an, for example, the shaykh and his disciplines drew upon the most traditional and popular Qur'anic exegetes of the Sunni world, including al-Tabari (d. 923), al-Baydawi (d. 1316), Ibn Kathir (d. 1373), and al-Suyuti (d. 1505).[84] Finally, it should be noted that he recognized the validity of the four legal schools of Sunni Islam. Each believer could, in his view, follow the school of his choice on the condition that he profess the Hanbali creed. The historiographer of the first Saudi Emirate, Ibn Ghannam (d. 1810), was thus Malikite in law and Hanbali in theology. This practice was perfectly in keeping with the history of Hanbalism, which is, it is to be recalled, at once a theological and a legal tradition.

The same continuity can be observed in the political domain, where Ibn Abd al-Wahhab contented himself with adopting the main ideas of Ibn Taymiyya and Ibn al-Qayyim. He believed that the main function of any political entity was to see to it that orthodoxy, orthopraxy, and the political order—that is, sharia, the real mystical body of the community—be respected. The nature and form of this entity was not important in his eyes. As a consequence, the Caliphate as an institution was not indispensable to the proper functioning of society.[85] According to Ibn Abd al-Wahhab, each sovereign in the lands of Islam is legitimate regardless of his origin or the manner in which he came to power provided that he sees to it that the three O's are respected. His subjects then owe him absolute fidelity whatever his policies, and all rebellion is categorically condemned.[86] Cooperation and good council are encouraged in order to reform those in power so that they will promote the interests of the population and the religion. Ibn Abd al-Wahhab thus in no way aspired to establish a universal Caliphate or compete with the Ottoman Empire. His fundamental objective was to create a sound and stable platform for spreading his ideas. In his view, there was absolutely no need for those who could already profess the True Religion where they found themselves to carry out a *hijra* (expatriation) to the territories under the control of the Saudi Emirate.[87]

As we have seen, jihad was only an emergent effect of Ibn Abd al-Wahhab's predication. This is reflected in his writings, which only rarely mention the practice. On the basis of the scant information available and in light of the shaykh's actions (and those of his followers), it can be concluded that Ibn Abd al-Wahhab's ideas on jihad were only a repetition of classic Sunni opinions, in particular, those expressed by Ibn al-Qayyim.[88] In many Islamic writings, the term "jihad" is used for the purposes of mobilization or even as a "catch-all" term rather than as a juridico-religious concept. There is thus nothing extraordinary about Ibn Abd al-Wahhab's understanding of jihad: in his case, one finds neither an outrageously aggressive attitude nor a plan for expansion or desire to subjugate others by force. In sum, he had no messianic conception of "holy war." On the contrary, as we have seen, the better part of his writing on the subject concerns defensive jihad.[89]

PROVIDING FOR THE FUTURE: THE ESTABLISHMENT OF THE CORPORATION

While the actions of Ibn Abd al-Wahhab were initially a matter of individual initiative, he quickly realized that it would be necessary to establish a corpus, train disciples, and acculturate the population. His objective was not simply to successfully revive the True Religion but also to perpetuate and spread it. In other words, the charismatic leader aspired to perpetuate his ideas and convictions by organizing a tradition and establishing a corporation responsible for protecting and transmitting them. It goes without saying that organization, training, and transmission were overlapping processes. For the sake of convenience, however, I will discuss each separately.

As I have already indicated on many occasions, Ibn Abd al-Wahhab did not stand out for his intellectual production. His writings are a near systematic reprise of the classic Hanbali corpus, his main contribution being to render this generally very elitist production accessible to a larger public. It seems clear that his primary preoccupation was not to produce original work but rather to pass on what he believed to be eternal ideas. This desire is reflected in his writing style: the use of flowing, sometimes dialect-inflected language featuring frequent enumeration to assist in memorization of the articles of faith and legal orders. These were short texts aimed at facilitating learning and diffusion in a region where paper was a rare commodity and few knew how to read.[90]

We can divide the writings of Ibn Abd al-Wahhab into five categories:

1. Catechisms: These are small works that present the main articles of Hanbali-Wahhabi faith and morality, with examples drawn from Qur'anic verses and prophetic traditions. The main catechisms are *The Book of the Unity of God* (Kitab al-tawhid), *Clarification of the Doubts* (Khashf al-shubuhat) *The Three Fundamental Principles* [of Divine Unity] (al-Usul al-thalatha), *The Excellent Virtues of Islam* (Fada'il al-islam), and *The Inculcation of the Foundations of Dogma in the Population* (Talqin usul al-'aqida lil-'awamm).[91]

2. Anthologies: These are collections bringing together most Qur'anic verses and prophetic traditions, interspersed with brief commentaries on specific questions such as the deadly sins and the end of the world.[92]

3. Précis: These take the form of books in which he sought to condense and render clearer and more accessible other works considered indispensable to the training of his disciples and followers. He thus summarized Ibn Hisham's hagiography of the Prophet (al-Sira), the legal works of Ibn al-Qayyim, Shams al-din ibn Qudama and al-Mardawi, and several works of Ahmad ibn Taymiyya.[93]

4. Commentaries: Notes of various length on aspects of Muslim Law, treating them from a methodological (ijtihad, disagreements between ulama, etc.) or practical (prayer, ablutions, death, etc.) point of view.[94]

5. Letters and fatawa: These bring together the missives and responses that Ibn Abd al-Wahhab addressed to his followers or enemies at various points in his career. While they contain invaluable historical information, they simply reiterate the shaykh's principal religious ideas.[95]

Simplicity, brevity, and above all coherence are the common denominators of Ibn Abd al-Wahhab's writings. His aim was clear: to restore the three O's around the concept of divine unity, *al-tawhid*. Some of his texts—in particular, those concerning questions of dogma—were to become key elements in the formation of the Hanbali-Wahhabi tradition.

Like all charismatic leaders, the Najdi preacher surrounded himself from the start of his predication with faithful disciples and oversaw their instruction so that they might help spread his ideas. Indeed, he believed that *'ilm* (religious knowledge) was the noblest vocation and entailed the heaviest responsibilities since those who practice it are seen as the heirs of the Prophets. In this respect, they are responsible for protecting the mystical body of Islam: sharia. Ibn Abd al-Wahhab thus attached particular importance to training his disciples. As we have seen, following the conquest of Riyadh in 1773, the shaykh withdrew from worldly affairs in order to devote himself fully to writing and, above all, teaching. He was no doubt aware of the fact that the entire edifice he had constructed depended on the solidity of the nascent tradition and the body that would protect it after his death.

The methods of instruction and sites of socialization Ibn Abd al-Wahhab chose hardly differed from those found throughout the Muslim world since the High Middle Ages. Courses were held at the mosque or in the shaykh's home. Instruction was for the most part based on reading, annotation, and systematic memorization of the Qur'an, the Sunna, and several classical textbooks of law and theology. As the shaykh's ideas gained ground, Al-Dir'iyya became a meeting place for many student delegations, most of which lacked resources. Ibn Abd al-Wahhab did everything in his power to ensure them decent living conditions. This is why, for a long period, he sought loans from the notables of the oasis. The spoils that had been amassed through military conquest allowed him to reimburse his debts and also pay the salaries of all religious personnel.[96]

At the end of their training, the apprentice ulama received an *ijaza* from the master authorizing them to teach and issue fatawa in keeping with his doctrine. Thus, the principal disciples of Ibn Abd al-Wahhab became officials who occupied the main juridico-religious posts within the Saudi Emirate, including the prestigious office of judge (*qadi*). Less accomplished disciples, for their part, were dispatched to the region's major tribes to spread the teachings of the "new" tradition. But while the preacher had disciples from all regions of Najd and all social categories, he showed a clear preference for his descendants. Born into an important kindred of ulama, he tried to perpetuate this heritage by giving his children and grandchildren the best training and granting them the most prestigious offices. Toward the end of his life, his sons controlled the main religious posts of the capital, overseeing the largest mosques, education, and the magistrate.[97] In 1792, one of them, Abd Allah, succeeded him at the head of the religious establishment. By favoring his descendants, Ibn Abd al-Wahhab consciously perpetuated the local patrimonial system, in which offices and privileges were passed on within a single line. Unconsciously, he drew upon the Sufi model, which he had tirelessly condemned throughout his life. In this model, the descendants of a tradition's founder are the nearly exclusive heirs of his charisma and thus of his ideas and duties. Over time, the patrimonial tendency within the Hanbali-Wahhabi tradition and corporation would only deepen.[98] I will return to this point again.

The establishment of a corpus and the creation of a corporation not only aimed to preserve and transmit the True Religion but also sought to oversee the population and lead it to salvation.[99] One of the main objectives of any religious tradition and its representatives is to have followers. Ibn Abd al-Wahhab endeavored to "convert" the local population by means of teaching, writing, and coercion.

Throughout his career, Ibn Abd al-Wahhab organized simplified instruction for the benefit of the population.[100] He wrote several simplified textbooks intended to be read or recited before popular assemblies, particularly after prayers.[101] He also held special meetings to answer the population's various questions.[102] He sent dozens of disciples to all regions of Najd, in particular, to the Bedouin tribes.[103] In order to impose his doctrine in the public sphere, he obliged the people to perform collective prayer, respect the law in their commercial transactions, and so on.[104] In sum, Ibn Abd al-Wahhab established a veritable acculturation machine. The results were more than encouraging. Toward the end of his life, the district of Al-'Arid, in the heart of Najd, had been once and for all "Hanbali-Wahhabized." The region's other districts, which had been politically subjugated, were to gradually follow suit.

3

HANBALI-WAHHABISM IN THE NINETEENTH CENTURY

Grandeur and Decadence

POLITICAL EXPANSION AND THE FIRST ATTEMPT AT DOCTRINAL ROUTINIZATION

Muhammad ibn Abd al-Wahhab's death in 1792 does not seem to have diminished the determination of his descendants and disciples, who continued to actively promote his ideas. A genuine and nearly permanent division of labor between the religious and political authorities emerged: the Sauds henceforth dominated the political, military, and financial space while the shaykh's descendants and followers monopolized the juridico-religious space. Political power and religious authority worked side by side to impose the three O's. Emir Abd al-Aziz ibn Muhammad ibn Saud (d. 1803) continued to oversee politico-military affairs, while Abd Allah ibn Muhammad ibn Abd al-Wahhab (d. 1829) took charge of the Hanbali-Wahhabi corporation.[1]

Emir Abd al-Aziz pursued the attacks he had begun against the province of Al-Ahsa' in 1784. Profiting from dissension within the Banu Khalid confederation, he intensified raids between 1790 and 1795. The military effort was coupled with a religious polemic led by the ulama against other Muslim traditions, in particular, Shiism. Abd Allah ibn Muhammad ibn Abd al-Wahhab's main work, now lost, was a refutation of Shia doctrines. In one of his fatawa, he accused the Shiites of associationism (*al-shirk*) because of their cult of the saints. He nevertheless pulled back from once and for all excommunicating them. In keeping with a classic Hanbali opinion, he considered imprisonment or flagellation sufficient to bring them to repent or withdraw from the public sphere.[2] The province of Al-Ahsa' was conquered by preaching and the sword in 1795. With this done, Hanbali-Wahhabi preachers, imams, and judges were immediately dispatched to supervise and acculturate the local populations.[3] Apart from the moral and symbolic effects that it produced as a sign of divine election and support, the Hanbali-Wahhabi conquest also had clear economic consequences. The spoils amassed and taxes collected in Al-Ahsa', a prosperous commercial and agricultural province, considerably reinforced the power of the emergent Saudi Emirate.

The military victories scored by representatives of Ibn Abd al-Wahhab's predication worried the political and religious elites of Mecca, who vainly addressed a petition to Istanbul begging the Porte to intervene and put an end to this danger.[4] In late 1795, the emir of Mecca, Ghalib (1788–1812), thus decided to take matters into his own hands, launching a series of attacks on Saudi territories. The campaign ended with a crushing defeat.[5] Though they had not opened the hostilities, the shaykh's followers were the fortunate beneficiaries of the war's emergent effects. The Saudi Emirate no doubt realized that its mobilizing ideology gave it an advantage vis-à-vis the region's other forces, making it the Arabian Peninsula's leading military power. The time had come to profit from this to enlarge the emirate's territory and spread the Hanbali-Wahhabi tradition.

There seems to have been no precise plan of expansion for the preceding period, and the emir of Mecca's unexpected victory gave rise to a policy of conquest. Between 1796 and 1798, the Saudi Emirate easily seized the province of Asir after winning over several local chiefs attracted by the ideas of Ibn Abd al-Wahhab and the dynamism of the Saudi Emirate. In 1796, a number of raids were launched against the region of Najran, which was obliged to recognize the sovereignty of Al-Dir'iyya and pay tribute. The same year, Qatar was conquered. Seven years later, the sultan of Oman paid tribute to the Saudi Emirate and gave a free hand to Hanbali-Wahhabi preachers on his territory.[6] Military expansion thus went hand in hand with the spread of the shaykh's ideas, particularly among sedentary populations. Sometimes, the ideas preceded military conquest. For example, during the pilgrimage of 1800, an inhabitant of the southwestern province of Jazan was won over to Hanbali-Wahhabi doctrine. He thus decided to travel to Al-Dir'iyya in order to learn more about it. His stay in the Saudi capital only strengthened his beliefs. Returning home, he began to propagate Hanbali-Wahhabism, and his mission was a success: a large part of the population embraced the new tradition.[7]

Between 1795 and 1798, Mecca found itself nearly encircled by the Saudi Emirate. In order to calm the situation and dispel misunderstandings, Emir Abd al-Aziz sent a delegation of ulama to the holy city to explain the orthodox foundations of their actions and doctrine to local elites.[8] The effort met with failure, but several events obliged the emir of Mecca to reconsider his stance:[9] the conquest of Egypt by Napoleon Bonaparte in 1798, which had cut the Hijaz off from the Ottoman Empire (itself caught up in a host of economic and political problems); the failure of an attack launched on Saudi territory by Iraqi tribal confederations at the instigation of the Ottoman governor of Baghdad; and the victory of Saudi troops against the emir himself. The two parties thus entered negotiations, the main outcome of which was a six-year truce, authorization for Saudi subjects to participate in the pilgrimage to Mecca, and an agreement to share influence over nomadic tribes on the frontiers of Najd and the Hijaz.[10] Far from being a concession on the part of the Hanbali-Wahhabis, this negotiated settlement was yet another example of action modeled on prophetic gesture. Had not the Prophet of Islam signed the al-Hudaybiyya agreement with the inhabitants of Mecca, an agreement that stipulated a ten-year truce, authorization for Muslims to carry out the pilgrimage, and shared influence over certain tribes?[11] Thanks to the intense activity of Hanbali-Wahhabi agents and the economic advantages offered by the possibility of future conquests, the tribes under joint guardianship ultimately decided to follow the example of this "blessed" epoch and joined ranks with the Saudis around 1802.[12] By winning them over, Emir Saud ibn Abd al-Aziz (1803–1814) was able to tighten his vise grip on Mecca before once and for all conquering it in 1806.[13]

According to available Saudi, Ottoman, and European sources, once most of the Hijaz had been conquered, the emir imposed orthodoxy and orthopraxy in the public sphere with help from the ulama. This move was reflected in the destruction of certain places of popular worship, the organization of obligatory collective prayer, a prohibition on silk clothing and the use of tobacco, the abolition of extracanonical taxes, the application of legal punishments, and so on.[14] It also brought order and security, allowing Mecca and its dependencies to once again find prosperity.[15]

While these measures were being pursued on the ground, the head of the Hanbali-Wahhabi establishment, Abd Allah ibn Muhammad ibn Abd al-Wahhab, issued a fatwa setting out the foundations of his ideology in clear and simple language. This document can be seen as the first systematic exposition of Hanbali-Wahhabi doctrine as well as a (timid) first attempt to routinize it—that is, to move from the stance of counterreligion to that of a religion that interacts with other religions.

Abd Allah ibn Muhammad ibn Abd al-Wahhab began by remarking that the fundamental objective of the message preached by his father was the need to reestablish the pure and absolute unity of god via the promotion of virtue and the prevention of vice (al-*amr bi al-ma'ruf wa al-nahy 'an al-munkar*). He next enumerated the main guidelines of Hanbali-Wahhabism:[16]

- The pious ancestors (*al-salaf al-salih*), that is, the generations of Muslims who lived between the first and third centuries of the Hegira, are to be scrupulously imitated. In a certain manner, this authorized the ulama to call into question legal arrangements elaborated after this period.

- Saintly intercession (*al-shafa'a*) with God is an illusion. Anyone practicing it is automatically excommunicated and liable to capital punishment, even if he believes in divine superiority.
- Collective prayers in the Grand Mosque of Mecca and elsewhere must be led by a single imam from one of the four schools of Sunni Islam. An end should thus be put to the harmful innovation of the Mamluk sultans (1250–1517), who divided the community of believers by permitting each school to have its own imam to lead prayer.
- It is forbidden to speculate on the matter of divine attributes on the basis of the speculative theology of Ash'arism and Maturidism. One need simply believe without trying to go further, in keeping with the famous remark of Malik ibn Anas (d. 795): "The how of the thing escapes us. Believing in it is a duty, asking questions on this subject is blameful." In other words, only the Hanbali *'aqida* is valid.
- While the disciples of Ibn Abd al-Wahhab are Hanbalis in the area of law (*al-fiqh*), they nevertheless recognize the authenticity and validity of the other legal schools of Sunnism.[17]
- No Hanbali-Wahhabi *'alim* claims to be an absolute *mujtahid*, that is, to have the intellectual capacity necessary to deduce a legal norm directly from the Qur'an and the Sunna without reference to the juridico-theological production of his predecessors. This, however, does not prevent some of them from deducing new legal norms by drawing upon a clear scriptural source.
- The reference works used by the Hanbali-Wahhabis for Qur'anic exegesis are classics of Sunnism: al-Tabari (d. 923), al-Baghawi (d. 1122), al-Baydawi (d. 1292), al-Khazin (d. 1341), Ibn Kathir (d. 1373), al-Haddad (d. 1398), al-Suyuti (d. 1505), and so on. In what concerns the prophetic tradition, they used the six works that are regarded as authoritative in the Sunni world,[18] accompanied by commentaries on these texts by al-Nawawi (d. 1278), al-Qastalani (d. 1517), and al-'Asqalani (d. 1448).
- With the exception of a few Sufi works that were considered heretical—in particular, those of Muhammad ibn Sulayman al-Jazuli (d. 1465) and Abd Allah al-Yafi'i (d. 1367)[19]—no book was to be destroyed.
- The prophets, particularly Muhammad, and the angels can intercede on behalf of mankind on the condition that it is recognized that absolute authority belongs to God in conformity with a procedure that is well-defined by the tradition.
- Muslim saints, who strictly observe orthodoxy and orthopraxy, can perform some miracles (*al-karamat*). Nevertheless, they are not to be the objects of any form of worship.

- All men are equal before God. As a consequence, the descendants of the Prophet are to be loved and respected in conformity with the tradition and no more than that. The descendants of the Prophet can marry any Muslim.[20]
- Hanbali-Wahhabis do not excommunicate earlier generations of Muslims. They exclude only those who have heard their call and yet fail to apply the divine precepts they have defined.
- All religious rites established after the third century of the Hegira are blameworthy innovations (*bida'*) and categorically condemned.
- Poetry and some genres of music—in particular, military music and the music played on feast days—are lawful.
- Ibn Taymiyya and Ibn al-Qayyim are seen as great Sunni authorities, and their works are deeply respected. Nevertheless, Hanbali-Wahhabis do not hold to all of their opinions.
- Sufi brotherhoods that respect orthodoxy and orthopraxy are recognized and accepted.

This presentation of the main articles of Ibn Muhammad ibn Abd al-Wahhab's Hanbali-Wahhabi doctrine calls for a few remarks. First of all, it shows that the successor of Ibn Abd al-Wahhab adopted an ethic of responsibility in the interests of preserving his father's heritage. While the father had in one way or another excluded all of his adversaries and opponents, the son located this *in* the framework of the Islamic practice of promoting virtue and preventing vice. However, this practice can be exercised only *within* the Islamic community. This means that he situated his father's struggles with his adversaries *within* Islam. It was no longer a combat between the True Religion and false religions, in other words, but rather a struggle to redeem "brothers" who had strayed from the straight and narrow path. Ibn Muhammad ibn Abd al-Wahhab thus indirectly returned to the concentric circle of the *umma* drawn by Ibn Taymiyya.

As we have seen, Ibn Abd al-Wahhab categorically condemned Sufism. Conscious that he had to make concessions on certain points if he was to win acceptance from all of the region's religious elites, nearly all of whose members were tied in one way or another to the brotherhoods, Ibn Muhammad ibn Abd al-Wahhab decided to rehabilitate mysticism on the condition that its followers respect orthodoxy and orthopraxy.

From the very beginning, the Hanbali-Wahhabis were accused by their detractors of blindly following the teaching of Ibn Taymiyya despite the fact—once again, according to these detractors—that he had been condemned by all Sunni schools. To counter this accusation, the religious chief of the Saudi Emirate claimed that, while the Hanbali-Wahhabis certainly respected this *'alim* and his main disciple, they did not follow all of his teachings. What is certain is that, for all Sunni legal schools, legal and theological norms established after the third century of the Hegira are of relative value, at least in theory.

While Ibn Muhammad ibn Abd al-Wahhab was generally uncompromising with regards to his father's thought, he nevertheless had to mitigate certain aspects of it in order to meet the new situation. The Saudi Emirate was no longer a small local entity; it had risen dramatically to the rank of Islamic power thanks to the conquest of Mecca. Hanbali-Wahhabism was thus no longer a peripheral phenomenon but a reality at the level of the *umma*. As a consequence, its content was no longer solely of interest to local elites; leaders throughout the Muslim world were intrigued, to say the least, by this rising power.

In the same spirit, Emir Saud—no doubt on the advice of the ulama, who once again drew inspiration from the Prophet's example[21]—sent delegations of ulama[22] and several letters to the various Muslim countries in order to explain the dogma and legal practices of Hanbali-Wahhabism.[23] He also saw to it that he met with the heads of pilgrim delegations from Muslim countries in order to supply all necessary explanations regarding the tradition he defended and to reassure them with regards to the future of the pilgrimage.[24]

It seems clear that the Hanbali-Wahhabi tradition began its process of routinization thanks to very rapid political expansion, which obliged its representatives to engage with other actors on the Islamic scene. The experience of temporal and spiritual power, in other words, constrained the most uncompromising actors to adapt to the new situation. Yet the Saudi Emirate was not particularly prepared for such rapid growth, and as a result, there was a limit to how far its representatives could go in this process. The representatives showed themselves to be inflexible with regards to the Ottoman Empire, for example, treating the Sultan like a simple tribal chief,[25] forbidding the Ottoman governor of Damascus from joining the pilgrimage,[26] and continuing to publicly accuse the Ottoman authorities of associationism.[27] These affronts could not go unpunished, all the more so given the symbolic importance that the Ottoman Empire attached to the holy cities of Islam: was not one of the sovereign's titles Custodian of the Two Holy Mosques (*Khadim al-Haramayn al-Sharifayn*)? Losing control of these holy places signified a loss of religious power at a time when the Ottoman sultans had begun seeking to impose themselves as the caliphs of all Muslims in order to better confront the European threat.

Napoleon Bonaparte's capture of Egypt and the Ottoman Empire's European dilemma encouraged the expansion of the Saudi Emirate. Yet the retreat of the French from Egypt in 1801 and the coming to power in Istanbul and Cairo of two strong, ambitious, and equally uncompromising men—Mahmud II (1808–

1839) and Muhammad Ali (1805–1849)—were to call into question the very existence of the Saudi entity and constitute a turning point in the history and ideas of Hanbali-Wahhabism.

POLITICAL WITHDRAWAL AND RELIGIOUS CONTRACTION

In 1807, Sultan Mustafa IV (1807–1808) ordered the governor of Egypt, Muhammad Ali, to conduct a military expedition to dislodge the Hanbali-Wahhabis from the holy places. The unstable situation in the Ottoman province, however, meant that the governor was unable to immediately act on this order. By 1811, Sultan Mahmud II had reestablished order in Istanbul and undertaken political and military reforms. Once again, he ordered the governor of Egypt (who had in the meantime also secured his position) to put down this politico-religious entity that was challenging the legitimacy and hegemony of the empire in the region.

In late 1811, Muhammad Ali launched a long and bloody military expedition. After having chased Saudi troops from Hijaz, in 1815 his army began to make its first incursions into Najd. Three years of heavy combat were necessary to destroy the Saudi Emirate. The capital Al-Dir'iyya was laid waste, several hundred dignitaries were massacred, and approximately 31 ulama and 250 members of the Saud kindred were deported to Cairo or Istanbul, where they were put under house arrest or executed—as was the case of Emir Abd Allah ibn Saud (1814–1818).[28] Several survivors, particularly some ulama,[29] were able to flee to other regions of the Arabian Peninsula, while the portion of Al-Dir'iyya's population that escaped the massacres settled in the oasis of Riyadh.[30]

The brutality of the Ottoman attack was a traumatic experience for the Hanbali-Wahhabi religious elite. The spectacle of a local population that surrendered without resistance, negotiated with the enemy, and even went over to the Ottoman side in the hope of returning to the state that had prevailed before the emergence of the Saudi Emirate persuaded Hanbali-Wahhabi ulama that their world was in the process of collapsing. Some of them were convinced that the Ottoman attack was divine punishment for failure to respect orthodoxy and orthopraxy in Najd together with the recent openness shown the Other (that is, the first moves in the direction of routinization discussed above).

The result was a firm resolve on the part of the Hanbali-Wahhabis to protect their beliefs and identity by rigorously distinguishing (at least at the intellectual level) between true and false religion in the hope of remobilizing the population and preventing the worst. Convinced that the Ottoman offensive was intended to destroy the True Faith, nineteenth-century Hanbali-Wahhabi ulama developed a system of distinction that Abd al-Rahman ibn Hasan (d. 1868), grandson of Muhammad ibn Abd al-Wahhab and leader of the corporation, would term *al-wala' wa al-bara'* (allegiance [to the Muslims] and rupture [with the infidels]).[31]

While the war was still raging between Ottoman troops and the Saudi forces, yet another of Ibn Abd al-Wahhab's grandsons and one of the bravest defenders of the emirate, the *'alim* Sulayman ibn Abd Allah (d. 1818), drafted a number of fatawa to give systematic expression to the attitude that Muslims—that is, Hanbali-Wahhabis—should adopt in regards to coreligionists and enemies of Islam.

In the first fatwa, Ibn Abd Allah claimed that all Muslims must show hostility to infidels. They must also abstain from all contact with them. This order held as much for individuals—in particular, political leaders—as it did for the collectivity. Adherents of the True Religion thus had to radically break (*bara'a*) with infidels and associationists. For them, the only appropriate attitude was one of uncompromising enmity (*mu'adat*). According to Ibn Abd Allah, any Muslim who showed kindness toward an infidel or associationist or helped him in any way was himself considered to be an infidel or associationist. Neither fear nor weakness could excuse the believer from performing this duty, nor did they authorize him to behave otherwise.[32]

In a second fatwa, Ibn Abd Allah drew upon scriptural evidence to describe the relations that should obtain between a Muslim and his coreligionists. In keeping with the principle of *al-muwalat*, every Muslim owed absolute fidelity and loyalty to all other members of the community as well as assistance and support in all hardship. Since they are based on faith, the ties between Muslims must be indissoluble.[33]

In a third fatwa, finally, Ibn Abd Allah went so far as to forbid Muslims— meaning, once again, Hanbali-Wahhabis—from traveling to infidel territories (that is, the Ottoman Empire). According to him, this ban was intended to guard against any corruption of the True Faith.[34]

Unable to reverse the situation on the ground, Ibn Abd Allah used all of his ideological authority to construct a virtual world characterized by clear and insurmountable frontiers between true and false religion. For him, the best way to live better and protect the faith was to withdraw into oneself and completely break with infidels and associationists. His target here was neighboring Muslim countries, which he saw as a source of corruption and thus eternal damnation.[35]

The process of routinization of the Hanbali-Wahhabi tradition, which began with the conquest of Mecca in 1806, thus abruptly came to an end with the Ottoman offensive. What's more, Ibn Abd Allah challenged some of his grandfather's ideas. Though Ibn Abd al-Wahhab distinguished between true and false religion, he nevertheless authorized his followers to adopt a sort of *taqiyya* (dissimulation), allowing them to hide their opinions and beliefs in the event of weakness. He also authorized them to travel to so-called hostile territories—particularly for the purposes of trans-Saharan trade, one of Najd's principal economic resources—on the condition that they were able to freely exercise their faith there.[36]

At first, Ibn Abd Allah's positions probably went largely unnoticed by the population and its rulers, who at the time were busy ensuring their survival. Hoping to spare his power and the autonomy of his territory, Saudi sovereign Abd Allah ibn Saud thus went so far as to declare that he was "only a slave of the Sublime Porte and a loyal servant."[37] The ethic of conviction expressed by Ibn Abd Allah, which consisted of rigidly applying the ideal in which one believes without regard to the consequences that may result, could lead only to destructive confrontation or total withdrawal into oneself.

Consciously or not, Ibn Abd Allah was only reproducing a schema long familiar to Islamic history. Since the seventh century, several groups and currents in Islam—in particular, some Kharijite and Shiite groups—had claimed to adhere to the principle of allegiance and rupture, establishing a fundamental distinction between true and false religion and forbidding all interaction with infidels (that is, other Muslims).[38] This principle had been denounced as a blameworthy innovation by the Sunni (in particular the Hanbali) religious authorities as early as the ninth century.[39] That did not prevent its limited application for the purpose of inciting the population to abandon religious and social practices suspected of being non-Muslim in origin (including Jewish, Christian, Zoroastrian, and Mongol practices).[40]

The stance of allegiance and rupture adopted by certain Islamic currents at one moment or another of their historical trajectory was doubtless inspired by the Jewish principle of *amixia* (exclusivism or misanthropy), that is:

> [the] preference for living in an exclusively Jewish milieu cut off from all communication with idolators, the burning desire to render such communication ever more difficult, if not impossible. The duty to conserve a pure and unalloyed monotheism by means of a complete separation between Jews and pagan nations was always imposed on the former as an essential condition of Judaism. The Pentateuch contained a large number of precepts in this sense, and historical books seem to have been composed with the firm intention of demonstrating, through a narrative of events, the importance and holiness of this duty.[41]

This *amixia* gave rise to an "enclave culture," to borrow Mary Douglas's expression—that is, the establishment on the part of a community surrounded by enemies of a set of absolute norms and intellectual barriers to prevent absorption by a generally hostile majority.[42]

Throughout the nineteenth century, the memory of the trauma provoked by Ottoman military intervention and the destruction of the Saudi Emirate in 1818 remained keen in the minds of the corporation's leaders. The reestablishment of the Saudi Emirate in Najd and Al-Ahsa' beginning in 1823 in no way changed this situation. Haunted by the prospect of corruption of the True Religion through contact with the various provinces of the empire as well as further Ottoman intervention—which in fact occurred on two occasions (1838 and 1871)—the ulama selectively revisited the ideas of Ibn Abd Allah in order to develop an enclave culture capable of saving the tradition. In doing so, they continuously mulled over the following themes: the Islamic character of the Ottoman Empire, the lawfulness of calling upon infidels for help, the legal status of travel in associationist countries, and the attitude to be adopted by believers in infidel lands who are unable to profess the True Religion. Throughout the century, this intellectual project was led by Muhammad ibn Abd al-Wahhab's grandson, Abd al-Rahman ibn Hasan (d. 1868), and great-grandson, Abd al-Latif (d. 1876), as well as by the *'alim* Hamad ibn Atiq (d. 1889).[43]

For them, the Ottoman Empire was the temple of associationism and the nonapplication of the precepts of the Law, the source of all the ills of Muslims and a genuine antimodel. Its military interventions had only sown destruction and desolation by encouraging the return of heretical practices and the political fragmentation that had prevailed in Najd and its environs before the predication of Muhammad ibn Abd al-Wahhab.[44] The Ottomans merely reproduced the atrocities that the Mongols had inflicted on Muslims in the thirteenth century. These ulama thus established a parallel between the situation of Najd in the nineteenth century and the trauma experienced by a portion of the Muslim world six centuries earlier.[45] The influence of Ibn Taymiyya's writings is obvious here. Ibn Taymiyya regarded the Mongol invaders, though recently converted to Islam, as infidels because they gave scant attention to orthodoxy and orthopraxy. In his view, moreover, they encouraged heresy, applying their own customs in place of sharia and unjustly attacking Muslim lands. The Ottoman Empire was thus seen as an infidel state (*al-ta'ifa al-kafira* or *al-dawla al-kufriyya*[46]) that was to be resisted in case of attack in the framework of defensive jihad.[47] Contact with the aggressor was synonymous with apostasy.[48]

On the basis of this, the ulama concluded that any political alliance with the Ottoman Empire was illicit. However, the history of the Saudi Emirate in the nineteenth century was shaken by struggles within the royal house. In order to seize or monopolize power, certain pretenders did not hesitate to call upon Ottoman troops stationed in the Hijaz and southern Iraq. This was the case, for example, in 1838 and 1871. The ulama urged them to not act in that way, however grave the situation.[49] But the representatives of the Hanbali-Wahhabi tradition never excommunicated offspring of the House of Saud who called upon the Ottomans for assistance. Instead, they contented themselves with "affectionately" reprimanding them.[50] To all appearances, this was due to their awareness that, without an alliance with the Saud, the tradition would not endure.[51] The support of a political authority was indispensable if orthodoxy and orthopraxy were to be applied.

Concerning travel to Ottoman territory, the ulama adopted an intermediary position between the ideas of Ibn Abd Allah and those of the tradition's founder. Holding that travel to impious territory, whatever the reason, corrupts the faith, they judged that certain conditions had to be met before it was undertaken: an unshakeable faith, a disdainful attitude towards infidels and their beliefs, and the ability to freely profess one's faith and perform its rites. According to the ulama, any Muslim who does not respect these conditions must be reprimanded or even punished so that he learns to behave in an orthodox manner in the future.[52]

The last theme addressed was the legality of residing in territory (re)conquered by the Ottomans. On this issue, the ulama reiterated the same conditions they required of believers who wished to travel to "impious" countries. Should all conditions not be met, the believer was to leave his country and take up residence in Hanbali-Wahhabi territories in the framework of *hijra*, or expatriation.[53] They took the duty of *hijra* very seriously. For example, during the Ottoman invasion of Najd in 1838, which ended with the appointment of a vassal emir, the leading ulama—and, in particular, Abd al-Rahman ibn Hasan and Hamad ibn Atiq—quit the latter's territory, judging it to be impious.[54]

These positions nevertheless remained ideal-typical. In reality, they were generally less uncompromising and could change with events: one must never overlook the fact that the ulama's responses depended on the historical context as well as psychological and legal variables. As in any ideological group, divergent opinions can thus be noted within the corporation concerning exclusivism in all of its forms, the attitude to adopt vis-à-vis infidels, and so on.[55] Individual ulama sometimes even adopted contradictory stances over the course of their careers. While Abd al-Latif ibn Abd al-Rahman described the Ottoman Empire as an infidel, associationist, and hypocritical state, he did not hesitate to remark, in a letter addressed to a colleague from Mecca, that the empire had since the sixteenth century jealously and generously watched over the holy places of Islam. He even claimed that failures to respect orthodoxy and orthopraxy in the two holy cities and elsewhere in the empire were not the fault of the Ottoman sultans but rather that of their viziers and governors, who were led astray by ignorance.[56] He called upon the latter, as Muslims, to apply the three O's. There was thus no question of exclusivism. It should also be recalled that this leader of the corporation spent more than thirty years of his life in the Ottoman Empire. In 1818, at the age of eight, Abd al-Latif ibn Abd al-Rahman was deported to Cairo together with the principal members of the religious elite and ruling house. But while his father and most Saudi dignitaries returned to Najd to reconstruct the emirate alongside Emir Turki ibn Abd Allah,[57] Abd al-Latif for his part chose to remain in Egypt in order to finish his studies at Al-Azhar. Before returning to Najd in 1848, he spent several months in Mecca and probably also Medina. It seems that the fact of having spent fully thirty years in "infidel" countries presented no problem for him. It was only after he returned to the country to accept the family inheritance that he adopted the Hanbali-Wahhabi habitus in order to preserve the unity and strength of the corporation he was meant to lead.

Moreover, the break with false religion and the withdrawal into oneself did not indicate that the Hanbali-Wahhabi establishment was cut off from the world. On the contrary, these ulama waged intellectual war with their critics throughout the second half of the nineteenth century. Indeed, the region's various rival corporations of ulama put a number of polemical texts into circulation that sought to denigrate Hanbali-Wahhabism and systematically disfigure its teaching. The themes addressed in this literature generally corresponded to the politico-religious allegiances of its authors. Aside from the classic grievances against medieval Hanbalism (anthropomorphism, excess zeal in the promotion of virtue and the prevention of vice, etc.), the Hanbali-Wahhabis were accused of sectarianism, Kharijism, Qarmantianism, and, finally, exclusivism and narrow-mindedness. Abd al-Rahman ibn Hasan, his son Abd al-Latif, and his disciple Hamad ibn Atiq, wrote refutations (*rudud*) in response to these accusations, which they considered slanderous. Written in a simple and pedagogical style, these texts endeavor to deconstruct the arguments of their adversaries before proceeding to define and illustrate their authors' theological, legal, and religious positions.[58]

THE RELIGIOUS HOMOGENIZATION OF NAJD

The uncompromising rhetoric of allegiance and rupture allowed the representatives of Hanbali-Wahhabism to stake out genuine intellectual frontiers between true and false religion and thereby protect their tradition. They realized, however, that one of the main factors contributing to the failure of the first politico-religious experiment was the absence of doctrinal homogeneity, which was the result of rapid expansion. Although the tradition had spread to several regions of the Arabian Peninsula, it only did so in a superficial manner. Hostile to the predication of Muhammad ibn Abd al-Wahhab and very favorable to Sufism, traditional Hanbali ulama were thus able, not only to keep their positions, but also to profit from Saudi defeat to recuperate their status and influence with the support of different centrifugal forces. Only the districts of Al-'Arid and Al-Washm—that is, the heart of Najd and fief of the Saudi Emirate—had been truly and lastingly "Hanbali-Wahhabized."

The ulama made this observation in religious terms. For them, the disaster of the Ottoman invasion was only an expression of the divine anger provoked by failure to strictly observe orthodoxy and orthopraxy in the regions subjugated by the Saudi Emirate and the fact that associationist pockets persisted. It was thus necessary to remedy the situation and avoid once again provoking God's fury by completing the religious homogenization of Najd. To this end, the ulama could count on the coercive force of the Saudi Emirate, which was reborn from the ashes in 1823. Indeed, Emir Turki ibn Abd Allah (1823–1834), the grandson of Muhammad ibn Saud, succeeded in obliging Ottoman troops to gradually withdraw. In a reign that lasted fewer than eleven years, he extended his control over the entirety of Najd and Al-Ahsa'. In order to consolidate his power and legitimate his approach, Turki ibn Abd Allah called upon the ideological authority of the ulama. Political power and its religious sanction were thus once again indissolubly linked. The alliance between the House of Saud and the ulama was strengthened as a result. It is thus not surprising that Ibn Taymiyya's treatise on public law, *al-Siyasa al-shar'iyya*, became the most widely read book by the elites of the time: there, the author advocated close collaboration between emirs and ulama in order to impose the three O's.[59]

Scattered across Egypt and the eastern region of Arabia, Hanbali-Wahhabi ulama gradually returned from their exiles and rallied to the banner of Muhammad ibn Abd al-Wahhab's grandson, Abd al-Rahman ibn Hasan, who set up residence in a new capital, Riyadh. The process of religious homogenization that had begun under the reign of Turki only really got under way during the long reign of his son, Faysal (1843–1865).[60] In order to give concrete expression to the radical distinction between true and false religion, the ulama and their emirs sought to impose the Law in three complementary ways: control of the public sphere, inculcation of Hanbali-Wahhabi ideas, and elimination of traditional Hanbali ulama.

In order to control the public sphere, the ulama mobilized the concept of the promotion of virtue and the prevention of vice (*al-amr bi al-ma'ruf wa al-nahy* '*an al-munkar*). Abd al-Rahman ibn Hasan claimed that this fundamental injunction was the main path to achieving salvation, and his son and successor at the head of the religious establishment, Abd al-Latif, went so far as to write that it was more important than armed jihad.[61] The ulama and emirs incited the agents of the state and all religiously trained individuals to enforce orthodoxy and orthopraxy in the public sphere.[62] This included obligatory participation in collective prayers, the wearing of beards by men, the organization of the pilgrimage, the establishment of circles of exhortation (*halaqat al-waʿz*), respect for the Law in commercial transactions, observance of sartorial rules, and so on.[63] In order to show that their approach was in earnest, the ulama advocated merciless punishments: anyone who did not perform their prayers because of laziness had to repent. If that person continued to fail in this duty, he was to be executed as an apostate.[64] The residences of those who shut themselves indoors during collective prayers were to be burned.[65] Individuals who resisted those who promoted virtue and prevented vice were to be banished from the country. Finally, those who poked fun at the ulama or religious agents responsible for enforcing the Law were to be immediately excommunicated and were thus liable to capital punishment.[66]

An epidemic of cholera that struck the region between 1854 and 1855 was seen by the ulama as a new manifestation of God's wrath. According to the testimony of a British Jesuit named William Palgrave, who is said to have visited Riyadh in 1862, the Saudi political and religious authorities decided that

> twenty-two were to be selected, and entitled "Meddey'yeeyah," "men of zeal," or "Zelators," such being the nearest word in literal translation, and this I shall henceforth employ, to spare Arab cacophony. Candidates of the requisite number were soon found and mustered. On these twenty-two Feysul conferred absolute power for the extirpation of whatever was contrary to Wahhabee doctrine and practice, and to good morals in general, from the capital firstly, and then from the entire empire. No Roman censors in their most palmy days had a higher range of authority, or were less fettered by all ordinary restrictions. Not only were these Zelators to denounce offenders, but they might also in their own unchallenged right inflict the penalty incurred, beat and fine at discretion, nor was any certain limit assigned to the amount of the mulct, or to the number of the blows. Most comprehensive too was the list of offences brought under the animadversion of these new censors: absence from public prayers, regular attendance five times a day in the public mosques being henceforth of strict obligation; smoking tobacco, taking snuff, or chewing (this last practice, vulgarly entitled "quidding," had been introduced by the jolly tars of Koweyt and other seaports of the Persian Gulf); wearing silk or gold; talking or having a light in the house after night prayers; singing, or

playing on any musical instrument; nay, even all street-games of children or childish persons: these were some of the leading articles on the condemned list, and objects of virtuous correction and severity. Besides, swearing by any other name save that of the Almighty, any approach to an invocation, or even ejaculation directed to aught but Him; in short, whatever in word or deed, in conversation or in conduct, might appear to deviate from the exact orthodoxy of the letter of the Coran and the Wahhabee commentary, was to be denounced, or even punished on the spot. Lastly, their censorship extended over whatever might afford suspicion of irregular conduct; for instance, strolling about the streets after nightfall, entering too frequently a neighbour's house, especially at hours when the male denizens may be presumed absent, with any apparent breach of the laws of decorum or decency; all these were rendered offences amenable to cognizance and correctional measures.[67]

This lengthy extract of eyewitness testimony demonstrates how the desire to apply orthodoxy and orthopraxy in the public sphere in order to obtain divine favors led the Saudi authorities to institutionalize the practice of promoting virtue and preventing vice. The body that resulted from this institutionalization was to play a fundamental role in the construction and spread of Hanbali-Wahhabi identity and the configuration of the Saudi public sphere. It is a matter to which we will return.

But the ulama's efforts to ensure that the Law was respected in the public sphere could not bear fruit without an extended pedagogical campaign. In order to acculturate the sedentary and Bedouin populations of Najd, the ulama persuaded the emirs to send them official religious agents.[68] According to Abd al-Rahman ibn Hasan, each of Najd's oases generally possessed two or three religious personnel responsible for supplying the population with a rudimentary religious education.[69] Most of this information is confirmed by a report supplied by British voyager Lewis Pelly, who traveled to Riyadh in 1865.[70] As in the time of Muhammad ibn Abd al-Wahhab, the pedagogical material they employed mainly consisted of the catechisms Ibn Abd al-Wahhab had written, particularly *The Book of the Unity of God* and *The Three Fundamental Principles*. In order to provide "high-quality" instruction, the representatives of Hanbali-Wahhabism set about training competent personnel who were faithful to the tradition. The personnel were then to see to the task of "spreading divine unity and scriptural proofs among the elites and ordinary people."[71] As we will see, in the interest of preserving doctrinal purity and the corporation's power, the Al al-Shaykh—that is, the descendants of Ibn Abd al-Wahhab—retained a near monopoly on teaching. This allowed them to control the religious elite's networks of socialization. All apprentice ulama and religious personnel who aspired to a career in the service of the tradition were required to reside for a time in Riyadh.[72] This measure allowed the corporation to maintain its cohesion and identity, which in turn reinforced filial procedures for passing on Islamic scholarship.

The final phase in the effort to homogenize the population and monopolize the public space of Najd consisted of eliminating all rival corporations and figures. I mentioned above that adherents of traditional Hanbalism, with their ties to Sufi Islam, profited from the defeat of the Saud in 1818 to resume their religious activities, particularly in the district of Al-Qasim in the northwestern corner of Najd. These ulama were active in this region for two main reasons: the desire of local chiefs to distinguish themselves from Riyadh in order to maintain their autonomy, and the close economic and cultural ties that had for several centuries linked them with Syria and Iraq.[73] Saudi sovereigns and the Hanbali-Wahhabi corporation did everything in their power to rid themselves of these brother-enemies. Though the available sources do not allow us to rigorously reconstruct this process, we may nevertheless form a rather clear idea of it thanks to the following examples.

'Alim Abd Allah Aba al-Khayl (d. 1835) had a traditional Hanbali education in Mecca and Al-Zubayr, in southern Iraq. Upon returning home, he held the post of judge in the oasis of Unayza between 1824 and 1827. Despising the Hanbali-Wahhabi ulama, he had close ties with their enemies, with whom he regularly corresponded. This hostility led to a counterattack on the part of the ulama, who questioned his beliefs. When the oasis was conquered by Emir Turki ibn Abd Allah, they immediately had Aba al-Khayl stripped of his duties and marginalized.[74] They similarly regarded the judge of Burayda, Sulayman ibn Muqbil (d. 1887), with suspicion. This judge had long been a student of the Damascene Sufi 'alim Hasan al-Shatti (d. 1858), one of the most virulent adversaries of Muhammad ibn Abd al-Wahhab and his predication.[75] Ibn Muqbil was accused of encouraging worship of the saints and all of the heretical rites which that entailed. He was summarily dismissed from his duties as a result.[76]

The case of Uthman ibn Mansur (d. 1865) was more complicated. Having spent time in Iraq and Hijaz after an initial period of training at the hands of local ulama, he occupied the post of judge on behalf of the Saudi Emirate in several oases of Najd.[77] Regarded with suspicion because of his relations with anti–Hanbali-Wahhabi corporations, his commentary on Ibn Abd al-Wahhab's *Book of the Unity of God* was dissected by the leaders of the corporation, who wrote several epistles to discredit it.[78] But it was only after his death that they achieved victory. Indeed, Abd al-Rahman ibn Hasan ordered that Ibn Mansur's personal library be confiscated. It was thoroughly examined, and all anti–Hanbali-Wahhabi material was purged from it.[79] In the same spirit, all books circulating in Najd that appeared to contain "heretical" content were immediately confiscated and destroyed.[80]

Even the political leaders of Al-Qasim were subjected to homogenization. The emir of Burayda, who favored the traditional Hanbali ulama as a prop to his autonomy, was executed in 1861. Control over the oasis of Unayza, meanwhile, was entrusted to a family with several members who had received extensive training from Hanbali-Wahhabi ulama in Riyadh.[81]

The ferocious combat conducted against competing ulama persuaded most of them to quit Najd. A number of them set up residence in the holy cities of Islam. One such was Muhammad ibn Humayd (d. 1878), the author of a famous collection of Hanbali biographies and a mufti of the same school in Mecca. Most took refuge in the oasis of Al-Zubayr, in southern Iraq. This became the center of traditional Hanbalism and a locus of active opposition to Hanbali-Wahhabism, which it remains partially to this day.[82]

Though actively supported by the political authorities, the efforts of Hanbali-Wahhabi ulama to eliminate the Sufi-inflected current of Hanbalism were not entirely successful, particularly in some oases of Al-Qasim. After roughly thirty years of painstaking effort, they nevertheless succeeded in extending the tradition's domination over nearly all oases of Central Arabia by imposing the tradition on the vast majority of the region's sedentary population.

THE ULAMA SEEK PEACE, KNOWLEDGE, AND A MESSIAH

These efforts at homogenization would not have been so effective without the support of the political power. The emirate, which was only an emergent effect of Muhammad ibn Abd al-Wahhab's predication, became indispensable to the maintenance and spread of Hanbali-Wahhabism among the sedentary population of Najd during the nineteenth century. Had it not been restored by Turki ibn Abd Allah, this nascent tradition, the representatives of which were scattered across the entire region, no doubt would have been permanently marginalized or simply wiped out.[83] Without political order, the application of orthodoxy and orthopraxy is impossible. The leading ulama realized the important role played by the state structure in their efforts to reach salvation. They thus put all of their ideological authority in the service of the Saudi Emirate.

In keeping with medieval Hanbali tradition, Abd al-Rahman ibn Hasan and his son Abd al-Latif advocated absolute obedience to the House of Saud, which they saw as the True Religion's only supporter. As a result, they vigorously condemned all insubordination vis-à-vis Saudi authority.[84] In the tradition of Ibn

Taymiyya and Ibn al-Qayyim, they advocated close cooperation between subjects and sovereign by way of the classic practice of good advice (*al-nasiha*). And in order to legitimate the emirs' power—particularly, that of Faysal, who scrupulously observed the precepts of sharia—the ulama gave them the titles of imam and caliph.[85] These emirs' political and military projects were therefore considered acts of faith. Military operations intended to bring Bedouin tribes under Saud authority were thus described as instances of jihad.[86]

The death of Emir Faysal in 1865 once again called into question the hegemony of Hanbali-Wahhabi discourse in Najd and its dependencies. This time, the danger did not come from the Ottoman Empire but rather from the very heart of the Saudi political system. Indeed, the political structure established by Faysal proved fragile and did not survive him: for about a quarter century, his sons and grandsons constantly fought one another. Though it is true that his son Abd Allah (1865–1871, 1871–1873, and 1876–1889) legally came to power as presumptive heir (*waliyy al-'ahd*), Abd Allah's brother Saud (1871 and 1873–1875) was quick to challenge his claim. After several years of battle, alliance, and counteralliance, Saud ultimately won, but Abd Allah continued to attack the territories subjugated by his brother. He thus dangerously weakened the Saudi political structure and permitted regional powers—in particular, the Ottomans—and centrifugal forces to extend their influence in the region. While the Ottomans seized the eastern province of Al-Ahsa', various tribes and oases recovered their autonomy. Over most of the territory of Najd, the Saudi sovereigns no longer had more than nominal power.[87]

Abd Allah was able to return to power following the death of Saud in 1875 and an intermission of several months during which their brother, Abd al-Rahman, the father of future King Abd al-Aziz, reigned. But Abd Allah was unable to overcome the political problems engendered by so many years of conflict and dissension. In addition to being obliged to confront the many pretenders in the House of Saud who threatened his power, he also had to put an end to the centrifugal aspirations of certain tribal chiefs and reckon with the region's emergent power: the Ha'il Emirate in the northern Najd, led by Muhammad ibn Abd Allah Al Rashid (1869–1897).[88] Muhammad ibn Rashid profited from the House of Saud's weakness and the chaos reigning in Najd to expand his territory and impose a "protectorate." He ultimately captured Riyadh in 1888 and put Emir Abd Allah and his brother Abd al-Rahman into captivity. Toward the end of 1889, Abd al-Rahman succeeded in escaping and attempted to restore the authority of the House of Saud in the region. In 1891, however, he was driven away by Muhammad ibn Rashid and found refuge in Qatar and then Kuwait.[89]

During the war of succession between the offspring of the House of Saud, the leaders of the Hanbali-Wahhabi corporation adopted an attitude characteristic of all schools of Sunnism: recognizing a fait accompli, which consists of swearing allegiance and legitimating the power of the emir who succeeds in subjugating the majority of the population and imposing a minimum of order, in the interest of facilitating religious and social transactions.[90] *Fitna*, the disorder that gives rise to chaos, was and remains the most feared socioreligious situation of the Arab-Muslim imaginary.[91]

But the political situation was more complex. In order to maximize their chances, each of the pretenders in turn appealed to the Ottomans. Without ever excommunicating the Saudi emirs, for the reasons mentioned above, the ulama forcefully reiterated that it was forbidden to call upon "infidels," citing scripture in their support.[92] Yet these calls to order went unheeded. The emirs continued to seek Ottoman support, and the ulama continued to recognize their power, making due most often with an act of public repentance (*al-tawba*) on the part of the victorious emir for having entered into contact with the infidels.[93] The Hanbali-Wahhabi ulama's ethic of responsibility thus led them to recognize the fait accompli in order to save the bulk of the religious structure. This same pragmatism is to be observed in the attitude of Abd al-Latif concerning the *hijra* (expatriation) of populations whose territory had fallen into the hands of the enemy.[94] Indeed, the Ottomans seized the region of Al-Ahsa' in 1871. While he initially adopted an uncompromising stance, forbidding all contact with this province and ordering Hanbali-Wahhabis to immediately leave it,[95] he later changed his position, encouraging them to enter into contact with the Ottomans and the local population in the hope of "converting" them.[96] He took as his example Ibn Taymiyya, who preached in the military camps of the Mongols—considered to be infidels—while the latter prepared to attack Mamluk territory in Syria in the early fourteenth century.

The struggles of succession among offspring of the House of Saud, which led to the gradual weakening of their emirate in favor of centrifugal entities and, above all, the Ha'il Emirate, did not prevent the ulama from unconditionally supporting the reigning house. For example, when the oasis of Burayda broke with Riyadh around 1876, the ulama excommunicated its elites as enemies of the True Religion. After the fall of the Saud in 1891, they remained faithful to them despite Al Rashid efforts to co-opt them. The chief of the Hanbali-Wahhabi establishment, Abd Allah ibn Abd al-Latif Al al-Shaykh (d. 1921), was even called to Ha'il, where he began to give courses. But that in no way prevented him from propagandizing in favor of the House of Saud, forcing the emir to order him to leave his capital.[97]

As traditional Hanbalis, moreover, the Rashid favored the ulama of their camp, particularly in the oases of Burayda and Unayza.[98] These ulama profited from the conjuncture to propagandize against Hanbali-Wahhabism, an effort in which two ulama in particular distinguished themselves. The first, Ibrahim ibn Jasir (d. 1920), accused his adversaries of excluding all non–Hanbali-Wahhabis from the Muslim community and plotting on behalf of the House of Saud. He therefore encouraged Emir Muhammad ibn Abd Allah (1869–1897) to punish them.[99] The second, Abd Allah ibn Amr (d. 1908), sent a letter to the emir of Ha'il in which he presented the following arguments: the Hanbali-Wahhabi ulama were ignoramuses, megalomaniacs, and extremists who excommunicated all neighboring countries and forbade all contact with them. Enjoying much popular support in Najd, their temporal submission to the authority of the House of Rashid was only a subterfuge while they awaited a liberator.[100]

The incessant political and military struggles that followed the death of Emir Faysal provoked upheaval within the Hanbali-Wahhabi religious elite. In an atmosphere dominated by uncertainty and insecurity, the elite could no longer enforce orthodoxy and orthopraxy in the public sphere. In his lifetime, Abd al-Rahman ibn Hasan more or less succeeded in limiting the damage. He sent his disciples to several regions of Najd to oversee the population and sent letters to encourage sedentary and Bedouin chiefs to enforce the norms of the Law in the territories under their control.[101] His son, Abd al-Latif, tried to follow in his footsteps, though the situation became increasingly untenable because of the exacerbation of conflicts among the offspring of the ruling house. The death of Abd al-Latif in 1876 ushered in a period of chaos: his son Abd Allah (d. 1921), who succeeded him at the head of the corporation at the age of twenty-eight, was doubtless too young to assume the lineage's inheritance. It took him a dozen years to establish his personal authority and reputation. During this time, the power of the House of Saud crumbled under the weight of fratricidal struggles. While the local population suffered from this instability, centrifugal powers and the Al Rashid profited from it. This situation also worried the Hanbali-Wahhabi ulama, some of whom were very concerned about the failure to apply the three O's. Two phenomena reflect the ulama's response to this crisis: voyages outside of Najd to acquire religious knowledge and flee chaos, and growing expectations of a coming messiah.

With the exception of Muhammad ibn Abd al-Wahhab and two ulama sent on diplomatic missions to Egypt in the early nineteenth century, all of the Hanbali-Wahhabis trips abroad had been involuntary. This was of course the case of the deportation to Egypt following the destruction of the Saudi Emirate in 1818, which allowed Najdi ulama to establish their first contacts with other

Sunni ulama corporations. Indeed, many of Ibn Abd al-Wahhab's descendants enrolled at Al-Azhar to complete their studies. Abd al-Rahman ibn Hasan studied and taught at Al-Azhar for eight years, and his son, Abd al-Latif, received most of his institutional training there.[102] Thanks to this involuntary period of residence, the representatives of Hanbali-Wahhabism were able to enrich their literature through the inclusion of medieval Hanbali theological and juridical works hitherto unknown in Najd. Thanks to the ulama of Cairo, they were also able to link themselves to Egyptian, Syrian, and Iraqi schools via an uninterrupted chain of transmission of religious authority (*al-sanad*).

After the restoration of the Saudi Emirate and Abd al-Rahman ibn Hasan's return to Najd in 1826, Hanbali-Wahhabi ulama ceased traveling abroad to acquire knowledge. As their writings suggest, the religious authorities believed that they possessed truth and knowledge, excusing them from the need to travel. But this changed with the death of Abd al-Latif in 1876. Prevailing insecurity in Najd no doubt perturbed networks for acquiring knowledge. This phenomenon likely intensified after the fall of the House of Saud in 1891 and the placement under house arrest in the Rashid's capital, Ha'il, of Abd Allah ibn Abd al-Latif, leader of the clerical corps. Several ulama thus decided to leave Najd and pursue their education in less chaotic surroundings.

While a few ulama visited traditional places of learning, such as Mecca and Cairo, others traveled to India. This destination may at first seem surprising. What would a Hanbali-Wahhabi ulama, who prohibits travel to the Ottoman Empire, be doing in India of all places, a cosmopolitan country under British domination? Yet there is a simple explanation: the presence on site of the Ahl al-Hadith, a movement that, *grosso modo*, professed a doctrine similar to that of Hanbali-Wahhabism. Indeed, this group, which emerged in northern India in the nineteenth century, preached strict application of orthodoxy and orthopraxy by means of a direct return to the Qur'an and the Sunna. As a consequence, the members of this movement regarded all popular Islamic practices as forms of associationism that were to be combatted by all means necessary.[103] While only minor differences existed between these two traditions in the area of dogma, there was nevertheless a significant discrepancy with regards to the Law. Whereas one group was Hanbali, the other called for legal schools to be abandoned, seeing them as blameworthy innovations. Since the Hanbali-Wahhabis believed that dogma took precedence over Law, however, this divergence was not a source of real conflict. Moreover, the Najdis mainly traveled to India in order to profit from the encyclopedic knowledge of the prophetic tradition possessed by members of the Ahl al-Hadith corporation.

How did the Hanbali-Wahhabi ulama learn of the existence of the Ahl al-Hadith? Two complementary factors favored this encounter: annual contacts in Mecca during the pilgrimage season, and the commercial relations linking a number of Najdi kindreds with India. Beginning in 1884, several ulama traveled there. Relations intensified after the fall of the Saudi Emirate and were maintained up until the 1930s. No fewer than seventeen ulama went to stay with the Ahl al-Hadith over this period—an extremely high figure when one considers that Najd had only around fifty "highly" trained religious personnel at this time.[104] Some of the ulama who traveled to India to complete their training were to play a leading role in the restoration of the Saudi Emirate beginning in 1902.[105]

After receiving an education from his father, in 1884 Sa'd ibn Hamad ibn Atiq (d. 1930) traveled to India, where he stayed for approximately nine years. While there, he studied under the undisputed leader of the Ahl al-Hadith corporation, Siddiq Khan (d. 1890). He then traveled to Mecca for the pilgrimage and to study the thought of Indian, North African, and Meccan ulama. After the restoration of the Saudi Emirate, he became a judge and imam of the Grand Mosque of Riyadh. The principal religious figures of Saudi Arabia during the first half of the twentieth century—in particular, grand mufti Muhammad ibn Ibrahim Al al-Shaykh (d. 1969)—were his students.[106]

For its part, the career of Abd Allah ibn Muhammad ibn Abd al-Latif Al al-Shaykh (d. 1922) was atypical. After following a classic course of study in Riyadh under the direction of the most authoritative Hanbali-Wahhabi scholars, he became a veritable globe trotter. In order to acquire knowledge and experience of the world, he traveled to the Hijaz, Egypt, Tunisia, Morocco, Iraq, Iran, Afghanistan, and India. He ultimately joined the Saudi exiles in Kuwait and became one of the royal house's most faithful supporters. Abd Allah ibn Muhammad actively participated in efforts to acculturate, render sedentary, and mobilize the Bedouin tribes from which the Ikhwan army, which I discuss below, was to emerge.[107]

Placed in their historic context, the travels of the Najdi ulama in various Islamic countries, particularly India, expressed a desire to flee the unenviable situation of their country and an undeniable thirst for ever greater religious knowledge. From the perspective of the *longue durée*, however, this phenomenon allowed Hanbali-Wahhabism to expand its references, legitimate its positions, and endow itself with genuine historical depth via the accumulation of *ijazat* (authorizations to transmit juridico-religious knowledge). The representatives of this tradition once again demonstrated how an ethic of responsibility allowed them to adapt to a new situation in order to almost fully preserve their symbolic capital and ideological authority.

The second phenomenon that merits attention is the search for a messiah: by all appearances, some ulama expected a messianic event to bring a close to the cycle of political instability that had roiled Najd. Although he had adopted a messianic attitude, Muhammad ibn Abd al-Wahhab claimed only to be the reformer (*al-mujaddid*) whom God sent once every century of the Hegira in order to restore the three O's, in accordance with a tradition attributed to the Prophet of Islam.[108] His stance therefore excluded the idea of the end of the world. Indeed, in his work *Traditions concerning Discord and the End of the World*, the preacher from Najd adopted an extremely classical and orthodox position concerning the figure of the Mahdi, the messiah of Islam. For him, the Mahdi was a descendant of the Prophet who would emerge at the end of time to establish peace, security, and prosperity.[109]

It seems that the descendants and disciples of Ibn Abd al-Wahhab contented themselves with the founder's production on this subject. The prevailing chaos of Najd haunted the ulama to such an extent that some of them—in particular, those from Al-Qasim—imagined that only messianic action could deliver the region. It was for this reason that '*alim* Ali ibn Numayy (d. 1941), who had carried out his studies in Riyadh and India, traveled to Sudan in 1882 in order to verify the messianic claims of Muhammad Ahmad al-Mahdi (d. 1885). Once there, he realized that al-Mahdi's pretensions were unfounded, but that in no way prevented him from continuing to seek the providential man. After returning home the next year—that is, in the year 1300 of the Hegira (a significant date from a messianic point of view)—he went to meet Emir Muhammad ibn Abd Allah Al Rashid, Najd's new strongman. Ibn Numayy told him that the ulama of Sudan mentioned a number of prophetic traditions concerning the Qahtani who was to dominate the world.[110] According to traditions attributed to the Prophet Muhammad and reported by al-Bukhari and Muslim, an offspring of the Qahtan tribal confederation would reign over the world until the end of time.[111] As the House of Rashid belonged to the Qahtan confederation, their leader was doubtless this providential figure. It seems the Al-Qasim ulama hoped these messianic expectations would bring them peace and stability, whatever the government, and thereby allow them to resume their peaceful lives and lucrative commercial activities.

Although they did not contest the veracity of the prophetic traditions, the Hanbali-Wahhabi ulama of Riyadh claimed that there were objective reasons proving that Muhammad ibn Abd Allah Al Rashid was not this figure. To that end, the '*alim* Hamad ibn Atiq mobilized all available scriptural resources.

In order to be valid and in keeping with the most authoritative traditions, al-Qahtani's claims had to meet two necessary conditions: the Qahtani figure in question had to emerge after the Mahdi[112] and would take all necessary steps to implement the Law. According to Ibn Atiq, Emir Muhammad ibn Abd Allah Al Rashid fulfilled neither of these conditions. He was therefore not the Qahtani announced by the Prophet.[113]

The Hanbali-Wahhabi religious establishment thus expressed its refusal of any form of messianism not in conformity with the sacred texts as well as its rejection of the House of Rashid's pretensions to legitimate domination. Far from endorsing "extravagant" messianism, the corporation aspired to and actively sought the restoration of the Saudi Emirate, the only possible guarantor, in its eyes, of the three O's.

4

THE BIRTH OF A KINGDOM AND THE RENAISSANCE OF A TRADITION

THE SYMBIOTIC RELATIONSHIP IS CONFIRMED

The ulama's wish came true when a grandson of Emir Faysal ibn Turki, Abd al-Aziz ibn Abd al-Rahman, undertook to restore the house's power in the first years of the twentieth century. Following several unsuccessful attempts, in 1902 he succeeded in seizing Riyadh and expelling the Rashid's small garrison. This initial victory was the founding act of a military and political epic that resulted in the creation of the Kingdom of Saudi Arabia in 1932. Conscious of the ideological importance of the Hanbali-Wahhabi tradition, King Abd al-Aziz (1902–1953) hastened to resume the historic alliance that had united his predecessors with the ulama.[1] The reactivated symbiotic relationship between the political power and the religious authority was expressed in the language of kinship: Abd al-Aziz married the daughter of Abd Allah ibn Abd al-Latif Al al-Shaykh, the head of the clerical corps. In 1906, Prince Faysal, king of Saudi Arabia between 1964 and 1975, was born of this symbolic and carnal union.

Once again, one cannot help but note the elective affinities between the House of Saud and the Hanbali-Wahhabi tradition. While the ulama mobilized all of their symbolic resources to sanctify Saudi political ambitions in the belief that this house alone was capable of guaranteeing the application of the Law, Abd al-Aziz, eager to legitimate his position, fully employed his coercive power to ensure that his faithful partners were able to impose and spread their religious discourse.

The ulama and their king initially joined forces to (re)unify Najd. Between 1902 and 1906, the districts of Al-'Arid, Al-Washm, Al-Dilam, and Sudayr, where Hanbali-Wahhabi influence was uncontested, joined the Saudi cause. By contrast, the district of Al-Qasim, where traditional Hanbali ulama were still very active, preferred to remain under the nominal suzerainty of the Rashids.[2] It was to become the main theater of conflict between the two powers.

In order to sanctify the action of Abd al-Aziz and mobilize the population, the ulama fully drew upon their ideological authority. As Abd Allah al-Anqari

(d. 1954),³ judge and religious referee (*marji'*) for the district of Sudayr, wrote: "God granted Muslims a religious government, represented by the imam Abd al-Aziz ibn Abd al-Rahman ibn Faysal [Al Saud], God grant him victory and give him the strength to enforce the Law and destroy blameworthy innovations."⁴

The population of Najd had to respond to the call of its legitimate leader and mobilize itself for jihad, which had become an individual obligation (*fard 'ayn*), in order to liberate its territory from the hands of infidels and associationists.⁵ To this end, the ulama once again mobilized the concept of *al-wala' wa al-bara'* (allegiance [to Muslims] and rupture [with the infidels]) against the Rashid and their supporters in the Qasim. Abd Allah ibn Abd al-Latif Al al-Shaykh considered the Rashid and their lackeys the greatest enemies of the True Religion because they had called for military and financial support from the "Ottoman associationists."⁶ They thus had to be not only excluded from the community, but also combatted in the framework of jihad. He even claimed that, in his view, fighting and subjugating the Rashid was the best form of jihad.⁷ Finally, he added that any person who refused to carry out this sacred obligation would be seen as a hypocrite and condemned to eternal damnation;⁸ for in the view of these ulama, Abd al-Aziz's project sought to put an end to the *fitna* (disorder) that had for decades rocked Najd in order to reestablish political and religious unity.⁹

Thanks to the ideological authority of its representatives and the various resources at their disposal, the Hanbali-Wahhabi corporation was able to use "psychic coercion by distributing or denying religious benefits."¹⁰ To persuade the population, the ulama mobilized affective and rational arguments, the two principal motors of which were seduction (such as the promise of material advantage and symbolic gratifications) and threats (such as excommunication, eternal damnation, the throes of hell, and chaos). Their monopoly over access to the sacred texts, instruction, and high culture no doubt facilitated this task. Indeed, the concepts, symbols, and images in which the ulama traded structured the better part of the local social imaginary, rendering it amenable to manipulation under the weight of their ideological authority.

With the support of energetic politico-military action on the part of the king and his collaborators, the efforts of the clerical corps soon bore fruit. Fewer than four years after the capture of Riyadh, Abd al-Aziz succeeded in subjugating most of Najd, particularly the district of Al-Qasim. Following the conquest of Al-Qasim in 1906, the religious establishment decided, with the consent and support of King Abd al-Aziz, to conduct a veritable campaign of "purification" against the traditional Hanbali ulama and have done with them once and for all. Three methods were used to this end: execution, elimination from the public sphere, and co-optation. As we have seen, Abd Allah ibn Amr, an *'alim* from the oasis of Burayda, was one of the most dogged adversaries of Hanbali-Wahhabism and the House of Saud. The letter he addressed to Emir Muhammad ibn Abd Allah Al Rashid in which he described the ulama as ignoramuses, megalomaniacs, and extremists left no doubt as to how he felt about them. Once the situation had stabilized, the Hanbali-Wahhabi ulama seized upon the first occasion to eliminate him. In 1908, they issued a fatwa of excommunication and execution. Abd al-Aziz immediately ordered that Abd Allah ibn Amr be put to death. Yet this killing was a unique case, the reflection of a very particular situation in which religious hostility had become mixed with a desire to settle personal scores. Traditional Hanbali ulama were for their part silenced by means of house arrest, a permanent ban on teaching and writing, and exile. Following a period of quarantine, some of them were later co-opted by the corporation after having completed a program of training and acculturation in Riyadh.[11]

The corporation was not content with permanently eliminating traditional Hanbalism; it also purged its ranks of what it saw as unreliable, politically quietist elements. This included such figures as Ahmad ibn Isa (d. 1911), despite the fact that he had been trained by leading Hanbali-Wahhabi authorities, some of them descendants of Muhammad ibn Abd al-Wahhab. As we have seen, the chaos to which the fratricidal struggles among descendants of Emir Faysal ibn Turki gave rise obliged dozens of ulama to leave Najd. Ibn Isa was one such. He took up residence in Mecca, where, alongside a thriving commercial activity, he set about proselytizing on behalf of his tradition among the local elite. He is said to have thereby "converted" the emir of Mecca, Sharif Awn (1882–1905), persuading him to destroy popular places of worship and put an end to heterodox practices. Similarly, he succeeded in "converting" several of the holy city's notables, including Muhammad Nasif (d. 1971), who played an important role in the process of restoring the Hijaz to Hanbali-Wahhabism and integrating it into the Saudi state. But, for unknown reasons, Ibn Isa rallied to the cause of the Rashids after they conquered and temporarily pacified Najd. He then returned to the province, where he served as a judge in the district of Sudayr. This willingness to collaborate with the Saud's political enemies was considered an act of treason by the religious establishment. The first sovereign act of King Abd al-Aziz after the conquest of the district of Sudayr in 1906 was thus to dismiss Ibn Isa.[12]

Membership in the corporation at the start of the twentieth century thus supposed both scrupulous observance of the Hanbali-Wahhabi tradition and allegiance to the House of Saud. These two elements today remain the two inseparable pillars of the habitus of the religious elite in Saudi Arabia. The slightest lapse is seen as "high treason" by the political power and the religious authority. We will return to this question below.

While the purge campaigns were under way, the leaders of the corporation, once again acting in complicity with the political authorities, set about appointing members of their circle to head the religious bodies of the conquered regions. Closely associated with descendants of Muhammad ibn Abd al-Wahhab and the House of Saud, the Silim lineage thus was given the task of reestablishing the Hanbali-Wahhabi discursive monopoly in the district of Al-Qasim. Throughout the first half of the twentieth century, the members of this lineage, their clients, and their followers occupied the principal juridico-religious offices there.[13] Similarly, trained and trusted religious agents were dispatched to enforce orthodoxy and orthopraxy among the sedentary populations of territories subjugated by the House of Saud.[14]

Along the same lines, the religious elite saw to reorganizing and overseeing the networks for transmitting knowledge in Najd in order to maintain control over the market for the goods of salvation. Indeed, the representatives of the tradition attempted to strengthen the unity and homogeneity of the corporation around the Al al-Shaykh, the descendants of Muhammad ibn Abd al-Wahhab. In a letter addressed to the notables and people of Najd, the leading figures of Hanbali-Wahhabism claimed that God had sent Muhammad ibn Abd al-Wahhab to combat blameworthy innovation and impose the three O's. Having succeeded in his mission, his descendants followed his example, doing everything in their power to preserve the living tradition. As their teaching was the only path to eternal salvation, their fatawa must be scrupulously respected and their doctrine followed to the letter in order to escape the torments of hell.[15] This centralizing desire was reflected in practice. Around 90 percent of the religious personnel I have been able to identify spent time in Riyadh in order to receive instruction from the Al al-Shaykh and their followers.

STABILIZING THE FRONTIERS OF THE FAITH

Abd al-Aziz devoted the first ten years of his reign to consolidating his power and subjugating the main sedentary population centers of Najd. But he soon realized that in order to perpetuate his regional hegemony, it was absolutely necessary to once and for all subjugate the Bedouin tribal confederations. Indeed, the confederations profited from every crisis and moment of tension to recover autonomy and maximize their politico-economic advantages. This was the case in 1910, when a tribal confederation from the southern Najd rallied behind a rebellion that had been launched by some of the king's cousins.[16] Similarly, the periodic struggles between various tribes for control over the region's meager resources disturbed trade routes and called into question the security and stability of the revived Saudi state. The religious factor must also be taken into consideration. Since the nineteenth century, the Hanbali-Wahhabi establishment had regarded these tribes as bands of infidels and heretics in desperate need of "Islamization" if they were to be saved from eternal damnation.

For reasons that remain obscure because of a paucity of sources, the idea emerged of sedentarizing and acculturating the Bedouin tribal confederations. Some sources attribute this idea to King Abd al-Aziz, others to the ulama. Although the origin of this idea remains unknown, the two partners actively participated in bringing it about. This undertaking allowed the political power and the religious authority to closely supervise the ideas and actions of the tribes. Starting in 1912, the authorities set up camps (*al-hijar*, sing. *al-hijra*) intended to receive Bedouin groups at watering places. The use of the term *hijar* to describe these sedentarization camps is particularly significant. In the Arab-Islamic imaginary, this notion evokes a veritable rite of passage: leaving an impious life and place in order to return to one in which the True Religion is practiced. Once again, the example of the Prophet was evoked in order to legitimate action: in 622, Muhammad left Mecca and moved to Medina, where a new phase of Islamic history began.

The phenomenon of sedentarization must not be seen as without precedent. On the contrary, it is part and parcel of the long-term history of the Arabian Peninsula. Since the pre-Islamic period, the sedentarization of Bedouin groups was encouraged via the establishment of enclosures and sacred territories (*haram*, *hima*, *hawta*, etc.). These constituted havens of peace where the Bedouin could perform religious rituals, carry out commercial transactions, and graze their herds in total security. After a period of more or less gradual development, this system, which was at first only temporary—it lasted no more than a few months each year—generally led to the emergence of centers of integration and stabilization for the Bedouin population. What's more, it must not be forgotten that, in several dialects of the Arabian Peninsula, the term *hijra* means village or place of sedentarization.[17] The modern *hijar* were original in two respects: their scale and the speed with which the process of sedentarization took place. Between 1912 and 1926, hundreds of *hijar* were created and approximately 150,000 Bedouin sedentarized. This undertaking was accompanied by a process of inculcation overseen by the Hanbali-Wahhabi corporation, with unconditional support from King Abd al-Aziz. It consisted of two ideal-typical phases: acculturation and mobilization.

During the first phase, the establishment made significant efforts to impose orthodoxy and orthopraxy on these groups. Agents of socialization known as *al-mutawi'a*—we will consider the history and meaning of this term later—responsible for overseeing the inhabitants and teaching them the basics of the religion were sent to the *hijar*. Several clerics made frequent trips to the various sites of sedentarization in order to strengthen ties with the tribes and ensure that instruction, supervision, and acculturation were being properly seen to.[18] The pedagogical material these agents used was entirely drawn from the classical repertoire of Hanbali-Wahhabism: the catechisms of Ibn Abd al-Wahhab and several of his descendants' epistles and fatawa. The little anthology put together by the *'alim* Sulayman ibn Sahman (d. 1930) is a good example of the type of pedagogical material that was circulating in Najd during the first years of the twentieth century.[19]

The objective of the second phase was to impose the habitus and vision of the Hanbali-Wahhabi world on the recently sedentarized Bedouin. To this end, the concept of culturally and geographically distinguishing between true and false religion by means of allegiance and rupture (*al-wala wa al-bara'*) was once again mobilized. For example, Hasan ibn Husayn Al al-Shaykh (d. 1921), an *'alim* who actively participated in the creation of the Al-Artawiyya *hijra*—one of the country's largest—wrote an epistle in which he reiterated the exclusivist ideas of the nineteenth century: all peaceful contact with impious territories and populations, particularly southern Iraq and Kuwait, was prohibited. The only possible site of interaction was the battlefield in the framework of jihad.[20]

In just a few years' time, this process of acculturation and mobilization resulted in the Bedouin tribes' conversion to Hanbali-Wahhabism. This was a great victory for the tradition and its representatives: after several decades of fruitless efforts, they had succeeded in homogenizing and unifying the religion over nearly the entire Najd. The most vivid symbol of their success was the creation of an army of sedentarized Bedouin: al-Ikhwan (the Brothers [in religion]). Between 1914 and 1927, this army played an active role in the process of constructing the Saudi state and spreading its doctrine.[21] The aim of the following pages is not to describe the history and sociology of the Ikhwan—a task that has already been seen to by other scholars[22]—but rather to examine the attitude of the religious establishment vis-à-vis the ideological positions and intrigues of some of their leaders.

Just a few years after this army was created, some of its leaders began to adopt a hardline religious and political stance, provoking alarm and suspicion in the religious authority and the political power. Tensions between some of the Ikhwan and the authorities were aggravated by a fundamental question of identity: what were the symbolic, cultural, and geographic frontiers of the True Religion? Though couched in religious language, this question concealed a number of sociopolitical problems, the most important of which were the conflict between the sedentary population and the Bedouins, the centrifugal aspirations of certain tribal chiefs, and the ambitions for social promotion of certain peripheral religious agents.[23]

Beginning in 1914, some of the Ikhwan leaders took the liberty to indiscriminately attack and ransom members of the Bedouin tribes of Najd, southern Iraq, and Kuwait. On the king's request, the ulama sent them several letters and fatawa ordering them to immediately cease their attacks. According to Hanbali-Wahhabi doctrine, only the leader of the community has the privilege of declaring jihad, collecting taxes, and carrying out legal punishments.[24] Calling royal prerogatives into question amounted to transgressing one of the main precepts of sharia.[25] The ulama also drew the attention of the Ikhwan's leaders to the fact that no qualified and recognized religious figure—in particular, none of Ibn Abd al-Wahhab's descendants—authorized such a breach of the three O's. They therefore advised the leaders to stop blindly following the teachings and fatawa of the agents of socialization, whom they described as extremists and ignoramuses.[26] Between 1916 and 1920, several of the agents were dismissed from their posts. During the same period, some recently sedentarized tribes attempted to leave the *hijar* and return to their former lifestyle. The ulama held that such an act constituted a grave sin—indeed, an act of apostasy—for it resulted in sociopolitical disorder and a failure to apply the Law.[27] By contrast, Bedouin who pledged their allegiance to King Abd al-Aziz and accepted the teachings of Hanbali-Wahhabism were considered genuine Muslims. It was thus forbidden to attack or capture them for ransom.[28]

The clerical corps, in complicity with the king, hoped to impose politico-religious centrality and verticality. Its members were well aware of the fact that only political unity and stability favored the application of sharia, the sole means for achieving salvation. From a sociological point of view, the religious elite also aspired to maintain the homogeneity of their religious group and discourse in order to preserve the unity of the corporation and tradition. While the ulama disapproved of only a portion of the Ikhwan's action and the teaching of socialization agents, they condemned their insubordination, which they feared would threaten the ideological authority and unity of the political entity that protected them. Future events were to confirm this hypothesis.

Despite the remonstrance of the king and the ulama, some of the Ikhwan continued to attack the Bedouin groups of the region with impunity, in particular those among them that recognized the power of Abd al-Aziz. Meanwhile, other groups of Ikhwan attempted to return to a nomadic lifestyle. The Ikhwan reproached Abd al-Aziz with favoring the sedentary population on the grounds that it had embraced the True Religion much earlier. They perceived themselves to be second-class subjects, despised by a sedentary population that did not even deign to eat their food.[29] This escalation, which threatened to call into question the entire process of state construction that had begun two centuries earlier, forced the king to come to grips with the situation. In 1919, he thus called a secret meeting during which he asked the leading figures of the Hanbali-Wahhabi establishment to once again give their opinion on all of these questions.[30]

Between 1919 and 1920, the ulama issued a number of collective and individual fatawa presenting the official positions of the corporation. They thus affirmed that all subjects of King Abd al-Aziz—whether sedentary, sedentarized Bedouin, or nomadic Bedouin—are Muslims.[31] They reiterated that the Qur'an, the Sunna, the acts of the companions, and the teachings of the four legal schools of Sunnism are the foundations of the True Religion. As long as all observed the same credo—that is, the Hanbali 'aqida—certain discrepancies among the practices of these four schools were of no consequence.[32] The ulama called upon all subjects to unite around their monarch and obey the teachings of the great figures of the corporation, reaffirming that only the king could declare jihad, apply punishments, grant protection to non-Muslims, and sign truces with foreign powers.[33] They alone were in possession of religious truth; the only path to salvation was to follow their teachings and instructions.[34] To all appearances, their conclusions were well-received by King Abd al-Aziz, who reiterated his desire to perpetuate the alliance with his faithful partners by applying the three O's in the public sphere.[35]

In order to effectively regain control of the situation and bestow the principles of obedience and centrality upon these unmanageable, recently sedentarized Bedouin populations, several figures from the corporation took up residence in the main recalcitrant *hijar*.[36] In 1920, even Abd Allah ibn Abd al-Latif Al al-Shaykh visited several *hijar*, where he provided instruction.[37] The political power and the religious authority sought to use all of their influence to prevent cracks from appearing in the edifice of the Saudi state,[38] for both had reached watershed moments in their respective histories: while the state was being transformed from an insignificant little emirate into a genuine regional power, Hanbali-Wahhabism, once a strictly local phenomenon, was on its way to becoming a global Islamic tradition.

After the end of the First World War, which resulted in the collapse of the Ottoman Empire and the consecration of British hegemony in the region, King Abd al-Aziz, a British ally, looked unstoppable. In fewer than eight years, he had succeeded in overcoming all of his adversaries and conquering the better part of the Arabian Peninsula—in particular, the two holy cities of Islam (1924–1925). This is why the king and the ulama, in keeping with the ethic of responsibility, took care to avoid all *fitna* and adopt a conciliatory tone in their dealings with the Ikhwan, whose strength and cohesiveness significantly contributed to this epic conquest.

The situation changed radically beginning in 1926. With the exception of a few military raids to the southwest to stabilize the frontier with Yemen, which continued through the mid-1930s, the large-scale military operations that had led to the creation of the present-day Saudi Kingdom came to an end. The geographical and political frontiers of the True Religion reached their maximal limits for a simple reason: Saudi territory was now encircled by British colonies and protectorates. Thanks to a good reading of the geopolitical situation and innate practical understanding, Abd al-Aziz, formerly the great conqueror, transformed himself into a skillful diplomat in order to preserve his possessions. Starting in 1921, he signed a number of agreements with the British authorities fixing the northern borders of the nascent kingdom.

With support from the religious authority, the king's recognition of the modern frontiers brought the period of jihad to an end and had several repercussions on the domestic scene, particularly in what concerned certain Ikhwan factions. For these factions, the cessation of military operations meant an end to the substantial revenues they had gained through plunder and royal gifts as well as to various forms of symbolic gratification (such as glory, honor, and chivalry). It also meant that they had to return to their *hijar* to resume their peaceful but impoverished existence as farmers, merchants, and artisans. What's more, the political and social ambitions of some Ikhwan leaders—in particular, Faysal al-Duwaysh (d. 1931), Sultan ibn Bajad (d. 1934), and Daydan ibn Hathlin (d. 1929)[39]—were disappointed. Though these leaders had aspired to high military and political posts in the new entity, nothing came of it. With a few exceptions, Abd al-Aziz preferred to co-opt and retain local elites in important posts in order to profit from their influence, reassure the native population, and stabilize his power. To this must be added the centrifugal temptations driving several tribal groups that had never accepted the idea of submitting to a central power.

To crown it all, the religious factor excited the passions and accentuated the bitterness of the Ikhwan and their leaders. While the ulama and the agents of socialization constantly invoked the principle of allegiance and rupture, according to which any peaceful contact with infidels was prohibited, in order to sedentarize and mobilize the Bedouin tribes, the king and his advisors established diplomatic relations with foreign powers and tolerated "associationists" (that is, the other Muslim currents present on Saudi territory). Indeed, the ulama claimed that diplomatic relations with non-Muslim powers were permis-

Birth of a Kingdom, Renaissance of a Tradition

sible and in practice adopted a less aggressive attitude toward the kingdom's non–Hanbali-Wahhabi populations. While some of the Ikhwan attempted to impose orthodoxy and orthopraxy by violence in certain regions—in particular, that of Mecca and the eastern region—religious dignitaries disapproved of their actions and called for the use of milder and more "intelligent" methods.[40] It seems that some agents of socialization profited from the situation to further exacerbate tensions by whispering to leaders of the Ikhwan that the king no longer observed sharia and that the leading religious figures of the kingdom were hypocrites in the pay of a corrupted power.[41]

Whatever the case, some Ikhwan leaders decided to act. In December 1926, they organized a sort of special meeting in the *hijra* of Al-Artawiyya. At the end of this meeting, they expressed their resentment and disappointment by recording a number of grievances against the king and the ulama.[42] Although their grievances consisted of social and political demands, they were couched in religious language; as the dominant idiom, it alone was capable of bestowing legitimacy and intelligibility upon them. The following points succinctly capture the Ikhwan's main grievances:[43]

1. Use of the telegraph, which was seen as a blameworthy innovation (*bidaʻ*).
2. The voyages of the king's sons, Saud and Faysal, in infidel countries (specifically, Egypt and England) despite the fact that the Law forbade all peaceful contact with these countries.
3. The imposition, also forbidden, of extracanonical taxes on the populations of Najd.
4. The fact that the Bedouin tribes of Iraq and Transjordan had been given permission to graze their herds on Muslim territory even though they were considered infidels.
5. The ban on all trade with Kuwait: if the Kuwaitis were held to be infidels, jihad had to be declared against them; otherwise, trading with them should be permitted.
6. The fact that the presence of Shiites—infidels who had to be either converted or massacred—was tolerated in the eastern region.
7. The application of positive laws in the province of Hijaz.
8. The fact that Egyptians were authorized to introduce the *mahmal* into the holy enclosure of Mecca.[44]

In January 1927, realizing that the Ikhwan's demands could degenerate into an open rebellion that would threaten to disrupt the process of Saudi state construction, Abd al-Aziz called for a meeting of the new kingdom's main elites to discuss the situation. At the end of negotiations, the king once again expressed his commitment to scrupulously observe sharia. The ulama issued several fatawa partly responding to the Ikhwan's grievances:[45]

1. The telegraph is a modern invention and no classical legal text makes mention of it. Given the present state of knowledge, it is thus impossible to express an opinion regarding its legality.
2. The positive laws applied in the Hijaz must be immediately repealed and replaced by sharia.
3. Places of popular worship must be immediately destroyed, in particular the mosques of Hamza and Abu Rashid.
4. Extracanonical texts are illicit. The king will be acting in conformity with the Law if he suppresses them, but failure to do so on his part does not justify rebellion.
5. The *mahmal* will no longer have access to the Grand Mosque of Mecca, and all popular rituals involving it are prohibited. But the question of whether to ban it from Mecca is left to the judgment of the king, who will act in keeping with the diplomatic interests of the kingdom.
6. The king alone has the right to declare jihad.

While these fatawa appeared to respond to the temporal and spiritual concerns of the Ikhwan, in reality they only reaffirmed the prerogatives of the religious authority and the political power. While nothing was said about the foreign travels of the king's son, the conversion of populations to Hanbali-Wahhabism was hardly mentioned, the problem of technological innovation was dismissed, and the need to respect royal prerogatives and the three O's was unambiguously and forcefully reiterated. The claim that only the sovereign could declare jihad and the formal ban on rebellion, whatever its causes, were merely the religious expressions of a desire to centralize and monopolize all of the ideological tools of domination. The ulama hoped to establish a genuine vertical power transcending all of the social components of the developing Saudi Kingdom. The order imposed by this coercive power would allow them to implement the principles and interests of the corporation in the public sphere. The only two points on which the ulama showed themselves inflexible were the full application of the Law and the destruction of places of popular worship. The corporation first of all wished to control the public sphere and the legal domain in order to give expression to its victory and domination before subsequently imposing its convictions on the native populations. As we will see, this strategy was to prove effective.

In order to reaffirm his commitments and strengthen his position, in April 1927 Abd al-Aziz convened a second meeting which brought together hundreds of notables from all regions of the Saudi state. This extraordinary assembly resulted in a genuine symbolic victory: the notables renewed their pledges of allegiance to Abd al-Aziz, who was officially proclaimed king of the Hijaz, Najd, and its dependencies.[46] Yet one false note blemished the festivities: the absence of Sultan ibn Bajad and his supporters. In their role as spokesmen of the monarchy, the ulama took the initiative to reprimand him. They reiterated the political and religious benefits of unity in this world and beyond. One must therefore obey the king and the ulama, the exclusive keepers of the truth.[47]

Neither the actions of the king nor the words of the ulama lastingly influenced the Ikhwan, who, after several months of respite, reactivated their grievances and resumed their attacks on southern Iraq and Kuwait between October 1927 and April 1928. On several occasions, their repeated attacks provoked intervention by the British air force, alarming Abd al-Aziz. He realized that the English could use these incidents as a pretext to interfere in the affairs of his kingdom. But for all that, he did not decide to use force to rid himself of the Ikhwan rebels. Instead, he convened a new conference in April 1928 in the hope of bringing their leaders to reason. The Ikhwan leaders, however, declined the royal invitation and are said to have worked out a plan for dividing up Saudi possessions among themselves: the Hijaz would revert to Sultan ibn Bajad, Najd to Faysal al-Duwaysh, and Al-Ahsa' to Daydan ibn Hathlin. They even carried out a defamation campaign against the king and the ulama: Abd al-Aziz was accused of failing to apply the Law and consorting with infidels, and the ulama were accused of hypocrisy because they hid the truth from the population.

Confrontation had become inevitable. The king preferred to play for time in order to ensure popular support and British help. In May 1928, he signed a friendship and cooperation agreement with the representative of the Crown, according to which the latter recognized the full independence of the Saudi Kingdom. On the ground, the English continued to supply Abd al-Aziz with all of the weapons and ammunition he needed. Internally, he mobilized the sedentary population of Najd, most of which firmly supported the House of Saud, and co-opted the tribal chiefs. These efforts were crowned by a general assembly (*al-jam'iyya al-'umumiyya*), which first met on 6 December 1928. There, the notables and the religious establishment of Najd reiterated their unconditional support for the king and strongly condemned the Ikhwan's schemes.[48]

Confident of British support and the fidelity of the local elites, Abd al-Aziz decided that the time had come to rid himself of this burdensome group. With help from the religious establishment, he began to recruit new contingents among the sedentary population of Najd in anticipation of the decisive battle. The Ikhwan, for their part, implicitly declared themselves rebels by attacking local populations and taking prisoners for ransom. Even as he prepared for the worst, the king still hoped to peacefully bring them to reason. To this end, he sent a delegation of ulama under the leadership of Abd Allah al-Anqari (d. 1954) and Abd al-Aziz al-Shathri (d. 1967) to negotiate with them and meet with some of their leaders, in particular Faysal al-Duwaysh. Once again, the king's efforts ended in failure, and negotiation gave way to military operations. Six months of campaigning followed, the main episode of which was the Battle of Sbilla on 30 March 1929, before royal troops put down this uprising that had mixed religious feeling, centrifugal desires, and social demands. Henceforth, Abd al-Aziz was the uncontested master. After having finished pacifying the southwestern provinces of the kingdom and having reiterated his commitment to respect the frontiers that had resulted from the First World War, the king officially proclaimed the birth of the Kingdom of Saudi Arabia on 18 September 1932.[49]

During the conflict between King Abd al-Aziz and the Ikhwan, the Hanbali-Wahhabi corporation once again made full use of its ideological authority to defend the policy of the monarchy and its own spiritual and temporal interests. Between December 1928 and January 1930, the ulama issued no fewer than seventeen collective and individual fatawa solemnly reiterating the principal themes mentioned above:[50]

- The defense of the monarchy: For the ulama, Saud domination meant security, prosperity, and salutary unity. In order to avoid chaos, the king was to be obeyed in all circumstances as he alone was competent to oversee the affairs of the community. If the king happened to make mistakes, he was to be secretly lavished with good advice (*nasiha*, pl. *nasa'ih*). As a consequence, his royal prerogatives were to be scrupulously respected (declaration of jihad, application of legal punishments, collection of canonical taxes, signature of truces and international agreements, etc.).
- The defense of the corporation's interests: The ulama claimed that they alone and to the exclusion of all other social categories were legitimately placed to define and possess religious truth. As heirs of the prophets, they maintained that the religious establishment was the only body responsible for overseeing the goods of salvation and thus of monopolizing meaning. They sharply criticized certain agents of socialization, whom they saw as the main vector of evil. Indeed, the agents' teachings, which were inspired by a literalist interpretation and a thirst for power, had not only led some of the population astray, but had been at the origin of Ikhwan extremism and the dissension that had shaken the kingdom. Consulting the Hanbali-Wahhabi corpus without the mediation of the ulama could only lead to false interpretations.

As a result, King Abd al-Aziz had to forcibly put down the Ikhwan groups and religious agents who had challenged the centrality and verticality of the political power and the religious authority. The principle of obedience thus became one of the key words of the Hanbali-Wahhabi tradition and remains so to this day. Similarly, in keeping with the ethic of responsibility, the preservation of the tradition and the privileges of its representatives led the ulama to challenge the inviolability of one of the doctrine's fundamental principles: allegiance and rupture (*al-wala' wa al-bara'*). In a fatwa addressed to the Ikhwan, the *'alim* Abd Allah al-Anqari, a religious figure in Najd during the first half of the twentieth century, explained that they had misunderstood the exclusivist fatawa of Sulayman ibn Abd Allah Al al-Shaykh and Hamad ibn Atiq. These had to be put into historical context. The fatawa of Ibn Abd Allah Al al-Shaykh had been written in the course of the Ottoman invasion that had resulted in the destruction of the Saudi Emirate in 1818; those of Ibn Atiq had been written after the capture of Al-Ahsa' by the same power in 1871. The contents of these legal judgments responded to particular situations and therefore had no universal validity. Moreover, for the purposes of realpolitik, it was permissible to meet, sign truces, and exchange ambassadors with infidels without pledging allegiance to them (*muwalat*); King Abd al-Aziz had merely applied these principles.[51] As David Easton has thoroughly demonstrated, the ulama, like the actors of any political system, could "regulate their own behavior, transform their internal structure, and even go so far as to modify their fundamental aims" in response to the internal and external constraints that threatened the unity and homogeneity of their tradition.[52] In other words, a new process of routinization was now under way. The declaration of the end of jihad, the recognition of frontiers, the authorization of diplomatic relations, the tacit acceptance of the Other (above all, other currents of Islam), and so on could mean only one thing: Hanbali-Wahhabism was in the process of shifting from a counterreligion to a religion. The king took note of this change and tried to encourage this process of routinization.

ATTEMPTS TO DILUTE HANBALI-WAHHABI IDENTITY

The propaganda of the Ottomans and their associates gave the Hanbali-Wahhabi tradition a bad image, not only in the Muslim world, but also in Europe. From the second half of the eighteenth century, information about Hanbali-Wahhabis spread like wildfire. The more objective descriptions of some Muslim and European travelers and chroniclers failed to challenge stereotypes that depicted them as fanatical, ignorant, bloodthirsty Bedouin.

Fully aware of the stereotypes that circulated among his contemporaries, King Abd al-Aziz realized that only a large-scale public relations campaign could restore the prestige of the Najdi doctrine and give it its place among the traditions of Islam. This was especially true after the conquest of Mecca and Medina in 1924–1925. The task was twofold: to reassure Muslims and Europeans, and to make them accept the power of the House of Saud and Hanbali-Wahhabi hegemony over the Arabian Peninsula. To this end, Abd al-Aziz played upon the emotions and idealized representations of the Arab-Muslim elites in order to demonstrate the exemplary nature of the Saudi state construction. He presented himself as the only independent Muslim ruler—a valid claim, as it happens—and the only defender of the Arabs' cause, values, and identity. He claimed that the emergent Saudi Kingdom was alone in applying sharia and fighting blameworthy innovation, the main cause, according to him, of the *umma*'s decadence. The king's declarations quickly won the approbation of several Arab-Muslim groups that hoped to implement this new ideal in their own countries.

As we have seen, the Hanbali-Wahhabi ulama had been in continuous contact with the Indian Ahl al-Hadith group since the late nineteenth century. Interaction between the two corporations resulted in genuine cooperation. The Ahl al-Hadith possessed a large number of printing houses in Delhi and Bombay. Beginning in 1891, they put this technological advance to work in the service of their Najdi counterparts by publishing a number of classic works, the first of which was, of course, Muhammad ibn Abd al-Wahhab's *Book of the Unity of God*. This cooperation intensified under Abd al-Aziz, who funded the publication of a large number of Hanbali-Wahhabi works and anthologies, the most important of which was Ibn Ghannam's *History of Najd* and *Anthology of Najd Unity*, which gathered together the epistles and legal opinions of leading ulama. Many of these works were subsequently offered to Muslim elites to help them directly familiarize themselves with the true foundations of Najdi preaching.[53] Moreover, several Ahl al-Hadith ulama came to the defense of Hanbali-Wahhabism in their writings, explaining to their readers that this tradition reflected the authentic Islam of the pious ancestors.[54] Ultimately, this movement of defense and apology even spread beyond the Ahl al-Hadith group to Abul Ala Maududi's (d. 1979) Jamaat-e-Islami. In 1942, one of Maududi's most faithful lieutenants, Mas'ud al-Nadawi (d. 1954), wrote a laudatory biography of Muhammad ibn Abd al-Wahhab that is to this day widely read throughout the Muslim world in Arabic and Urdu.[55]

Yet the rehabilitation of Hanbali-Wahhabism mainly took place via the mediation of representatives of the Muslim reform movement that had been inspired by Jamal al-Din al-Afghani (d. 1897) and Muhammad Abdu (d. 1905). Beginning in the first decade of the twentieth century, Iraqi, Syrian, and Egyptian figures[56] wrote articles and books reiterating the slogans of King Abd al-Aziz.[57] The crushing defeat of the Ottomans at the end of the First World War and the embezzlement and mismanagement committed by Emir Hussayn and his sons in Mecca pushed a large number of reformers into the arms of Abd al-Aziz. In their eyes, the developing Saudi Kingdom was the only glimmer of hope in a Muslim world subjugated by European powers.

While such figures as Muhammad Shukri al-Alusi (d. 1924), Muhammad Hamid al-Fiqi (d. 1959), and Muhibb al-Din al-Khatib (d. 1969) played significant roles in normalizing and rehabilitating Hanbali-Wahhabism via the publication of classics of the tradition and apologetic writings,[58] the leading role was held by Muhammad Rashid Rida (d. 1935), the head of the reformist movement. After the fall of the Caliphate in 1924, Rida threw his unconditional support behind the Saudi monarchy. In a series of articles published in the newspaper *Al-Ahram* and the journal *Al-Manar*, probably the most widely read outlets of the Arabic language press of the period, he took a staunch position in favor of the Saudi monarchy before the conquest of the Hijaz and promoted Hanbali-Wahhabism.[59] Simultaneously drawing on religious terminology and rational argument, Rida sought to demonstrate that, in contrast to the Hashemite family and its supporters, the House of Saud and its faithful allies were pious Muslims endeavoring to apply orthodoxy and orthopraxy in keeping with the doctrines of the pious ancestors and the renaissance of the Arab nation.[60] He had no doubt that leadership of the holy places of Islam was incumbent upon them since their leader was "the sultan who worked silently, [while the Hashemites] were only kings of propaganda and empty talk." He even concluded one of his articles with an observation borrowed from the Lebanese-American traveler Amin al-Rihani (d. 1947): "the subjects of King Hussayn obey and fear him; those of Abd al-Aziz obey and love him; those of Imam Yahya [the ruler of Yemen] obey him without loving or fearing him; those of King Faysal of Iraq do not fear him, do not love him, and only obey when forced to do so [by the British authorities]. Who therefore deserves to rule over the Arabs of the Peninsula?"[61]

The answer went without saying.

Thanks to Rida's reputation throughout the Muslim world, his apologetic writings allowed the Saudi monarchy and the Hanbali-Wahhabi tradition to partly rid themselves of the stereotyped image that had pursued them for more than a century. But he did not stop there. With Saudi funding, he edited and published a large number of Hanbali-Wahhabi classics. At the same time, he tried to convince a number of ulama—particularly the guardians of the Al-Azhar mosque-school—to reconsider their anti–Hanbali-Wahhabi positions. Rida's opinions were widely known in reformist circles. Their echoes, for example, can be heard in the Algerian reformist review *Al-Shihab*, which took up the defense of the political project of Abd al-Aziz (depicted as the king of Islam) and Hanbali-Wahhabism (depicted as an integral part of Sunni Islam).[62]

Rida's efforts at rehabilitation seem to have gone beyond reformist circles properly so called. A number of very famous authors of various cultural and political sensibilities, including Amin al-Rihani (d. 1947), Muhammad Kurd Ali (d. 1953), Ahmad Amin (d. 1954), Mahmud al-Aqqad (d. 1964), Taha Hussayn (d. 1973), and Abd Allah al-Qasimi (d. 1996), devoted laudatory passages to the Hanbali-Wahhabi tradition and its founder. Indeed, most of these writers saw Hanbali-Wahhabism as the tradition closest to original Islam. In his book *The Leaders of Reform [in the Arab World] in Modern Times*, Ahmad Amin claimed not only that Hanbali-Wahhabism was the purest form of Islam, but also that Muhammad ibn Abd al-Wahhab was the indisputable leader of the movement for religious reform, inspiring such emulators as al-Shawkani (d. 1834) in Yemen and Muhammad Abdu (d. 1905) in Egypt. Amin also sang the praises of the Saudi monarchy, which had in various domains succeeded in reconciling the purest form of Islam with modern progress.[63]

To this list must be added the usual sycophants of the Saudi monarchy, among them Hafiz Wahba (d. 1967) and Khayr al-Din al-Zirikli (d. 1967), who contributed to popularizing a romantic image of Saudi Arabia, mixing religious values, a chivalric spirit, and historical sequences recalling the Golden Age of Islam. In *al-A'lam*, one of the Arab world's most widely consulted biographical dictionaries, al-Zirikli dedicated eulogistic entries to the clerical corps and the most eminent members of the House of Saud. He described Muhammad ibn Abd al-Wahhab, in particular, as "the initiator of modern religious renaissance and reform in the Arabian Peninsula."[64]

Beginning in the late 1920s, these favorable writings encouraged Abd al-Aziz to forge ahead with the process of routinizing the tradition in order to (re)integrate it into the bosom of Sunni Islamic schools and currents. The king more particularly profited from the affinities between Najdi tradition and Syro-Egyptian reformism that were very much in vogue at the time in all Muslim circles to attempt to dilute the former in the latter. On 10 May 1929, in the presence of several members of Muslim pilgrim delegations, he declared: "We are described as Wahhabis in order to give the impression that we have a separate school [*madhhab*]. This is a serious mistake born of hostile and malicious propaganda. Muhammad ibn Abd al-Wahhab preached nothing new. We are thus not followers of a new school or a new dogma ['*aqida*]. Our doctrine is that of the pious ancestors who recommended the Qur'an and the Sunna. We respect the four legal schools. In our eyes, there is no difference between Malik, al-Shafi'i, Ahmad, and Abu Hanifa."[65]

The rest of the king's speech insisted on the fact that the government scrupulously applied sharia in all domains, as doing so was the only legitimate and possible means for the Muslim community to recover its strength and power. Abd al-Aziz profited from the presence of pilgrim delegations to affirm that Hanbali-Wahhabism was only one of several expressions of the modern Muslim reformism known as *al-salafiyya*, Salafism. In doing so, he drew upon, with the help of his Egyptian and Syrian advisors, all of the reformists' fondest catchwords and slogans: the dogma of the pious ancestors, the application of the Law, and the overcoming of distinctions between the four legal schools of Islam.

The king's efforts to accelerate the process of diluting Hanbali-Wahhabism in reformism had in fact preceded these statements. As early as 1926, he ordered the creation of a high school known as the Islamic Institute (Al-Ma' had al-Islami) and appointed the Syrian reformist *'alim* Muhammad Bahjat al-Baytar (d. 1976) as its director. Al-Baytar assembled an Egyptian and Syrian staff to teach an academic program mixing religious and modern lessons. For reasons that will be discussed later, this attempt at ideological and pedagogical hybridization displeased the ulama. The representatives of Hanbali-Wahhabism discouraged families from sending their children to this institution. Such was their influence that, after just one year, the establishment closed its doors for lack of students.[66]

The failure of this first attempt did not prevent the king and his advisors from repeating the experiment a second time roughly twenty years later. In 1945, he ordered the creation of a religious studies institute in the town of Ta'if, naming it Dar al-Tawhid (The House of Unity). The site and name chosen for the school were highly symbolic. Located at the crossroads of the Hijaz and Najd, Ta'if symbolized the permanent unity of these two provinces and their populations under the Saudi aegis after several decades of combat. This choice was also no doubt a matter of distancing the students from the Hanbali-Wahhabi corporation. Furthermore, the institution's name expressed the desire for religious and political unity that had driven the king since the start of his reign. In sum, the creation of Dar al-Tawhid was meant to symbolize the unity of the kingdom on new foundations and its (re)integration into the Sunni world. In order to confer prestige upon it in the eyes of the population and a degree of independence vis-à-vis the dominant tradition, the institution was placed under the direct authority of the royal cabinet.

Al-Baytar was named its director and once again staffed it with foreigners. Of the twenty-three professors who taught there between 1945 and 1957, only three were Saudi. The majority came from Egypt.[67] In addition to the Hanbali-Wahhabi *'aqida*, the other religious subjects taught there were based on the scholarly programs of Cairo and Damascus. Even Asharite theology was taught.[68] In other words, reformism and even the Muslim Brotherhood must have had a significant influence on the students, who were intended to become the future hybrid religious elites of Saudi Arabia. In order to ensure the loyalty of these callow leaders, moreover, the students were exclusively chosen, in keeping with patrimonial practice, from the province of Najd—the bastion of the royal house and center of power. After four years of instruction, those who passed their exams could join Mecca's Faculty of Sharia—later to become Umm al-Qura University—which was founded in 1949 expressly to receive graduates of Dar al-Tawhid.[69]

Once again, this effort was very poorly received by the guardians of ideological authority, who saw it as an attempt to put an end to their hold over the Saudi juridico-religious space. Determined to retain what they had won after one hundred years of struggle and intellectual effort, the ulama decided to thwart this dangerous attempt at dilution without entering into conflict with their political partner. With help from their agents of socialization, they initially discouraged the population of Najd from sending their children to this institution, arguing that all the knowledge they needed was available onsite. This apparently simple tactic proved highly effective:[70] a majority of families refused to send their children, and many students, recruited by force, escaped.[71] Next, the ulama decided to marginalize Dar al-Tawhid. As we will see, this process was facilitated by the emergence, beginning in 1950, of competing religious institutes throughout the provinces of the kingdom under the aegis of the Hanbali-Wahhabi corporation. Young people from Najd no longer needed to travel to Ta'if. The result was the gradual decline of Dar al-Tawhid, which little by little transformed into a simple provincial institute. Moreover, the graduates of this institute, particularly those from the first classes that were chosen, were systematically excluded from high-ranking clerical offices. Only two of them succeeded in reaching the summit of the clerical hierarchy.

The Hanbali-Wahhabi tradition nevertheless profited from the Saudi monarchy's rapprochement with the reformists: it allowed its representatives not only to rid themselves of the bad reputation that had pursued them since the second half of the eighteenth century, but also to achieve symbolic and real gains. Indeed, the ulama gradually appropriated the *al-salafiyya* name—as we have seen, a not insignificant source of legitimacy. From 1950 onward, they drew upon the experience of reformists in various domains—in particular, publishing and teaching—to build their own structures. But their ecumenism stopped there. The ulama refused to allow their tradition to become diluted in this movement on the grounds that they did not share all of its religious and political leanings, on the one hand, and firmly believed that they were the sole keepers of religious truth, on the other. It was up to others to join their religious movement, not the other way around.

EXPANSION OF THE HANBALI-WAHHABI TRADITION

The expansion of Saudi power between 1902 and 1932 went hand in hand with the corporation's growing field of action. Confined to Najd for most of the nineteenth century, it could henceforth control the public sphere in the conquered regions—in particular, the holy places of Islam—and spread its doctrine among recently subjugated populations.

Following the conquest of Al-Ahsa' province in 1913, King Abd al-Aziz tried to reassure the local population, which mainly consisted of non–Hanbali-Wahhabi Sunnis and Shiites, by promising to respect their freedom of worship. In exchange, they were to pay a tribute, after which they would be protected and excused from contributing to the military effort.[72] The ulama contented themselves with reminding their followers that it was forbidden to speak to, greet, or eat with the Shiites, as socializing with them was dangerous for the faith.[73] But this situation did not last long. Beginning in the early 1920s, the religious establishment profited from the death of the province's Malikite judge, Isa ibn Akkas (d. 1920), by appointing a Hanbali-Wahhabi judge in his place and sending several socialization agents to oversee the public sphere and the juridico-religious offices of the province.

The simultaneous rise to power of the Ikhwan only complicated matters for the province's Shiite and Sunni populations. The Ikhwan were not satisfied with imposing orthodoxy and orthopraxy in the public sphere; they hoped to immediately "convert" local populations. They did not hesitate to use force to this end and were criticized for doing so by the ulama, who saw it as threatening the order necessary for the performance of religious duties.[74] At the 1927 meeting, the Ikhwan's demands included immediate conversion of the Shiites to Hanbali-Wahhabism and the dispatch of massive numbers of religious personnel to the eastern province. In order to calm the situation, the ulama, with the king's approval, issued a fatwa recommending that the population of this province be acculturated and agents of socialization be sent to all of its villages and hamlets.[75] But nothing came of it on the ground, especially after the Ikhwan rebellion was crushed between 1929 and 1930. The clerical corps contented itself with controlling the public sphere, monopolizing juridico-religious offices, and supervising the instruction of religious subjects in the modern schools that were created starting in 1937.

Nearly the same phenomenon was repeated in the towns of the Hijaz after it was conquered (1924–1926). The stakes were high in this province, as it contained the two holy cities of Islam. In this case, all Muslim countries—and not just the heterogeneous local population—were in need of reassurance. Abd al-Aziz therefore promised to preserve local traditions and institutions unchanged in order to ensure that the pilgrimage, an event of worldwide symbolism, took place without a hitch.[76] Once he was certain of being firmly in control of the province, the king gave his religious partners free reign: popular places of worship were destroyed, the mortmain goods (*al-awqaf*, sing. *waqf*) associated with them were confiscated, public consumption of tobacco and mixing of the sexes were prohibited, collective prayer became obligatory, and so on.[77] They also did away with the tradition established by the Mamluk sultans (1250–1517) in keeping with which each Sunni legal school possessed its own judge and its own imam to lead prayers—in particular at the Grand Mosque of Mecca.[78] Henceforth, only Hanbali-Wahhabi judges and imams would see to the religious life of the native inhabitants and pilgrims traveling from the four corners of the world. In order to enforce orthodoxy and orthopraxy in the public sphere, the Saudi authorities decided in 1926 to institutionalize the practice of promoting virtue and preventing vice (*al-amr bi al-ma'ruf wa al-nahy 'an al-munkar*).[79] This change was overseen by religious officials under the joint authority of the monarchy and the corporation (we will return to this subject). Moreover, the religious practices of the inhabitants of the Hijaz, though considered heterodox, were tolerated in private spaces.[80]

The Hanbali-Wahhabi establishment showed little interest in "converting" the native population, for two main reasons. The towns of these provinces were populated by structured communities with deep-rooted traditions and educated, influential elites. In the short term, acculturating them would be a difficult task. Similarly, the ulama were busy reaping the fruits of more than a century of labor: the monopoly of religious duties, particularly in the two holy places, and control of the public sphere. And even when, following a period of institutional "digestion," the establishment decided to take action in the early 1940s, it preferred to begin with more vulnerable, "easier-to-convert" regions. In Medina, for example, it set to work on Bedouin groups—in particular, the Harb and the Juhayna—whose religious structures were more than receptive.[81] Agents of socialization were also sent to the various towns of the Hijaz under the leadership of the *'alim* Muhammad al-Shawi (d. 1935).[82] Thanks to a process of implacable indoctrination, these groups were ultimately won over en masse to Hanbali-Wahhabism. The corporation's most resounding success, however, took place in the province of Asir.

Located in the southwestern corner of the Arabian Peninsula and subjugated by the Saudi Emirate at the start of the nineteenth century, Asir had been only superficially converted to Hanbali-Wahhabism. Most of the elites belonged to the Shafi'i school. Several forms of Shiism—in particular, Zaydism—and several Sufi brotherhoods also had followers there. Most of the population, however, was under no form of structured religious supervision.[83] After the conquest of this province in 1920, the corporation had to (re)build everything from scratch. To this end, Muhammad ibn Abd al-Latif, a leading *alim* and brother of the head of the establishment, was dispatched to the province.[84] He wrote a simplified credo, probably intended to be read to the population, in which he reiterated the main ideas of the tradition in regards to orthodoxy, orthopraxy, and political order (divine unity, the ban on popular cultural practices, the application of the Law, absolute obedience to the political authorities, etc.).[85]

The region's unstable political situation, however, did not permit Ibn Abd al-Latif and the religious agents who accompanied him to carry out their mission. Indeed, Saudi forces were only able to effectively control it in 1932, while its frontiers with Yemen were only stabilized in 1934 because of clashes with Yemen and local resistance. After this interlude, Ibn Abd al-Latif gradually resumed the work of acculturation with the support of the monarchy,[86] but it seems that between 1934 and 1939, he did not achieve the expected results. The head of the religious establishment, Muhammad ibn Ibrahim Al al-Shaykh (d. 1969), thus took matters in hand, choosing one his best disciples, Abd Allah al-Qar'awi (d. 1969),[87] to inculcate the True Religion into the "poor" inhabitants of the Asir.

Born around 1898 in Unayza, an oasis in the district of Al-Qasim, al-Qar'awi began his religious studies under the best-known ulama of the region, members of the Silim lineage. Like many of his contemporaries, he undertook a voyage in search of religious knowledge, resulting in two stays in India (1926–1927 and 1934–1938). Between these two peregrinations, al-Qar'awi frequented the country's main Hanbali-Wahhabi teaching circles. He became particularly interested in the teachings of Muhammad ibn Ibrahim. Upon returning to his native oasis, he distinguished himself by his exceptional devotion and zeal for enforcing orthodoxy and orthopraxy in the public sphere. His mentor ultimately appointed him to carry out the noblest mission that a religious agent could perform: saving souls from eternal damnation.

Accompanied by a dozen disciples, al-Qar'awi set up residence in the village of Samita. Thanks to the recommendations of the king and the head of the establishment, he soon had obtained moral and financial support from the local notables and authorities. A long labor of acculturation followed. After thirty-one years there, he succeeded in constructing a number of schools throughout the province and dozens of mosques offering religious courses centered on Hanbali-Wahhabi doctrine. Accompanied by a number of disciples, he visited tribes and villages twice a week (usually Thursday and Friday) to give instruction, answer questions, and settle disputes. To encourage young people to attend his schools, he established a system of scholarships funded by the royal family and local notables. Thanks to these schools, approximately seventy-five thousand young Asiris, including ten thousand girls, received an education. Indeed, al-Qar'awi's activity was not limited to the educational framework. He also helped people dig wells, cultivate their land, and conduct trade.

His exemplary behavior, deep devotion, and intense activity allowed the Hanbali-Wahhabi tradition to supplant local traditions and permanently establish itself in the kingdom's southwest, where it became the majority religion.

As has already been mentioned, this religious expansion would have been impossible without the Najdi corporation's stranglehold over the juridico-religious space. In order to render their vision of the world victorious, the ulama pursued two complementary actions: they set about driving other traditions out of the public sphere, education, and religious offices; and they monopolized the main religious and judicial duties and promoted public events exalting their beliefs. Only the True Religion enjoyed full rights. This was the case of the Hijaz, despite the king's promise to maintain the status quo. Just a few months after the conquest, Hanbali-Wahhabi officials began to impose their vision of orthodoxy and orthopraxy in the public sphere.

The career of Abd Allah ibn Hasan Al al-Shaykh (d. 1959) closely reflects these changes. Trained in Riyadh by the most prominent members of his family, he began his career as imam in a Riyadh mosque before traveling to the Al-Artawiyya *hijra* to indoctrinate and mobilize the factions of the Mutayr tribe who had settled there. He subsequently became judge of King Abd al-Aziz's armies and one of the king's closest companions. After the conquest of Mecca in 1924, he became its first Hanbali-Wahhabi judge and from there began to accumulate offices and supervise the public sphere. He thus became grand judge of the entire Hijaz, president of the administration responsible for managing the two holy places of Islam (logistics, instruction, organization of worship, etc.), president of the Committee for the Promotion of Virtue and the Prevention of Vice (responsible for enforcing orthodoxy and orthopraxy in the public sphere), and president of the administration responsible for censoring foreign books and distributing religious works. He was also responsible for appointing

Birth of a Kingdom, Renaissance of a Tradition 117

and supervising all of the province's religious personnel, a post he retained until his death.[88] As one of his biographers aptly puts it, Abd Allah ibn Hasan considered himself "the eyes and ears" of the political power and the religious authority in the Hijaz.

During the first half of the twentieth century, the careers of most members of the Najd corporation resembled this one. As religious actors, the ulama were mainly interested in the religious domain, which facilitated access to eternal salvation; they thus rarely intervened in the political domain. When they did so, it was with the aim of preserving the political order and the unity of the corporation. They clearly expressed this starting in the late 1920s: politics and the general interest of the population were the exclusive responsibility of the monarchy.[89]

This division of labor meant that each partner was to respect the domain reserved for the other. In order to preserve theirs from any intrusion, on several occasions the ulama reminded the political authorities that those authorities were to respect their prerogatives and doctrine. They thus sent several letters to the king asking him to immediately repeal positive laws in certain sectors, particularly commercial transactions.[90] The existence of a parallel juridical corpus challenged the validity and adequacy of sharia as well as its representatives' monopoly over the legislative and regulatory domains. The king partly acceded to their demands. In order to display his power, Abd al-Aziz wished to imitate other monarchies by establishing a "Throne Day." The ulama rebelled against this blameworthy innovation (*bid'a*), which they saw as a pre-Islamic polytheistic practice (*jahiliyya*). Muhammad ibn Ibrahim Al al-Shaykh addressed two fatawa to the king forbidding it and pointing out that the only lawful celebrations in Islam were those of the sacrifice (*'id al-adha*) and the end of Ramadan (*'id al-fitr*). As stipulated by sharia, events, places, and persons were not to be honored outside of these two celebrations.[91] The king had no choice but to submit to the inviolable verdict of his faithful allies.[92]

Abd al-Aziz did not always obey the ulama's fatawa, particularly in regards to political questions. Initially, the ulama opposed the introduction of several tools of modern communication, including the telegraph, telephone, and automobile. In keeping with the principle of *maslaha*, or general interest, the monarch nevertheless adopted them to further his political designs.[93] Several ulama were against including in the Kingdom's academic curriculum the subjects of drawing (they believed that it was forbidden to represent living beings), geography (they did not belief the Earth was spherical in form or rotated around the sun), and foreign languages (a tool for discovering the infidels' perverse ideas, in their view). All of these threatened children's faith. The king is said to have tried to convince them of the utility of these subjects in the context of the process of state construction, but faced with their categorical refusal, he decided to forge ahead without their consent.[94]

Moreover, they refused to allow the presence of foreigners—particularly Westerners—on Saudi territory, holding that it could have serious consequences for the country's faith and independence. As early as 1929, they vainly advised the king to expel them.[95] A 1944 U.S. report informs us that an *'alim* named Abu Bahz [*sic*] denounced the foreign presence in the al-Kharj district.[96] Summoned by the king, he continued to state that calling upon the help of infidels was contrary to the precepts of the Law and unworthy of the protector of the two holy places. To be clear in his mind on this score, Abd al-Aziz consulted the other ulama, who declared that the Prophet had called upon assistance from non-Muslims for the good of the community. Abu recklessly refused to change his position. Faced with such unusual insubordination, the king had to resort to threats to oblige him to climb down.[97] This ulama, whose name had been erroneously transcribed in the U.S. report, was none other than Abd al-Aziz ibn Baz (d. 1999), the leading Hanbali-Wahhabi figure of the second half of the twentieth century and signatory of the fatwa authorizing U.S. troops to establish themselves in Saudi Arabia during the Iraqi invasion of Kuwait in 1990.

Their rejection of particular political, cultural, and diplomatic innovations involved in the establishment of state structures in no way expressed an uncompromisingly dogmatic position. Rather, it reflected a period of adaptation and routinization. As a matter of rational calculation, the ulama realized that systematic opposition threatened to lead to the corporation's marginalization, something that could jeopardize orthodoxy and orthopraxy. Occasionally making concessions to their political partner allowed them to continue their mission. Moreover, they ultimately realized that many modern inventions and institutions could aid in their efforts to consolidate their positions and spread their influence. They thus deployed an ethic of responsibility to preserve the Hanbali-Wahhabi tradition, upon which their personal salvation and ideological authority depended. This attitude established itself as a genuine strategy, which I henceforth refer to as the adaptive strategy.

5

ROUTINIZATION AND INSTITUTIONALIZATION OF HANBALI-WAHHABISM

THE CRISIS OF SUCCESSION AND THE IDEOLOGICAL AUTHORITY OF THE ULAMA

The question of political succession is the Achilles' heel of the Saudi monarchy. Since its emergence in the eighteenth century, the royal house has done its best to resolve this problem, which is principally due to the horizontal manner in which power is transmitted and distributed, after the model of the local kinship system. Phases of generational transition systematically coincide with periods of crisis, in the course of which each branch attempts to monopolize power. As we have seen, the instability and subsequent collapse of the Saudi Emirate in 1891 were mainly due to this structural problem.[1]

The prevailing conception of the transmission of power underwent no significant change after King Abd al-Aziz restored Saudi sovereignty in 1902. In keeping with patrimonial practice, he eliminated all other branches of the royal house—particularly his brothers and first cousins—from competition.[2] According to an "accord" signed with the Ottoman authorities in 1914, the government of Najd was to be passed on only to members of his lineage.[3] By the Treaty of Darin, the British also recognized this as his right.[4] But while Abd al-Aziz ensured the continuity of house power by means of these accords, he did nothing to establish a system of transmission capable of saving the third Saudi state from fratricidal conflict at the moment of succession.

This problem obsessed the kingdom's notables, particularly those of the Hijaz, who, on 23 September 1932, "implored the king ... to establish a Fundamental Law and a law of succession."[5] These dignitaries also asked him to confer the name of Saudi Arabia upon the new kingdom. Less than a week later, the new name was adopted, which suggests that the request had been formulated with the tacit agreement of the palace, and the king ordered the Advisory Council of the Hijaz to begin drafting a Fundamental Law and a law of succession.[6]

The Royal Order nevertheless remained a dead letter, and no law of this type saw the light of day under Abd al-Aziz. It can be supposed that this was merely a political maneuver intended to reassure the Hijazis concerning their future within the new state. By means of this institutionalization, the elites of the Hijaz, whose social capital was clearly superior to that of their Najdi rivals, hoped to play an important role in the new state.[7] The name chosen to refer to this new kingdom reflected a patrimonial conception of politics according to which conquered territory is the property of the House of Saud. As I specified in the introduction, Abd al-Aziz and his descendants in fact administered the country after the fashion of a "house."

Although he named his son Saud as presumptive heir to the throne, the king established a system of multidomination proper to some patrimonial states. He made house members partners in power, particularly his sons.[8] Each of them was assigned a sector of the kingdom's political, economic, or military activity. In the middle term, this distribution gave rise to a multiplication of centers of power and the routinization of Abd al-Aziz's authority. The preservation of the adelphic system of succession, meanwhile, meant that all descendants of the founder of the third Saudi state were potential pretenders. At times of generational transition, this situation could lead only to political crisis.[9]

The first years of Saud's reign (1953–1964) were marked by a distribution of power among the various members of the house, but it was not long before the new king sought to revive the house tradition: excluding his brothers and cousins from power in order to replace them with his own sons and trusted companions.[10] This effort ended in political crisis.[11] The royal house split into several factions, with the two main factions forming around King Saud and Crown Prince Faysal. Between 1958 and 1964, each of the two factions tried to monopolize power and permanently exclude the other. While the Faysal faction seemed to have the upper hand, Saud and his followers were far from having given up. On several occasions, these tensions almost degenerated into fratricidal war.

This situation could only reawaken the memory of nineteenth-century conflicts over succession and their politico-religious consequences, a trauma of Hanbali-Wahhabi collective memory. For the ulama, fratricidal struggles inevitably led to *fitna* (great discord): "Sedition, war in the heart of Islam, centrifugal force bearing in its wake the break-up of the community, its implosion, and ruin. . . . It is a permanent threat to the continuity of Muslim society that worries the conscience of the ulama, the doctors of the Law, and incites them to caution and prudence."[12] In other words, the disintegration of the political order can only disrupt the application and spread of orthodoxy and orthopraxy and disturb the paths of salvation. The weakening or disappearance of the political partner would once again challenge the hegemony of the Hanbali-Wahhabi corporation. This fear was no doubt fed by the fall of the Egyptian (1952), Tunisian (1957), Iraqi (1958), and Yemenite (1962) monarchies, which were overthrown by military juntas or ambitious politicians claiming to adhere in ideal-typical manner to Pan-Arabism and secular socialism. *Fitna* thus had to be avoided at all costs.

Starting in 1958, the ulama turned to the Islamic practice of good advice (*al-nasiha*) to encourage reconciliation or at least good relations and a fair distribution of powers within the royal house. To this end, Muhammad ibn Ibrahim Al al-Shaykh, who assumed the title of grand mufti in 1957, met with the most influential princes on several occasions and sent them letters backed up by scriptural citations insisting on the harm caused by *fitna* in all aspects of life and the benefits of unity.[13]

Beginning in the early 1960s, however, the ulama began to slowly adopt a position in favor of the faction headed by Prince Faysal. Several factors preceded this choice. First, Prince Faysal was, on his mother's side, first cousin of the grand mufti, himself a descendant of Muhammad ibn Abd al-Wahhab. The Al al-Shaykh, who at the time constituted a majority of all members of the religious establishment, doubtless saw the rise to power of a close relation in a positive light. Second, Faysal was known for his ostentatious piety and scrupulous observance of the precepts of sharia, in contrast to Saud, whose zeal was not outstanding. Third, Faysal was perceived as more experienced and more clever and therefore better suited to oversee the affairs of the kingdom. Fourth, some of King Saud's allies for a time consisted of princes and technocrats who were enthusiastic followers of Pan-Arabist, socialist, and secular ideas. The presence of these "leftists"—the expression in use in the clerical circles of the time—could only upset the guardians of the faith.

Faysal's faction decided to act in order to confront the economic, political, and diplomatic challenges that had for several years been facing the country. In March 1962, profiting from the poor health of his older brother, Faysal succeeded in obtaining full powers and appointing his main allies to key posts. From that point on, Saud had only an honorific role. But far from resigning himself, Saud attempted to retrieve his prerogatives after several trips abroad for medical treatment between October 1962 and September 1963.

In order to avoid a destructive confrontation, on 1 January 1964 the ulama met on the request of the most influential members of the royal house to pronounce a juridico-religious opinion on the issue—in other words, to legitimate moves to exclude the king from affairs of state. In keeping with a clerical habitus that had been codified in Islamic lands since the High Middle Ages, the ulama simply confirmed the decisions of the faction that was most capable of ensuring and maintaining order once in power. They did not deviate from the rule in this instance. After several days of deliberation, they advised the king to accept the fait accompli as that was the only way, in their view, to preserve the three O's. In order to spare the king public humiliation and encourage reconciliation, the ulama abstained from issuing a written fatwa on this subject.[14] But, against the advice of Grand Mufti Muhammad ibn Ibrahim, who wanted to preserve social peace and the unity of the community, Saud continued maneuvering to recover his lost power.[15]

Prince Faysal and his allies had little choice but to make a show of force to persuade Saud to give up his pretensions. Units from the National Guard and army encircled the royal palace and skirmishes occurred. Saud faced facts and accepted the winner's diktat: he gave up all of his powers and most of his privileges, including those of a financial nature. In order to confer a legal character upon this palace revolution, however, Faysal and his allies requested that a fatwa be issued.

Meeting at the home of Muhammad ibn Ibrahim, on 29 March 1964 the kingdom's twelve most important Hanbali-Wahhabi ulama[16] issued a brief fatwa in which they insisted on two points:[17]

1. Saud was the country's sovereign and must be respected and revered by all.
2. As prime minister, Prince Faysal could freely manage the kingdom's internal and external affairs without consulting the king.

This text, which served to ratify the fait accompli, calls for several remarks. In order to justify their position, the ulama drew upon no scriptural evidence. They contented themselves with using a few key words capable of catalyzing the imaginary of the elites and the population. They called upon homiletic terms and expressions in reference to mythical or historical situations that would be well-known to their audience, such as *fitna* (great discord), *fawda* (anarchy), *al-maslaha al-'amma* (the general interest), and *al-darar 'ala al-bilad wa al-'ibad* (harm to the country and to believers). To put it plainly, no text in the Hanbali-Wahhabi tradition or indeed the entire Sunni corpus authorized the ulama to act in this way or make this decision. The ethic of responsibility no doubt encouraged them to privilege the general interest in the aim of preserving sharia, even though this was to the detriment of one of the corporation's political principles: absolute obedience to the head of the community and the formal prohibition of any rebellion against him.

The ulama's position reflected their vision of the monarchy: after the death of Abd al-Aziz, the system of multidomination—that is, the horizontal distribution of power among members of the ruling house—very rapidly established itself. The House of Saud was no longer a dynasty in the classic sense of the term—a monocephalic and monocratic power transmitted in lineal-agnatic manner—but rather a collegial-familial administration. As a result, while the king could, like a tribal chief, wield influence in several domains, he could not pretend to monopolize power. He was, in short, only primus inter pares. The Hanbali-Wahhabi corporation saw the monarchy as a sort of collective actor composed of several dozen individuals; its stability took precedence over the king's personal interest. This was no doubt why, in their fatwa, the ulama departed from standard usage, employing the term *wulat umurina* (the holders of power [in our country]) in its plural and not singular (*waliyy al-amr*) form, and in this way clearly expressed the collegiality of the Saudi monarchical system.

The faction led by Prince Faysal was not satisfied with its overwhelming symbolic and political victory. Many still feared an about face on the part of King Saud, who would have constituted a not insignificant nuisance were he to have mobilized his resources. Starting in late 1964, Faysal and his partisans considered deposing Saud. The most prominent princes set out on tours through the kingdom's provinces to mobilize, co-opt, and reassure notables. Once this fieldwork had been carried out, they moved on to the next step. On 28 October 1964, under the leadership of Prince Fahd, the members of Faysal's faction called for a meeting of the ulama to ratify in religious terms—the unique source of legitimacy—the decision they had already taken to depose King Saud and enthrone Faysal. An important contemporary religious figure who participated in the negotiations as the disciple and close collaborator of Grand Mufti Muhammad ibn Ibrahim gave me the following account of events:

> Kings Khalid and Fahd[18]—may God have mercy upon them—on several occasions contacted Shaykh Muhammad ibn Ibrahim—may God have mercy upon him—to persuade him to issue a fatwa deposing King Saud— may God have mercy upon him—for the situation had become untenable and the country was on the verge of *fitna*, may God save us from it. Action was necessary in order to preserve the unity of the community and of the Islamic state. The ulama had to support the decision of the royal house. Shaykh Muhammad therefore decided to gather together the ulama at his home in the Dakhna neighborhood. After a brief discussion of the country's situation, they concluded that it was necessary to confirm the royal house's choice. Accompanied by a large number of his colleagues and disciples, Shaykh Muhammad next went to the Sahara Hotel, where members of the ruling house— may God guide them in the straight and narrow path—had for several hours been meeting, in order to assure them of his support.

The main points of this account have been confirmed by other interviews carried out in Saudi Arabia as well as by contemporaneous European sources.[19]

While the ulama were, as we have seen, very familiar with the way in which the royal house operated, this brief passage shows that the princes were in their turn just as familiar with the mentality of their faithful allies. In order to mobilize the latter, Khalid and Fahd insisted on the issue that had haunted the clerical imaginary since the High Middle Ages: *fitna*—the source of chaos and destruction and the main obstacle to salvation. In order to preserve the three O's, the only way to save their souls and those of their followers, the ulama had no choice but to accept the proposals of the faction supporting Faysal. These metaphysical interests were tied to quite earthly interests of economic advantage, social status, and political influence. Far from being contradictory, worldly and otherworldly interests are organically related in Islam. As a maxim wrongly attributed (in order to confer performative value upon it) to the Prophet of Islam has it, "work for your life here below as if you were going to live eternally and work for your life in the beyond as if you were going to die tomorrow."[20]

Following this meeting with the princes at the Sahara Hotel, on 1 November 1964 the ulama issued a fatwa consisting of no more than a few lines.[21] Without surprise, it merely legitimated the resolutions of the victorious faction by deposing (*khal'*) King Saud and calling for allegiance to be sworn (*mubaya'a*) to Prince Faysal. Once again, the ulama drew upon no scriptural source. Instead, they contented themselves with briefly indicating that this fatwa was based on realist justifications (*mubarrirat waqi'iyya*) and juridico-religious foundations (*qawa'id shar'iyya*), something obviously not mentioned in the document itself. For all that, Faysal ibn Abd al-Aziz was enthroned the very next day. Several weeks later, King Saud went into exile.

The religious establishment thus played an extremely important role during the period of generational transition that followed the death of King Abd al-Aziz in 1953. The ideological authority of the ulama allowed the faction of Prince Faysal, henceforth King Faysal (1964–1975), to legitimate his political action in religious terms. In a region in which coups d'état and palace revolutions were commonplace, no other way existed for the princes to justify their deed without undermining the image—and even the legitimacy—of the royal house. Theological argument thus proved crucial in sanctifying political action. As the sacred and dominant idiom, it conferred a religious dimension, historical depth, and performative force—that is, legitimacy—upon Faysal's supporters, allowing them to take power without incurring collateral, material, or symbolic damage.

The intervention of the ulama in the political space reserved to the royal house must not be seen as interference or interventionism: they became involved only on the explicit invitation of the most influential members of the House of Saud and then as strictly religious actors. For the ulama, preserving the unity and power of the royal house was above all a religious duty.

THE STRUGGLE AGAINST PAN-ARABISM AND ITS BENEFICIAL EFFECTS

Since its emergence in the second half of the eighteenth century, the ideological confrontations of Hanbali-Wahhabism had been limited to other religious traditions. Essentially theological questions were at the heart of the conflict. But the situation radically changed with the rise of socialist-leaning Pan-Arabism in its various forms and denominations across the Arab world during the 1950s and 1960s. This ideology immediately presented itself as a modern alternative to local religious traditions. Its adherents, for their part, hoped to replace old elites and regimes, which they considered obsolete. Egyptian President Gamal Abdel Nasser (d. 1970) was without doubt the leading figure of this secularist movement (which, it should be noted, did not shy away from using religion as a symbolic resource in the event of need). That he pursued a hegemonic policy in the Middle East is well-known and requires no argument.

Thanks to the charisma and effective propaganda of the rayyis (the president), Egyptian influence in Saudi Arabia, as in other countries in the region, made itself felt with the appearance of several more or less well-organized, socialist-leaning Pan-Arab movements demanding constitutional reform and even the overthrow of the monarchy. Several members of the royal house, led by Prince Talal ibn Abd al-Aziz (b. 1932), were attracted to these ideas. They demanded constitutional monarchy and to that end founded the Movement of Free Princes in 1962. The 1950s witnessed the outbreak of several worker strikes in the oil-producing region of Al-Ahsa', the leaders of which were followers of the various forms of Pan-Arabism. At the same time, several planned coups d'état organized by officers seeking to imitate the Free Officers who had overthrown the Egyptian monarchy in 1952 were thwarted by the Saudi authorities.[22]

In order to counter Egyptian pretensions to hegemony, which depended on Pan-Arabism for legitimacy, the Saudi authorities decided to adopt a foreign policy based on Islamic solidarity (*al-tadamun al-islami*). As sacred media of communication, religious discourse and action seemed the most appropriate means for catalyzing the imaginary of Arab populations and thereby containing

Pan-Arab discourse. Similarly, the protectors of the holy places presented themselves as the heirs of various Pan-Islamic projects, whether Ottoman (the reign of Abd al-Hamid II, 1876–1909) or Muslim reformist (Jamal al-Din al-Afghani [d. 1897], Muhammad Abdu [d. 1905], Abd al-Rahman al-Kawakibi [d. 1902], and Muhammad Rashid Rida [d. 1935]).[23] They thereby hoped to profit from the symbolic capital of these great figures of contemporary Islam to legitimate their efforts.

In the 1950s and 1960s, the struggle for influence between Saudi Arabia and Egypt resulted in a veritable cold war.[24] As faithful allies of the House of Saud, representatives of ideological authority, and guardians of religious values, the ulama intellectually and institutionally participated in this struggle.

In the intellectual domain, the corporation set about attacking the ideological and historical foundations of Pan-Arabism by drawing upon religious language as well as rational, historical, and even political arguments. Several written and oral fatawa were issued by the ulama during this period. The most important remains that of Abd al-Aziz ibn Baz, judge of the al-Kharj district. In 1961, on the request of the grand mufti and with financial support from the government, he wrote a long epistle titled *Critique of Arab Nationalism in the Light of Islam and Reality*.[25] Printed by the thousands in Damascus and Cairo, it was distributed in Saudi Arabia and several Arab Muslim countries.[26]

For Ibn Baz, the Arabs were no more than a marginal people foundering in anarchy and ignorance. The Muslim religion had given them a global system of values capable of meticulously governing all aspects of their existence. Thanks to this, they were able to unite and grow strong, allowing them to conquer a large portion of the world and construct a brilliant civilization. In his view, the Arabs had no particular merit without Islam. Ibn Baz was thus astonished to see some of them distance themselves from the values of Islam, "which makes no distinction between Arab and non-Arab, white and black, rich and poor, Eastern and Western; for they are all brothers who love one another in God and help one another for the common good."[27] Was not the Pan-Arabist ideology, by contrast, whatever its political and social demands, a *jahiliyya* practice (*jahiliyya* refers to the pre-Islamic period, to which a pejorative connotation attaches in the Arab-Muslim imaginary), as it called for the fragmentation of the Muslim community along racial lines (Arabs as opposed to non-Arabs)?

The author also reminded his readers that all of the positive principles advocated by Pan-Arabism (such as unity, solidarity, and the realization of common interests) are also recommended by Islam but on foundations that are infinitely more noble and sacred. Indeed, the nationalists rely on relative and utilitarian human opinions whereas the values of Islam are of divine origin and therefore impartial and eternal. What's more, Pan-Arabism is an extremely dangerous ideology: its proponents do not defend Islam or encourage people to observe and apply its precepts, the only means for achieving salvation. Worse, they demand the separation of church and state, the repeal of sharia in favor of positive laws, the creation of a multiconfessional Arab identity, and the participation of non-Muslims in managing affairs of state. They also call upon non-Muslim powers to provide them with military support, something that is contrary to the principle of allegiance and rupture, or *al-wala' wa al-bara'*: "if there were a higher interest in allying with Arab or other infidels or calling upon their assistance, then God would have authorized and allowed his creatures to do so. But as he knows the considerable evils and disastrous consequences that it entails, God forbade it and condemned whoever did so."[28]

In sum, Ibn Baz believed that Pan-Arabism was a plot hatched by the West to split Muslims and destroy Islam in keeping with the principle of divide and conquer. Muslim youth and intellectuals thus had to beware of falling into this trap, while preachers and ulama were to use all means necessary to denounce this plot and support Islam.

Despite its simple style and modest proposals, Ibn Baz's fatwa marked a new phase in Hanbali-Wahhabi thought in more than one way. *The Critique of Arab Nationalism* was the first writing of this tradition to take a stand against a non-religious ideology of Western origin. The ulama had realized that their fight to preserve the three O's could no longer be reduced to the religious space but rather concerned the entire social realm. The new enemy that threatened to upset the dominant position of the tradition, its guardians, and its protectors was no longer so much other currents of Islam as secularizing ideologies. In order to better combat this enemy, a new strategy had to be adopted.

At the stylistic and formal levels, Ibn Baz alternated between two arguments in order to reach the general public targeted by Pan-Arabist and secularist writings. Throughout his fatwa, as one might expect, the judge from al-Kharj used arguments from authority, scriptural citations, and anecdotes featuring the first Muslims (*al-salaf al-salih*) to emotionally influence his readers. As a professional manager of religious meaning, he was quite aware that recourse to key themes and "psychic constraint by dispersion or refusal of the spiritual goods of salvation" gave historical depth and a symbolic dimension to his remarks.[29] He was conscious of the fact that the audience for his message, many of whom were familiar with the modern educational system, was receptive to "rational" and "historicist" arguments. In order to shore up his critique of Pan-Arabism, he thus drew upon historical facts (though often deformed to suit his polemical ends) and rational argument.

On this occasion, the term *mu'amara* (conspiracy) made its entrance into the Hanbali-Wahhabi glossary. Following the example of his Pan-Arabist enemies, from whom he very likely borrowed the term, Ibn Baz made conspiracy theory key to the explanation of all of the evils afflicting Muslims. But while the word *mu'amara* was new, the notion of conspiracy was for its part very old. Classic authors used several terms, particularly *kayd*, to designate this notion. In order to reach a broad public and grab the imagination, in other words, the fatwa's author preferred to use modern idiom rather than religious terminology as the former was part of contemporary vocabulary and thus intelligible to most people.

In theory, the fatwa was addressed to all Muslims—not just Hanbali-Wahhabis—to warn them of the dangers and ravages of Pan-Arabism. Ibn Baz even cited long passages from the diatribes of the Egyptian *'alim* Muhammad al-Ghazali (d. 1996) against secularist Pan-Arabism as well as the Indian *'alim* Abu al-Hasan al-Nadawi's (d. 1999) advice to Arab Muslims to unite around religion. Al-Ghazali was Ash'arite and a member of the Muslim Brotherhood, and al-Nadawi was a Maturidite and Sufi. This was not the first time that a Hanbali-Wahhabi *'alim* cited authorities from other Islamic currents. Texts and citations from Ash'ari, Mu'tazili, and Sufi ulama, such as al-Ghazali (d. 1111), al-Zamakhshari (d. 1148), Ibn Rushd (d. 1198), and al-Razi (d. 1209), were used by the guardians of the Najdi tradition to reinforce their legal or theological arguments.[30] But never before had non–Hanbali-Wahhabi authors been deliberately and consciously used to give the impression that the author spoke in the name of universal Islam and not solely that of the corporation. This reflects a genuine desire for Islamic ecumenism to confront an external threat. Far from being an isolated personal act, this initiative was part of a global strategy that had for several years been pursued by the political power and the religious authority.

As we have seen, in the late nineteenth century Hanbali-Wahhabi ulama began to slowly open themselves to other Muslim corporations and traditions. This process accelerated after the conquest of the two holy places of Islam, which made Saudi Arabia a de facto Islamic power. Reassuring Arab-Muslim elites and managing the flow of heterogeneous pilgrims required a certain religious flexibility and some political skill. In 1926, representatives of twenty-six Muslim countries from a variety of different traditions met in Mecca at an Islamic congress organized by King Abd al-Aziz to discuss the question of the Caliphate and the status of the holy cities of Islam.[31] The Hanbali-Wahhabis rubbed shoulders and signed several official documents with the representatives. Shakib Arslan (d. 1946), a Druze, was appointed to head the organization that resulted from this congress. Nevertheless, nothing concrete immediately came from this first instance of direct contact with the representatives of Islam. For the Muslim world, the historical context was very delicate; every party to the congress was absorbed with its own social, political, and religious problems.

The religious establishment nevertheless maintained its relationships with its traditional partners and established new contacts. Despite their refusal to dilute themselves in the reformist movement, the ulama continued to interact with its most prominent figures. Some of the latter even settled in Saudi Arabia and put themselves in the service of the state in various sectors. The Najd corporation consolidated its relations with the Ahl al-Hadith and established occasional exchanges with Jamaat-e-Islami and Tabligh, both of which originated on the Indian subcontinent. The ulama also drew closer to figures and groups that, like Ansar al-Sunna al-Muhammadiyya in Egypt, adopted the Hanbali-Wahhabi tradition.[32] Moreover, the annual pilgrimage to Mecca was no doubt a privileged moment for encounters and interactions with other currents of Islam. Unfortunately, no source allows us to consider this hypothesis in greater depth.

The year 1954 represented a turning point in relations with other Islamic traditions. Saud ibn Abd al-Aziz, who had been king of Saudi Arabia for only four months, tried to impose himself in the kingdom and on the international scene. He thus held an Islamic congress to which he invited several heads of state and Arab-Muslim figures. In August 1954, Grand Mufti Muhammad ibn Ibrahim Al al-Shaykh received in his home Muhammad al-Aziz J'ayt (d. 1970), the Ash'ari and Sufi mufti of Tunisia; Hasanin Muhammad Makhluf (d. 1990), an Ash'ari and Sufi former mufti of Egypt with ties to the Muslim Brotherhood; and Muhammad al-Shadhili (d. 1978), an eminent Maturidite and Sufi judge from Tunisia. The official Saudi newspaper reported the news in the following way: "The great ulama of Islam meet with his eminence the grand mufti of Saudi Arabia to discuss the steps to follow to reform Muslim nations in the aim of restoring their power and glory."[33] At the end of this meeting, the ulama called for the application of all aspects of sharia, educating young people in a healthy Islamic culture, and cooperation between Muslims in all domains. On this occasion, the head of the religious establishment not only explicitly recognized the Islamic nature of other Sunni Muslim religious traditions, but also called for strengthening ties between Muslim nations to meet external challenges. Several of Ibn Ibrahim's letters and fatawa addressed to religious figures and the populations of the Muslim world show all of the marks of respect and recognition due one's coreligionists.[34]

Beginning in the second half of the 1950s, this process of recognizing the Other was reinforced by the exacerbation of tensions between Saudi Arabia and

Egypt. In the framework of its policy of Islamic solidarity, the Saudi government decided, in complicity with the religious establishment, to create a Saudi-financed nongovernmental organization to counter Egyptian influence and promote Islam and its values throughout the world: the World Islamic League (Rabitat al-'Alam al-Islami), which was founded in 1962. The league's Constituent Assembly (al-Majlis al-Ta'sisi li-Rabitat al-'Alam al-Islami) clearly reflects the desire to institutionalize the new openness to other Sunni traditions. The profiles of its twenty-seven members represented most of the theological and mystical sensibilities of the Muslim world.[35] The Hanbali-Wahhabis, a minority group within the assembly, there rubbed shoulders with Asha'rites, Maturidites, and Sufis. The grand mufti of Saudi Arabia even delegated the presidency of the inaugural session of the first meeting of the World Islamic League to the Indian *'alim* Abu al-Hasan al-Nadawi, who was, as we have seen, a Maturidite and a Sufi.

The cold war between Nasser's Egypt and Saudi Arabia also allowed the corporation to forge ahead in the process of transforming a counterreligion into a religion. The ulama realized that the new enemy could permanently challenge the application of orthodoxy and orthopraxy by means of secularization, positive legal codes, control of religious institutions, a stranglehold over mortmain goods, the conversion of ulama into state employees and their marginalization, and so on. They also understood that the Egyptian example threatened to undermine the political order, possibly leading to the overthrow of the Saudi monarchy, the protector of the tradition and its representatives. The ulama thus agreed to make ideological efforts to preserve the core of their tradition. In doing so, they were acting in conformity with an Islamic legal principle (*al-qa'ida al-fiqhiyya*) which stipulates that, between two evils, the least must be chosen (*mura'at akhaff al-dararayn*): with the support and encouragement of the political power, they therefore opted to open up to other Sunni traditions.

But this openness did not mean that the ulama recognized the validity of other Muslim religious traditions in the theological and ritual domains: they believed in the absolute validity of their principles, particularly in the theological domain. They simply toned down their positions by holding that certain beliefs and practices differing from their own were merely blameworthy innovations:[36] as was the case following the conquest of Mecca in the early nineteenth century, the struggle with other traditions was located within the *umma* and not between believers and infidels. A marked change is nevertheless to be noted. As religious actors, the ulama no doubt hoped to win the adherents of other traditions over to the doctrines of the pious ancestors (*'aqidat al-salaf al-salih*)—that is, to the Hanbali credo.

While the struggle against the Ottoman Empire throughout the nineteenth century and the deterioration of the Saudi political entity led the clerical corps to adopt an exclusivist ideology—*amixia*—and withdraw into itself, the cold war with Egypt had the opposite effect. From its beginning as a local phenomenon, Hanbali-Wahhabism gradually transformed into a global one. Since the end of the nineteenth century, their interaction with the reformist movement and Indo-Pakistani corporations had allowed the ulama of Najd to appropriate a certain number of ideas—in particular, that of religious cooperation between Muslims and spreading the faith via preaching (*al-da'wa*). Together with Islamic political solidarity, the material and symbolic resources available to Saudi Arabia—the two holy cities of Islam and growing petroleum revenue—allowed the ulama to succeed where the reformists had failed: the creation of an Islamic university intended to train Muslim religious personnel from the four corners of the world and the establishment of an international Islamic body intended to produce works and fatawa for the entire *umma*.

Starting in 1899, the reformist ulama Muhammad Rashid Rida published a large number of articles in which he called upon the Ottoman authorities to adopt a new religious strategy in the framework of the caliphal and Pan-Islamic policy of Sultan Abd al-Hamid II. Among other things, he recommended that an institution for training future ulama in a uniform manner be created as well as another responsible for promulgating fatawa and discussing the religious affairs of the community.[37] But the historical conjuncture was profoundly unfavorable to carrying out these projects, with nearly all Muslim countries under European tutelage. Rida's ideas nevertheless remained vivid in the minds of his readers and disciples—particularly those belonging to the Muslim Brotherhood—who never abandoned the idea of making them a reality.

In 1957, Amjad al-Zahhawi (d. 1967), an *'alim* and founding member of the Iraqi branch of the Muslim Brotherhood, suggested that King Saud finance the creation of an ecumenical institute. To be based in Jerusalem or Medina, the institute would be devoted to studying the religious affairs of the Muslim community. The Saudi sovereign immediately sought the opinion of Grand Mufti Muhammad ibn Ibrahim, who was in favor of the project but on three conditions: (1) that the institute be under the control of the corporation (he feared that it would otherwise become a scene of politico-religious conflicts between Islamic actors); (2) that it address matters only on which there was consensus; and (3) that its headquarters be in Mecca.[38] In 1962, al-Zahhawi's idea, which had been adopted by the Saudi monarchy, seized upon by the religious establishment, and encouraged by the Arab cold war, gave birth to the World Islamic League.

While the main objective of this organization was to support the policy of Islamic solidarity pursued by the Saudi monarchy, it also sought to spread the Hanbali-Wahhabi tradition throughout the world. The first such efforts, which were directed at African and Asian populations, got off to a timid start in the 1960s.[39] Concomitant with the political collapse of Pan-Arabism after Egypt, Jordan, and Syria were defeated in the Six-Day War in 1967 and substantial growth in petroleum revenue, the success of the policy of Islamic solidarity allowed the organization to concentrate on the religious domain: sending preachers, constructing mosques and social centers, distributing books, creating schools and other educational institutions, supplying financial and food support, and so on. To this end, no fewer than eleven specialized organizations dependent on the World Islamic League were created between 1978 and 2000.

Just one year before the league's creation, the Islamic University of Medina (Al-Jami'a Al-Islamiyya) was inaugurated.[40] In a letter to the leaders of the Muslim pilgrim delegations present that year in Mecca, King Saud remarked:

> it is an obligation for me to serve the two holy places [of Islam] and to work for the spread of Islam to the four corners of the world. I therefore ordered the creation of an Islamic university in Medina, the town of the Prophet, and it has been given all of the resources necessary to carry out its noble mission. I also called upon a large number of ulama from certain Muslim countries to establish scrupulous programs and regulations. This university will welcome students from throughout the world . . . particularly the Africans and Asians who hope to draw upon the precepts of Islam at its Source. The university will also welcome students from other parts of the world. At the end of their degree course, they will return to their countries to preach the True Religion [*al-din al-qawim*]. Several years of hard work will be necessary before we can gather the fruit of our efforts.[41]

The Saudi sovereign thus affirmed that the time of *amixia* had come to an end. It was time to export the True Religion to the rest of the Muslim world. One of the leading ideas of reformism was appropriated for this purpose: the creation of an international Islamic university that would over time participate in the standardization and homogenization of Sunni clerical elites. Because of the chronic shortage of Saudi religious personnel and to ensure the Pan-Islamic character of the institution, Muslim staff from Egypt, Syria, Iraq, Sudan, Algeria, Morocco, Mauritania, Pakistan, and India were called upon to provide legal (*fiqh*) and secular instruction. However, the job of teaching the credo—that is, the Hanbali *'aqida*, understood as the beliefs of the first generation of Muslims (*al-salaf al-salih*)—remained the preserve of Hanbali-Wahhabi ulama and religious personnel. Similarly, the principal positions of responsibility were given to high-ranking members of the corporation. The president and vice president of the university were, respectively, Muhammad ibn Ibrahim Al al-Shaykh, grand mufti of the kingdom, and Abd al-Aziz ibn Baz. The Islamic University of Medina thus became a tool for spreading Hanbali-Wahhabism in the world.[42] This expansion was encouraged by Abdel Nasser's reform of Al-Azhar in 1961, an effort to once and for all win control over this institution by making its members state employees and splitting it into several organizations.[43] Al-Azhar thus lost much of its influence and staff, who settled in several Arab-Muslim countries, particularly Saudi Arabia. Throughout the 1960s, the kingdom welcomed hundreds of Egyptian religious officials, who were employed by the Najdi corporation (which suffered from a severe shortage of competent personnel) to construct all of the country's religious institutions.[44]

The struggle against Egypt thus had beneficial effects for the Hanbali-Wahhabi tradition. The dynamics analyzed above allow us to throw new light on the process by which the tradition was routinized—a phenomenon most perceptible in its discourse and organization. In order to preserve the strength of the corporation and its defenders, the ulama once again turned to their ethic of responsibility. They brought their discourse up to date in order to confront the secularizing Pan-Arabist threat and appropriated reformist ideas in order to turn these ideas into a veritable repertoire of contention. The creation of international organizations, such as the World Islamic League and the Islamic University of Medina, were only a part of the process of institutional construction that began during the second half of the 1950s.

ESTABLISHING MODERN ORGANIZATIONS

Since its beginnings, the followers of Hanbali-Wahhabism were organized in an informal manner around one of the descendants of Muhammad ibn Abd al-Wahhab, who was referred to as the *marji'* (referent).[45] The *marji'* managed a large part of the religious and legal affairs of the Saudi Emirate: appointing judges, imams, *mutawi'a* (agents of socialization), teachers, administrators of mortmain goods, and so on; issuing fatawa on the various aspects of life; carrying out daily instruction in the capital's Grand Mosque in order to perpetuate the corporation; defending doctrine by writing responses and refuting adversaries; and legitimating the political undertakings of the House of Saud.

To assist him in performing his job, the *marji'* was surrounded by several colleagues and disciples. The teachings of Ibn Abd al-Wahhab, his descendants, and followers were scrupulously followed. As in the political domain, management of the religious domain was exclusively based on personal relations and ad hoc arrangements. The creation of the Kingdom of Saudi Arabia in 1932 changed little in this respect. About twenty years would pass before this informal structure began to give way to legal-rational organization.

This was in response to a particular sociopolitical context. As in other sectors of activity, the kingdom critically lacked religious personnel capable of managing a rapidly expanding market in salvation goods. In addition to Najd, the three O's now had to be imposed in the other provinces, particularly in the two holy places of Islam. In response to this situation, the Saudi authorities resorted to importing religious "labor," a process accelerated by the struggle with Pan-Arabism. In order to defend its religious values, social privileges, and political system, in other words, the corporation found itself obliged to construct institutions capable of confronting the Egyptian colossus.

Unique in the modern and contemporary history of the Arab-Muslim world,[46] this effort at institutionalization was the work of Muhammad ibn Ibrahim Al al-Shaykh (d. 1969), with support from the political power.[47] A descendant of Ibn Abd al-Wahhab and son of the Saudi capital's judge,[48] Ibn Ibrahim was born in Riyadh in 1893 and received a meticulous education. He frequented the most reputed coteries of his native city and the best-stocked libraries of Najd. At the age of eleven, he already knew the Qur'an by heart and began studying the Hanbali-Wahhabi corpus (the works of his grandfathers, those of Ibn Taymiyya and Ibn al-Qayyim, etc.) under the direction of his father and uncle, Abd Allah, head of the religious establishment. Under the supervision of Sa'd ibn Atiq—who had spent a long period among the Ahl al-Hadith in India—he then studied the prophetic traditions (*al-hadith*). Though he lost his vision at the age of sixteen, he nevertheless continued his education, which seems to have come to an end sometime around 1925.

Ibn Ibrahim made his entry onto the Saudi religious scene in 1926 when King Abd al-Aziz sent him to the Al-Ghatghat *hijra* to calm the zeal of the Ikhwan. He particularly distinguished himself in the course of the Ikhwan crisis (1928–1930), defending the Saudi order and the socioreligious prerogatives of representatives of Hanbali-Wahhabism.[49] Thanks to his genealogy, his theological-juridical knowledge, and his fidelity to the royal house, he was able to accumulate significant symbolic capital. This allowed him to become head of the corporation in the 1930s.[50]

Like his predecessors, the new *marji'* of Hanbali-Wahhabism supervised a large portion of the kingdom's juridico-religious space. Yet he continued to operate in a traditional manner. For example, instruction was always dispensed in the ulama's mosques and homes, and judges, who had no offices of their own, continued to resolve disputes in their homes and visit the markets several times a week.⁵¹ While this mode of operation functioned well enough for several decades, it seems that it reached its limits following the creation of the kingdom of Saudi Arabia in 1932.

Starting in 1926, King Abd al-Aziz, eager to control his territory and create an elite capable of effectively managing the kingdom, established a modern educational system and adopted a portion of the Ottoman judicial system, with positive laws inspired by the French example, particularly in the commercial domain.⁵² As we have seen, he even tried to dilute Hanbali-Wahhabi identity in reformism by recruiting foreign religious personnel and creating Dar al-Tawhid. Like other Arab-Muslim countries, Saudi Arabia slowly moved toward a degree of secularization, in Peter Berger's sense of the term—that is, "the process by which sectors of society and culture are removed from the domination of religious institutions and symbols."⁵³ These structural changes slowly marginalized religion and its representatives in the social space, which entailed a loss of socioreligious privileges.

Like their colleagues elsewhere in the Muslim world, the ulama initially resisted these developments. They refused all modern advances, which they described as blameworthy innovations (*bida'*).⁵⁴ This refusal was more a reflection of a crisis of transition than of a settled dogmatic position, and it was not long before the clerical corps realized that its services and structures had to be adapted if it was to maintain its central role in the Saudi social system.

As early as the second half of the 1940s, the erosion of the corporation's structures seems to have worried Ibn Ibrahim. One of his close disciples reported that

> Shaykh Muhammad—may God have mercy upon him—liked to meet all ulama and Islamic figures visiting the kingdom [of Saudi Arabia] in the framework of the pilgrimage or official business in order to inquire as to the state of Muslims in the world. He asked his guests a very large number of questions about religious institutions in their respective countries. In particular, he was interested in the Al-Azhar organization. . . . He also called upon graduates of the latter institution and, in particular, Shaykh Abd al-Razzaq Afifi—may God have mercy upon him—to profit from their knowledge and experience.⁵⁵

The grand mufti thus sought to acquire as much information as possible regarding the organizational frameworks of the religious space in other Muslim countries in order to find a model to follow. As might be expected, he turned to Al-Azhar, the region's oldest and most prestigious religious institution. In addition to the fact that several of Ibn Ibrahim's grandparents, masters, and colleagues had carried out part of their initiatory voyage there, Al-Azhar, thanks to the reforms of Muhammad Abdu (d. 1905) and Muhammad al-Maraghi (d. 1945), appeared to be a modern institution with a network of schools, a university, a body specialized in issuing fatawa, an administration responsible for managing mortmain goods, and so on. To import this model, Ibn Ibrahim invited Egyptian religious personnel—including Hanbali-Wahhabis such as Abd al-Razzaq Afifi (d. 1994), whose career I will examine more below—to settle in Saudi Arabia. He also sent a number of his young disciples to Al-Azhar to finish their studies and "observe all positive aspects of its pedagogical and administrative organization."[56]

The ethic of responsibility led him to open up to the Egyptian model in order to reinforce the positions of his own corporation. With financial support from the political power, he endeavored to endow the Hanbali-Wahhabi tradition with modern organizational structures in four complementary sectors: teaching, the promulgation of legal opinions and the management of religious affairs, justice, and the media.

In order to give his undertaking a formal, institutional character, Ibn Ibrahim first took the title of grand mufti (*al-mufti al-akbar*) of Saudi Arabia.[57] This title added charisma of office—necessary to establish a legal-rational hierarchy within the corporation—to his personal and familial charisma. It also allowed him, from a symbolic point of view, to locate himself in the *longue durée* of Islam and establish himself as a central figure in the national and regional religious space. The process of routinization was also reflected in the decision to abandon the traditional title of *marji'*, which evokes the Shiite clergy in the Arab-Muslim imaginary, and adopt in its place mufti, the dominant idiom in the Sunni world.

Creating educational institutions capable of training future clerics initially seemed to be Ibn Ibrahim's main concern. Without trained personnel, the corporation could not impose orthodoxy and orthopraxy on a heterogeneous Saudi space undergoing transformation. It also risked losing entire sectors of activity to new actors—the graduates of modern educational institutions, particularly in the judicial domain. A large number of personnel thus had to be trained in order to guarantee the application of orthodoxy and orthopraxy in the various spheres of society and preserve the privileges of the corporation. Inspired by the Egyptian model, the grand mufti founded the first religious studies institute (*al-ma'had al-'ilmi*) in 1950. A five-year course of study allowed adolescents who had attended a state-run primary school to acquire basic knowledge in various domains of religious studies.[58] The success of this first experiment encouraged the mufti to generalize it to all provinces of the kingdom. In only fourteen

Table 2. Religious Studies Institutes (1950–1964)

Place of Creation	Date of Creation
Riyadh	1950
Burayda	1953
Unayza	1953
Riyadh	1954
Al-Ahsa'	1954
Shaqra'	1954
Samita	1954
Al-Majma'a	1954
Huraymila'	1958
Abha	1961
Ha'il	1961
Najran	1963
Medina	1963
Baljurashi	1963
Hawtat Bani Tamim	1963
Al-Zulfi	1963
Mecca	1963
Al-Aflaj	1964
Tabuk	1964
Jeddah	1964
Al-Dilam	1964
Dammam	1964

years, twenty-two of these institutes were created, with the number of enrolled students growing from 75 to 3,570 over the same period (Table 2).[59]

To round off their training, in 1953 the mufti created the faculties of religious studies (*kulliyyat al-shari'a*) and Arabic (*kulliyyat al-lugha al-'arabiyya*) in Riyadh, which issued a diploma after four years of study. Substantial grants were established to attract students. These efforts also met with success: in fourteen years, the number of students enrolled in religious studies grew from 22 to 810 and those in the Arabic faculty from 22 to 471.[60] In 1965, Ibn Ibrahim created the Higher Institute of the Magistracy (*al-Ma'had al-'Ali li al-Qada'*) to supplement this system. This institute was intended to receive the best students of the religious studies and Arabic faculties for a period of three years, grooming them to become the kingdom's future judges.[61] The institute counted sixty-three students just four years after its creation.[62] The fusion of these three institutions in

1974 gave birth to Riyadh's Al-Imam University (Jami'at Al-Imam Muhammad ibn Su'ud al-Islamiyya), which as we will see was to become the human nursery and breeding ground of contemporary Hanbali-Wahhabism.

Centralization was the watchword in what concerned the promulgation of legal opinions and the supervision of religious affairs. In 1955, Ibn Ibrahim established a body responsible for issuing fatawa and managing religious affairs (Dar al-Ifta' wa al-Ishraf 'ala al-Shu'un al-Diniyya).[63] Supported by the entire clerical corps, the grand mufti's aim was doubtless to dominate the Saudi religious space by means of the state employment of religious agents: henceforth, all imams, preachers, stewards of mortmain goods, and so on, were to be officially appointed by him, and all religious questions, whether private or public, and books published regarding them were to be sent to Riyadh for examination by Ibn Ibrahim or his collaborators (see Figure 1).[64] The mission of Dar al-Ifta' was also to spread the Hanbali-Wahhabi tradition throughout the kingdom's various provinces, particularly among the Bedouin populations of the North.

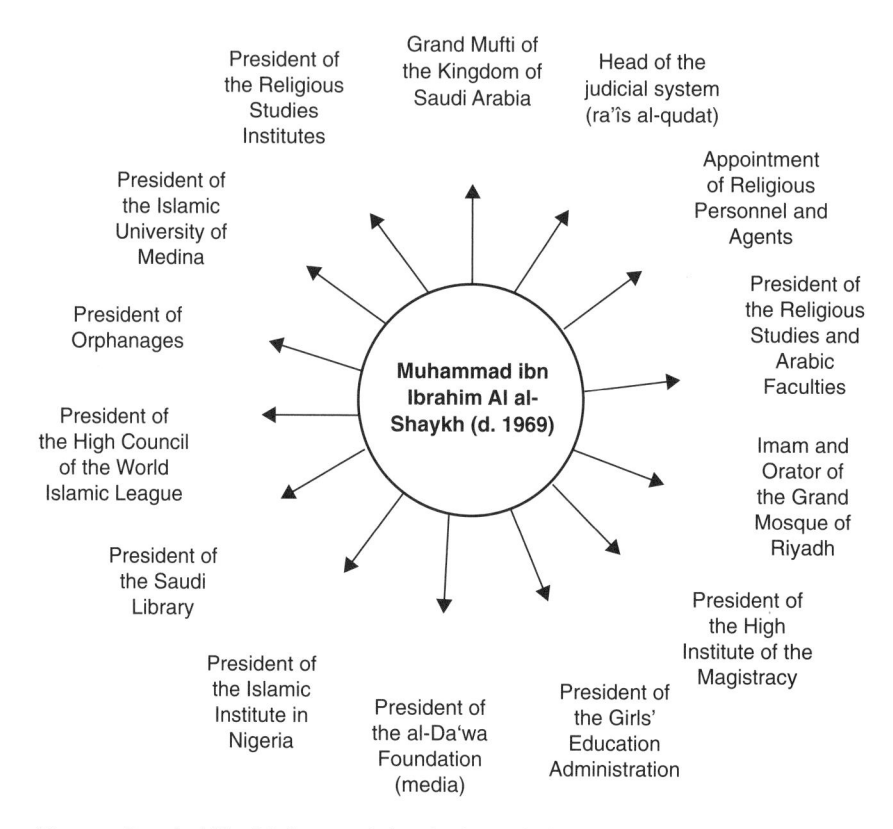

Figure 1. Posts held by Muhammad ibn Ibrahim Al al-Shaykh (d. 1969).

In the 1950s and 1960s, several delegations of ulama and agents of socialization were assigned the task of bringing them the "good news."[65]

Ibn Ibrahim pursued the same centralizing project in the judicial domain. Two systems had coexisted since the kingdom's (re)unification. While the traditional and informal organization continued to reign over Najd and Al-Ahsa', the Ottoman organization was maintained with several modifications (the Hanafi corpus was replaced with the Hanbali one) in the provinces of the Hijaz, Asir, and Jazan. The unification of the Saudi judicial system only took place in 1959. Two factors may explain this delay. On the one hand, King Abd al-Aziz insisted that the institutions of the Hijaz and its dependencies continue to function as before and autonomously, no doubt in the hope of extending this relatively modern system to the rest of the kingdom. On the other hand, justice in the Hijaz was administered by Abd Allah ibn Hasan Al al-Shaykh. As a descendant of Muhammad ibn Abd al-Wahhab, a high-ranking member of the religious establishment, and a former professor of Ibn Ibrahim, Ibn Hasan was a respectable figure who had the ear of members of the royal house, the support of the Hijaz elites, and the ulama's respect.[66] The grand mufti thus had to await a more favorable conjuncture.

In 1959, the death of Ibn Hasan and the crisis of generational transition that followed the death of King Abd al-Aziz gave Ibn Ibrahim the opportunity he was waiting for to carry out his project. Far from putting an end to the Hijaz's judicial system, however, he extended it to the entire kingdom. To all appearances, he was thus aware of the fact that, were the Hanbali-Wahhabi religious ideal and its monopolistic aspirations to be realized, a smoothly operating and efficient organizational framework—whatever its origin—was needed to oversee the application of sharia. Under his authority and the benevolent eye of the monarchy, the number of courts increased in all provinces of the kingdom throughout the 1960s.[67]

The media domain did not escape the vigilance of Ibn Ibrahim and his followers. During the 1950s and 1960s, a growing number of local and Arab newspapers representing various political and religious sensibilities became available in the kingdom. Hanbali-Wahhabi discourse no longer had a monopoly. Approached by a number of leading ulama, the grand mufti tried to ban certain newspapers[68] and called upon the population to boycott them.[69] But given the impossibility of such an undertaking, he had to face facts: ideas had to be fought with ideas. He thus gave his brother, Abd al-Latif (d. 1967),[70] and his leading disciple—now a prominent figure of the religious establishment—Salih al-Luhaydan (b. 1931), the task of creating a magazine to present and defend Hanbali-Wahhabi ideas. The first installment of *Rayat al-Islam* (*The Standard of Islam*) came out in June 1960. Yet "after two years, the review ceased to appear due to financial difficulties, its directors' inexperience, and understaffing."[71]

Far from resigning himself, Ibn Ibrahim decided to change strategy. In June 1964, he requested that Prince Faysal, as a personal favor and as prime minister, give him financial and logistical assistance for the creation of an Islamic (that is, Hanbali-Wahhabi) periodical and begged members of the royal house to follow suit. Finally, he sent a form letter to several members of the religious establishment and affiliated intellectuals to request that they submit articles on various questions from an Islamic point of view.[72] In fewer than six years, the grand mufti was able to launch a new weekly: *Al-Da'wa* (*The Mission*).[73] It soon became the leading large-circulation Hanbali-Wahhabi review, which it remains to this day.[74] The number of officially and unofficially supported reviews subsequently increased.

Ibn Ibrahim did not content himself with official activities, encouraging individual projects that sought to defend the corporation's principles and promote them among the population. In 1961, several members of the first cohort of graduates of the Riyadh Faculty of Sharia thus had the idea of founding a publishing house dedicated to printing the classics of Hanbali-Wahhabism and refutations of "deviant" doctrines and importing and translating Islamic newspapers, reviews, and books. In short, the recent graduates hoped to spread the Islamic heritage and Islamic values throughout the world. To this end, they called upon the support of the grand mufti. Taken with the idea, he asked Abd al-Aziz ibn Baz, one of the foremost members of the establishment, to be their patron.[75] In order to strengthen their effort and give it credibility in Saudi social space, which was dependent upon patrimonial relations, Ibn Baz sought moral and financial support from King Saud. He even asked him to encourage one of his sons to become a shareholder in this publishing venture. The king accepted Ibn Baz's request and bestowed four hundred thousand riyals upon this religious enterprise, a huge sum at the time.[76] The publishing house was subsequently absorbed by Dar al-Ifta'.[77]

Moreover, Muhammad Yusuf Siti, a wealthy Sikh Indian merchant and convert to Islam, undertook to found a school for Qur'anic study and memorization in his country. To this end, he traveled to Mecca to recruit a number of ulama and Qur'anic experts (*huffaz* or *muqri'un*) capable of accomplishing this religious task. The result, however, was disappointing: the religious capital of Islam possessed no official institution specializing in Qur'anic instruction and lacked the personnel capable of carrying out this religious duty. The convert's zeal led him to alter his plans: a structure of this type had first to be bestowed upon the holy city of Islam before there could be any thought of exporting it. After just a few months of negotiation with the Saudi religious and political authorities—particularly the grand judge of the Hijaz, Abd Allah ibn Hasan Al al-Shaykh—Muhammad Yusuf Siti succeeded in realizing his project. The first school specializing in Qur'anic instruction and memorization—Jam'iyyat tahfiz al-qur'an (Association for the Memorization of the Qur'an)—opened its doors in 1962. Two years later, Muhammad Yusuf Siti founded a second school, this time in Medina.

The success of these two establishments encouraged him to forge ahead. In 1966, he met with Ibn Ibrahim to suggest that the experiment be extended to the entire kingdom. Aware of the social and religious repercussions that such an undertaking might have, Ibn Ibrahim did not hesitate to adopt it. He sought political and financial backing from the monarchy to open Qur'anic study and memorization schools in the provinces of Najd, Al-Ahsa', and the Northern Frontier. As one of his former collaborators and disciples remarked: "By means of these establishments, our shaykh—God have mercy on him—sought to imprint Islamic values in the souls of young children in the aim of constructing a healthy Muslim society that fully applied the precepts of sharia. He also sought to combat destructive ideas that had appeared in the kingdom and were not in keeping with our religion."[78]

This type of establishment thus "democratized" access to the sacred text and encouraged better application of its precepts in all areas of life. It also allowed religious discourse to continue to influence the cultural and religious representations of the population. All processes of instruction and memorization require explanation and an attempt to put things into context; for the agents of the Hanbali-Wahhabi corporation, it was an occasion to promote their vision of the world. Finally, teaching the Qur'an and the religious-pedagogical system that accompanied it "immunized" Saudi society against the foreign ideologies that in the eyes of the clerical corps threatened to disrupt the three O's.

Just a few weeks after Muhammad Yusuf Siti's visit, Ibn Ibrahim received the funds necessary for these establishments from the authorities. The body charged with overseeing them was baptized the Charitable Association for the Memorization of the Holy Qur'an in the regions of Najd, Al-Ahsa', and the Northern Frontier (Jama'at Tahfiz al-Qur'an al-Karim al-Khayriyya fi al-Mintaqa al-Wusta wa al-Sharqiyya wa al-Hudud al-Shamaliyya).[79] The grand mufti gave the job of realizing this project to one of his disciples, Abd al-Rahman al-Faryan (d. 2004). Thanks to the generosity of the royal house and Saudi notables, forty-seven establishments were set up between 1966 and 1969, the year of Ibn Ibrahim's death.

Ibn Ibrahim's charismatic personality and entrepreneurial character had brought about profound changes in the structures of the clerical corps. In order to meet external challenges and respond to the growing demands of the market for salvation goods, Muhammad ibn Ibrahim—arguably the most important figure of Hanbali-Wahhabism after Muhammad ibn Abd al-Wahhab—did not hesitate to draw upon foreign models and adopt private initiatives to optimize the performance of his corporation. Together with the petroleum industry, the religious space was thus among the first sectors of society to move from informal to formal organization. The guardians of Hanbali-Wahhabism did not hesitate to adapt their structures in response to ecological change. In doing so, their aim was always to preserve the religious and social interests of their tradition in keeping with the requirements of an ethic of responsibility. But adaptation in no way meant abdication. When the fundamental interests of the corporation and tradition were threatened, the ulama did not hesitate to ferociously defend it, even against their political partner.

DEFENDING THE CORPORATION'S RELIGIOUS AND SOCIAL INTERESTS

The process of institutionalization went hand in hand with the establishment of modern state structures. Managing an extended territory, supervising a heterogeneous population, and administering petroleum revenue in the context of the struggle against Pan-Arabism required the existence of an operational bureaucratic system. Although a number of administrations were created under King Abd al-Aziz, it remains the case that he "did not govern by way of a bureaucratic apparatus but rather through personal networks consisting of trustworthy lieutenants, local intermediaries, and clients."[80] It was only under his sons and successors—Saud and, above all, Faysal—that administrative structures, those symbols of state domination, were gradually constructed.

The religious establishment broadly profited from this process, which allowed it, thanks to the political and financial support of the Saudi monarchy, to extend its domination across most of the Arab Peninsula and even beyond. Yet it very much frowned upon certain state practices that ran counter to its social and religious interests. Indeed, the construction of an administration required the adoption of a number of rules, statutes, and codes inspired by Western positive laws. The ulama were convinced that adopting and applying these laws ran counter to religious precepts and constituted a grave sin and even an act of impiety. In their opinion, this "innovation" would facilitate the emergence of a parallel legal system and judicial authority beyond their control. An end to their monopoly in the legal and judicial domains would not only diminish their influence over time, but also imperil orthodoxy, orthopraxy, and even the political order. This worrisome situation led the representatives of the Hanbali-Wahhabi tradition to rally around the grand mufti, who tenaciously fought to defend the religious interests and social privileges of the corporation until his death in 1969.

Starting in 1956, Ibn Ibrahim contested the legality of the courts and chambers of commerce responsible for investigating and resolving disputes in the financial and commercial domains.[81] He claimed that only Islamic courts were competent to do so, as eternal Islamic law is superior to and transcends human law. Recourse to these human institutions amounted to a "path toward impiety, injustice, and immorality," the equivalent of "blasphemy, meriting excommunication from the religion."[82]

In 1960, Ibn Ibrahim continued his fight against positive law by distributing an epistle titled *On the Application of Positive Laws* (*Risala fi Tahkim al-Qawanin*). This work mustered a large number of scriptural citations, theological arguments, and key words, condemning human laws:[83] those who applied them to the detriment of sharia were obeying the *taghut* (idol) and perpetuating the practices of the *jahiliyya* (the pre-Islamic period). To illustrate his remarks, he called upon the classic example of the thirteenth-century Mongols, who, though claiming to be Muslims, continued to apply their own laws, leading to their excommunication by Ibn Taymiyya and his colleagues—for "holding [human] laws to be superior to divine revelation is disbelief." As a consequence, Ibn Ibrahim excommunicated all Muslim rulers who resorted to it with the exception of "a ruler who, encouraged by his desires and whims, adopts positive laws concerning a particular case while recognizing that divine law is truth and that he acted poorly and departed from the straight and narrow path. While he is not to be excommunicated, [this ruler] has nevertheless committed a sin more serious than the capital sins [*al-kaba'ir*]—to wit, adultery, the consumption of alcohol, theft, false testimony, and so on."[84] There is no doubt that this latter passage referred to the Saudi government, whose action the grand mufti sought to justify while maintaining some pressure.[85]

In the hope of realizing his goal, Ibn Ibrahim "inundated" the king, the leading princes, and high-ranking personnel with courteous and paternal letters reminding them that Islamic courts were capable of investigating all sorts of civil, criminal, administrative, and commercial cases. The new "civil" judicial institutions and the codes governing them were therefore useless.[86] Whenever possible, he also refused to ratify the decisions of these bodies on the grounds that their judgments were not based on Islamic law.[87] Ibn Ibrahim also mobilized the ulama, urging them to use all available resources (such as sermons, cenacles, courses, and printing houses) to justify Islamic law and attack positive laws and those who supported them.[88] The ulama thus drew upon their entire repertory of action in their effort to sway the political partner.[89] Abd Allah ibn Humayd (d. 1982), the grand mufti's leading disciple and judge of the Al-Qasim district, particularly distinguished himself in the course of this episode. He wrote many letters to the most influential members of the royal house as well as several articles in defense of his religious ideal and the privileges of his corporation.[90] He devoted dozens of sermons and courses to this question,[91] and was particularly critical of the labor code, several articles of which, in his view, clearly contradicted precepts of sharia.[92]

Led by the energetic Ibn Ibrahim, the clerical corps tenaciously pursued their fight, attacking by turns the civil servant code, the labor code, and the Dispute Resolution Committee.[93] For all that, they did not entirely succeed in swaying their political partner.[94]

Far from abandoning the fight, the grand mufti adapted his strategy. Having failed to persuade the government to do away with these institutions, he accepted the fait accompli and sought to control them, appointing Hanbali-Wahhabi ulama and dignitaries to lead them while marginalizing jurists who had received a modern training:[95]

1. In 1926, a commercial court (*al-mahkama al-tijariyya*) was opened on the order of King Abd al-Aziz: seven magistrates, only one of whom was an *'alim*, were to preside over it. Profiting from the period of generational transition, Ibn Ibrahim persuaded King Saud to abolish this body in 1955. A dozen years later, King Faysal tried to restore the commercial courts. In 1967, he established three courts to settle commercial disputes in Riyadh, Jeddah, and Dammam, presided over by three modern jurists. The religious establishment mobilized all of its resources to put an end to what it considered an anti-Islamic situation. Aware that requesting these new bodies to be abrogated would have no effect, Ibn Ibrahim contented himself with telling the king that ulama had to sit in these new courts in order to see to it that the Law was applied. In 1968, the political power restructured them. Of the four magistrates who presided over each tribunal, two were ulama. One year later, two out of three magistrates were ulama. Ibn Ibrahim ultimately got his way, and the corporation continued to rule over the better part of the Saudi legal and judicial system.[96]
2. The foremost members of the religious establishment led a campaign to protest what they saw as content incompatible with sharia in certain codes. This obliged the king to appoint expert commissions whose mission was to use memoranda and meetings to convince the ulama of the Islamic nature of these modern legal measures. In 1968, for example, King Faysal gave his Syrian advisor Maruf al-Dawalibi (d. 2004) the task of organizing

working meetings with members of the religious establishment in order to find a compromise concerning the labor code. After long negotiations and several concessions, the king's advisor was able to persuade the ulama (led by Abd Allah ibn Humayd and Abd al-Aziz ibn Baz) to accept the content of this code and declare it in keeping with sharia.[97]

3. The first girls' school opened in Mecca in 1942.[98] The number of establishments of this type subsequently increased in the Hijaz, with thirty-three in operation in 1959; two of these schools were located in Riyadh.[99] These educational institutions were the result of private initiatives—they were financed and managed mainly by princesses and the wives of notables—and concerned only a small elite. In the framework of state construction, the political authorities had to monopolize the main sectors of social space, particularly the educational sector. The state decided to take back authority for managing existing schools and extend the system to the entire kingdom. In 1955, Ibn Ibrahim categorically refused this project.[100] Four years later, however, the political power decided to forge ahead, and the religious establishment rapidly altered its position to respond to the new situation. The ulama affirmed that it was permissible to educate girls provided that they supervised instruction.[101] The monarchy no longer had any choice but to accept the conditions of its religious partner, all the more so given that much of the population looked upon the project to extend girls' schools across the entire kingdom with suspicion and even hostility. Placing the schools under the direction of the clerical corps would give the schools legitimacy and reassure reluctant heads of family. In 1960, King Saud ordered the creation of the General Chancellor of Girls' Schools (al-Ri'asa al-'amma li-madaris al-banat) and confided its presidency to the grand mufti.[102] The religious establishment would retain control of the institution until 2002.

These three examples show how Ibn Ibrahim and his associates drew upon their ethic of responsibility to preserve the role and influence of the corporation.[103] Far from wanting to take a stand against their political partner, they defended a cause that appeared just from a religious point of view as well as their own status and all of the symbolic and material privileges it entailed. They were aware, however, that systematic opposition to government policy and a too inflexible socioreligious stance would only marginalize them over time, as had been the experience of their colleagues in nearly all Muslim countries. Saudi ulama therefore privileged negotiation and compromise. In this way, they sought to maintain a certain balance and prevent their political partner from taking away their prerogatives in the legal and judicial domains. The adaptive strategy thus appeared the best way to guarantee proper application of the three O's.

6

THE COMMITTEE OF GRAND ULAMA

An Organization in the Service of the Prince . . . and the Population

THE NEW FACE OF THE RELIGIOUS ESTABLISHMENT

The unity of the clerical corps and the energetic manner with which it defended its interests did not leave the monarchy indifferent. Though symbolic and without effect, the clerical corps' criticisms were no doubt seen by the country's rulers as a precedent that might have significant consequences in the future.[1] A structural consideration must be added to this purely conjunctural factor. All processes of state construction require the emergence of a central power that leads a monopolist and homogenizing policy in all domains. After the (re)unification of the kingdom, the monarchy became involved in this dynamic, which accelerated during the 1950s and 1960s. But it ran up against the Hanbali-Wahhabi corporation's desire to preserve its autonomy and privileges in keeping with the traditional division of labor with the religious authority.

Like most Arab countries of the period, all more or less inspired by the example of Egypt, the Saudi monarchy seriously considered asserting control over the ulama in order to free its hand in the institutional domain and make better use of the ulama's ideological authority. In 1961, Gamal Abdel Nasser instituted a reform of Al-Azhar that aimed to control and marginalize the ulama.[2] There is no doubt that this strongly influenced Prince Faysal, at the time Saudi Arabia's prime minister. The following year, Faysal set about imitating some aspects of his best enemy's policy. In a statement delivered on the occasion of the first meeting of the new Saudi cabinet (2 November 1962), the prince–prime minister made a commitment to step up efforts in his "program aimed at developing the country, consolidating the state, and improving the condition of citizens so that, having acted as the crucible of authentic Arab nationalism, they may occupy the rank they deserve as a people."[3] In order to accelerate the march of progress, King Saud's government drew up a large program of reform, with the following main components:[4]

1. His Majesty's government is eager to ensure the inviolability and prestige of the magistracy, for the magistracy is the guarantee of law and the symbol of justice. To the degree that we will have ensured that the magistracy can occupy the high rank that it deserves and enjoys full liberty, we will have consolidated one of the fundamental bases of our religion: to wit, the proper administration of justice. No effort will be spared to this end; a law will be issued assuring the independence of the magistracy and creating a high council responsible for enforcing it. What's more, we have decided to create a ministry of justice that will look after its administrative organization. A public minister will be part of this organization, the aim of which will be to uphold the interests of citizens and protect their rights. This institution will further collaborate with the courts of the judiciary in order to guarantee rights and the rule of justice.
2. We know that the texts of the Book of God [the Qur'an] and the [prophetic] Tradition are clear and do not lend themselves to any addition or interpretation, whereas legal situations and the requirements born of developing trade and progress are constantly changing. The government of our young state—God be praised for it—is inspired by the letter and spirit of the Book and the Tradition. However, it is of capital importance to accord a greater interest to the administration of justice and ensure that our jurists and scholars, the guardians of knowledge and enlightenment, are capable of taking an active part in finding solutions to the problems that arise for the nation, solutions that follow from divine law and guarantee the interests of the Muslim community. For these reasons, His Majesty's government has decided to establish an advisory council consisting of twenty-two members who will be chosen among leading jurists and scholars. The main duties that this organism will be called upon to carry out are:

    a. To examine legal questions taken up by the government;
    b. to issue rulings and give advice on questions of interest to members of the Muslim community;
    c. to serve as a source of enlightenment and a tool for overcoming obstacles to progress.

3. This noble Muslim nation—the best on Earth—promotes virtue and prohibits vice. However, Islam is aware of the need to maintain this duty; sharia exalts its merits as well as those who carry it out. This pious work obliges whoever devotes himself to it to always pursue the path of God through wisdom and good advice. He must do his utmost to see to it that law, virtue, and love take root in people's hearts. Also, His Majesty's government has decided to immediately reform the body responsible for promoting virtue

and preventing vice in keeping with the noble aims for which this body was originally created. This reform also seeks to employ resources appropriate for eradicating the roots of evil.

Any monopolist undertaking on the part of the Saudi political authorities was thus legitimated by appeal to populist rhetoric. Adopting a tone that was at once religious, nationalist, statist, and developmentalist—indeed, almost Nasserian—in order to reach out to a population that had become accustomed to the enflamed speeches of Nasser broadcast by Voice of the Arabs (Sawt al-'arab) radio, Prince Faysal aspired to achieve control over the entire Saudi social space, particularly the juridico-religious space. In the juridico-religious domain, it seems that his fundamental objective was to put an end to the monopoly of the grand mufti and thereby destroy the vertical organization of the corporation. Apart from "improving public services," the creation of the Ministry of Justice, the High Council of the Magistracy, a public ministry, and a twenty-two-member body responsible for issuing fatawa, as well as the reform of the Committee for the Promotion of Virtue and the Prevention of Vice, this program aimed to fragment the juridico-religious space and create a degree of collegiality within the religious establishment—that is, establish a horizontal organization after the image of the organization of the royal house. Some leading members of the ruling house, particularly Prince Faysal, looked askance upon the fact that a single figure dominated the religious authority, as this lent itself to abuse should the post fall into ambitious hands.

Faysal's project involved an attempt on the part of the royal house to partly free itself from Hanbali-Wahhabi discourse and create a differentiated religious legitimacy. Indeed, the prime minister's declaration insisted on the Saudi monarchy's responsibility for defending, consolidating, and spreading the Islamic faith in the world. The policy of Islamic solidarity initiated that same year is confirmation of this desire: while its stated objective was to counter the spread of Pan-Arabism, it also gave national legitimacy and international visibility to Saudi Arabia.

For all that, Faysal's project came to a successful conclusion only in 1969. Several factors may explain this delay. First, throughout the 1950s and 1960s, the religious establishment unconditionally supported the House of Saud against all enemies and deployed all of its ideological authority to legitimate the political and diplomatic choices of the political power (the crisis of succession, the various worker riots, the riots that followed the creation of the first television channel, the fight against Pan-Arabism, etc.). Second, the charismatic personality of Muhammad ibn Ibrahim no doubt prevented Faysal, first as prime minister and then as king, from forging ahead with his monopolist project. Apart from questions of precedence relating to the social anthropology of Saudi Arabia,[5] Ibn Ibrahim had accumulated broad institutional powers and such extensive symbolic capital that any maneuver on the part of the political partner was rendered difficult.

To this must be added the fact that, according to the meager information available to us, Ibn Ibrahim seemed to wish at all costs to avoid intervention in the religious space on the part of the political power. Aware of the fact that none of his sons or disciples had the charisma necessary to replace him at the head of the religious establishment (at least not immediately), he set about establishing a collegial board of his own to preempt King Faysal and his accomplices. Just a few months before his death, Ibn Ibrahim put the final touches on the Commission of Grand Ulama (Lajnat Kibar al-'Ulama'), whose budget had been approved by the government.[6] Up until the very end of his life, he was thus at great pains to assure the future of the corporation.

Ibn Ibrahim's death in 1969 opened the way for the monarchy to directly intervene in the religious space. Between 1969 and 1971, King Faysal set about creating a number of bodies, including the Ministry of Justice, the High Council of the Magistracy, and the Committee of Grand Ulama. In doing so, his aim was to split up the juridico-religious offices formerly held by the grand mufti (see Figure 1) and thereby routinize his charisma. The office of the grand mufti itself was eliminated and only reestablished in 1993. The objective of King Faysal's efforts was not to bureaucratize the ulama and thereby marginalize and weaken them, as other Arab countries had done. Rather, his aim was to fragment their religious authority in order to better control this "intellectual tool par excellence of political domination" and use it as he saw fit.[7] It must not be forgotten that, since the emergence of the Saudi political entity, the Hanbali-Wahhabi ulama had been an integral part of its political and administrative apparatus.[8] Contrary to the claims of some observers, the monarchy thus had no need to bureaucratize its operation.[9]

The shift from a monocephalic, centralized organization to a headless, fragmented one was made possible thanks to the charisma of King Faysal. The success of his policy of Islamic solidarity and his demonstrations of piety, combined with the fact that he was, on his mother's side, a descendant of Muhammad ibn Abd al-Wahhab, gave him great religious legitimacy in the eyes of the population. The explosion of the price of petroleum in 1973 crowned his successes.

For the Hanbali-Wahhabi corporation, the 1970s may be considered a time in the wilderness. The petroleum boom (*al-tafra*) allowed the political power to partly free themselves from religious discourse as the unique source of legitimacy by drawing upon developmentalist rhetoric and establishing a tacit social pact with the population based on the redistribution of a significant portion of petroleum revenue in exchange for popular renunciation of any form of political participation. Troubled by the death of its charismatic leader, the religious establishment found itself de facto sidelined.

But far from destroying the establishment, this attempt at fragmentation and marginalization allowed the ulama to exclusively concentrate on the religious space, assiduously pursuing the work of institutionalization begun by Ibn Ibrahim. They thus continued to modernize their organizational frameworks by endowing themselves with new infrastructures (such as middle schools, high schools, universities, courts, mosques, religious orientation offices, and nongovernmental organizations) and opening their minds to other religious institutions. The ulama thus entered into dialogue with the Vatican and the main Protestant churches,[10] drew upon the organizational experience of Muslim Brotherhood members residing in Saudi Arabia,[11] and opened up a bit more to Al-Azhar in Egypt.[12]

As I have underscored on several occasions, however, the ulama, as collective actors, did all they could to thwart Faysal's effort at fragmentation by individually overseeing the newly created institutions on behalf of the corporation. Starting in the late 1970s, they recuperated all of their prerogatives in the juridico-religious domain, strengthening their presence in the social space, and were able to find a leader, Abd al-Aziz ibn Baz, capable of expressing unshakeable unity and collective identity. It should be pointed out, however, that Ibn Baz never recovered all of Ibn Ibrahim's prerogatives.

In other words, the clerical corps very rapidly adapted to the new situation. More particularly, it once again adopted a strategy that would allow it, not only to preserve its interests by significantly reinforcing its social base and organizational frameworks, but also to impose itself as a reliable, long-term partner of the political power. When a series of events in the late 1970s called into question the religious legitimacy of the House of Saud and plunged its developmentalist rhetoric into disarray, the symbiotic relationship was reactivated.[13] It was, however, to be on a new basis. Henceforth, the political power had a right to monitor all questions touching upon the political domain in the broad sense of the term.

The Committee of Grand Ulama's structure (Figure 2) and mode of operation perfectly illustrate the new form taken by the symbiotic relationship. Created in 1971, the committee very rapidly established itself as the most important Hanbali-Wahhabi organization: it consists of the most eminent members of the corporation, acts as the country's main legislative body alongside the Council of Ministers, and serves as ideological shield to the ruling house. It thus became

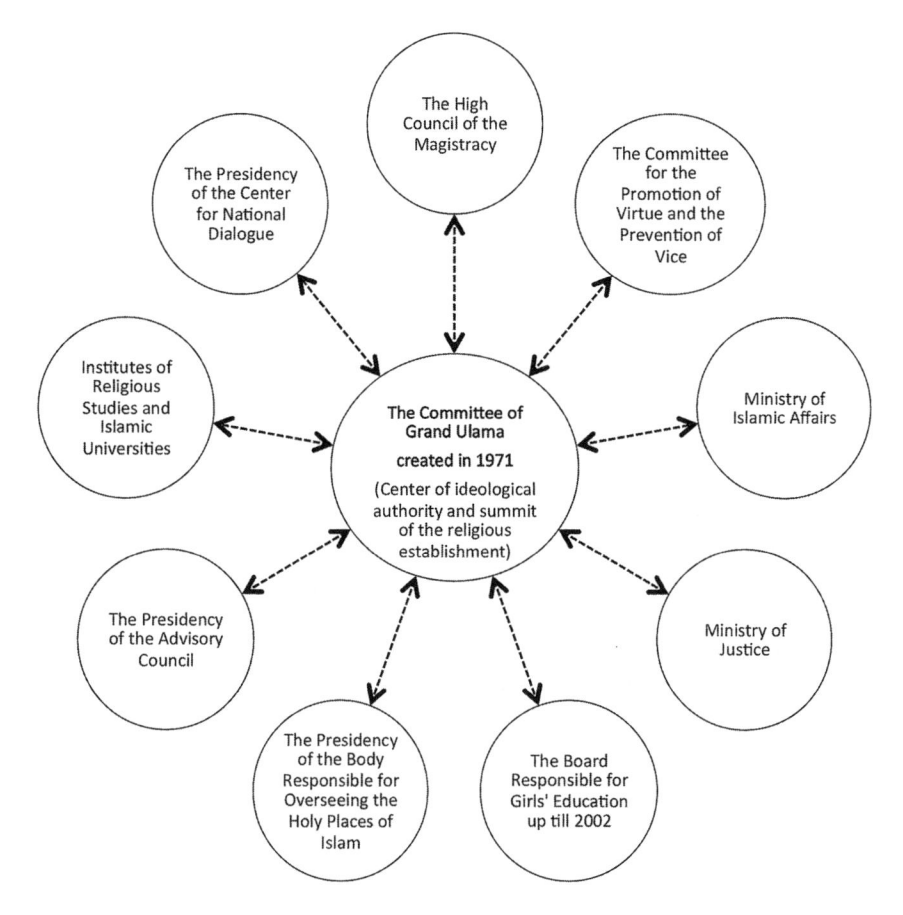

Figure 2. Sociogram of the religious establishment since 1971.

the headquarters of ideological authority in contemporary Saudi Arabia. The importance assumed by this federative state organization for the Saudi political authorities (equivalent to that of the Saudi Arabian Oil Company [Aramco] in the economic domain) encouraged those authorities to seek to control access to it and supervise its activity. The description of its structures and modes of operation will allow us to grasp the role of the religious corps as a collective actor and the holder of ideological authority as well as the extent of its activity in Saudi social space.

THE MORPHOLOGY OF A DUAL-PURPOSE BODY

Though Egypt was its rival, Saudi Arabia nonetheless considered it a model to follow. A large number of Saudi institutions and laws imitated those of Cairo.

This was because since the early twentieth century, Egypt had taken the lead in the area of modernization, much prestige had resulted from that fact, and many collaborators of the Saudi king, princes, and ministers were Egyptian. Al-Azhar, in particular, was a model of religious organization for the Middle East. The Saudi Committee of Grand Ulama was also inspired by its older brother, the Egyptian Committee of Grand Ulama, which was created in 1911.

The Egyptian committee consisted of thirty ulama drawn from the four legal schools of Sunni Islam. Its mission was to teach religious studies and Arabic, oversee academic programs in Islamic studies, and inspect the manner in which courses were taught. It was also capable of issuing fatawa and censoring books. The members of the Egyptian committee met once a month and more often in exceptional cases. The presence of at least half of its members was required for a meeting to take place. Final decisions were made by absolute majority. Clear conditions had been laid down in writing for those wishing to join it: the candidate had to be at least forty-five years old; hold the *'alimiyya*—the equivalent of a doctorate; hold the post of professor, judge, or high-ranking civil servant in the religious domain; meet the moral criteria defined by the committee; have written a noted work in the area of religion, Islamic history, or Arabic language and literature; and have at least fifteen years of experience in the religious domain. Finally, candidates to Egypt's Committee of Grand Ulama had to receive more than sixteen votes from their future colleagues.[14] New members were thus elected by senior ones and appointed by royal decree (the palace intervened neither in the choice of new members nor in the event of their dismissal). The grand shaykh or rector of Al-Azhar, who sat on the committee, was elected by his fellow members.[15]

This body's role was in reality rather restricted and concerned only the technical aspects of religious instruction, worship, and mores. It only rarely intervened in public affairs of a social or political nature and was only one body among others within Al-Azhar. Finally, the Egyptian Committee of Grand Ulama, first known as Hay'at Kibar al-'Ulama', twice changed its name: first it was called Jama'at Kibar al-'Ulama' (the Assembly of Grand Ulama) before taking the name of Majma' al-Buhuth al-Islamiyya (the Islamic Research Council) following the 1961 reform.[16] In the case of the committee he created in 1971, King Faysal chose to adopt the name that the Egyptian committee had borne during the time of the monarchy and thereby distinguish himself from the regime of his rival, Abdel Nasser.

Royal Order A/137 of 28 August 1971 established a supreme religious body in Saudi Arabia, the Committee of Grand Ulama (Hay'at Kibar al-'Ulama'), the seventeen members of which were specialists of Islamic law.[17] The mission of this body was to determine whether a given question raised by the king or his government was in conformity with sharia. It consisted of three parts: the Council of the Committee of Grand Ulama (Majlis Hay'at Kibar al-'Ulama'); the General Presidency for the Management of [Religious] Scholarship, Predication, and Guidance (al-Ri'asa al-'amma li-idarat al-buhuth al-'ilmiyya wa al-da'wa wa al-irshad); and the Permanent Commission on [Religious] Scholarship and *Ifta'* [the issuing of legal opinions] (al-Lajna al-da'ima lil-buhuth wa al-Ifta').

These three parts have distinct but complementary areas of competence. The Council of the Committee plays a role at the macro-social level; the General Presidency looks after macro-social, micro-social, administrative, and international questions and is, so to speak, the committee's mainspring. The Permanent Commission, for its part, has an exclusively micro-social role. The Saudi Committee of Grand Ulama thus possesses more parts than its Egyptian counterpart (three versus one) but has fewer members (seventeen to twenty-two versus thirty). Finally, the Saudi committee has more prerogatives: the only thing the two committees have in common is thus their name and a collegial organization. In what follows, we continue to examine the structures and prerogatives of the Saudi committee without further reference to the Egyptian model.

The members of the Permanent Commission issue fatawa concerning personal affairs (mainly questions of dogma and ritual). They are directly addressed by the population to the ulama or are gathered by post, telephone, or Internet. The ulama answer all questions: immediately for those that are addressed to them in person or by telephone; after a delay for all others. The most frequently raised questions and those of greatest concern to the population are discussed in the course of weekly meetings (generally on Sundays and Tuesdays).

The four to seven members who compose the Permanent Commission are chosen from among the members of the Council of the Committee of Grand Ulama.[18] As noted, this commission meets twice a week, and the most recurrent fatawa are gathered in a compendium and published at year's end. More than twenty volumes and a CD-ROM are available, and all can be downloaded via the Internet from a large number of Arabic-language religious websites.[19] To issue a fatwa, at least three members of the commission must be present, with the question decided by absolute majority. In the event of a split vote, the president's vote decides. The other days of the week, at least two ulama are on duty to directly respond to the population's questions.[20] The ulama of the Permanent Commission are, as its name suggests, permanently available and easy to reach. Indeed, five days a week, at least three members receive visitors in their offices and answer telephone calls (most of the calls are from women, though the ulama are also contacted by men living in the provinces or abroad).[21] Their fatawa concern all aspects of life. I was myself able to attend several of these consultations in 2005 throughout which the ulama were unaware of the reasons for my visit. While most fatawa corresponded to problems of ritual (such as prayer, ablutions, almsgiving, blood money, marriage, funerals, and vestimentary obligations), economic questions were heavily represented, particularly in what concerned the permissibility of investing in the stock market and other investment advice. But the most astonishing questions no doubt had to do with the private domain and above all concerned marital issues. Thus, one of the ulama whom I visited received a call (his secretary had plugged in the speaker phone) from a woman who asked him for advice about helping her impotent husband. In simple language and without any scriptural reference or aside (the conversation lasted thirteen minutes), the *'alim* lavished the young woman with what was, to say the least, unusual advice: "avoid wearing a slip that is pink or too short . . . do not walk ahead of him on the way to the bedroom . . . reassure him and tell him that you will be patient and will wait as long as necessary." Following this, the woman cried "Allahu Akbar!," warmly thanking him by calling upon God to give him a long life, and then hung up, delighted with what she had been told.[22] The versatility of the ulama is on full display here. They are not only technicians of the routine cults in the strict sense of the term, but also veritable agents of socialization who issue opinions that hold for all aspects of life and specialists of social questions who seek to ensure the symbolic superiority of Hanbali-Wahhabi discourse—the only way, according to them, of achieving earthly happiness and eternal salvation.

From 1971 to 1975, the presidency of the commission was in turn held by all of its members; in 1975, a permanent president, Abd al-Aziz ibn Baz (d. 1999), was appointed; the kingdom's grand mufti has been president since 1993.[23]

The Permanent Commission does not have the right to rule on questions falling outside of the micro-social domain, that is, everyday socioreligious questions. If it receives questions that exceed its domain of competence, it must prepare a research report and submit it to the Council of the Committee of Grand Ulama. In practice, the members sometimes exceed their field of competence by giving their opinions on macro-social or political questions.[24] During the Israeli attack against Gaza in December 2008, the commission published a communiqué online condemning the war and calling for support for the Palestinian people.[25] It seems that the ulama had recourse to this maneuver in order to get around the procedure that requires them, as we will see, to submit all macro-social questions to the royal cabinet for approval. In this way, they were able to both respond to popular expectations and present the government with a fait accompli. But the ulama only rarely resort to this type of behavior.

The General Presidency for the Management of [Religious] Scholarship, Predication, and Guidance is the keystone of the committee. During its first phase of existence, this apparatus had very broad prerogatives. Its raison d'être was to support the official ideology, consolidate the kingdom's religious prestige, and supply administrative oversight for the Committee of Grand Ulama. Indeed, it saw to the "promotion, defense, and propagation of Islam"—that is, Hanbali-Wahhabism—inside the kingdom and abroad.[26] Moreover, it was responsible for coordinating all of Saudi Arabia's pastoral associations and organizations. The aim of this "coordination" (in reality, near control) was to supervise the action of preachers and religious associations in order to rule out insubordination or ideological faux pas.

The General Presidency also gave itself the task of protecting and preserving "Islamic thought"—that is, the Hanbali-Wahhabi doctrine—through the publication of works of theology, jurisprudence, polemic, and propaganda.[27] Most of these works are sold at symbolic prices or freely distributed outside of mosques, schools, and universities and may also be downloaded from the Internet. During periods of pilgrimage, the General Presidency saw to the instruction and orientation of pilgrims and visitors to the two holy places and profited from the occasion of these great human gatherings to engage in proselytism. On the strictly interior level, it supported students of religious studies via educational grants, giving them free access to libraries and manuscript collections in the kingdom and elsewhere in the Muslim world.

Since 1975, the General Presidency has published a trimestrial review— *Majallat al-Buhuth al-Islamiyya (The Islamic Research Review)*—to promote Hanbali-Wahhabi theological and legal research, and since 2007, it has operated a website.[28] Finally, it reserves to itself the exclusive right to publish the Qur'an and the power to censor foreign books.

But things changed in 1993. The Ministry of Islamic Affairs, Predication, and Orientation was created. As can be seen in Figure 3, it inherited most of the General Presidency's prerogatives. The latter, now known as the General Presidency of Scientific Research [in the Area of Religion] and the Issuing of Fatawa (al-Ri'asa al-'amma lil-buhuth al-'ilmiyya wa al-ifta'), was to exclusively concentrate on managing the ideological authority of the Committee of Grand Ulama. Indeed, its role was now largely reduced to overseeing the *Islamic Research Review* and Internet site and a series of publishing activities covering fatawa by the Permanent Commission and the Council of the Committee of

```
                    ┌──────────────────────────────┐
                    │ The Committee of Grand Ulama │
                    │      (created in 1971)       │
                    └──────────────────────────────┘
         ┌─────────────────────┼──────────────────────┐
         ▼                     ▼                      ▼
┌──────────────────┐  ┌──────────────────┐  ┌──────────────────┐
│  The Permanent   │  │ The Council of the│  │ The General Presidency│
│  Commission of ifta' │  │ Committee of  │  │ of Scientific Research│
│ (meets twice a week and│  │ Grand Ulama   │  │ (active on a daily basis)│
│   is on call daily)  │  │ (meets twice a year│  └──────────────────┘
└──────────────────┘  │ and more often in │
                      │ case of a serious event)│
                      └──────────────────┘
         ▼                     ▼
   Private-type fatawa     Public-type fatawa      Defense, promotion,
    (dogma, ritual,       (questions of legitimacy  and propagation of
    everyday life, etc.)    and public order,       Hanbali-Wahhabism
                          important religious and    in Saudi Arabia
                          social questions)            and abroad.
```

The General Secretariat of the Committee of Grand Ulama
The General Secretariat of Islamic Predication
The Committee for Islamic Public Awareness during the Pilgrimage
The Agency of Information Predication
The Office of Predication in the Kingdom and the Countries of the Gulf
The Office for Foreign Predication
The General Direction of Koranic Vulgates and Oversight of Publications
The Office of Publication and Translation
The Saudi General Library

(With the exception of the General Secretariat of the Committee of Grand Ulama, all of these administrations were transferred to the Ministry of Islamic Affairs upon its creation in 1993.)

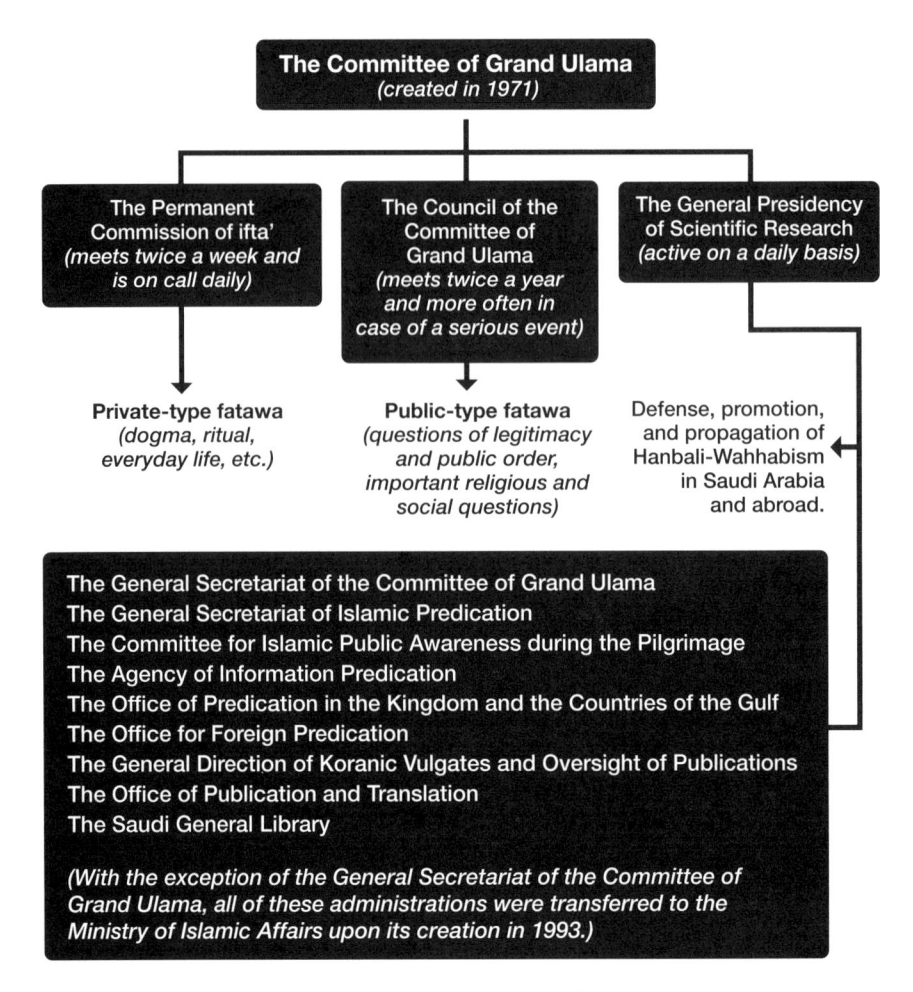

Figure 3. The structures of the Committee of Grand Ulama.

Grand Ulama, research, and theological-legal works (mainly Hanbali-Wahhabi classics and books written by certain members of the Committee of Grand Ulama). But its main mission still consisted of managing dozens of ulama and legal and theological scholars. The scholars were responsible for responding to the thousands of socioreligious questions (in fact, questions to which the members of the Permanent Commission could not respond) that daily arrived at the General Presidency's headquarters (conveniently referred to as Dar al-Ifta') on Asir Avenue in Riyadh and preparing research reports on various subjects on the request of the grand mufti or members of the Committee of Grand Ulama.[29] Since 1993, the General Presidency has been led by the grand mufti with help from a number of technocrats—in particular, a vice president who is the true chief of the administrative apparatus.[30]

The creation of the Ministry of Islamic Affairs did not represent a reduced role for the religious establishment. It was part of a process of institutionalization, rationalization, and optimization of the Hanbali-Wahhabi corporation's activities intended to meet the sociopolitical changes affecting Saudi Arabia and the world in the early 1990s. While the fall of the Berlin Wall offered formidable possibilities of expansion to Hanbali-Wahhabism, the Gulf War gave rise to an Islamist protest movement—to be discussed more in chapter 9—that obliged the clerical corps, with support from the political power, to reorganize its structures for better control. Separating management of socioreligious bodies and activities (such as mosques, Qur'anic learning associations, the printing and translation of the Qur'an, and preaching), human resources (such as the mosque imams and muezzins, preachers, translators, and administrative staff), and properly ideological work doubtless allowed its positions to be strengthened to better defend its socioreligious privileges and protect the three O's. Since its creation, moreover, the Ministry of Islamic Affairs has been directed by leading members of the religious establishment: Abd Allah al-Turki (b. 1940), a member of the Committee of Grand Ulama and a very active *'alim* whose career we will consider in the next chapter, followed by Salih Al al-Shaykh (b. 1958), grandson of Muhammad ibn Ibrahim.

Finally, the Council of the Committee of Grand Ulama for its part acts at the macro-social level. Its members generally meet twice a year: once in Riyadh and once in al-Ta'if. On the express request of the president of the council after consultation with the royal cabinet, they may also meet at any given time or place as the situation demands, and they can furthermore meet on the express request of the Council of Ministers presided over by the king or crown prince. Until 1993, the presidency of the council was entrusted by turns to its five oldest members. Since 1993, the kingdom's mufti has presided over its meetings, which in theory can take place only when at least two-thirds of its members are present.

The council addresses the great social and political questions that directly touch upon the monarchy's legitimacy. The social themes sometimes have to do with penal law (such as drug trafficking, alcohol trafficking, organized crime, and capital punishment), and sometimes with civil law (such as marriage, divorce, inheritance, and contracts).[31] Depending on the agenda, it can also respond to diverse and varied questions concerning, for example, the medical (brain death, abortion, etc.) or economic (bank interest, investing in the stock market, etc.) domains and issues relating to dogma and religious ritual.[32]

The aim of its responses to political questions is to legitimate and defend governmental positions or attack enemy or rival foreign governments. For example, the council supported the Saudi government's (unpopular) decision to call upon U.S. troops at the time of the Gulf War. It excommunicated and called for a boycott of Khomeini (d. 1989) and Saddam Hussein (d. 2006), who were seen as "enemies of Islam."[33] It condemned the intrigues of the Saudi Islamist opposition in the early 1990s as well as the attacks carried out by Al-Qaeda in Saudi Arabia, describing its members as heretics.[34] Finally, fatawa were issued to condemn suicide attacks and forbid young Saudis from going to fight in Iraq or elsewhere.[35]

THE PROCEDURE FOR ISSUING FATAWA

As we have seen, the Permanent Commission receives a large number of questions on all aspects of Saudi life. These questions are raised by natural or legal persons (such as the Council of Ministers, the governor-princes of the regions, and the universities). In 2005, for example, the commission received a question from Prince Khalid al-Faysal (b. 1947), the governor of Asir, regarding forced marriage.[36] This question, of interest at the national level, was immediately transferred to the Council of the Committee of Grand Ulama.

All questions transferred to the council must be accompanied by a research report prepared by a member of the Permanent Commission (the research is generally carried out by a graduate in sharia working alongside members of the commission or for the General Presidency). The Permanent Commission sets its agenda depending on the questions it receives. Once it reaches the royal cabinet, the agenda may be vetoed by the king, who can modify it at will. In other words, anything that precedes the king's decision is no more than a proposal. The importance of the agenda should be mentioned in passing: in the end, only questions authorized by the royal cabinet are handled by the Committee of Grand Ulama. This oversight clearly shows the importance of the committee, whose decisions legitimate a good part of the House of Saud's power.

In exceptional cases (mainly in the event of serious disturbances that threaten the country's stability or the future of the regime itself), the Committee of Grand Ulama is asked to hold an extraordinary session, and the agenda is directly set by the royal cabinet. As we have already seen, the purpose of such meetings is to legitimate a decision, discredit an enemy of the regime in the eyes of public opinion, or condemn what is seen as a dangerous event. The capture of Mecca by the Juhayman messianic group in 1979, the Iranian pilgrim riots of 1986, and the Iraqi invasion of Kuwait in 1990 are signal occasions on which the political power expressly requested a fatwa on the part of the ulama.[37]

The general secretary of the Committee of Grand Ulama, who is not himself a member of the committee, is an official directly appointed by the Council of Ministers to ensure a direct line to the palace.[38] He must nevertheless hold a diploma in religious studies. His work above all consists of seeing to it that research reports on the questions to be examined by the Council of the Committee are ready one month before the start of the session at which they will be discussed. He must also deliver these reports, together with the corresponding agenda, to members of the committee at least fifteen days before the start of the session. He plays the role of intermediary and also keeps an eye on this politico-religious body on behalf of the political power.

Depending on the importance of the question under examination and the gravity of the context, the ulama call upon specialists (who are not themselves members of the committee) capable of explaining, for example, a given scientific or security mechanism. For medical questions, teams of doctors are called upon to write reports and hold seminars. To clarify gray areas or delve more deeply into a question, the ulama may also be granted access to classified documents, particularly security service reports. In the case of less sensitive files, the ulama content themselves with reading research reports prepared by the Permanent Commission and/or examining decisions already made on the subject by other Islamic bodies in the Muslim world—in particular, Al-Azhar and the Council of Islamic Jurisprudence, which has its headquarters in Mecca (and is under the authority of the World Islamic League).[39]

After this phase of expertise, it is time for debate. Most ulama insist that the debates are free and transparent when social and religious questions are under discussion. But where political questions are concerned—above all, those touching upon the legitimacy and stability of the political system—their answers are more evasive. From this, it can be surmised that the ulama automatically and without discussion legitimate the government's positions, even when it may damage their own credibility (their vote to bless the request for U.S. troops in 1990 is the best illustration of this). This is less a matter of the grand ulama's allegiance to the regime than a form of association and alliance—that is, political co-optation in its purest form. They thus consider themselves part of the regime. This is due to the mentality of the Hanbali-Wahhabi ulama and their great pragmatism: they know very well that if the present regime, which they support, were to disappear, their status and privileges would likely be in danger and the three O's would be compromised.

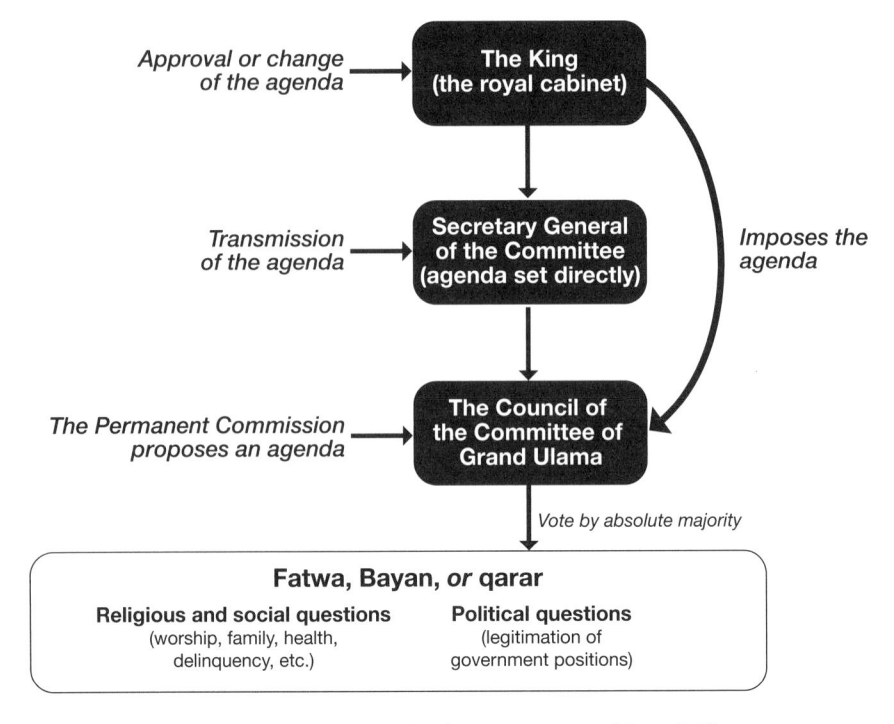

```
                    ┌─────────────────────┐
Approval or change ─→│    The King         │
   of the agenda    │ (the royal cabinet) │
                    └──────────┬──────────┘
                               │
                               ▼
                    ┌─────────────────────┐
   Transmission    │  Secretary General   │   Imposes the
   of the agenda ─→│   of the Committee   │     agenda
                    │(agenda set directly)│
                    └──────────┬──────────┘
                               │
                               ▼
                    ┌─────────────────────┐
The Permanent Commission │   The Council of   │
   proposes an agenda ──→│ the Committee of   │
                    │    Grand Ulama      │
                    └──────────┬──────────┘
                               │ Vote by absolute majority
                               ▼
              ╭──────────────────────────────────╮
              │      Fatwa, Bayan, or qarar      │
              │ Religious and social  Political  │
              │     questions         questions  │
              │ (worship, family,   (legitimation│
              │ health, delinquency,    of       │
              │       etc.)         government   │
              │                     positions)   │
              ╰──────────────────────────────────╯
```

Figure 4. Procedures for issuing fatawa by the Committee of Grand Ulama.

After this debate, the vote is taken by a show of hands. Decisions are reached by absolute majority. In the event of a split vote, that of the president in theory decides. In practice, however, a second vote is held. While the ulama are free to vote as they like in regards to social, legal, and legislative questions, those who wish to vote "no" in the case of the political questions debated at extraordinary sessions have no choice but to absent themselves from the meeting, something that may incidentally cost them their place on the committee. But such a scenario has yet to actually occur (see Figure 4).

The Royal Order of 1971, the only available document describing the operation of the committee, fails to specify the modes of deliberation. It was only by means of interviews that I was able to identify them. Three sorts of deliberation can be distinguished: the first type of deliberation is by *bayan* (declaration), a fatwa concerning political questions. Requested by the monarchy, a *bayan* only defends the regime's positions and sanctifies its action.[40] It thus has a largely ideological and symbolic value. The second type is the fatwa, which can sometimes take the name of *qarar* (resolution) in order to guarantee performative force. The fatwa covers religious, social, and legal questions. It has universal value only if it is approved by the Council of Ministers or the king. In other words, these legal opinions remain dead letters if the state, with all its coercive force, does not adopt them. Generally, the political power ratifies the legal-religious decisions of the Council of the Committee of Grand Ulama, but it sometimes happens that it refuses them because they run counter to the state's interests. Thus, in 2006, King Abd Allah asked the Committee of Grand Ulama to give a ruling on the legitimacy of a project to enlarge the *mas'a* of the Grand Mosque of Mecca in order to make room for a larger number of pilgrims.[41] After thoroughly studying the problem, the ulama held that enlarging the area was illicit because it did not conform with available scriptural attestations.[42] Outraged by this refusal, King Abd Allah decided to go over the heads of the committee members and sought the opinion of other ulama in the Muslim world. As expected, the latter approved his project.[43] Indeed, he saw this undertaking as an important economic and symbolic investment that would positively reflect on the kingdom and its rulers. In reaching their decision, the Saudi ulama had taken account of only religious considerations and the technical aspects of the question.

The broad prerogatives enjoyed by the Committee of Grand Ulama in the religious, social, and political domains thus explain the oversight exercised by the political power over certain aspects of its operation, particularly its agenda. This discrete form of supervision—much of the population and the elites are unaware that such mechanisms exist—aims to prevent the committee from becoming a competing platform or hotbed of insubordination, particularly during moments of transition and political crisis. The authorities seek less to control religious discourse—an inexhaustible source of legitimacy—than to master initiative. While the committee and its various components are practically independent in the domain of the goods of salvation (in the framework of the Hanbali-Wahhabi tradition), the grand ulama are not bothered by the supervision that is exercised over political questions. Since the Law cannot be enforced without the coercive force of the state, cooperation (*ta'awun*) and obedience (*ta'a*) to the prince (*waliyy al-amr*) are the foundations of Hanbali doctrine. And the spiritual and temporal interests of the corporation are intrinsically linked to those of the monarchy; were the latter to be jeopardized, the domination of Hanbali-Wahhabism on Saudi territory would be called into question, at least institutionally.

A PRACTICAL CASE: THE CODIFICATION OF LEGAL NORMS DEDUCED FROM SHARIA

In order to illustrate my remarks in what follows, I have chosen to study the codification of legal norms deduced from sharia (*tadwin al-rajih min aqwal al-fuqaha'*, commonly known as *taqnin al-shari'a*). Doing so will allow us to better observe the Committee of Grand Ulama's mechanisms for promulgating fatawa. It will also permit us to assess the Hanbali-Wahhabi tradition's long and complex process of routinization as seen through the prism of a particular issue and supply a glimpse of the debates that drive the corporation in this respect.

As we saw in the first chapter, ever since the failure of the first Abbasid caliphs' attempts in the second half of the eighth century to establish an imperial legal body with which to impose their theocratic power, the ulama had controlled the better part of legal and judicial systems in Muslim countries.[44] To this end, they drew upon a large juridico-theological corpus based on the interpretation of the Qur'an and Sunna: sharia, literally, the "path to be followed" for achieving eternal salvation.[45] This rich corpus, which they alone were able to manipulate, gave them much freedom to maneuver and broad autonomy. Most Muslim lands were governed by this system without significant problems throughout the Middle Ages and the modern era.

Yet the situation was to radically change in the nineteenth century. Under pressure from the European powers, the Ottoman Empire, the main Islamic power of its time, withdrew in all domains. The Ottoman authorities saw that the only way to slow this decline and close the technological and social gaps that separated them from their enemies was to take their enemies as their model. A process of structural reform (*al-tanzimat*) was officially launched in 1839. In order to homogenize, institutionalize, and centralize the empire's judicial system, the authorities officially issued the first precise code of Islamic rules and norms between 1849 and 1876: *Majallat al-ahkam al-'adliyya* (Code of Legal and Judicial Measures). This involved bringing together into a single collection a number of normative texts from the Hanafi corpus, the official legal school of the Ottomans, relating to particular issues (such as commercial transactions and legal penalties). All judges in the Ottoman Empire had to scrupulously respect this code, particularly in the province of the Hijaz. Though the Hijaz became independent in 1916, it nevertheless continued to rely upon the Ottoman code.

After King Abd al-Aziz conquered the two holy places of Islam in 1924–1925, he sought to adopt this model in order to ensure control over the recently conquered territories and legitimate his power. In 1927, he ordered that a commission be created to compile a code similar to that of the Ottomans but based on the corpus of the four legal schools of Sunni Islam.[46] This project displeased the ulama in more than one respect. According to them, the Hanbali-Wahhabi identity and corpus would be diluted in a larger corpus of this type, which constituted an imitation of the infidels and a roundabout path for introducing positive laws. They were convinced that such a project threatened to challenge the power of the corporation and compromise the path to salvation.

There is no doubt that they profited from the Ikhwan rebellion to dearly sell their support. In 1928, a Royal Order approved the decision that all Saudi courts would now hand down judgments in keeping with Hanbali methods and opinions.[47] The judges had mainly to rely on two large surveys of Hanbali legal norms compiled by Mansur al-Buhuti (d. 1641): *Sharh Muntaha al-Iradat* and *Kashshaf al-Qina' 'an al-Iqna'*. Judges were obliged to apply the norms on which the two works were in agreement as well as those that each separately contained. In the event of divergence between them, the norms of *Sharh Muntaha al-Iradat* were to have precedence. Moreover, if the judges were not in possession of these two books, they had to refer to *Dalil al-Talib li-Nayl al-Matalib* by al-Karami (d. 1624) and *al-Rawd al-Murbi' Sharh Zad al-Mustaqni'* by al-Buhuti. Recourse to other Hanbali works was permissible if the above-mentioned compilations did not address the question to be decided.[48]

This is what jurists call a codification-collection, a system that limits to a small number of texts the materials upon which judicial authorities may draw in handing down rulings. In contrast to the official thematic codification of legal norms, which implicitly or explicitly repeals precedent texts, whatever their origin, this form of semicodification has the advantage of giving actors a feeling of continuity. The establishment of *Majallat al-ahkam al-'adliyya* in the Ottoman Empire represented a genuine break with local legal practices. Little by little, the Islamic legal corpus and its representatives were marginalized in favor of European codes, with the exception of the family code (marriage, inheritance, etc.), which continued to be inspired by Islamic norms. Nearly all Arab countries followed this path, and the members of the religious establishment were conscious of this change.[49] It was mainly for this reason that the ulama blacklisted the code compiled by the Meccan Hanbali judge Ahmad Abd Allah al-Qari' (d. 1940).[50] Hoping to imitate the Ottoman *Majalla*, al-Qari thematically compiled into article form norms drawn from classic Hanbali works of jurisprudence: his collection was titled *Majallat al-Ahkam al-Hanbaliyya* (Code of Legal and Judicial Dispositions according to the Hanbali School).

The question of codification subsequently disappeared from the Saudi scene, reappearing only in the second half of the 1950s. The process of state construction required the introduction of a number of codes to govern various state sectors. The religious establishment was not opposed to the establishment of this system, but it did oppose the methods employed (the introduction of positive laws and the recruitment of jurists with a modern training), which reflected a lack of respect for sharia and the spiritual and temporal prerogatives of its representatives. The objective of Muhammad ibn Ibrahim and his accomplices was to "Islamicize" these codes and thereby achieve control over the new legal and judicial bodies.

That being said, the ulama remained opposed to any attempt at official thematic systemization of legal norms in the judicial domain *stricto sensu*. The first text that clearly expressed their position on this question was published in 1969. Abd al-Malik ibn Ibrahim Al al-Shaykh (d. 1984), brother of the grand mufti and head of the Committee for the Promotion of Virtue and the Prevention of Vice in the province of Hijaz, gave the young judge Abd Allah al-Bassam (d. 2004)—subsequently a member of the Committee of Grand Ulama and the corporation's main historiographer—the task of writing an epistle to refute an article published in a Saudi newspaper calling for sharia to be codified.

The argument that al-Bassam developed in his short letter, titled *The Codification of Sharia: Its Damaging Effects and Perversions* (*Taqnin al-shariʿa adraruhu wa mafasiduhu*), can be summarized in four main points: (1) sharia is eternal and cannot in consequence be set in the form of a code; (2) the Islamic legal corpus is so rich and vast that it cannot be contained in a simple code; (3) judges must preserve their freedom of conscience and of maneuver, which allows them to pronounce judgments in conformity with divine will; and (4) calls for codification are just an external plot to destroy Islam from within by alienating it from divine precepts.[51] The young judge obviously supported his remarks with scriptural citations, historical examples, and rational arguments. These have been reiterated and expanded upon by detractors of codification up until the present day.

Four years after al-Bassam's text appeared, King Faysal asked the ulama to officially express themselves on the question of the codification of legal norms deduced from sharia. It seems that the royal initiative was part of a dual dynamic: the process of constructing modern state structures and fragmenting religious authority in order to acquire control over its representatives.

Whatever Faysal's motivations, the procedure was launched. The secretary general of the Committee of Grand Ulama transmitted the king's request to the Permanent Commission, whose members, with assistance from a dozen religious personnel, set about preparing a detailed study of the issue of codification.[52] Indeed, all aspects of the question were reviewed and all opinions, for or against, presented. What's more, the report's authors did not limit themselves to examining the opinions of Hanbali ulama; they also called upon the authorities of other Sunni legal schools, both classical and modern. The study nevertheless remained biased, with its authors making no attempt to conceal their hostility toward any attempt at codification.[53] Once finished, the study was submitted, in keeping with the established procedure, to the general secretary of the committee responsible for transmitting copies to the other members and to the royal cabinet.

After receiving the study, the ulama had about one month to read it and reach their own opinions—in reality, nearly all of them already had a clear-cut opinion on the matter. The meeting of ulama led to a heated debate between opponents and supporters of codification. With a majority of ten out of sixteen votes, the opponents of codification carried the day. On 8 May 1973, a fatwa forbidding codification was issued by the Committee of Grand Ulama.[54]

According to the most eminent members of the religious establishment, codifying norms deduced from sharia and compelling judges to scrupulously apply such a system, far from being the best way to reform the Saudi judicial system, would for the following reasons produce undesirable consequences:[55]

1. Codification would oblige judges to use norms that were sometimes contrary to their opinions and convictions. This was a blameworthy innovation that had been rejected by the pious ancestors, in particular Malik ibn Anas (d. 795), when the Abbasid caliph Abu Ja'far al-Mansur (754–755) proposed imposing his collection of traditions, *al-Muwatta'*, on the entire empire (see chapter 1).
2. The undertaking sought to control judges, for over time the code would prevent them from directly referring to scriptural citations and classical sources.
3. Codification leads directly to the adoption of positive laws. In order to prevent vice in keeping with the legal principle of *sadd al-dhara'i'* (the prevention of risks of vice) and maintain the Law's sovereignty, it is imperative to forbid it.
4. Establishing a code, whatever its quality, cannot prevent various sentences from being handed down on affairs that at first glance appear similar. Countries that use these codes do not escape from this problem.
5. The population does not need to know the arguments of the judge and the various sources upon which he draws in handing down his verdict. The overwhelming majority of people in countries that use codes are ignorant of the law and need lawyers to defend their interests.

In order to make the judicial system more effective, the members of the Committee of Grand Ulama recommended the following measures:[56]

1. Giving special attention to the training of magistrates by establishing continuous education programs, internships, and sabbaticals that allow them to bring themselves up-to-date intellectually.

2. Reducing the number of courts and concentrating them in the kingdom's large cities. In this way, judges would be able to rapidly meet and exchange their points of view on a given matter. They would also be able to locate all of the bibliographical references they need. Only agents of socialization (such as imams, predicators, and notaries) need be sent to remote villages.
3. Imposing a draconian procedure for recruiting magistrates.
4. Establishing commissions consisting of leading members of the religious establishment responsible for studying delicate topical or unprecedented questions and issuing fatawa.

While the majority of the Committee of Grand Ulama's members supported this fatwa, a minority freely expressed a contrary opinion in writing, in keeping with legal procedure. Indeed, the six members of the committee who voted in favor of codification[57] wrote a joint text in which they defended their position, advancing the following arguments:[58]

1. The political power seems to be seriously considering the creation of codes. If the Committee of Grand Ulama refuses to oversee this enterprise, the authorities will have no other choice but to turn to modern jurists. That will have more than regrettable consequences since it will lead to the introduction of positive laws.[59]
2. Codification is a reality since magistrates are obliged to rely on a limited legal corpus (the Hanbali works cited above). The government is therefore seeking only to regulate and institutionalize an established fact.
3. Codification is not a blameworthy innovation but an historical reality that exists in all Muslim countries. The four legal schools of Sunni Islam long ago ratified it (several examples were cited in support of this claim).
4. Most contemporary magistrates have a modest intellectual level that does not permit them to directly interpret scriptural sources or the rich Hanbali corpus. One thus has a right to impose a code upon them in conformity with sharia in order to safeguard the general interest and protect the rights of believers.
5. The classic corpus supplies no response to contemporary legal problems such as bank transactions, insurance, import-export problems, public markets, and so on, and most judges have no competence in these domains. If the clerical corps does not take back control of things, the government will ultimately impose special courts where positive laws will be applied.
6. In the contemporary period, Grand Mufti Muhammad ibn Ibrahim and the kingdom's highest judicial bodies put out a number of decrees requiring magistrates to hand down a particular sentence in certain types of case.

7. Codification can help promote religious homogenization and unification around common principles. The examples of Caliph Uthman (644–656), who imposed a single revision of the Qur'anic text, and the famous Umayyad governor al-Hajjaj (d. 714), who established diacritic marks to standardize its reading, were cited in support of this point.
8. Several Muslim countries need a model to follow, and only Saudi Arabia can supply it.

The fatwa of the Committee of Grand Ulama and the text of its members who voted for or against codification call for several remarks. Despite their apparent disagreements, each of the two parties only sought to preserve the centrality of the Hanbali-Wahhabi tradition and the privileges of its representatives. While the ulama who voted against codification feared the introduction of positive laws and the emergence of a rival elite, that of the positivist jurists (as was the case in other Arab countries), those who voted for it feared de facto marginalization by the government. Their disagreement only concerned the strategy that was to be adopted vis-à-vis this threat. There was thus no fundamental disagreement. Like members of any ideologically based corporation, the representatives of Hanbali-Wahhabism presented various perspectives in pursuit of the same objective: to perpetuate the tradition while adapting it to political and historical imperatives.

Even if the Permanent Commission's study of codification drew upon several scriptural citations, neither of the two parties returned to them in defending their positions. Indeed, the citations in question were very vague and could be interpreted in several ways. Both groups of ulama thus preferred to base their position on logical argument, historical events, and the interpretation of classical Muslim jurists. Opponents and supporters of codification alike thus had recourse to *ijtihad*—that is, "the free exercise of personal opinion [in order to] draw valid conclusions from the Qur'an, the Sunna of the Prophet, and consensus, by analogy or by systematic reasoning."[60] All positions resulting from *ijtihad* respond to a particular situation and precise sociohistoric context. In contrast to positions based on scriptural citation, this allows them to be transformed in order to respond to the requirements of a fluid social space. In other words, there was nothing dogmatic or final about the ulama's stance. It reflected the concerns of a corporation that was undergoing institutionalization and feared a loss of influence and being cut off from the path to salvation.

Even if, for the political, economic, and social reasons briefly sketched above, the debate over codification no longer occupied the foreground for a period of thirty years, voices were raised from time to time to defend one position or another.[61] But a marked tendency gradually emerged from this debate. More and more ulama (particularly those drawn from the younger generations who had studied in the Islamic universities of foreign countries) joined the ranks of supporters of codification in the 1980s and, above all, the 1990s. This was due to several factors. Religious discourse now dominated the social space and constituted the main point of reference for all actors, particularly the monarchy. It could no longer easily be challenged. In this context, codification could render the judicial system more transparent, efficient, and modern, allowing it to further influence and homogenize the population. Codification could also serve the interests of foreign policy. What's more, the kingdom's political and economic partners could no longer reproach its leaders with having an archaic and nontransparent judicial system: it would facilitate Saudi Arabia's integration into the new world system, particularly in what concerned the World Trade Organization. At the same time, the kingdom would become a model for other Muslim states, proving to the entire world the eternal validity of sharia.[62] In short, the codification of norms deduced from sharia was a matter of general interest (al-maslaha al-'amma) in the eyes of the ulama. After rationally considering the matter, the ulama had realized that its benefits outweighed its costs.

Despite the reluctance of several of its leading members, the pro-codification stance thus slowly but surely gained ground within the corporation. The terrorist attacks against the United States on 11 September 2001, Al-Qaeda's attacks on Saudi territory in 2003 and 2004, and the arrival to power of Abd Allah in 2005 helped accelerate this process. On the one hand, the ulama wanted to once and for all distinguish themselves from Jihadist movements, part of an ideological readjustment to which we will return in chapter 9. On the other, they wanted to guarantee a place for themselves in the process of modernization and the reform of Saudi state structures begun by the monarchy. When the Saudi judicial system was placed on new foundations in 2007,[63] Minister of Justice Abd Allah Al al-Shaykh (b. 1948)—Grand Mufti Muhammad ibn Ibrahim's son and a member of the Committee of Grand Ulama—officially launched the process of codifying the legal norm deduced from sharia with the blessing of the palace and the support of a large number of his colleagues.

The first step consisted of publishing *Mudawwanat al-Ahkam Qada'iyya* (Anthology of Judicial Sentences), a collection of type-judgments and the decisions of the High Council of the Magistracy concerning personal status, criminal questions, commercial transactions, and so on.[64] The stated objective of this publication was uniquely pedagogical: to help familiarize judges and the actors of the judicial system with the judgments handed down by the kingdom's various courts so that they could better apply the procedure. Unofficially, however, this initiative sought to encourage the magistrates to refer to this collection in handing down their sentences, something that would over time allow the standardization of judgments on similar cases.[65] Three editions of the *Mudawwana* appeared between 2007 and 2008.[66]

As soon as he took office in February 2009, Muhammad al-Isa (b. 1965), minister of justice and a member of the Committee of Grand Ulama, declared that codification was one of the pillars of the reform and modernization of the Saudi judicial system. Work thus had to begin without delay. He therefore announced that several specialized commissions would be established to develop codes concerning the various domains of social life (*al-mu'amalat*).[67]

In order to confer real legitimacy upon this undertaking, however, it was necessary to receive the approval of the Committee of Grand Ulama, whose members held ideological authority. The question of codification was submitted to the Council of the Committee during its seventy-first session, which took place in al-Ta'if on 25 July 2009.[68] The debate was lively. For the first time, however, supporters of codification seemed to have the upper hand. Yet, as several reluctant members required an additional extension in order to further study this delicate question, the vote was postponed to the next session.[69] Supported by the monarchy, the supporters of codification decided to take no chances. An expert commission, led by members of the committee, was appointed to draft a new report that tipped the scales in favor of codification.[70] The seventy-second session of the Council of the Committee of Grand Ulama, held in Riyadh on 30 January 2010, marked a decisive step in the process of routinizing the Hanbali-Wahhabi tradition.[71] Apart from definitively condemning terrorism, a subject we will more extensively consider in chapter 9, the Saudi ulama issued a fatwa authorizing the codification of legal norms deduced from sharia according to specific procedures.[72] After receiving royal approval for this legal opinion, a long process of elaboration was launched. While it will no doubt be studded with pitfalls, it would constitute a first in Arab-Muslim history should it succeed.

The preceding discussion makes it clear that the Committee of Grand Ulama, a federative state body, had come to play a critical role for the Saudi monarchy in the political and religious domains. In addition to exercising control over this body's agenda, the royal house endeavored to control access to it. For its part, the religious elite sought, via its formal and informal networks, to impose more or less rigorous conditions on candidates for high clerical office in order to maintain its cohesion and homogeneity and perpetuate its discursive hegemony. Yet no document mentions the conditions that an *'alim* must meet to join the Committee of Grand Ulama. The only way to raise the veil on these tacit conditions of access is to examine the careers and processes of socialization of the fifty-two ulama who presently sit on the committee or did so in the past. Studying their social, "ethnic," and regional origins; education; *cursus honorum*; and mobility will allow us to clarify the conditions of access to this elite and shed new light on the main characteristics of this stratified and differentiated group. And, in the interests of comparison and historical perspective, we will set this elite in the context of its sociopolitical milieu, that of the kingdom's other elites—whether ministers, high-ranking civil servants, or members of the Advisory Council (Majlis al-Shura). This will allow us to enumerate the main conditions, more or less implicit, of access to this elite and consider its evolution. It will also allow us to analyze the extent to which the Hanbali-Wahhabi establishment shows signs of self-policing, self-regulation, reproduction, and adaptation under the benevolent eye of the political authorities in order to better dominate the Saudi religious space and shine forth as an example for the Muslim world.

7

Raising the Veil on the Conditions of Access to the Religious Establishment

From Self-Made Men to Heirs: The Social Origins of the Ulama

The predication of Muhammad ibn Abd al-Wahhab made many disciples. In the founder's lifetime, several of his followers showed great devotion and zeal to propagate *al-daʿwa*.[1] Upon the master's death, his charisma was "routinized" in Max Weber's sense of the term: while the members of his family inherited a large part of this charisma, his disciples also benefited from routinization. The result was the creation of a number of "houses" of ulama (*buyut ʿilm*, sing. *bayt ʿilm*) that monopolized the religious space of the successive Saudi emirates up until the middle of the twentieth century (though several isolated cases of individual success did exist). The most important of these houses of ulama included those of Al al-Shaykh, direct descendants of Ibn Abd al-Wahhab; Al Slim; Al al-Qadi; and Al ʿAtiq. Beginning in the 1950s, however, the Saudi Arabian clerical corps underwent a degree of "democratization." This can be seen in the membership rolls of the Committee of Grand Ulama since its creation in 1971. My interviews with and study of the biographies of members of the committee have allowed me to identify three broad categories of ulama: the self-made men, the children of midlevel religious personnel, and the heirs of the houses of ulama.

In the first category, I include foreign and Saudi-origin ulama from socially and economically "modest" backgrounds. Study and promotion to high religious offices offer incalculable opportunities to clerics from this category and guarantee them upward social mobility. Few, however, experience this type of ascent. In a society of houses based on personal relations and networks of solidarity, social mobility is in theory possible only for individuals possessing a degree of social and cultural capital—something that, by definition, self-made men do not possess. This is reflected in the committee itself: though highly respected for their personal qualities and knowledge, its self-made men are "looked down upon" by their colleagues because of their social origins. In fact, the appointment of self-made men to the Committee of Grand Ulama has taken place only on four occasions since its creation: in 1971, 1977, 1987, and 2005.

The second category, offspring of midlevel religious personnel, consists of ulama whose kinsmen held religious posts in the magistracy or public instruction or were not especially renowned imams or preachers at mosques. I have also included in this category ulama whose relatives were "experts" on the Qur'an or an area of Hanbali-Wahhabi theology and held posts in the liberal, administrative, or manual professions. Ulama drawn from this category have constituted more than 67 percent of the committee's members since its creation.

Family background plays a decisive role in their social promotion. Midlevel religious personnel themselves initiate their children into religious knowledge or sometimes confide it to trusted tutors. Their family networks allow them to study under the guidance of the most renowned and influential masters and to frequent the best-stocked libraries. What's more, the apprentice ulama of the generation preceding the petroleum boom were not obliged to work or simultaneously pursue other studies in order to provide for their needs. Indeed, it is important for midlevel religious personnel to train "prodigal" sons as great ulama in order to ensure social mobility for the entire lineage, for becoming a member of the Committee of Grand Ulama brings affluence and social influence alike.

Yet few of these ulama succeed in accumulating symbolic capital.[2] Ulama who succeed in transmitting this capital to their heirs are even more rare. When such transmission occurs, one witnesses the creation of a house of ulama. This was the experience of Ibn Humayd's family.

Born into a lineage of midlevel religious personnel, Abd Allah ibn Humayd (d. 1982) climbed one by one all of the rungs of the religious establishment.[3] After an extensive course of study in Islamic law and theology under the supervision of Riyadh's best-known masters of religious studies, he became the main disciple of Grand Mufti Muhammad ibn Ibrahim. His close relations with Ibn Ibrahim led him to be appointed to juridico-religious offices that otherwise would have been inaccessible to a debutant (which is what he then was). At the age of twenty-eight, he became of one of Riyadh's foremost judges, a post to which a man is normally appointed only at the end of his career. Three years later, he was named judge of the important region of Sudayr. In 1944, Ibn Humayd became the grand judge of the Al-Qasim. He was now considered the *marji'*, or religious reference, for the entire region. Several months before King Abd al-Aziz died in 1953, he appointed Ibn Humayd judge of Mecca.

Unhappy with the policies of King Saud and seeking to avoid becoming compromised in the conflict between the king and his brother Crown Prince Faysal, Ibn Humayd resigned from his duties to exclusively focus on teaching. His apparent neutrality was nevertheless entirely relative: in reality, the 'alim was on Faysal's side. He was thus one of the signatories of the fatwa confirming Saud's deposition in 1964. Several weeks after this legal opinion was issued, he resumed his duties as president of the body responsible for overseeing the holy places of Mecca and Medina. At the same time, he became the chief preacher (*khatib*) of the Grand Mosque of Mecca. This post gave Ibn Humayd a national profile, and he gradually became one of the kingdom's leading religious figures. In 1971, he was appointed to the newly created Committee of Grand Ulama. Four years later, he reached, so to speak, the summit of his career, becoming the president of the High Council of the Magistracy and thus the supreme magistrate of Saudi Arabia.[4]

Ibn Humayd is not the only example of success in the kingdom during the second half of the twentieth century—Abd al-Aziz ibn Baz (d. 1999) and Muhammad ibn Uthaymin (d. 2001) also reached the summit of the religious establishment. But the novelty of Ibn Humayd's dazzling career resides in the fact that he succeeded in transmitting his symbolic capital to his heirs and in creating a new house of ulama. His son Salih inherited his father's main prerogatives.[5]

Born in 1950, under the benevolent eye of his father, Salih pursued a simultaneously traditional and modern education, which was crowned with a doctorate in Muslim law. He then began a university career, which rapidly led him to the summit of the religious establishment. In the space of just a few years, he became dean of the Department of Sharia at Mecca's Umm Al-Qura University. His new duties and "knowledge" of the English language allowed him to participate in international meetings and present a modern image of the clerical corps. At the same time, he replaced his father at the head of the body responsible for overseeing the holy places. He simultaneously took the very prestigious and prominent position of imam and preacher of the Grand Mosque of Mecca. In 1993, Salih was named a member of the Advisory Council (Majlis al-Shura). In December 2001, he became a member of the Committee of Grand Ulama. Several months later, he took over leadership of the Advisory Council. In 2009, he inherited his father's post as president of the High Council of the Magistracy. Salih Ibn Humayd is already preparing his children to take over from him: a house of ulama is born.[6]

The provinces of Hijaz and Al-Ahsa', known for their religious heterogeneity, have supplied many midlevel religious personnel. Most members of the

Committee of Grand Ulama from these regions come from lineages of midlevel religious personnel, while a few are self-made men or belong to houses of ulama. More important is the fact that the families of these ulama belong to the four legal schools of Sunni Islam. For example, the Meccans Mihdar Aqil (d. 1984), Abd Allah Khayyat (d. 1995), and Abd al-Wahhab Abu Sulayman (b. 1937), all from families of midlevel religious personnel, are Shafi'i, Hanafi, and Maliki, respectively. Ali al-Duwayhi (b. 1956), originally from the eastern province and a self-made man, is Hanbali. Qays al-Mubaraki (b. 1960) is the offspring of the oldest line of Maliki ulama in Al-Ahsa'.

THE AL AL-SHAYKH: THE LEVITES OF HANBALI-WAHHABISM

The portrait of ulama would be incomplete if one omits the country's largest religious lineage, which reigned supreme over the clerical corps from the second half of the eighteenth century: the Al al-Shaykh, direct descendants of Muhammad ibn Abd al-Wahhab and the kingdom's second most eminent lineage after that of the ruling house (see Figure 5). Indeed, since the advent of the Saudi Emirate, its members have held the highest religious offices. Its symbolic capital has been transmitted uninterrupted from generation to generation ever since Hanbali-Wahhabism first emerged (Figure 6).

Upon the death of Ibn Abd al-Wahhab, his descendants received a good portion of his spiritual and temporal inheritance. Thanks to the ideological support they brought to the House of Saud, the Al al-Shaykh were able to freely oversee the religious space.[7] In addition to their position at the head of the religious establishment (*marji'* and, later, grand mufti), they took control, as we have seen, of the main juridico-religious offices (imam in the largest mosques of the emirate, then kingdom; the main offices of the magistracy; leadership of the Committee for the Promotion of Virtue and the Prevention of Vice, etc.). They also controlled all networks of socialization by managing the domains of education and high culture with an iron fist. Indeed, up until the 1960s, 90 percent of the Hanbali-Wahhabi corpus consisted of works written by Ibn Abd al-Wahhab and his descendants. The delegation of ulama who swore allegiance (*al-bay'a*) to King Saud in 1953 was made up of seven individuals, six of whom were Al al-Shaykh.[8] Of the twelve signatories to the fatwa giving full authority to Prince Faysal in 1962, five belonged to this lineage.[9] Between 1950 and 1960, the grand mufti and head of the judicial system was of course Muhammad ibn Ibrahim Al al-Shaykh, the vice mufti and administrator of Dar al-Ifta' was his son Ibrahim,[10] the vice president of the judicial system was his other son Abd al-Aziz,[11] and the director of the religious education system (of the religious studies institutes and

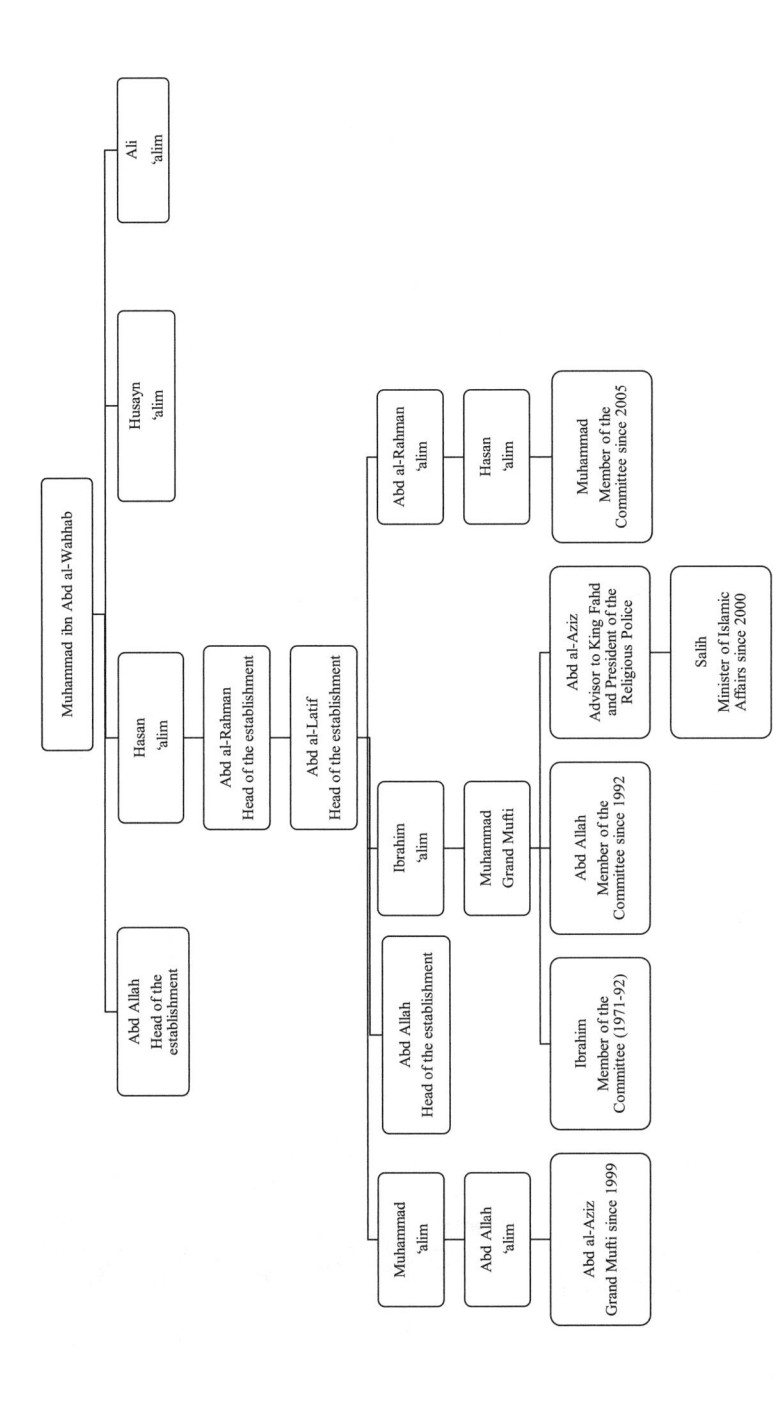

Figure 5. Genealogy of the Al al-Shaykh.

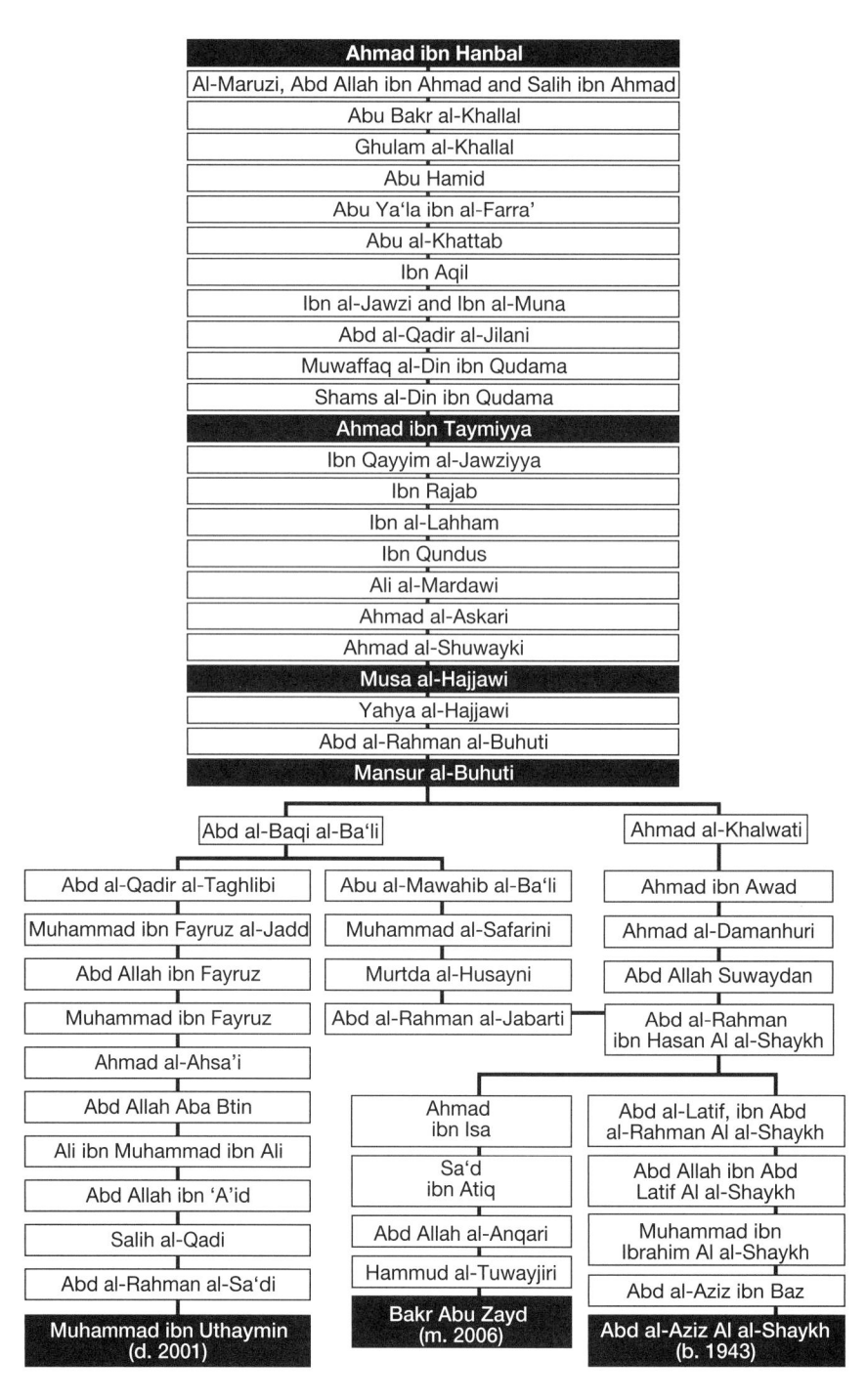

```
Ahmad ibn Hanbal
├── Al-Maruzi, Abd Allah ibn Ahmad and Salih ibn Ahmad
│   └── Abu Bakr al-Khallal
│       └── Ghulam al-Khallal
│           └── Abu Hamid
│               └── Abu Ya'la ibn al-Farra'
│                   └── Abu al-Khattab
│                       └── Ibn Aqil
│                           └── Ibn al-Jawzi and Ibn al-Muna
│                               └── Abd al-Qadir al-Jilani
│                                   └── Muwaffaq al-Din ibn Qudama
│                                       └── Shams al-Din ibn Qudama

Ahmad ibn Taymiyya
├── Ibn Qayyim al-Jawziyya
│   └── Ibn Rajab
│       └── Ibn al-Lahham
│           └── Ibn Qundus
│               └── Ali al-Mardawi
│                   └── Ahmad al-Askari
│                       └── Ahmad al-Shuwayki

Musa al-Hajjawi
├── Yahya al-Hajjawi
│   └── Abd al-Rahman al-Buhuti

Mansur al-Buhuti
├── Abd al-Baqi al-Ba'li
│   ├── Abd al-Qadir al-Taghlibi
│   │   ├── Muhammad ibn Fayruz al-Jadd
│   │   ├── Abd Allah ibn Fayruz
│   │   ├── Muhammad ibn Fayruz
│   │   ├── Ahmad al-Ahsa'i
│   │   ├── Abd Allah Aba Btin
│   │   ├── Ali ibn Muhammad ibn Ali
│   │   ├── Abd Allah ibn 'A'id
│   │   ├── Salih al-Qadi
│   │   ├── Abd al-Rahman al-Sa'di
│   │   └── **Muhammad ibn Uthaymin (d. 2001)**
│   └── Abu al-Mawahib al-Ba'li
│       ├── Muhammad al-Safarini
│       ├── Murtda al-Husayni
│       ├── Abd al-Rahman al-Jabarti
│       ├── Ahmad ibn Isa
│       ├── Sa'd ibn Atiq
│       ├── Abd Allah al-Anqari
│       ├── Hammud al-Tuwayjiri
│       └── **Bakr Abu Zayd (m. 2006)**
└── Ahmad al-Khalwati
    ├── Ahmad ibn Awad
    ├── Ahmad al-Damanhuri
    ├── Abd Allah Suwaydan
    ├── Abd al-Rahman ibn Hasan Al al-Shaykh
    ├── Abd al-Latif, ibn Abd al-Rahman Al al-Shaykh
    ├── Abd Allah ibn Abd Latif Al al-Shaykh
    ├── Muhammad ibn Ibrahim Al al-Shaykh
    ├── Abd al-Aziz ibn Baz
    └── **Abd al-Aziz Al al-Shaykh (b. 1943)**
```

Figure 6. The main chains of transmission of Hanbali jurisprudence (ninth to the twenty-first centuries).

faculties) and editor-in-chief of the corporation's leading journal was his brother Abd al-Latif.[12] Abd Allah ibn Hasan controlled the religious space of the Hijaz (justice, education, the Committee for the Promotion of Virtue and the Prevention of Vice, etc.) until his death in 1959—he was replaced as head of the latter committee by the brother of Grand Mufti Abd al-Malik—and Salih ibn Abd al-Aziz was Riyadh's leading judge.[13] Finally, 80 percent of the future members of the establishment who carried out their initiatory voyage between the 1940s and the 1960s were disciples of Ibn Ibrahim and more or less closely frequented the circles of other offspring of the lineage.

The predominant position occupied by the Al al-Shaykh lineage in Saudi religious space must not be seen as an exceptional phenomenon. It is a matter of social reproduction commonplace in Muslim societies (with lineages controlling Sufi brotherhoods and ulama lineages in urban contexts) and elsewhere (the families of Jewish and, more generally, Semite priests, African and Asian sorcerers and shamans, Protestant pastors and Catholic prelates, etc.).[14] Like some of the holy lineages that have emerged in all cultural zones since antiquity, the descendants of Ibn Abd al-Wahhab were in all probability seen as symbols of historical continuity and guarantors of the preservation and transmission of the True Religion, that is, as a reference point of collective identity. Moreover, the heritage of the Al al-Shaykh constituted genuine material and immaterial capital to be jealously preserved and put to service. From an economic point of view, the monopoly in Arabia over writing, reading, and religious studies (which, it is to be recalled, governed all aspects of life) before the petroleum boom was a significant source of revenue, all the more so given that the heirs of the Najdi preacher had no other resources—neither a territorial base nor trade, agriculture, or artisanal activity. As we have seen, this monopoly, a true source of ideological authority alongside genealogy, allowed them to wield great sociopolitical influence. Finally, the cultural privileges afforded by the family milieu must not be overlooked. Thanks to their acquaintance with the libraries and teaching circles of their relatives, the Al al-Shaykh were very familiar with the Hanbali-Wahhabi corpus and the clerical habitus, something that immediately granted them the "body of knowledge, skills, and, above all, modes of expression which constitute the heritage of cultivated classes."[15]

The absolute control exercised by the Al al-Shaykh over the Saudi religious space came to an end with the death of Muhammad ibn Ibrahim in 1969. Several factors explain this change. The expansion of Hanbali-Wahhabism across most of the Arabian Peninsula and its institutionalization thanks to the flow of petroleum revenue required that the number of religious clerics be increased to oversee the market on the goods of salvation. The result of this was a democratization of clerical education, bringing a de facto end to the Al al-Shaykh monopoly. The vocational crisis within the lineage and the desire to discover new horizons are two other important elements that need to be considered. Indeed, the petroleum boom (*al-tafra*) offered opportunities for work and social promotion in all domains. Once it had begun, several offspring of the religious lineage set out on careers as politicians, military officers, businessmen, engineers, and doctors.[16] Finally, as we have seen, it seems that the strength and unity of the corporation as incarnated by the Al al-Shaykh lineage was a matter "of concern" to the monarchy. In the framework of King Faysal's policy of fragmenting religious authority, everything possible was done to "decapitate" the establishment by marginalizing its "natural" leaders in favor of newcomers. While Abd al-Aziz ibn Baz, a *khadiri* (a nontribal sedentary, implying lower status in the local social hierarchy) from a kindred of midlevel religious personnel, was appointed to head the corporation, only two members of the lineage—Ibrahim ibn Muhammad ibn Ibrahim Al al-Shaykh (d. 2007), initially intended to succeed his father in the post of grand mufti, and his brother, Abd al-Aziz (d. 2005)—held high-ranking clerical posts between 1971 and 1987.[17] The former was interim president of Dar al-Ifta'; a member of the Committee of Grand Ulama; director of the General Presidency for the Management of [Religious] Scholarship, Predication, and Guidance; minister of justice; and interim president of the High Council of the Magistracy.[18] The latter was director of the University of Riyadh from 1974 to 1976, president of the Committee for the Promotion of Virtue and the Prevention of Vice, member of the Advisory Council, and advisor to the royal cabinet.[19]

During the Islamist protests that followed the Iraqi invasion of Kuwait in 1990, the political authorities needed unwavering ideological support of a type that Abd al-Aziz ibn Baz seemed unable to supply as a result of his social profile and position in Saudi religious space (see chapter 9). In Saudi Arabia, as in many other countries, social interactions are based on personal relations and ties of kinship. Yet given his *khadiri* origin, Ibn Baz had no ties of kinship or clientelism with the ruling house and was associated with the interests of no lineage. Similarly, his entire image had been built on his consensual character. Indeed, he saw himself as *al-walid*, a term that can be translated as patriarch—that is, the spiritual father of most actors of the Saudi religious space. While such a stance could be an asset during periods of stability, it became a handicap during periods of crisis, when the political partner required full commitment on its behalf. It can even be said that Ibn Baz's ultimate condemnation of Islamist demands was due to the fact that some of their intrigues threatened one of the pillars of Hanbali-Wahhabi doctrine: the political order (a member of the

Al al-Shaykh, by contrast, would have taken the alliance with the ruling family into consideration). Aware of how dangerous a socially unmoored holder of religious authority could be for the future of the regime, the monarchy decided to return to its traditional alliance with the Al al-Shaykh, who were indissolubly linked with it by historical, matrimonial, and economic ties. Unable to sideline Ibn Baz, however, because he was widely respected by the population, King Fahd (1982–2005) created the post of vice grand mufti and appointed Abd al-Aziz ibn Abd Allah Al al-Shaykh to this position in 1993 to prepare the way for the old religious leader's succession.

The death of Ibn Baz in 1999 marked the return to normalcy in relations between the royal house and the descendants of Muhammad ibn Abd al-Wahhab: Abd al-Aziz ibn Abd Allah Al al-Shaykh was named grand mufti of the kingdom and president of the Committee of Grand Ulama. Since then, members of the Al al-Shaykh lineage have gradually reinvested the better part of the posts they had formerly occupied. Apart from the grand mufti, two members of the family sit on the Committee of Grand Ulama, another Al al-Shaykh is minister of Islamic affairs, and yet another was minister of justice and has since February 2009 served as president of the Advisory Council (see Figure 5).

THE PREDOMINANCE OF THE NAJDI CRESCENT

While the familial factor is certainly important, it must be noted that "tribal" membership remains a criterion of communalization—that is, of the creation of a subjective feeling of belonging to a given group, a matter of fundamental importance in Saudi Arabia.[20] After religion, membership of this type, which is generally invented,[21] is the main criterion of identity among the better part of the population. While the process of sedentarization put an end to the tribe as a social reality over the course of the twentieth century, it has nevertheless continued to serve as an undisputed symbol of reference. In a society that is for the most part based on personal relations reflected in real or fictive ties of kinship, the mobilization of a "genealogical network" also plays a fundamental role in social status and the group promotion of the individual.

It is thus not surprising to discover that ulama with tribal origins broadly dominate the Committee of Grand Ulama. They make up forty-one of the fifty-two members who have sat on the committee since its creation in 1971, or 79 percent of the total. They thus represent the lion's share. The eleven remaining seats have been occupied by ulama from various backgrounds: Hijaz town-dwellers of various origins (co-opted to represent their regions, an effort is made to choose the most "Hanbali-Wahhabized" or, failing that, quietist among

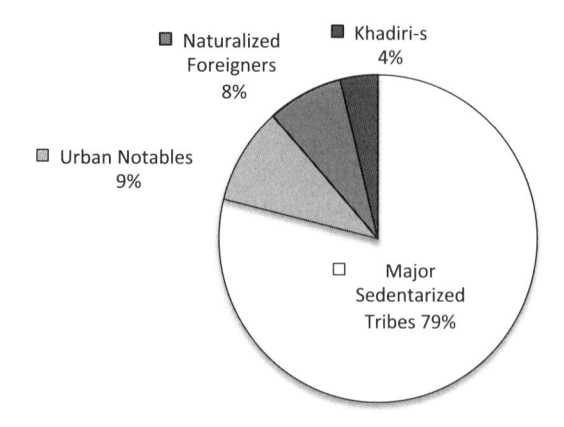

Figure 7. The "ethnic" origins of members of the Committee of Grand Ulama (1971–2010).

them), naturalized foreigners (they are Hanbali-Wahhabi, have "exceptional" talents, and have defended Hanbali-Wahhabism and the Saudi state), and inhabitants of Najd without tribal affiliation or *khadiri* (in principle, the latter owe their social promotion only to their personal abilities).

It can be observed from Figure 7 that belonging to the sedentarized tribal milieu plays a decisive role in the social promotion of ulama, with *'asabiyya* constituting a major added value for the accumulation of social capital. Although the tribes clearly dominate the committee in absolute terms, they are not representative of the Saudi ethnographic landscape. Indeed, some "tribes", such as the Banu Tamim, the Banu Zayd, and the Banu Khalid, are "overrepresented," whereas others, like the Utayba, have only a single "representative" despite their numeric importance in the population. Finally, other tribes, such as the Shammar, the Harb, the Mutayr, the Ajman, the Ghamid, and so on, have no representatives on the committee. While the marginalization of the Shammar, the Utayba, the Mutayr, and the Ajman can be explained by their participation in past rebellions,[22] the marginalization of other tribes can only be due to religious and, above all, regional factors. In some cases, the personal charisma of an *'alim* allows his *khadiri* origins to be overlooked. This is the case of Ibn Baz, who was able to rise to the very summit of the corporation solely on the basis of his theological knowledge, moral integrity, popularity, and services to the monarchy. His charisma and symbolic power have made him the most famous contemporary Hanbali-Wahhabi dignitary.

The Kingdom of Saudi Arabia is a Najdi kingdom. Most members of the Saudi elite are from the region of Najd, a fief of the dynasty and of the Hanbali-

Wahhabi doctrine. More recent studies (dating from the past decade) demonstrate this by use of statistical data; however, they examine only ministerial elites, the high civil service, and members of the Advisory Council. They thus offer no information regarding the ulama. In what follows, we attempt to make up for this lacuna. Of the fifty-two individuals who have been members of the committee since its creation in 1971, almost three-quarters have come from Najd (see Figure 8).

Two things might be said about the fact that the majority of the Committee of Grand Ulama's members have come from Najd. It is easy to understand why only 4 percent of the grand ulama have been from Al-Ahsa' given that a significant part of the eastern province's population is Shiite or non–Hanbali-Wahhabi Sunni. It is similarly easy to understand why only 9 percent of them have been from the Hijaz, where the population, though Sunni, is not generally Hanbali-Wahhabi. The figure of 6 percent for ulama from the country's South, by contrast, may seem absurd given that it is a majority Hanbali-Wahhabi region. The hypothesis of regional preference thus can be reasonably maintained: if 73 percent of grand ulama are from Najd, it is because it is the fief of Hanbali-Wahhabism and the House of Saud. For these reasons, their fidelity to both is beyond question.

If one compares the figures put forward for the Committee of Grand Ulama with those for the Council of Ministers, within which Najdi constitute 72 percent of members; the Advisory Council, where Najdi hold a majority of 51 percent;

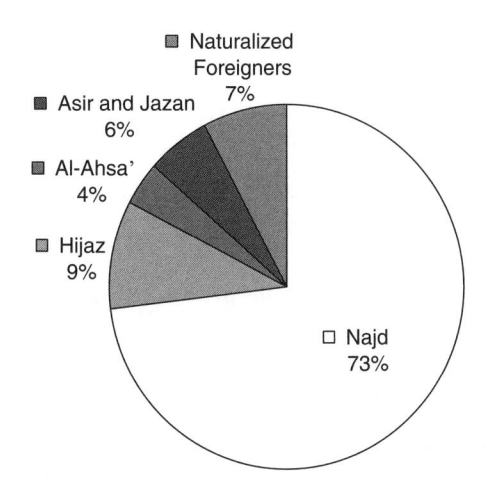

Figure 8. The regional origins of members of the Committee of Grand Ulama (1971–2010).

the plenipotentiary ministers, 78 percent of whom are from Najd; and high-ranking civil servants, 67 percent of whom are Najdi; it is clear that most of the ruling class, whether religious or political, is drawn from Central Arabia.[23] Though mainly Hanbali-Wahhabi, those from the South represent only 1 percent of ministers, 7 percent of members of the Advisory Council, less than 5 percent of plenipotentiary ministers, and less than 9 percent of high-ranking civil servants:[24] the argument presented above can be applied here as well.

Let's take a closer look at the figures: while only 9 percent of ulama are from the Hijaz, 20 percent of the Council of Ministers, 29 percent of the Advisory Council, and 22 percent of high-ranking civil servants are from this region. Moreover, looking yet closer at the figures, it seems that at the moment of the committee's creation, 29 percent of the ulama were from the Hijaz as opposed to 9 percent today, as we have seen. As it becomes established and no longer needs senior personnel, the committee, like all other state bodies, thus tends to close itself to anything that is not Najdi. To this it must be added that once they have won a place on the committee, non–Hanbali-Wahhabi ulama conceal their beliefs—or at least avoid speaking of them—and very much fill the role of "extras."

The Committee of Grand Ulama thus seeks to give an illusion of openness: the main regions are generally all "represented," even if only in small proportions. But in reality the Najdi element still dominates the committee by a large margin. What's more, even if there were to be more openness, with the committee accepting Sufis and Shiites of all persuasions in the framework of routinization, it would need to retain only a 51 percent majority of Hanbali-Wahhabis—Najdis—to ensure that votes pass with an absolute majority in the committee and that the Hanbali-Wahhabi vision continues to dominate.

Finally, in what concerns ulama of foreign origin: they were allowed to join the committee (three of them) only at the moment of its creation. They were co-opted because of the religious establishment's lack of senior personnel. Devoted to the Saudi state and the corporation but born non–Hanbali-Wahhabi,[25] these foreigners "converted" out of personal conviction. Without a social or tribal base in Saudi Arabia, they owed their rise to the state. While the Islamic solidarity initiated by King Faysal favored the integration of such foreign elements, the committee has since closed its doors to additional co-optation.

To conclude this point, if one were to trace a line between the towns in which the Najdi members of the Committee of Grand Ulama originated, it would form a crescent. I call this the "Najdi crescent" (Map 2). It constitutes the epicenter of Saudi Arabia as well as that of Hanbali-Wahhabism. Yet, while the ulama of

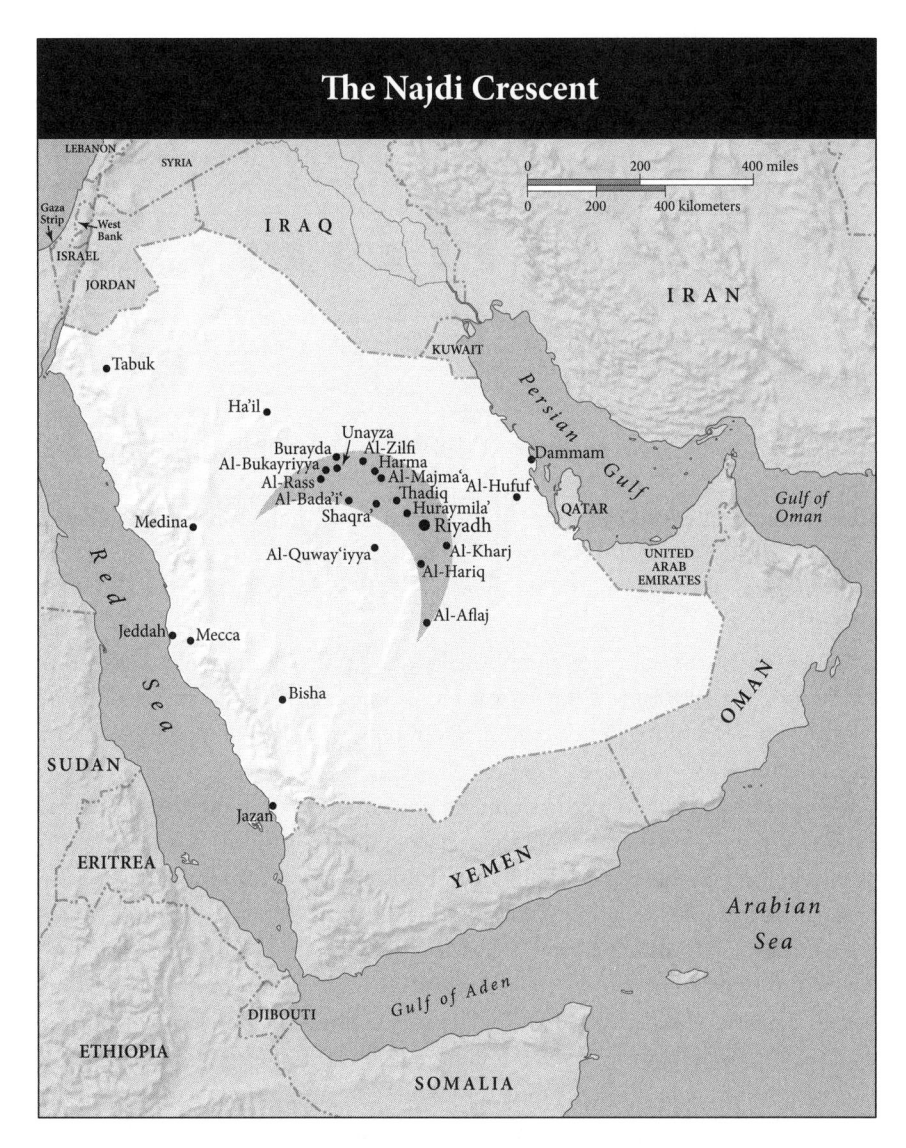

Map 2. The Najdi crescent.

Najd hold a clear majority within the committee, one must not suppose that all of the towns and districts of this region are equally "represented" on it. Najd contains three main districts: the region of Riyadh (Al-'Arid, Al-Washm, Al-Dilam, Sudayr, etc.) has supplied twenty-seven ulama, Al-Qasim ten, and Ha'il none. The first two districts present a near balance in the distribution of ulama:

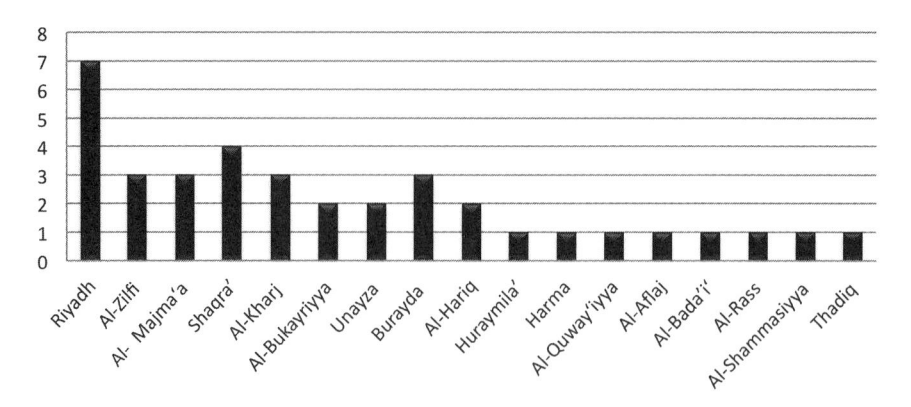

Figure 9. Distribution of grand ulama among the towns of Najd (1971–2010).

in the region of Riyadh (outside of the city itself, which alone supplies seven ulama), the towns have each supplied between one and four ulama. Similarly, in the region of Al-Qasim, the number of ulama varies between one and three (Figure 9).

Ha'il, for its part, has been intentionally marginalized for an obvious historical reason: the Al Rashid Emirate was long a direct rival of the House of Saud. Just one representative of this region is found on the Council of Ministers and one on the Advisory Council.[26]

It should finally be noted that some regions of Najd are totally excluded and have not supplied a single *'alim*: the example of Al-Dawadmi, to cite just one, is due to the fact that most inhabitants of this town are from the Utayba tribe, some members of which are of doubtful loyalty to the House of Saud. There is thus subregionalization within the larger scheme of regionalization. Similarly, no grand *'alim* comes from the regions of the North, where the population, which became Hanbali-Wahhabi in the 1960s, possesses no clerical tradition. Finally, no Shiite has ever been admitted to the Committee of Grand Ulama.

The Saudi religious elite is thus subject to the same rule that governs other categories of the ruling class: endo-recruitment. This is a commonplace phenomenon encountered in all societies, particularly those with patrimonial systems. In order to maintain its cohesion and strength, the dominant group, whatever its vocation or the disagreements among its members, must maintain endogamous networks founded on, in the Saudi case, kinship, common cultural reference points in the broad sense of the term, and regional belonging. That said, family, tribal, and regional advantages do not alone suffice: the apprentice grand *'alim* must also have followed a particular course of study in order to join the committee.

FROM THE *IJAZA* TO THE DOCTORATE: THE INSTITUTIONALIZATION OF CLERICAL EDUCATION

Of the fifty-two ulama who have been members of the Committee of Grand Ulama since its creation in 1971, 25 percent (or thirteen of them) received a traditional education and 75 percent (or thirty-nine of them) a "modern" one. Fewer than a quarter of the ulama thus followed a traditional degree course. My interviews, together with Hanbali-Wahhabi biographical collections, have allowed me to identify these paths of initiation and describe the "ideal-typical" traditional cursus followed by members of the establishment.

In keeping with a tradition that has been current in the Muslim world since the High Middle Ages, apprentice ulama (*talib al-'ilm*, pl. *talabat al-'ilm*) study the Qur'an between the ages of five and eight. Candidates for the clerical profession from a modest background—those who will later be self-made men—learn the Qur'an at a Qur'anic school (*kuttab*) under the direction of a moderately well-known shaykh. The children of midlevel religious personnel and the offspring of houses of ulama, for their part, learn the Qur'an directly under the supervision of their father, a member of their lineage, or a well-known private tutor. One can easily imagine the difficulties that face apprentice grand ulama from modest backgrounds and the discrepancies that exist from the outset among the various sociocultural classes.

Following this phase of apprenticeship, they begin studying Arabic grammar and rhetoric, indispensable tools for a better understanding of the holy texts, and learn by heart the three main works of Muhammad ibn Abd al-Wahhab on divine unity (*al-tawhid*), the foundation of Hanbali-Wahhabism: *Kitab al-Tawhid* (*The Book of the Unity of God*), *Kashf al-shubuhat* (*Clarification of the Doubts*), and *al-Usul al-thalatha* (*The Three Fundamental Principles [of Divine Unity]*).

The third moment in the classical program of study is the quest for knowledge (*talab al-'ilm*) under the guidance of renowned ulama. Indeed, future grand ulama must bring together a large number of *ijazat* (sing. *ijaza*), or authorizations, in all available branches of Islamic knowledge, particularly the law and prophetic tradition. In order to do this, they more or less regularly attend the circles of knowledge (*halaqat 'ilmiyya*) that are held daily in mosques or the homes of ulama. These consist of mechanical reading sessions, followed by commentary on the works of hadith, Qur'anic exegesis, law, and theology, with particular attention given to the study of classic Hanbali works. The *ijaza*, however, must not be seen as the equivalent of the *licentia docendi*—permission to teach—of medieval European universities. The *ijaza* is not the permission to teach that crowns an institutional course of study[27] but merely an authorization to transmit a prophetic tradition, a book, or sometimes an entire corpus thanks to the disciple's nearly filial relationship with a master.

For a clear idea of traditional instruction, it may be useful to describe a typical day in the life of Grand Mufti Muhammad ibn Ibrahim. After the dawn prayer (*al-subh*), Ibn Ibrahim began the day with three successive courses of grammar for beginner (*sighar al-talaba*), intermediary (*mutawassitu al-talaba*), and advanced (*kibar al-talaba*) disciples. His teaching was based on the reading and commentary of classical works—to wit, *al-Ajrumiyya* (by Ibn Ajrum) for the first category, *Sharh qutr al-nada wa ball al-sada* (by Ibn Hisham) for the second, and *al-Alfiyya fi al-nahw wa al-sarf* (by Ibn Malik) and *Sharh Ibn 'Aqil 'ala alfiyyat Ibn Malik* (by Ibn 'Aqil) for the third. These grammar courses were followed by a session dedicated to the study of the main works of Hanbali jurisprudence. The works of Ibn al-Qayyim, al-Hajjawi, al-Buhuti, and al-Makrami were read by one of the attendees and commented on nearly word for word by Ibn Ibrahim. After a break between noon prayer (*al-zuhr*) and afternoon prayer (*al-'asr*), Ibn Ibrahim devoted a session to the prophetic tradition (*al-hadith*) and its methodology (*mustalah al-hadith*) and another to theology, where the main works of Ibn Taymiyya, Ibn Abd al-Wahhab, and their descendants were read, explained in simple terms, and illustrated by way of examples. In the evening, he taught inheritance law (*'ilm al-fara'id* or *al-mawarith*) and Qur'anic exegesis by reading and commenting on the work of Ibn Kathir (*Tafsir al-qur'an al-'azim*), a disciple of Ibn Taymiyya.[28]

Following these *halaqat* (the most important of which were of course those of the descendants of Ibn Abd al-Wahhab) and once he had properly absorbed all of the *'alim*'s teaching, the disciple submitted an *istid'a'*—that is, a request for *ijaza* corresponding to the works he had studied and the prophetic traditions he had learned by heart. The most brilliant disciples became assistants to the master, a step that opened the door for them to becoming professors or judges. Their careers were thus launched. This was the case of Muhammad al-Sbayyil (d. 2012), the last member of the Committee of Grand Ulama to have received a traditional education.

Born in the oasis of Bkiriyya in the region of Al-Qasim in 1926, al-Sbayyil came from a lineage of midlevel religious personnel. His father was a bookseller and copyist with a perfect knowledge of the Qur'an and a portion of the Hanbali-Wahhabi corpus. His older brother, Abd al-Aziz, had sufficient religious knowledge to give courses in the Grand Mosque of the oasis and settle disputes between inhabitants.[29] At the age of five, al-Sbayyil began his apprenticeship of the Qur'an under the supervision of his father and later his brother.

Around the age of ten, he embarked on the study of the three main works of Ibn Abd al-Wahhab under the direction of his brother and later several local religious figures. He also studied jurisprudence and the prophetic tradition under the direction of several ulama from Al-Qasim. After learning the *mukhtasarat*, or synopses of works of Islamic jurisprudence, al-Sbayyil devoted himself to the study of classic works—in particular, those of Ibn Taymiyya, Ibn al-Qayyim, al-Buhuti, and al-Makrami. According to his own statements, he read and commented on these works with his masters three or four times. At the age of twenty, he had already received several *ijazat*, which allowed him to become the assistant and main disciple of Abd Allah ibn Humayd, judge of Al-Qasim and a leading member of the corporation.

The traditional education that had up until the early 1950s been indispensable gradually lost ground. Indeed, ulama who had received this education had difficulty adapting to the requirements of the contemporary Saudi market in the goods of salvation due to the fundamental structural changes that had occurred during the second half of the twentieth century. In order to reinforce the unity of the country's religious elite and preserve its ideological authority, train personnel and religious agents capable of responding to the population's expectations, and enforce respect of the three O's in the social space, it was necessary to create a complete, homogenous, and institutionalized course of study that was at once national in scale and modern. The Hanbali-Wahhabi school system underwent radical change. Informal education based on circles of knowledge, individual initiative, and personal relations gave way to education based on a Western-type organization. The representatives of Hanbali-Wahhabism had no trouble adopting this organizational framework in the educational domain on their own initiative, as it appeared to them to be the most effective way of preserving and stimulating their tradition. This is yet another example of the ethic of responsibility at work.

While only 47 percent (or eight of seventeen) of the ulama had received a "modern" education in 1971, 100 percent of them have in the twenty-first century. After a cycle of primary studies in public schools,[30] disciples intending to pursue a juridico-religious career attend religious studies institutes (*al-maʿahid al-ʿilmiyya*). The first such institute was opened in Riyadh in 1950 on the instigation of Grand Mufti Muhammad ibn Ibrahim.[31] Very quickly, however, the government adopted the project and institutes were opened in all regions, with sixty-two of them in existence in 2010. In order to study at these institutes, children must have a solid dossier and have learned at least two parts of the Qur'an (*juz'an*, sing. *juz'*). Instruction is free. The religious studies institutes offer a six-year course of study: three years of middle school, resulting in a certificate of success, a sort of middle-school diploma (*shahadat itmam al-dirasa al-mutawassita*), and three years of high school, resulting in another certificate of success, a sort of high-school diploma (*shahadat itmam al-dirasa al-thanawiyya*). The subjects covered by this education have evolved since the 1950s. At first, instruction consisted of four common areas: religious studies, Arabic studies, the "social sciences," and mathematics. Over the years, the study of English and computer science was added (Table 3).

These religious studies institutes are unevenly distributed across the country (see Figure 10). Many are located in regions in which Hanbali-Wahhabism enjoys majority status: in Najd, the South, and the North.

While the proportion of institutes created in the Hijaz is roughly equivalent to that of the proportion of Hijazi ulama who sit on the Committee of Grand Ulama, the proportion between the number of institutes in the three other Hanbali-Wahhabi regions and that of their respective ulama admitted to the committee is significantly uneven. Indeed, one would expect there to be more religious institutes in Najd, fewer in the South, and none in the North. While such institutes have been established in the North and South, the aim of doing so is less to train grand ulama than to further efforts to bring these regions (which, as we have seen, do not possess deeply rooted local religious traditions) into the Hanbali-Wahhabi fold and train technicians of the routine cults and midlevel religious personnel.

When the disciple has successfully finished his secondary studies within the institute, he can present himself as a candidate for a place at the country's three large universities: the Islamic University of Medina (Al-Jami'a Al-Islamiyya), Umm Al-Qura University in Mecca (Jami'at Umm al-Qura), and Al-Imam University in Riyadh (Jami'at Al-Imam Muhammad ibn Saud Al-Islamiyya). The diplomas offered by these universities are the license (three years), the master's (two years, in theory, but generally more), and the doctorate (three years, but generally more).

Founded in 1961, the Islamic University of Medina mainly receives Muslim disciples from foreign countries. The Saudis who study there generally aspire to preach abroad. Only one grand *'alim* has come from this university: Muhammad ibn Muhammad al-Mukhtar al-Shanqiti (b. 1961).

Umm Al-Qura is the oldest university in Saudi Arabia. Yet despite its seniority—it was founded in 1949—it has trained only six grand ulama. Should this be seen as yet another expression of Saudi regionalism? Since the 1970s, it has welcomed professors, personnel, and disciples of various politico-religious tendencies, in particular, the Muslim Brotherhood and their Sahwist disciples.[32] The Saudi government and religious establishment have no confidence in

Table 3. Hourly Volume of Subjects Taught in the Religious Institutes

Subjects Taught	Middle School 1st year	Middle School 2nd year	Middle School 3rd year	High School 1st year	High School 2nd year	High School 3rd year
Religious Studies						
Qur'an	3	3	3	3	3	3
Exegesis	2	2	2	2	2	2
Tradition	2	2	2	2	2	2
Theology	2	2	2	2	2	2
Law	3	3	3	3	3	3
Inheritance Law	—	—	—	2	1	—
Methodology of the Tradition	—	—	—	—	1	—
Foundations of Law	—	—	—	—	—	2
Total	12	12	12	14	14	14
Arabic Studies						
Grammar and Conjugation	3	3	3	3	3	3
Style	2	2	2	2	2	2
Study of Texts	1	1	1	—	—	—
Eloquence	—	—	—	2	2	1
Meter	—	—	—	—	—	1
Literature and Literary History	—	—	—	1	1	1
Rules of Writing	2	2	2	—	—	—
Total	8	8	8	8	8	8
Social Sciences						
History	1	1	1	2	2	2
Geography	1	1	1	1	1	1
Total	2	2	2	3	3	3
Other Subjects						
Mathematics	3	3	3	—	—	—
English	4	4	4	4	4	4
Computer Science	1	1	1	1	1	1
Sciences	3	3	3	—	—	—
Sport	1	1	1	1	1	1
Total	12	12	12	6	6	6
Total	34	34	34	31	31	31

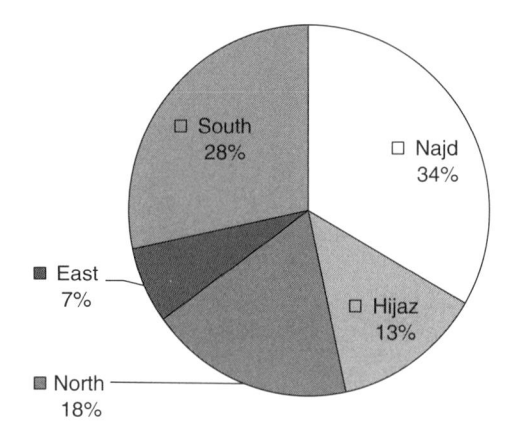

Figure 10. Distribution of religious institutes in the principal regions of Saudi Arabia (1950–2010).

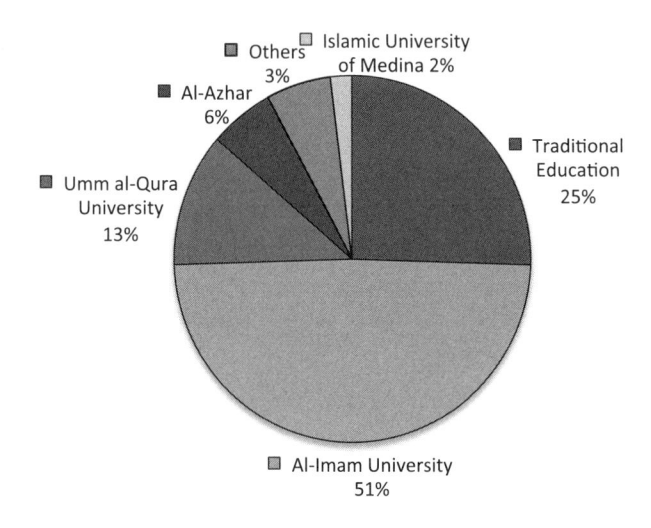

Figure 11. Education of members of the Committee of Grand Ulama (1971–2010).

the Sahwists, so they therefore are not recruited by the Committee of Grand Ulama. I return to this issue in chapter 9.

Al-Imam University, created in 1974 from the fusion of the Faculty of Sharia and the Faculty of Arabic, is indisputably the most important for our study. It has educated twenty-five ulama, or 48 percent of the committee's members since its creation in 1971 (Figure 11). It has also supplied by far the greater part of its members who have followed a modern course of study: 75 percent.

Riyadh's Al-Imam University, or Imam Muhammad ibn Saud Islamic University, is named after Muhammad ibn Saud (1744–1765), the faithful ally of Ibn Abd al-Wahhab. Since its creation, it has been seen as the breeding ground of grand ulama as well as of most of the religious personnel and technicians of the routine cults required by the religious establishment. The university's "pharaonic" campus (a veritable city within the city, with its own infrastructure, a small hospital, a supermarket, residential neighborhoods for the disciples, professors, and administrative staff, and so on) includes eleven faculties (faculties of sharia, theology, Arabic, [Islamic] social science, preaching, public relations, language and translation, computer science, economics and administrative sciences, natural science, medicine and engineering) and two institutes of advanced study (the Advanced Institute of the Magistracy and the Institute for Arabic Language Instruction [for foreigners]).[33] The grand ulama are drawn exclusively from the faculties of sharia and theology and the Advanced Institute of the Magistracy. Disciples in these three domains benefit from a grant and, at the end of their first year, obtain the highly esteemed title of shaykh. The success of Al-Imam University is such that it has adopted a policy of expansion, leading to the creation of two satellite campuses in Saudi Arabia and three abroad.[34]

In the 1960s and 1970s, some disciples prepared their doctorates in religious studies at Al-Azhar University in Egypt for reasons of prestige and in order to observe the organization, structures, and operating mechanisms of this institution with an eye to "importing" them to Saudi Arabia. As the corporation now possesses all of the necessary material and symbolic resources onsite, this practice has nearly ceased in the twenty-first century.

During their period of advanced study, the ulama all follow the same tripartite syllabus, which consists of courses in the foundations of theology (*al-'aqida*), Qur'anic exegesis (*al-tafsir*), and jurisprudence (*al-fiqh*). During the first year of the master's program (copied from the Anglo-Saxon system), 74 percent of the ulama specialize in jurisprudence—more specifically, the foundations of Islamic jurisprudence (*usul al-fiqh*)—in order to obtain the diploma required to issue fatawa. Meanwhile, 26 percent of them specialize in theology, more specifically, comparative religion (in order to demonstrate the superiority of Hanbali-Wahhabi Islam).[35] Given that these disciples all aspire to careers as technicians of the routine cults and managers of the goods of salvation, there is nothing surprising about their fields of specialization. Without going into the details of these specializations, I will give a few examples: Abd al-Wahhab Abu Sulayman (b. 1937), Abd Allah ibn Mani' (b. 1930), and Abd Allah al-Mutlaq (b. 1954) are specialists of economics, more particularly, of banking and stock market investment, and Qays al Mubarak is a specialist of medical questions. This is a nearly universal phenomenon. As several studies have shown, the representatives of all great religions have had to diversify their activities and adapt their goods of salvation in order to maintain their influence in the public sphere.[36]

The university education of the ulama is crowned by receipt of a doctorate. Most members of the Committee of Grand Ulama call themselves *al-shaykh al-duktur*. This title reflects the double legitimacy to which, like many ulama in the Muslim world, Hanbali-Wahhabi clerics aspire. While the title of shaykh places them in the long-term history of Islam and adorns them with a religious aura,[37] that of *duktur* anchors them in their epoch and grants them the status of highly trained expert. With the Westernization of the educational system in the various countries of the Arab-Muslim world and the growth in the number of diplomas offered by European and American universities, the title of doctor has become the pillar of all academic capital, conferring social prestige and legitimacy in a given domain of specialization. This dominant idiom is indispensable to the ulama if they are to preserve their legitimacy and influence vis-à-vis the other actors with whom they are in competition. The adoption of this title is thus neither a fad nor a form of Westernization, as some opponents of the practice (including a few ulama[38]) claim. Rather, it is an appropriation of the dominant language that clearly reflects the ulama's desire to adapt in order to better consolidate their ideological authority. As was the case with Ottoman titles (such as *pasha, beg, agha,* and *afandi*)—to go no further into the history of the region—the Western title will fall into disuse once it no longer expresses ideas of prestige and domination.

Although the modern degree course is a well-established part of the Saudi landscape, the *ijaza* nevertheless remains a source of prestige as well as a significant source of social capital.[39] I found that all ulama who followed the modern degree course had also obtained one or more *ijazat*. In theory, this is optional. In practice, however, obtaining it allows the *'alim* to establish a link with an uninterrupted chain of transmission (*al-sanad*) going all the way back to the Prophet, legitimate his position and knowledge, locate himself in the long religious history of Islam, and establish privileged relations with one *'alim* or several ulama. In this way, he begins to build the network that will be necessary if he is to reach the summit of the clerical corps.[40] The *ijaza* is also an efficient means for controlling access to the corporation for it supplies "a filiation better than biological filiation. If the sire is the father of the body, the master [*al-shaykh*] is the father of the soul. A being is what he is thanks to his soul and reason and not thanks to his body."[41] It therefore gives rise to an indissoluble tie of kinship. In practice, an autodidact, whatever his knowledge, cannot join the corporation without an *ijaza*: this was the case of Syrian-born Nasir al-din al-Albani (d. 1999).[42] The *ijaza* can be seen as a rite of transubstantiation, investment, and legitimation of the ulama's status. In this sense, it nicely corresponds to what Pierre Bourdieu called a rite of institution.[43]

MAKING A CAREER: THE CURSUS HONORUM OF THE ULAMA

Since the High Middle Ages, teaching and the magistracy have been the preferred occupations of ulama. The members of the Committee of Grand Ulama, like all representatives of the Hanbali-Wahhabi tradition since it first appeared in the second half of the eighteenth century, are no different: 96 percent of them exercise at least one of these two professions; 50 percent (twenty-one of them) are or were professors of Islamic jurisprudence and/or theology; 31 percent are magistrates in the various institutions of the Saudi judiciary; and 15 percent officially exercise both occupations simultaneously (Figure 12). Indeed, in their weltanschauung, justice and teaching are seen as the two indispensable conditions for preserving and applying the three O's. In their writings, interviews, and speeches, they thus insist on the following maxim: justice is the foundation of all power (*al-'Adl asas al-mulk*). And who better than the heirs of the prophets to apply justice, maintain order on earth, and please God? However, the application and preservation of the Law necessarily depends on its transmission by way of teaching and writing.

Both teaching and the magistracy are suffused with prestige. Furthermore, the magistracy allows the ulama to observe, examine, and rule on concrete cases

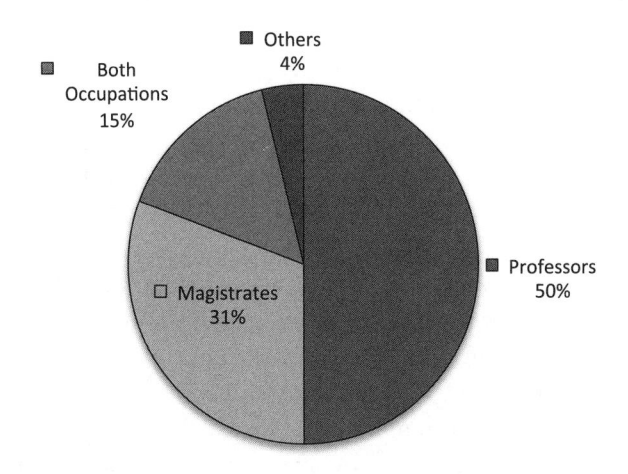

Figure 12. Distribution of grand ulama by type of profession (1971–2010).

in constant contact with social reality. Teaching, by contrast, supplies them with the resources necessary to rationalize and codify this practical knowledge in the interests of better transmitting and diffusing it. It is thus not astonishing that so many grand ulama should exercise both occupations: in reality, they are inseparable as theory and practice. The phenomenon of simultaneously exercising these two occupations is above all apparent in the first generation, something that can be explained by reference to the shortage of available religious personnel at the time of the creation of the Committee of Grand Ulama. Indeed, between the 1940s and the 1970s, Saudi Arabia was obliged to "import" personnel from abroad. Egyptian-born cleric Abd al-Razzaq Afifi (d. 1994), for example, arrived in Saudi Arabia in 1949 to teach Arabic and religious studies, climbed the rungs of the establishment one by one, and eventually reached its summit. Initially a professor at Dar al-Tawhid in al-Ta'if, in 1950 he was transferred to the Institute of Religious Studies in Unayza, in the region of Al-Qasim. He subsequently settled in Riyadh, where he actively participated in the foundation of the faculties of sharia and Arabic. His competence and devotion led to his appointment as director of the Advanced Institute of the Magistracy from 1965 to 1973. In 1971, he became a member of the Committee of Grand Ulama, the Permanent Commission on [Religious] Scholarship and *Ifta'* (the issuing of legal opinions), and vice director of the General Presidency for the Management of [Religious] Scholarship, Predication, and Guidance.[44] His case is a clear instance of the contemporaneous Saudi practice of recruiting foreigners to teach because of a lack of trained personnel in all domains. In this system, the more perseverant Hanbali-Wahhabi foreigners, well-placed to smoothly integrate into the host society, could succeed in reaching the summit of the Saudi religious establishment.

Together with these two preferred occupations, the grand ulama are of course technicians of the routine cults, and many of them are or were imams in mosques. For example, the present grand mufti of the kingdom, Abd al-Aziz Al al-Shaykh, is an imam in the Grand Mosque of Riyadh, Salih ibn Humayd is the grand mufti of that of Mecca, and so on. Finally, their other essential occupations should not be forgotten: issuing fatawa and listening to the population. And while they monopolize the most important religious and judicial posts, they do not for all that hesitate to encroach upon the domains of other elites.

To begin with, it should be emphasized that, once admitted to the committee, a grand *'alim* automatically obtains the rank of high-ranking civil servant (*al-martaba al-mumtaza*) or even minister. Of the committee's fifty-two members, twenty-two have occupied posts of responsibility other than that of magistrate and teacher. Nine are or were ministers. The ministries they control (whether directly or by the intermediary of a member of the corporation) are the ministries of Justice, Islamic Affairs, the Pilgrimage, and Girl's Education (before its incorporation into the Ministry of National Education in 2002). Since its creation in 1971, the Ministry of Justice has been led by a member of the committee.[45] Nine were members of the Advisory Council, and since its creation in 1992, its presidency has been held by a member of the committee. From 1992 to 2002, this office was held by Muhammad ibn Jubayr (d. 2002), a member of the committee (1971–2002). He was succeeded in 2002 by Salih ibn Humayd (b. 1950), a member of the committee since 2001. In 2009, Ibn Humayd was in his turn replaced by Abd Allah Al al-Shaykh (b. 1948), a member of the committee since 1992. Three members were advisors to King Fahd (1982–2005) and two are presently advisors to King Abd Allah (2005–). Four are university deans or presidents: up until his death in 1999, Abd al-Aziz ibn Baz presided over the Islamic University of Medina. Sa'd al-Duwayhi (b. 1956) was dean of the Al-Ahsa' Faculty of Theology. Abd Allah ibn Abd al-Muhsin al-Turki (b. 1940), no doubt presently one of its most active members, presides over the World Islamic League after having held, among others, the posts of president of Al-Imam University and minister of Islamic affairs.

The career of al-Turki is a remarkable illustration of the ease with which ulama pass from one sector to another. Born in Harma, a small oasis in the Nadji crescent, in 1940, he received both a modern and traditional education in religious studies. After having obtained his high school diploma in 1959 from the Institute of Religious Studies in Al-Majma'a, he joined the Faculty of Sharia in Riyadh, where he received a master's degree in jurisprudence at the Institute for Advanced Studies of the Magistracy. Al-Turki also regularly attended the *halaqat* of Grand Mufti Muhammad ibn Ibrahim. In 1970, he enrolled at Al-Azhar in order to prepare a doctorate in jurisprudence. This resulted in a dissertation titled "The Foundations of the Legal School of Imam Ahmad b. Hanbal" (*Usul madhhab al-imam Ahmad: dirasa usuliyya muqarana*). His stay in Cairo allowed him to further develop his theoretical knowledge while closely observing the university's administrative and pedagogical organization, with a view to adapting it to the Saudi context. Upon his return, al-Turki spent several months teaching before becoming the director of a religious studies institute. He subsequently joined the Faculty of Sharia as a professor. On the strength of his Egyptian experience and privileged relationship with the highest-ranking members of the religious establishment, al-Turki was in 1974 given the task of establishing Al-Imam University in Riyadh.[46] The twenty years during which he presided over this university was a period of tremendous expansion: a gigantic campus was constructed and endowed with administrative and pedagogical structures similar to those of Al-Azhar. Thanks to his efforts, Al-Imam University thus became renowned and the veritable breeding ground of the ulama. In 1992, al-Turki was named a member of the Committee of Grand Ulama and, two years later, minister of Islamic affairs. In 2001, he became secretary general of the World Islamic League, a post that he still occupied in 2014. Alongside these official duties, he has been a member of several national and international organizations: in Saudi Arabia, al-Turki is, among other things, a member of the High Council of Information, the King Faysal Foundation, the Education Policy Institute, the Governing Council of Abd al-Aziz Library, and the Foundation for Handicapped Children. At the international level, he presides over the World Islamic Council in London, the League of Islamic Universities, and the Islamic University of Islamabad in Niger. He is a member of the Governing Council of Oxford University's Center for Islamic Studies, the Islamic faculty of Chicago, and the Institute for the History of Arabic-Islamic Sciences in Frankfurt. In all, al-Turki is involved with nearly twenty different organizations. Apart from these institutional commitments, he pursues extensive intellectual activity. With the help of several collaborators, he has written seventeen books and edited twenty works of exegesis, jurisprudence, theology, history, and hagiography.[47]

For at least two decades, then, the ulama have pursued an adaptive strategy. Their desire to enforce orthodoxy and orthopraxy while adjusting, not always without difficulty, to the changing face of Saudi society has led them to become involved in several sectors of activity. Apart from the religious, legislative, and educational domains, they are involved in charitable associations, governmental and nongovernmental organizations, and the economic and financial fields. In the latter two areas, Abd Allah ibn Mani' (b. 1930), Abd Allah al-Mutlaq (b. 1954), and Salih al-Sadlan (b. 1941) have become experts and consultants de rigueur of the Saudi financial world. In the framework of what is referred to in Saudi Arabia as *al-lijan al-shar'iyya* (juridico-religious commissions)—that is, the body that guarantees the permissibility of transactions within a banking establishment—these three ulama, together with their colleagues and disciples, are also members of several governing boards of banks and businesses. In Saudi Arabia, the very appearance of a grand *'alim*'s name on a business brochure in this sector is the best kind of publicity. The ulama thus enjoy real influence in this domain. According to a survey of a representative sample of fifteen hundred investors, part of a 2007 Saudi stock market study, 73.9 percent claim to follow the ulama's advice. Of these, 73.2 percent depend on the analyses and opinions of the three members of the Committee of Grand Ulama mentioned above: Abd Allah ibn Mani' (30.5 percent), Abd Allah al-Mutlaq (28.6 percent), and Salih al-Sadlan (14.1 percent).[48]

THE ACCUMULATION OF SUPPORT NETWORKS

The ulama's mobility, however, requires that they develop support networks to supplement their cultural and economic capital. Future members of the Committee of Grand Ulama nearly always rely on three types of network: family networks, "tribal" networks, and *mulazama*—that is, a long-standing relationship with a master of the religious sciences.

Family networks constitute their first resource. I have identified at least three examples of this. That of the Al al-Shaykh is, without doubt, the oldest and densest. The importance of this family has already been discussed above; here, I fill in the portrait. The example of Grand Mufti Muhammad ibn Ibrahim's two sons, Ibrahim and Abd Allah, is significant: while the eldest of the two brothers, Ibrahim, hardly stood out among his father's collaborators and disciples, Muhammad Ibn Ibrahim nevertheless appointed him vice mufti of the kingdom.[49] By way of a "consolation prize" after his father's death and the suppression of the post of mufti, Ibrahim, who had been tapped as his father's successor, became a member of the Committee of Grand Ulama and was appointed director of the General Presidency for the Management of [Religious] Scholarship, Predication, and Guidance and, indeed, minister of justice. When Ibrahim retired, his replacement at the ministry and on the Committee of Grand Ulama was none other than his younger brother, Abd Allah, sitting president of the Advisory Council.

Another striking example of the Al al-Shaykh network is Muhammad ibn Ibrahim's grandson, Salih ibn Abd al-Aziz (b. 1958). After studying science in high school and receiving a diploma in engineering, Salih decided to take up the family heritage by enrolling at Al-Imam University. Thanks to his prominent name and the intervention of his father, president of the Committee for the Promotion of Virtue and the Prevention of Vice, Salih was allowed to transfer his credits and directly begin work on his master's degree. He thus got around a rule that, however strict, easily ceded to the advantage of an Al al-Shaykh. He is presently minister of Islamic affairs and potentially a member of the Committee of Grand Ulama.

A third example concerns the most recent member recruited to the committee, Muhammad ibn Hasan. Thanks to his relations with his cousin, the present Grand Mufti Abd al-Aziz Al al-Shaykh, Ibn Hasan has enjoyed a meteoric assent: after rapidly climbing the rungs of the university, he became the grand mufti's private secretary. The latter has helped and supported him, proposing him as a candidate to the Committee of Grand Ulama, which he joined in April 2005. The Al al-Shaykh family network and the influence that flows from it significantly exceed the confines of the religious sphere: several members of the household have occupied important civilian and military posts.

The second family network is that of the Ibn Humayd, which I presented above and so will here turn to the al-Shathri family network. This Najdi family has supplied several ulama and political figures. Abd al-Aziz al-Shathri (d. 1967) was a somewhat well-known *'alim* who participated in the acculturation of the sedentarized Bedouin tribes of the *hijar* before devoting himself to teaching.[50] His close ties to the ruling family allowed his son Nasir to embark on a brilliant political career as councilor to kings Khalid (1975–1982), Fahd (1982–2005), and Abd Allah (2005–). Despite the social promotion afforded by Nasir's position, the Shathri could not claim to be a "grand house" (*bayt karim* or *bayt sharaf*), as they had produced no grand ulama. The kings' councilor thus did everything in his power to see to it that his son Sa'd (b. 1967) reached the summit of the religious establishment. From an early age, Sa'd was entrusted to the care of the most eminent ulama, including Abd al-Aziz ibn Baz (d. 1999), Muhammad ibn Uthaymin (d. 2001), and Abd al-Aziz Al al-Shaykh (b. 1943). Sa'd then enrolled at Al-Imam University. He sped through the Hanbali-Wahhabi *cursus honorum*, becoming a professor at the university in record time. In March 2005, the family supported his candidacy to the Committee of Grand Ulama (his father, Nasir, is a member of the royal cabinet, which transmits candidacies to the king). Sa'd was finally appointed in April 2005 and at age thirty-eight became its youngest member.

Regionalism and segmentation dominate the Saudi politico-religious landscape. The second resource of future grand ulama is therefore the "tribal" network—a nominal expression that I use by default to designate a complex configuration—which goes hand in hand with the Najdi regional network. As we have seen, ulama are generally drawn from the largest tribal confederations and lineages of Najd: the Banu Khalid have supplied four, the Banu Zayd seven, the Banu Subay' three, the Banu Tamim eight (to which the four grand ulama of the Al al-Shaykh must be added), the Qahtan three, the Unayza three, the Bahila two, and the al-Dawasir two as well. That translates to thirty-six of the committee's fifty-two grand ulama. The "tribal" network is very dense, and nominations are made (consciously or not) with an eye to maintaining a balanced distribution among the large lineages of Najd. And "tribal" and regional networks are not limited to the religious space; these same configurations play a significant role in the politico-administrative domain as well.[51]

The last resource available to future grand ulama is the long-standing relationship with a reputed and influential master of the religious sciences—*mulazama*. The personal relations that result from such contact can lead to marriage between disciples and their masters' daughters or nieces. Salih al-Luhaydan (b. 1931), for example, was for several years one of Grand Mufti Ibn Ibrahim's favorite disciples. This privileged relationship truly launched al-Luhaydan's career. He became the mufti's son-in-law and personal secretary as well as editor-in-chief of *Rayat al-Islam*, the leading official journal of Hanbali-Wahhabism. Personal relations with the head of the religious establishment and the charisma of office conferred by these posts contributed to his rise. Just one year after the master's death, al-Luhaydan was admitted to the Committee of Grand Ulama. He also inherited the office of judge. Several years later, he became president of the High Council of the Magistracy, a post that he occupied until February 2008. Al-Luhaydan is the most senior member of the Committee of Grand Ulama, on which he has sat since 1971. He is also one of its most influential members.

Muhammad al-Sbayyil, who was the disciple of Ibn Humayd during the latter's tenure as judge of Al-Bukayriya, is another example. When Ibn Humayd was promoted to grand judge of the region of Al-Qasim, he called al-Sbayyil to Burayda and appointed him to the posts of teacher and director of a religious studies institute. The relationship between the two men was so strong that, when Ibn Humayd became grand judge of the Hijaz, he had his disciple come to Mecca, where he was appointed imam and chief preacher of the Grand Mosque as well as vice president of the administration responsible for managing the two holy places. Following his protector's death, al-Sbayyil presided over this body (until 2005). After arriving in Mecca, he established close relations with the leading members of the religious establishment, particularly Ibn Baz, who requested that he become a member of the Committee of Grand Ulama in 1992. Ibn Baz also kept an eye on the career of his closest disciple, Abd Allah ibn Qa'ud (d. 2006). At the first opportunity (the death of two members of the committee), he proposed Ibn Qa'ud for a place on the royal cabinet, to which he was appointed in 1977.

Until his death in 1969, Ibn Ibrahim occupied the center of the establishment and its various networks of socialization and solidarity. From the second half of the 1970s until his death in 1999, Abd al-Aziz ibn Baz held the same key position. He enjoyed the respect and esteem of the other grand ulama and, for this reason, had considerable influence over those around him, all of whom took his advice into consideration and generally followed his suggestions. Ibn Baz thus occupied a central place in the establishment, and many roads passed through him. Eighteen members of the Committee of Grand Ulama were his disciples, and several of them were appointed on his recommendation.

POLITICAL QUIETISM

None of the grand ulama have been past opponents of the regime, expressed demands for reform, or criticized the decisions of the committee or one of its members, even when their personal positions ran counter to official decisions.

Abd Allah ibn Jabrin (d. 2009), a high-ranking religious official and potential candidate to the committee, was a patron of the Islamist opposition of the early 1990s. His support for them was an affront to both the regime and the grand ulama. The ulama did not fail to publicly disavow him, and he was relieved of his official duties. Though this renowned *'alim* was subsequently rehabilitated, the "stain" on his record meant that he was never able to pretend to a place on the committee: having openly opposed the government and participated in political activities that ran counter to Hanbali doctrine and official policy, his "redemption" and subsequent support for the monarchy were insufficient: political quietism, if not active support for the political authorities' decisions, is a key criterion of selection for candidates to the Committee of Grand Ulama. Ali al-Duwayhi (b. 1956) supplies an example of a politically engaged *'alim*—in support of the regime, of course—who succeeded in being appointed to the committee. Dean of the Al-Ahsa' Faculty of Theology, since 2001 he has signed several political petitions defending Saudi school programs, rallied in support of municipal elections, and so on.

Abd al-Muhsin al-Ubaykan (b. 1956), by contrast, openly called upon the government to undertake reforms between 1990 and 1992. As a result, he was marginalized and stripped of his various duties (losing his post as judge at the court of Riyadh and mosque imam). Though rehabilitated in 1999–2000, he nevertheless continued to criticize the judicial system and the decisions of the committee (above all in the area of jurisprudence), even going so far as to issue fatawa contradicting those of the committee. To compensate for these faux pas, he subsequently attempted to issue fatawa on the permissibility of saluting the national flag and the prohibition of Saudis to engage in jihad in Iraq, among other things.[52] Once again, the government agreed to rehabilitate him, but the grand ulama categorically refused to admit him to the committee. Al-Ubaykan was ultimately named advisor to the Ministry of Justice and a member of the

Advisory Council. In 2009, he became an advisor to the king; he was dismissed in 2012.

The leaders of the Saudi Islamist movement of the 1990s, Safar al-Hawali (b. 1950), Salman al-Awda (b. 1955), and Muhsin al-Awaji (b. 1961), admit that quietism in regards to the political and security domains is among the criteria of access to the Committee of Grand Ulama. They therefore accept being excluded from it because of their very extensive political involvement. "For the government," says al-Hawali, "grand ulama must be apolitical men, men who know nothing about politics."[53] Al-Awda adds that "future members of the committee have to be men with spotless pasts."[54] For al-Awaji, "access to the committee is purely a matter of state security criteria."[55]

The "ideal-typical" committee member is a Hanbali-Wahhabi issued from a lineage of midlevel religious personnel or a house of ulama from the large sedentarized tribes of the Najdi crescent. He will have been the disciple of renowned masters (in the case of grand ulama who have followed a traditional education) or carried out his studies at a religious studies institute and Al-Imam University (in the case of grand ulama who have received a modern education). He is a specialist in Islamic theology or jurisprudence and is generally a university (Al-Imam) professor and/or magistrate. The committee member is not politically engaged, or if he is, his engagement exclusively supports the regime, in keeping with Hanbali tradition. Above all, he is a religious actor.

Members of the committee hold their seats for an average of fifteen years. While it is difficult to determine the circumstances of access to the summit of the religious establishment, the reasons for departure are perfectly clear: a grand 'alim obviously quits the committee when he dies, is seriously ill, or has committed an act seen as reprehensible by the monarchy or the corporation. In 1986, Abd Allah ibn Qa'ud was dismissed from the committee for two main reasons: his suspect relationship with Islamist circles and the fact that some of his fatawa contradicted the consensus within the corporation. In October 2009, Sa'd al-Shathri was summarily dismissed because he dared criticize the practice of coeducation at King Abd Allah University (KAUST), which is seen as a royal fief. This amounted to trespassing on the domain reserved for the monarchy in keeping with the symbiotic relationship between the political power and the religious authority.

Thus defined, the habitus of members of the Committee of Grand Ulama—the product of historical and social conditioning—consciously or unconsciously generates behavior adapted to the logic of the Saudi politico-religious space. In the Hanbali-Wahhabi conception, the role of the ulama is to support the political authorities and manage the official market of salvational goods in accordance with the three O's. The extensive prerogatives enjoyed by the committee in the political, social, and religious domains, together with its basic function as an ideological stronghold and device for legitimating the actions of the government, justify oversight of its agenda by the political authorities and encourage the application of very rigorous criteria of selection. The symbiotic relationship between the political power and the religious authority must be scrupulously respected by the ulama. They must fully support the House of Saud and intervene in the political domain only at the express wish of the latter. In other words, they must remain exclusively religious actors.

8

Religious Authority in Practice
The Promotion of Virtue and the Prevention of Vice

According to Jürgen Habermas, before the emergence of a bourgeois public sphere tied to the spread of capitalism and the rationalization of state structures, the European public sphere, still dominated by feudalism and personal relations, was structured by representations. These consisted of a particular display of symbols, style, attitude, and rhetoric—"in a word, a strict code of 'noble' conduct . . . for virtue must be embodied, it has to be capable of public representation."[1] The public sphere thus became a space of regulation and control in the sense that the holders of power defined acceptable and legitimate conduct in keeping with the dominant culture. This definition, it seems to me, nicely characterizes the Saudi public sphere. The patrimonial nature of the local political system and a "tribal" culture that has been for the most part "invented" obliges the Saudi population to adopt a quasi-permanent representational behavior, something further reinforced by Hanbali-Wahhabi tradition. Like any other corporation founded on ideological principle, this tradition has since its emergence in the second half of the eighteenth century sought to impose its cognitive, normative, and symbolic principles upon the Saudi public sphere—that is, on every domain open to all.

In order to legitimate this ambition, the ulama turned to the Islamic principle of promoting virtue and preventing vice (*al-amr bi al-maʿruf wa al-nahy ʿan al-munkar*), the main objective of which is to promote a society that observes orthodoxy and orthopraxy, at least in public. While the duty to promote virtue and prevent vice is in theory incumbent on the entire community, the political power and the religious authority do everything in their power to quickly regulate and institutionalize it in order to preserve the political order—in the clerical imaginary, a necessary condition of any effort to achieve salvation. To that end, the first Abbasid caliphs created the office of *muhtasib*.

Classical legal texts claim that the bearer of this juridico-religious responsibility (*wilaya diniyya*) disposes of the following ideal-typical prerogatives. He verifies the propriety of commercial transactions and the quality and price of merchandise in markets. He also sees to it that the principal religious duties are observed (such as collective prayer, the upkeep and use of places of worship, and the keeping of fasts), public mores are respected (including current vestimentary practices and the bans on prostitution, alcohol, drugs, and tobacco), the ban on mixed-sex groups in some spaces is maintained, and so on. He also sees to it that labor laws are respected in regards to scribes, public notaries, and defense attorneys. In addition to ensuring that orthodoxy and orthopraxy are respected in the public sphere, the muhtasib fulfills aedile functions (such as street cleaning, repairs to city walls, ensuring the urban water supply, oversight of certain trades, and protecting animals). In order to carry out these tasks, the muhtasib disposes of a variable number of assistants and auxiliaries and can turn to the forces of order for help. He also possesses significant repressive power (including reprimand, censure, confiscation, imprisonment, banishment of recidivists, and the power to close stores and forbid an individual from exercising a given profession).[2]

In reality, the power and influence of this office depends on several environmental and psychological parameters: the place of Islam in the state system, the social atmosphere, and the historical context as well as the character, competencies, and, above all, convictions of particular officeholders. The discussion that follows seeks to compare this ideal-typical model of *hisba* with Saudi reality.[3] Doing so allows us to understand the dynamics that structure, stabilize, and regulate this institution in a particular ecological system. We also test the hypothesis of the routinization and institutionalization of Hanbali-Wahhabism by studying the history, structures, and mechanisms of the hisba system's operation as formalized by the Committee for the Promotion of Virtue and the Prevention of Vice (Hay'at al-amr bi al-ma'ruf wa al-nahy 'an al-munkar). This demonstration, which as far as possible draws on statistical data, also allows us to explore the theologico-juridical positions of the religious establishment on several social questions. Lastly and more generally, studying the institution of hisba in the *longue durée* of Saudi history can be considered an indicator of the process of state construction. As elsewhere in the world, this process is characterized by a monopolistic will to power on the part of a (political and religious) central authority and the various types of resistance to which this dynamic gives rise.

A LONG PROCESS OF INSTITUTIONALIZATION . . .

As Michael Cook observed in his book on the practice of promoting virtue and preventing vice in Islamic thought, Muhammad ibn Abd al-Wahhab assigned almost no importance to this religious duty despite the central place it occupies in Islamic history and the Islamic imaginary.[4] Indeed, I have been able to find only a few passages in all of the Najdi preacher's oeuvre that succinctly mention it in generic terms.[5] The explanation for this near total absence is simple: promoting virtue and preventing vice occurs only *within* the framework of the Islamic community. Yet the doctrine preached by Ibn Abd al-Wahhab sought not to reform the practices and mores of local populations in the framework of an existing system, but rather to "convert" them to genuine monotheism. Once this crucial step had been taken, the duty of promoting virtue and preventing vice would once again come into force. According to the meager information that we possess, the shaykh charged certain disciples and followers with the task of ensuring that orthodoxy and orthopraxy were observed in the public sphere in territories controlled by the Saudi Emirate. Needless to say, this practice was continued after his death.

Yet the strengthening of the Hanbali-Wahhabi tradition and the rapid expansion of the Saudi Emirate in the early nineteenth century obliged the shaykh's heirs to soften their stance in order to gain acceptance from the other Muslim populations of the region. After the conquest of Mecca in 1806, Abd Allah ibn Muhammad ibn Abd al-Wahhab (d. 1829) made his father's approach part of the framework of promoting virtue and preventing vice, a move that implied de facto recognition of other Muslim traditions. This initiative was the first Hanbali-Wahhabi attempt at routinization.[6]

While hisba was used to justify the expansion of the Saudi Emirate at the beginning of the nineteenth century, as has been the case of several Islamic countries since the High Middle Ages, it subsequently served—particularly during the second reign of Emir Faysal ibn Turki (1843–1865)—as a device for homogenizing the population of Najd in order to provide the Hanbali-Wahhabi tradition and the House of Saud with a solid territorial base. This period was also characterized by a desire to institutionalize this religious practice in the interests of efficiency. Religious agents from each oasis were appointed by Hanbali-Wahhabi judges to carry out this salvationist mission. For reasons already discussed in chapter 3, around 1854–1855, the authorities even gave a group of twenty-two pious men the task of seeing to it that orthodoxy and orthopraxy were respected in the Riyadh public sphere.[7] This measure was later extended to the provinces of the Saudi Emirate. But the death of Emir Faysal in 1865 and the outbreak of the war of succession among his sons put an end to this first attempt at institutionalizing hisba. During this period of instability, the religious establishment attempted to organize itself in an informal manner in order to carry out the duty of promoting virtue and preventing vice. Several pious figures voluntarily participated in this. But the lack of order—an indispensable condition for carrying out religious duties—frustrated their attempts to adequately do so.

The expansion and renaissance of the Saudi Emirate that began in 1902 went hand in hand with the reestablishment of hisba as a tool for homogenizing and dominating a public sphere structured by representation. As long as this office efficiently accomplished its mission, no change was made to its mode of organization. With assistance from a variable number of auxiliaries, each judge was responsible for ensuring that the precepts of the Law were observed in his jurisdiction (commercial transactions in the markets, religious obligations, mores, etc.).[8] During his stay in Riyadh in 1922–1923, the voyager Amin al-Rihani noted that the religious establishment scrupulously saw to it that orthodoxy and orthopraxy were respected in the public sphere. Those who transgressed the Law were subjected to corporal punishment. If a believer failed to attend one of the public prayers, a delegation of notables went to his home in order to ascertain the reasons for his absence. In case of recidivism, he was to be whipped.[9] This system was extended to conquered territories, in particular the holy cities of Islam.[10]

On the basis of the above, we can deduce that since the emergence of the Saudi Emirate, hisba has never been an autonomous office and has always lacked aedile prerogatives. The characteristics of the Saudi apparatus thus depart from the model presented by the classical theologico-juridical texts. This specificity resulted from the symbiotic relationship between the political power and the religious authority, according to which the two partners observe a rigorous division of labor. To this, another characteristic must be mentioned: voluntary work (*al-tatawwu'*). Although not specific to the Saudi case, it has played an important role in the process of institutionalizing hisba. Individuals known for their piety and religious commitment were also to freely carry out this duty. But while almost no one objected to the action of a few isolated and pious volunteers, this practice threatened to become a genuine danger to the established order when carried out by a more or less organized group. Such was the case of the Ikhwan during the 1910s and 1920s.

The brutal manner in which some Ikhwan treated subject populations in the growing Saudi kingdom was a matter of concern for the political power and the religious authority. As we have seen, King Abd al-Aziz (1902–1953) and the ulama were constantly calling these turbulent troops to order. The ulama did not hesitate to use strong-arm measures to ensure rigorous observance of the Law in the public spheres of the oases, conquered villages, and towns. On several occasions, this gave rise to bloody clashes between local populations and foreign delegations, in particular during the 1926 pilgrimage known as the *mahmal* incident.

In order to symbolize their presence in the annual pilgrimage to Mecca and display their power, the sovereigns of Egypt have since the thirteenth century sent a chief of the official delegation (*amir al-hajj*) with a richly decorated camel. Draped with covers embroidered in plumes and precious metals and carrying a sumptuously adorned litter, the camel was preceded by a detachment of soldiers and musicians and followed by a crowd of pilgrims.[11] We can well imagine how this spectacle could have shocked many Ikhwan, who no doubt considered it an act of idolatry. They tried to put an end to it by seizing the camel, but the Egyptian detachment fired upon them. The volley, which resulted in approximately twenty deaths and one hundred wounded, nearly led to a bloodbath in this holy territory and sacred month. But King Abd al-Aziz, who was himself in Mecca, arrived on the scene of the incident in time to bring it to a peaceful end.[12]

Aside from the loss of life, the *mahmal* affair was worrying in more than one respect. The friends and enemies of Abd al-Aziz could now wonder how, if he was not even capable of controlling his own troops, he could succeed in administering the holy places of Islam and protecting pilgrims. International Islamic opinion seconded these negative judgments of Hanbali-Wahhabism, which the king endeavored to change. The Saudi monarchy thus needed to show that it was capable of managing the holy places in an efficient manner and that the tradition could be adapted to its new status as state religion. Apart from the local and international loss of prestige, the Saudi political power and religious authority risked losing power should they fail to demonstrate their ability to control the public sphere with an iron fist. By giving rise to a desire to preclude international criticism and put an end to all private initiatives, the *mahmal* incident was thus the catalyst that precipitated the institutionalization of hisba.

Just a few weeks after the end of the pilgrimage, the king called upon Abd Allah ibn Blihid (d. 1940),[13] the judge of Mecca, to appoint an official body responsible for hisba in the holy city and its immediate environs.[14] On 10 September 1926, the official Saudi newspaper published a royal decree ordering the creation of the Company for the Promotion of Virtue and the Prevention of Vice (Jama'at al-amr bi al-ma'ruf wa al-nahy 'an al-munkar).[15] Consisting of twelve members,[16] the mission of this new body was to see to it that collective prayers were performed and customs (*al-'adat*) and social transactions (*al-mu'amalat*) were in conformity with sharia as well as to monitor the muezzins and imams of mosques and prevent people from using insults in the public sphere (*al-badha'a al-lisaniyya*). A guide to the pilgrimage, drafted in 1928 by an Egyptian in the service of the Saudi monarchy, added to this list a ban on mixed-sex groups and the consumption of alcohol and use of tobacco.[17]

The creation of this system was accompanied by a pedagogical exercise. At the beginning of 1927, Judge Abd Allah ibn Blihid and Muhammad Bahjat al-Baytar (d. 1976), a Syrian *'alim* in the service of the monarchy, wrote seven articles that were published on the front page of the official newspaper. Drawing on arguments developed by al-Ghazali (d. 1111) (an Ash'ari *'alim*) and Ibn Taymiyya in their writings on the hisba, they underscored the importance of this religious obligation to safeguarding orthodoxy, orthopraxy, and the political order. In particular, they insisted on the fact that only the competent authorities could use coercive force to ensure that the Law was respected to the exclusion of all other natural or legal persons.[18] The members of the corporation also issued several fatawa in keeping with this stance.[19]

In order to monopolize the public sphere and reassure the population of the Hijaz and the Islamic world more broadly, the king went further yet in the process of institutionalizing hisba. In 1928, he decided to unify all of the companies under a single leadership, giving it the name the Committee for the Promotion of Virtue and the Prevention of Vice. Regulations (*anzima*, sing. *nizam*) were drawn up for the committee setting its mode of operation and prerogatives on the ground.[20] And in order to leave nothing to chance, the king also promulgated a second series of regulations in which he strictly codified the functions of the volunteer muhtasib, referred to in the text as honorary members of the committee (*a'da' sharafiyyun*) but commonly known under the name of *mutawi'a* (sing. *mutawi'*).[21] From that point on, no one could carry out this religious duty on his own volition. Henceforth, each volunteer muhtasib had to be officially recognized by local committee leaders and report to them on his activities at least once a week. The crowning achievement of this institutionalizing drive was the nomination to the head of the committee of the Egyptian Abd al-Zahir Abu al-Samh (d. 1951). Although Hanbali-Wahhabi in point of dogma, this man belonged to the reformist current in the broad sense of the term.[22] In addition to reassuring local and international opinion, this choice was meant to allow the king to attract the sympathy of reformists who could mobilize their networks and media on his behalf.

The struggle with the Ikhwan pushed Saudi authorities to extend this institutionalization to the main administrative centers of the kingdom, particularly in Najd. On 2 August 1929, the king thus announced the creation of an administration (*idara*) for the Promotion of Virtue and the Prevention of Vice in Riyadh.[23] Umar ibn Hasan Al al-Shaykh (d. 1975), who had formerly carried out this duty on a volunteer basis, was chosen to lead the new administration, which was directly funded by the royal purse. With this announcement, it seems that Abd al-Aziz was in part seeking to respond to the grievances of the Ikhwan, who had been defeated several months earlier, by demonstrating that the state venerated and ensured respect for the precepts of the Law even as it cordoned off the public sphere to preclude the emergence of new actors and their attendant demands and impose the official vision on the majority.

Yet the extension of institutionalization to the principal regions of the kingdom did not mean that the founder of Saudi Arabia aspired to create a "national" administration for the promotion of virtue and prevention of vice directed by the religious establishment. On the contrary, there is ample reason to believe that he wished for purely political reasons to exclude at all costs the ulama from this function in the Hijaz: Hanbali-Wahhabi rigor in the area of religion could lead to a bad image for the young kingdom abroad and create problems with the local population. Indeed, in 1930 this concern for appearances led Abd al-Aziz to merge the Hijaz Committee for the Promotion of Virtue and the Prevention of Vice with the police. That same year, a new regulation consisting of thirty-one articles was issued to precisely address all technical, administrative, legal, and financial aspects of the hisba.[24] It remained in force in the Hijaz until 1980.

When the king tried to create hybrid institutes of religious sciences (al-Ma'had al-Su'udi in Mecca and Dar al-Tawhid in Al-Ta'if) or codify sharia in the province of the Hijaz, he met with sharp resistance on the part of the religious establishment, which no doubt saw such schemes as violating the terms of their symbiotic partnership. Unfortunately, the paucity of our sources does not allow us to follow this "struggle." We do know, however, that it resulted in a victory for the ulama: in 1937, a royal decree announced that the Committee for the Promotion of Virtue and the Prevention of Vice would henceforth be placed under the authority of Grand Mufti Muhammad ibn Ibrahim, who at the time held the title of chief judge (*ra'is al-qudat*).[25] After having consolidated the positions of the Hanbali-Wahhabi corporation in the Hijaz, Asir, and Jazan, Ibn Ibrahim in 1952 decided, with the blessing of the palace, to appoint his youngest brother, Abd al-Malik (d. 1984), to the head of the Committee for the Promotion of Virtue and the Prevention of Vice in these provinces.[26]

. . . PUNCTUATED BY CRISES

Like all of the religious establishment's activities, that of promoting virtue and preventing vice underwent significant expansion during the 1950s. Profiting from generational transition within the reigning house, the ulama sold dearly their unconditional support. Under the aegis of Muhammad ibn Ibrahim, the presidents of the Committees for the Promotion of Virtue and the Prevention of Vice of the provinces of the Hijaz and Najd—respectively, Abd al-Malik ibn Ibrahim Al al-Shaykh and Umar ibn Hasan Al al-Shaykh, who also controlled the provinces of Asir, Jazan, and Al-Ahsa'—began moving into new rural and urban centers. To do so, a recruitment campaign was launched.[27] Between 1956 and 1960, the number of field agents rose from 1,350 to 2,467.[28] The budget also rose from several hundred thousand riyals in 1956 to more than 12 million riyals in 1964, the year King Saud was deposed.[29]

These material resources were accompanied by symbolic resources. Ibn Ibrahim wrote several epistles intended to raise awareness among the muhtasib concerning the importance—indeed, the centrality—of their profession/vocation in the economy of Islamic salvation. He thus encouraged them to be strong, tightly bound to one another, and above all active so that orthodoxy and orthopraxy might be imposed in the public sphere—the only way, according to him, to save the souls of believers.[30] Conscious of their identity and their mission, Saudi muhtasib fulfilled their salvationist duty with zeal and efficiency.

The dynamism of the corporation and the criticisms of ulama concerning the introduction of positive laws were not matters of indifference to Prince/Prime Minister Faysal, who seems in all likelihood to have hoped to create a pole of authority uniquely centered on the royal house. As early as 1962, Faysal had considered taking over the Committees for the Promotion of Virtue and the Prevention of Vice,[31] but the weight of the religious establishment and the charisma of Ibn Ibrahim prevented him from doing so. Faysal thus tried to hinder their actions. For example, between 1966 and 1970, only forty-one people joined the various committees of the country. The number of members thus grew from 2,950 to 2,991 in four years.

But aside from these tactical maneuvers, Faysal and his followers above all counted on developmentalist discourse and policy to supply the monarchy with its own legitimacy and thus marginalize its religious partner. This policy led to a gradual change in the lifestyle of the populations of large Saudi towns in contact with foreign workers and the material and immaterial consumer goods imported from abroad. From the point of view of the ulama, the result was a loosening of mores and a drop in religiosity heralding, according to Ibn Ibrahim, an imminent catastrophe.[32] But instead of combatting this "devastating plague"[33] by supporting the agents of hisba, the political authorities adopted positions that were, in the eyes of their religious partners, at the very least underhanded: insults and mistreatment of certain muhtasib, permission given to some journalists to criticize their work, nonapplication of the punishments sought by the committee against offenders, and so on.[34]

The principal religious figures of the period—in particular Ibn Ibrahim and Ibn Humayd—came to the defense of the prerogatives of the religious establishment by deploying all of their ideological authority to weaken the political partner. While strongly condemning several foreign tools of amusement (such as alcohol, the cinema, foreign newspapers and books, Western dress, photography, portraits of heads of state, songs on the radio, and football)[35] and accusing foreign workers and executives of being responsible for all of the evil afflicting Saudi society,[36] they never for all that expressed criticism of the House of Saud. On the contrary, they constantly lavished the king and the leading princes with advice (nasa'ih, sing. nasiha) in what they described as an attempt to lead them back to the path of righteousness.[37] The two partners finished by finding common ground, of course, with each party making concessions to the other. The ulama thus conceded the legitimacy of radio and television on the condition that they not broadcast songs, films, or programs that could be perceived as running counter to the Law. The state could extend education to all girls in the kingdom while respecting Hanbali-Wahhabi precepts: a ban on mixed-gender groups, the generalization of the traditional dress of the sedentaries of Najd to the entire kingdom, and so on.

The ethic of responsibility and the Hanbali habitus of obedience prevented the ulama from going further in their demands. They accepted the ongoing social changes on the condition that most of the representations that structured the Saudi public sphere—such as shop closings during prayer hours, the ban on mixed-gender groups in open spaces, and the application of legal sentences in accordance with sharia—be maintained. But several peripheral actors—mainly belonging to the neo–Ahl al-Hadith movement[38]—did not accept the establishment's stance, which they saw as conflicting with sharia. They decided to respond by reactivating the notion of promoting virtue and preventing vice. Starting in 1965, photographic studios and women's clothing stores displaying mannequins were vandalized in Medina.[39] But such disorganized action very rapidly gave way to an ever more structured movement with the creation in 1966 of al-Jama'a al-Salafiyya al-Muhtasiba (the Salafi company for the hisba) founded by Juhayman al-Utaybi (d. 1980). To win legitimacy and gain official support, this group sought and obtained the blessing of Abd al-Aziz ibn Baz (d. 1999), who was then vice president of the Islamic University of Medina. Its principal objective, however, was to take over the functions of the Committee for the Promotion of Virtue and the Prevention of Vice (organization of training and awareness-raising circles, distribution of tracts, admonition, and even the promulgation of fatawa). In the space of ten years, Juhayman and his companions had extended their activity to several towns in the kingdom, particularly Najd. Following a pattern that has been familiar to the Muslim world since the High Middle Ages, the chief of this company began to gradually transform himself into a political actor, legitimating his actions by reference to the duty to promote virtue and prevent vice. But this parallel hisba, which threatened to metamorphose into a genuine protest movement, ultimately drew the attention of the political authorities and the religious establishment. In order to reenergize the system of official hisba, in 1976 King Khalid (1975–1982) issued a royal decree ordering that all committees in the country be unified under a single leadership, known as the General Presidency of the Committee for the Promotion of Virtue and the Prevention of Vice (al-Ri'asa al-'amma li-Hay'at al-amr bi al-ma'ruf wa al-nahy 'an al-munkar).[40] Abd al-Aziz ibn Abd Allah ibn Hasan Al al-Shaykh (d. 1990), the new president of the Committee for the Promotion of Virtue and the Prevention of Vice, announced that his mission was to restructure this system and recruit additional field agents in order to give further impetus to this sacred duty.[41] Other acts confirmed the political authorities' desire to recover their monopoly on hisba. In 1977, the representatives of the corporation, who were in a way honorary members of the Juhayman Jama'a, broke all ties with it. During the months that followed, its leading activists were hit by a wave of arrests. Known for his dynamism and organizational talents, the oldest son of Ibn Ibrahim, Abd al-Aziz (d. 2006), was appointed head of the committee with the rank of minister. This series of events could not have been a coincidence.

But governmental action only pushed Juhayman and his followers to adopt an ever more extreme stance. In 1979, this process of radicalization resulted in armed rebellion. Our aim here is not to reconstruct the history and sociopsychological causes of the storming of the Grand Mosque of Mecca, something that has already been done elsewhere,[42] but rather to demonstrate that this politico-religious crisis played an important role in the process of institutionalizing hisba. As with the Ikhwan rebellion, the Saudi authorities responded to a portion of the insurgents' demands while seeking to monopolize hisba as a tool for dominating the public sphere. It must be added that, the same year, the Saudi state was confronted by armed Shiite insurrection in the province of Al-Ahsa', which echoed the revolution of Khomeini (d. 1989) in Iran.[43]

Just a few months after these two events, a new *national* regulation for the Committee for the Promotion of Virtue and the Prevention of Vice was issued.[44] Still in force in 2014, it sets out the committee's prerogatives and mechanisms in a more or less detailed manner. It was supplemented by an organic regulation (*la'iha tanfidhiyya*) and a series of instructions (*ta'mimat*). Abd al-Aziz ibn Muhammad Al al-Shaykh also completely replaced the foundations of committee structures in the interests of a better division of responsibilities and greater efficiency in the field. Finally, its budget grew from more than 85.7 million riyals in 1979 to more than 203 million riyals in 1985. The funds allocated by the state to the "prevention" sector thus more than doubled in five years despite the fact that Saudi Arabia was then going through its greatest economic crisis in recent history.[45] This increase concerned not only the committee, but all of the country's juridico-religious institutions. It was occasioned by the rebellion of the Juhayman, the Shiite insurrection, and the failure of developmentalist policy due to the fall in the price of petroleum. Weakened by this latter event, to which it failed to effectively respond, the Saudi monarchy was henceforth required to draw upon the ideological legitimacy of the Hanbali-Wahhabi establishment in order to legitimize its power and efficiently control the public sphere.[46] After having passed through a period in the desert in the 1970s, the Committee for the Promotion of Virtue and the Prevention of Vice thus made a comeback in the 1980s.[47] As in other societies structured by representations and symbols, cinemas were closed and female singers gradually disappeared from Saudi television in order to clearly mark this return.[48]

Two other crises that shook Saudi Arabia at the beginning of the 1990s and the first decade of the twenty-first century also allow us to closely trace the long and difficult process of institutionalizing the practice of promoting virtue and preventing vice. These were the Islamist protests that followed the end of the 1990–1991 Gulf War and the combination of Jihadist threat and U.S. pressure that followed in the wake of the terrorist attacks of 11 September 2001.

For religious, political, and social reasons, Islamist protests demanding that the Saudi system be profoundly reformed broke out in 1991.[49] Invoking the duty to promote virtue and prevent vice, the leaders of this movement did not content themselves with simply addressing petitions to King Fahd (1982–2005) but also carried out genuine actions on the ground, organizing meetings, creating commissions, distributing printed and audio material, and so on.[50] The political power and the religious authority realized that all of the measures taken to monopolize the practice of promoting virtue and preventing vice had failed to stop the concept from being appropriated by a seditious group. In 1992, they thus decided to launch a new phase. While leading ulama reiterated that in keeping with the most orthodox Hanbali tradition, only holders of power had the right to promote virtue and prevent vice in the public sphere,[51] article twenty-three of the new Fundamental Law (al-Nizam al-asasi lil-hukm) of 1992 stipulated that "the state protects Islamic dogma, applies sharia, promotes virtue, prevents vice, and fulfills the duty of religious predication."[52] By writing hisba into the "constitution," the Saudi regime (including the ulama, who saw themselves as an integral part of the state system) declared their determination to monopolize this religious duty.

In the framework of a global reconstruction of the religious space in response to the Islamist protest movement,[53] the monarchy and the religious establishment gave new impetus to the work of the Committee for the Promotion of Virtue and the Prevention of Vice. By doing so, they sought, on the one hand, to respond to a portion of Islamist grievances and, on the other, to more efficiently control the public sphere. In other words, Saudi authorities hoped to burnish their image while improving the performance of the hisba system. Legitimacy and efficiency were thus the two motors driving this move toward further institutionalization, which was reflected on the ground by the emergence of a plan for professionalizing the muhtasib. In addition to the fact that the committee's budget grew from more than 172.7 million riyals in 1990 to more than 242.3 million in 1994—an increase of 40 percent—continuing education programs supported by modern pedagogical material and a policy of proximity were unveiled.

Starting in 1994, the committee began to regularly organize conference series, round table discussions, and internships for its employees in all provinces of the kingdom.[54] These activities were overseen by figures from the religious establishment, in particular members of the Committee of Grand Ulama.[55] Some muhtasib could even follow an intensive training program held in collaboration with Riyadh's Al-Imam University.[56] In 1996, forty training internships were organized for employees from the various provinces of the kingdom.[57] In addition to creating ʽasabiyya within this body, the objective of these training programs was to supply committee employees with the religious and legal backgrounds necessary to carry out their duties. Indeed, up until the mid-1990s, the employees generally had little training. Recruitment policy gradually changed, however, and well-educated candidates were increasingly sought after.[58]

In 1994, the committee also began publishing a monthly newsletter for its employees, *Akhbar al-hisba* (the *Hisba News*), to reinforce corporate identity and culture. The newsletter contained information concerning the various activities of the committee in the kingdom and articles by ulama justifying hisba and giving practical advice to field agents. This brochure met with such success in religious circles that, two years later, it was decided to transform it into a monthly review titled *Majallat al-hisba* (the *Hisba Review*). In addition to articles, fatawa, and interviews with leading figures of the religious establishment concerning various juridico-religious issues, the review continued to present the activities of the committee in the field. It also included a monthly rubric in which the editors presented—from a Hanbali-Wahhabi point of view, of course—a social phenomenon relating to hisba (mixed-sex groups; satellite channels; foreign travel; the damage done by rumors, tobacco, and drugs; the problems facing young people; the fight against terrorism, etc.), reviews of classic and modern works concerning the promotion of virtue and the prevention of vice, and idealized portraits of the careers of retired field agents, intended to serve as examples and inspire dedication.[59]

Nearly all of the training program material, articles, interviews, presentations, and book reviews at our disposal insist upon one point: the centrality of the duty of promoting virtue and preventing vice in Islamic society, seen as "preventive medicine for souls"[60] and an indispensable "ark" for reaching the banks of eternal salvation (*safinat al-najat*).[61] As a result, the muhtasib—"shadow soldiers in the service of virtue," to borrow a phrase from the *'alim* Muhammad ibn Uthaymin (d. 2001)[62]—were to act with dynamism and gentleness in order to save the greatest possible number of souls.[63]

On the advice of Abd al-Aziz ibn Baz and his colleagues, who recommended that all forms of modern communication be employed to propagate the good word (such as books, brochures, posters, films, telephone, fax, and the Internet),[64] the committee launched a policy of proximity with the population. This involved reappropriation by the religious establishment of the preaching media that had made the fortune of Saudi Islamism at the end of the 1980s and early 1990s. Indeed, between 1993 and 2000, the number of print media publications (books, fatawa, guidebooks, instructional works, etc.) increased from 238,563 to 5,733,029, and the number of audio recordings (sermons, commentary on dogma and rituals, Islamic history, etc.) grew from 100,000 to 671,950. The number of conferences intended for the general public grew from 911 to 12,611 and that of orientation visits—that is, visits by muhtasib to schools, universities, and government bureaucracies to preach to students and officials—grew from 871 to 3,682.[65]

The religious establishment, which sixty years earlier had wanted to forbid the study of foreign languages, no longer hesitated to have Hanbali-Wahhabi works translated and to call upon interpreters to communicate with non-Arabic-speaking populations. During the 1995 pilgrimage, the Committee for the Promotion of Virtue and the Prevention of Vice recruited thirty-five interpreters (including English, French, Indonesian, Turkish, and Persian) in order to facilitate the work of its field agents.[66] This system was complemented by the publication each Friday of a page in the Al-Jazira newspaper devoted to religious affairs and the duty of hisba,[67] the creation of a website,[68] and participation in several Saudi radio and television programs.

The process of institutionalizing the promotion of virtue and the prevention of vice and professionalizing its agents further accelerated after the September 11 attacks and the arrival of King Abd Allah to power in 2005. Indeed, international stigmatization, U.S. pressure, and Al-Qaeda attacks against Saudi territory pushed the authorities to try to remake the country's image in the eyes of international public opinion. To that end, a timid policy of openness was launched in various domains (such as partial reform of academic programs, a national dialogue among the country's various components and sensibilities, the organization of municipal elections, and relative liberty for the press). The domain of hisba was a priority for this policy. The excessive zeal shown by some muhtasib in carrying out their duties had earned the Committee for the Promotion of Virtue and the Prevention of Vice a sinister reputation among some groups of foreign workers and the local population. This in turn reflected unfavorably on the monarchy and the Hanbali-Wahhabi tradition, which was attempting to routinize itself.

The aforementioned system was strengthened via the creation of a number of university chairs charged with studying the technical and theoretical aspects of hisba and proposing practical solutions adapted to contemporary Saudi Arabia[69] as well as the establishment in 2004 of the Higher Institute for the Promotion of Virtue and Prevention of Vice (al-Ma'had al-'ali lil-amr bi al-ma'ruf wa al-nahy 'an al-munkar) to oversee the continuing education of muhtasib.[70] In 2009, the committee, then presided over by Abd al-Aziz al-Humayyin (b. 1964), launched a strategic plan known as the Hisba Project (Mashru' al-hisba).[71] Drafted and developed by a research team from King Fahd University, this strategy aimed to reorganize the committee's administrative structures, working methods, and human resource management over a period of twenty years.

While the stated objective of this strategic plan was to improve committee performance,[72] it sought above all to preserve the committee's legitimacy by permitting it to adapt to the social changes that had affected Saudi Arabia and to cope with the external constraints of a kingdom that would henceforth seek to play a significant role on the international scene. In 2009, for example, the committee sent one hundred of its field agents on language-learning trips abroad in order to allow them to better communicate with pilgrims and foreign workers.[73] It also organized training programs to raise awareness among its agents concerning the plurality of traditions and customs in the Muslim world so that they might learn to tolerate the religious practices of pilgrims to Mecca as long as those pilgrims did not threaten public order.[74]

As a collective actor possessing ideological authority, the religious establishment already supported this new strategy at the discursive level. The ulama called upon the agents of this system to show greater finesse in their interactions with society (as rudeness and even violence were the main reproaches

Religious Authority in Practice

made against them by the public). They asked them to privilege dialogue, prevention, and advice—in other words, to place greater emphasis on promoting virtue than on preventing vice. In short, the trustees of Hanbali-Wahhabi tradition recommended that committee agents shift their focus from supervision and repression to awareness-raising and prevention.[75] Although this process has only just begun, it allows us to anticipate (provided, of course, that there is no sudden change in the Saudi politico-religious landscape) the transformation of hisba as an institution and the emergence of a new manner of supervising the Saudi public sphere.[76]

STRUCTURE OF THE HISBA SYSTEM

Before describing the structures of the Committee for the Promotion of Virtue and the Prevention of Vice, we should elucidate the symbolism of its logo (Figure 13), as this visual identity nicely reveals the manner in which the Hanbali-Wahhabi establishment perceives the committee.[77]

In keeping with prophetic tradition, the three concentric circles represent the three different manners of preventing vice: "If someone among you sees something reprehensible [*munkar*], he is to change it with his hand; if that proves impossible, with his tongue, if not with his heart: [but] that is the lowest degree of faith."[78] The heart of the first circle is occupied by three symbols. The first form represents a V-shaped open book. This is very likely the Qur'an, the book par excellence and foundation of the social order. The map of Saudi Arabia embossed

Figure 13. Seal of the General Presidency of the Promotion of Virtue and the Prevention of Vice.

with the arms of the royal house symbolizes the monarchy's support, the official nature of the institution, and the territorial framework in which it is to carry out its mission. The state is thus represented as the protector of religion and the promoter of sharia. The third symbol—the veil— evokes what is referred to as the prophetic tradition of the ark (*hadith al-safina*). This tradition describes the promotion of virtue and the prevention of vice as an ark conducting believers to salvation (*safinat al-najat*) by means of the strict observance of orthodoxy and orthopraxy.[79] These three inseparable and complementary symbols representing the historical alliance between political power and religious authority are surrounded by the color blue, which recalls the sea of temptation and sin that the believer must confront and defeat in order to reach the good port—that is, to attain eternal salvation. To do this, the population must obey the government and follow the teachings of the religious establishment. The two partners thus monopolize the practice of hisba in the public sphere.

This desire for monopoly is eloquently expressed in the second and third circles. The space accorded to speech—that is, to exchanges and debate in the public sphere—is extremely narrow, as the second circle makes clear. And the area in white, the color of purity and absolute truth, here indicates that this sphere must be devoid of destructive debates and that only official truth is to reign over Saudi social space. The golden color of the third circle for its part without doubt refers to the Arab maxim "if speech is silver, silence is golden." Private individuals are invited to keep their silence and let the competent authorities act. The choice of Kufic calligraphy (*al-khat al-kufi*) to retranscribe the official name of the committee is also significant. Reputed to be the oldest, most elegant, and most majestic style of Arab calligraphy, *al-khat al-kufi* was used during the first centuries of the Hegira and later to retranscribe Qur'anic texts, make caliphal inscriptions, and engrave the epitaphs of believers. Its use thus allowed the committee to inscribe itself in the *longue durée* of Islamic history.

Elucidating the visual identity of the Committee for the Promotion of Virtue and the Prevention of Vice underscores two facets of its existence: first, this official apparatus is the product of a symbiotic relationship between the House of Saud and the religious establishment, one of the pillars of which is the observance of orthodoxy and orthopraxy in the public sphere; second, in keeping with the Hanbali-Wahhabi tradition, the committee must monopolize this religious duty in order to preserve public order. As mentioned above, this claim is reinforced by article twenty-three of the 1992 Saudi Fundamental Law.[80]

In keeping with the regulation (*al-nizam*) that organizes its operation, the Committee for the Promotion of Virtue and the Prevention of Vice is deemed an autonomous apparatus (*jihaz*) under the direct authority of the king as head of the executive branch and leader of the community. By Royal Order, the king appoints a president with all of the prerogatives of a minister to head the committee.[81]

With the exception of the Meccans Abd Allah al-Shaybi and Ahmad Jamal al-Layl and the Egyptian Abd al-Zahir Abu al-Samh, who successively served as presidents of the Mecca committee from 1926 to 1930, all other presidents through the early 1990s were drawn from the Al al-Shaykh line (Table 4). Following the retirement of Abd al-Aziz ibn Muhammad ibn Ibrahim in 1990, the profile of those who headed the system began to change. Although natives of the Najdi crescent, they no longer (with one exception) issued from the priestly lineage of Hanbali-Wahhabism but rather belonged to the families of midlevel religious personnel. Following the example of the grand ulama, the recruitment pool was enlarged to make room for the new elites coming out of the academic system that Muhammad ibn Ibrahim had begun constructing in 1950.

The new presidents of the Committee for the Promotion of Virtue and the Prevention of Vice were not ulama but rather were technocrat-clerics. Though they had studied religion under the great authorities of Hanbali-Wahhabism or at Al-Imam University, they were not renowned in the intellectual domain (writings, preaching, fatawa) but were instead distinguished for their brilliant careers in the country's juridico-religious administration. Ibrahim al-Ghayth (b. 1940) scaled all of the ranks of the clerical technocracy within the committee. After receiving his diploma at the Faculty of Sharia (the future Al-Imam University) in 1969, he joined the committee as an official in the accounting department. He then became director of a neighborhood committee center and, later, director for the entire city of Riyadh. In 1985, he took over the reins of the Riyadh province committee and seven years later became general secretary of the General Presidency of the Committee for the Promotion of Virtue and the Prevention of Vice. In 2002, he was appointed its president through 2009.[82]

The choice of these new profiles was in response to the Saudi authorities' desire to institutionalize and professionalize the system. Indeed, the presidency of the committee is an administrative post dedicated to executing the orders of the political power and the teachings of the religious authority in keeping with the regulations in force. The holder of this office must have administrative experience.

In order to carry out his mission, the president of the committee disposes of structures befitting a modern minister: financial, administrative, and legal affairs; human resources; planning studies; inspection; and public relations. These services are directed by three general secretaries (*wukala'*, sing. *wakil*),

Table 4. The Presidents of the Committee for the Promotion of Virtue and the Prevention of Vice

Name	Date and Place
Abd Allah al-Shaybi (d. ?)	(1926–1927) Mecca
Ahmad Jamal al-Layl (d. ?)	(1927–1928) Mecca
Abd al-Zahir Abu al-Samh (d. 1951)	(1928–1930) Hijaz
Attached to the Police	(1930–1937) Hijaz
Attached to the Grand Mufti	(1937–1952) Hijaz
Abd al-Malik ibn Ibrahim (d. 1984)	(1952–1976) Hijaz, Asir, and Jazan
Umar ibn Hasan Al al-Shaykh (d. 1975)	(1929–1975) Najd and Al-Ahsa'
Abd al-Aziz ibn Abd Allah Al al-Shaykh (d. 1990)	(1976–1977) Entire territory
Abd al-Aziz ibn Muhammad Al al-Shaykh (d. 2006)	(1977–1990) Entire territory
Abd al-Aziz ibn Abd al-Rahman al-Sa'id (b. 1937)[a]	(1990–2002) Entire territory
Ibrahim ibn Abd Allah al-Ghayth (b. 1940)	(2002–2009) Entire territory
Abd al-Aziz ibn Humayyin al-Humayyin (b. 1965)	(2009–2011) Entire territory
Abd al-Latif ibn Abd al-Aziz Al al-Shaykh (b. 1948)	(2011–) Entire territory

[a] Abd al-Rahman ibn Ahmad Al al-Shaykh (b. 1953) served as interim president for several months between the departure of Abd al-Aziz Al al-Shaykh and the appointment of Abd al-Aziz al-Sa'id.

who are themselves supervised by the vice president of the committee (*na'ib al-ra'is al-'amm*). The central administration of the committee principally sees to the distribution of the state-allocated budget, drafts strategies and action plans at the national level, supervises and organizes the work of regional centers, investigates complaints, organizes continuing educational sessions, and arranges partnerships with various state agencies.

As fieldwork constitutes its principal mission, the Committee for the Promotion of Virtue and the Prevention of Vice also has at its disposal offices (*furu'*, sing. *far'*) and centers (*marakiz*, sing. *markaz*) in most of the districts, towns, and villages of the kingdom's thirteen provinces.[83] Led by a president (*ra'is*) or director (*mudir*), each of these local systems has administrative employees and field agents, the number of whom depends on the sector to which they have been assigned. Table 5 summarizes the distribution of offices and centers across the territory of Saudi Arabia.[84]

Several remarks are in order concerning this distribution, as it seems to reflect the religious positions and acculturation strategies adopted by the religious establishment since the 1950s. The fact that Najd possesses 39 percent of the committee's offices and centers is explained by the authorities' wish to maintain

Table 5. Distribution of Committee Center Offices in the Provinces of the Saudi Kingdom in 2008

	Riyadh	Mecca	Medina	Al-Qasim	Al-Ahsa'	Asir	Tabuk	Ha'il	The North	Jazan	Najran	Al-Baha	Al-Jawf
Town office	1	1	1	1	1	1	1	1	1	1	1	1	1
District office	19	11	6	10	10	11	5	3	2	12	5	6	2
Local center	97	69	19	29	25	41	4	2	7	11	5	11	5

the socioreligious homogeneity of the Hanbali-Wahhabi tradition's historical stronghold and demographic center of gravity in order to maintain its dominance over the rest of the kingdom.

The location of the holy places of Islam explains why 28 percent of committee centers and offices are concentrated in the Hijaz, particularly in Mecca and Medina. Indeed, by energetically enforcing orthodoxy and orthopraxy in keeping with their vision of the universe, the religious authority wishes to impress pilgrims from the four corners of the world with a massive display of power. Saudi Arabia wants to be seen as a state that respects the Law by applying those precepts that are closest to the practices of the earliest generations of Muslims (*al-salaf al-salih*). But apart from the holy places, hisba offices and agents are hardly present: this is, for example, the case of Jeddah, where one sees people walking in town during hours of prayer, a phenomenon that is almost unimaginable in Najd.

The 23 percent of the offices and centers located in the South of the kingdom reflect a policy of "Hanbali-Wahhabization" that has been imposed on this region since its conquest by King Abd al-Aziz. In tandem with the dispatch of socialization agents and the establishment of educational and religious structures, the establishment endeavored to impose its representations in the local public sphere. As early as 1954, Grand Mufti Muhammad ibn Ibrahim gave his brother, Abd al-Malik, the task of creating an autonomous regional office. The number of offices and centers subsequently increased in the provinces of Al-Baha, Asir, and Jazan, reaching ninety-five in 2008.[85]

By contrast, the province of Najran, also located in the southern part of the kingdom, was provided with only a small number of hisba offices. This was for a simple reason: a good number of its inhabitants belong to the Shiite branch of the Isma'ilis, who are considered heretics and even infidels by all Sunni schools. The mission of the local apparatus is to prevent these populations from displaying their beliefs in the public sphere, not to impose the Hanbali-Wahhabi vision on them. This is also the case in the province of Al-Ahsa' (8 percent of all offices and centers), where a large portion of the population is Twelver Shiite or non–Hanbali-Wahhabi Sunni. Finally, the 6 percent of centers and offices that are located in the North is explained by that region's sparse population, only 1.2 percent of the kingdom's total.

The Committee for the Promotion of Virtue and the Prevention of Vice locates its offices and centers in a given region only for historical or symbolic reasons. We are thus far from observing a vast and extensive network designed to oppress minorities. There are of course excesses, something that is moreover to be expected in an authoritarian system, but these excesses must be put into

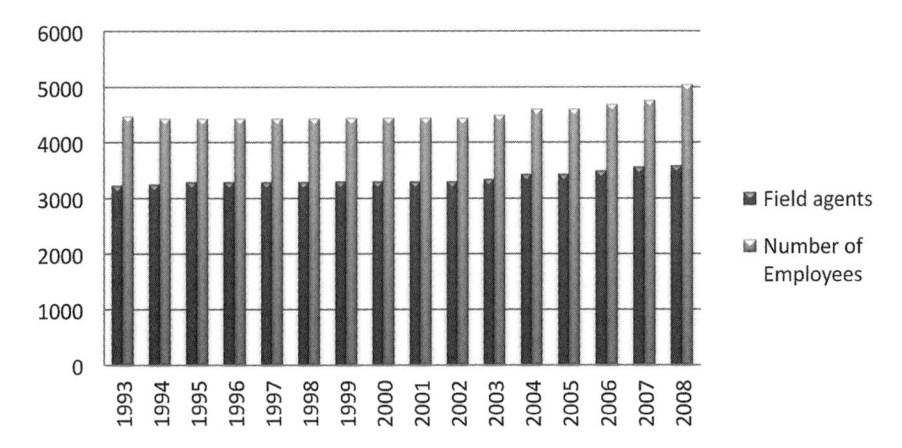

Figure 14. Number of employees of the Committee for the Promotion of Virtue and the Prevention of Vice (1993–2008).

proper perspective. An examination of the number of agents in the committee's service confirms this initial conclusion (Figure 14).

The number of committee employees across the territory was initially very modest and has hardly changed over the past fifty years. From a total of 1,350 in 1956, that number grew to 5,045 in 2008. Over the same period, by contrast, the kingdom's population grew from 4 million to more than 27 million. Therefore, the number of hisba employees per thousand inhabitants diminished from 0.3 to 0.2 in half a century. It thus cannot be said that field agents, who represent the majority of the system's employees (71 percent in 2008), thoroughly "police" the Saudi public sphere. But how are we to explain the fact that such a small number of field agents are able, not only to patrol a large part of the public sphere, but also to whip up the imagination of Saudis, immigrants, and pilgrims to such an extent that these three categories engage in self-regulation and even self-censorship?

Before answering this question, we should briefly consider the etymology and history of the name given to the committee's field agents, the infamous *mutawiʻa* (sing. *mutawiʻ*). This term is derived from the Arab root *t w ʻ* and refers to notions of obedience, submission, and the fact of allowing oneself to be led. In the juridico-religious semantic field, the various schema deriving from this root designate obedience to God in the observance of religious duties or volunteer religious work beyond the call of duty. Beginning with the first century of Islam, the combatants who participated in the expansion and defense of the empire solely in order to please God were called *mutawiʻa*, or *mutatawwiʻa*—that is, volunteers. But the sociopolitical troubles stirred up by the city of Baghdad during the war of succession that pitted the sons of Abbasid caliph Harun al-Rashid (786–809) against one another brought an end to this new meaning. Several groups of pious figures took the name of *mutawiʿa* and volunteered to reestablish order and the Law in the framework of the promotion of virtue and the prevention of vice.[86]

Over the course of the following centuries, it was this meaning that ultimately prevailed. In classical Iraq and Syria, *mutawiʿ* referred to a pious and moderately educated man striving individually or as part of a group to ensure that sharia is observed in the public sphere. Because of the paucity of sources, we do not know when the figure of the *mutawiʿ* first made its appearance in Najd with new social functions. Thanks to his moderate education, the *mutawiʿ* became a technician of the routine cults in the various oases of Central Arabia: he was responsible for elementary instruction, the organization of prayers, responding to the population's juridico-religious questions, and so on. In short, he fulfilled the role of ulama in a region that lacked religious personnel. Most opponents of the preaching of Muhammad ibn Abd al-Wahhab were thus *mutawiʿa*.

The success of Ibn Abd al-Wahhab in no way changed the status of this category, with many *mutawiʿa* placing themselves in the service of the Hanbali-Wahhabi tradition. While fulfilling their duties among the populations that had been won over by Ibn Abd al-Wahhab's predication, they also became agents of socialization sent to convert recently subjugated (or soon to be subjugated) sedentary or Bedouin populations. Alongside the ulama, they thus played a prominent role in the homogenization of Najd in the nineteenth century and in the acculturation of the sedentary Bedouin at the outset of the twentieth. The majority of the figures presented in biographical dictionaries devoted to the religious figures of Najd come from the *mutawiʿa* category.

The unification of the kingdom and the gradual institutionalization of Hanbali-Wahhabism no doubt rendered the office of *mutawiʿ* useless, particularly in the kingdom's rapidly growing cities and towns. As a result of this change, many *mutawiʿa* put themselves into the service of the nascent hisba apparatus.[87] It is for this reason that the population continued to refer to them as such. Officially, the field agents initially carried the title of lieutenant (*nuwwab*, sing. *naʾib*) before taking on the name of hisba agents (*rijal al-hisba*, sing. *rajul al-hisba*) or committee agents (*rijal al-hayʾa*, sing. *rajul al-hayʾa*).[88]

The myth according to which, despite their limited number, the *mutawiʿa* are omnipresent in the Saudi public sphere may be explained in terms of a series of complementary objective and subjective factors. The *mutawiʿa* are known for their dynamism and sometimes excessive zeal, and most see themselves as agents of salvation for the community. Their self-esteem is the product of a laudatory discourse transmitted by the entire establishment and a significant part of the royal house, which considers hisba as "preventative medicine for souls" and "society's safety valve" whose agents only "carry out the duty that had once devolved upon the Prophets."[89] Allowing for what several contemporary studies have shown to be the important place occupied by emotion and belief in the action of social actors,[90] we can easily understand the overflowing energy of hisba agents that is at the basis of the illusion that they are everywhere.

This dynamism is reinforced by a very good field deployment strategy: the *mutawiʿa* generally choose only very crowded zones (such as souks, shopping malls, the areas around mosques, public gardens, and restaurants) and very precise moments of the day (evening and late afternoon hours of prayer) to stage their interventions and thereby whip up the crowds. To this must be added the mobile character of hisba units, which renders their action unpredictable. The committee's various offices and centers also draw upon informal networks of informers (such as neighborhood imams, pious individuals, and shopkeepers) and closely collaborate with various police services, in particular the narcotics brigade.

But the imagination itself no doubt remains the most formidable arm in the *mutawiʿa*'s arsenal. As Georges Balandier writes, "power can only be brought to bear on persons and things if it turns to symbolic tools and the imagination as much as to legitimated constraint."[91] In order to establish their reputation and keep the respect of the majority, hisba agents generally have recourse to spectacular raids and arrests, which create quite a stir in the national and even international press. Indeed, the treatment of hisba in the Saudi media (amplified online at the hands of detractors and supporters alike) gives the uninformed observer and common citizen the impression that this system is omnipresent. We have collected hundreds of anecdotes spread by Saudis and expatriates insisting on the very conservative nature of this body (its raison d'être, after all) as well as the large number of hisba agents and their near ubiquity. These last two claims are, of course, empirically false. But spectacular actions, media amplification, and popular rumors have become the foremost assistants of hisba agents. Thanks to their symbolic charge, they have marked the popular imagination, provoking self-regulated—and even self-censored—behavior in the public sphere.

THE PREROGATIVES OF HISBA: REGULATIONS, STATISTICS, AND LEGAL RULINGS

According to its regulation (*nizam*), the mission of the Committee for the Promotion of Virtue and the Prevention of Vice is to guide people toward the path of righteousness. Its agents must encourage the population to carry out its religious duties and combat reprehensible behavior according to the prescriptions of sharia.[92] In addition to these general considerations, the organic regulation (*al-la'iha al-tanfidhiyya*) specifies the following prerogatives:[93]

1. Seeing to it that collective prayers are organized at canonical hours and encouraging people to perform them. Verifying that shops and administrations respect the obligation to remain closed during prayers.
2. Keeping watch over markets, shopping malls, streets, gardens, women's fashion boutiques, and so on in the aim of preventing mixing of the sexes and obliging women to respect the vestimentary tradition that the Hanbali-Wahhabi ulama consider Islamic. The agents of the committee must also energetically call to order men who do not respect the local vestimentary code.
3. Preventing people from turning on televisions or radios in the vicinity of mosques in order to not disturb prayer.
4. Preventing non-Muslims from professing their religion in public, donning ostentatious signs of their affiliation, or showing any form of contempt for Islam.
5. Forbidding the exhibition or sale of printed, audio, or video material that runs counter to Hanbali-Wahhabi precepts or contradicts the public mores advocated by the corporation.
6. Fighting against the production and commercialization of drugs and alcohol.
7. Identifying and closing brothels and illicit gambling rings.
8. Fighting all blameworthy innovations in the religious domain, particularly popular rituals and sorcery.
9. Inspecting weights and measures in the markets and ensuring the propriety of sacrifices in the slaughterhouses.

Although exhaustive, this list supplies us with only an approximate image of the real prerogatives enjoyed by agents of the Committee for the Promotion of Virtue and the Prevention of Vice. Only a statistical study of *mutawi'a* interventions in the field allows us to form a clearer image. In the pages that follow, I thus try to study all quantitative data concerning the various cases handled by the committee in the thirteen provinces of the kingdom between 1991 and 2008 (Figure 15). I have chosen to begin the survey in 1991 for the simple reason that statistics are not available before that.

Since 1991, infractions against ritual (*al-'ibadat*)—failure to attend group prayers, working during prayer time, eating in public during Ramadan, and so

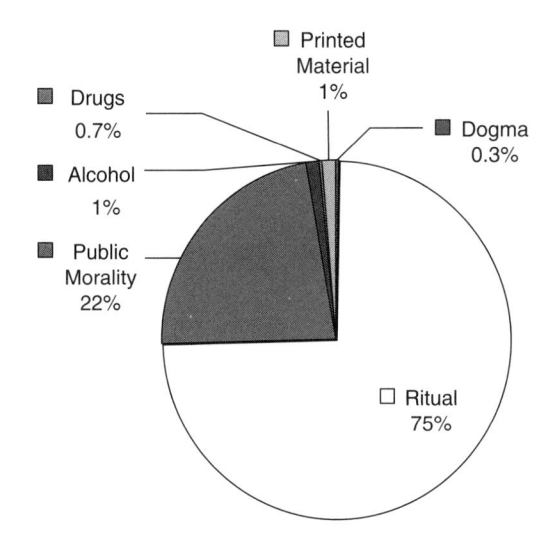

Figure 15. Cases handled by the Committee for the Promotion of Virtue and the Prevention of Vice (1991–2008).

on—represent 75 percent of the cases handled by the committee. Almost all of these infractions involve the failure to communally carry out one or several daily prayers. The importance granted to ritual is due to the fact that it is considered by all Sunni schools, and the Hanbali-Wahhabi tradition in particular, as the main pillar of Islam and "the first thing that man has to account for on the last day of judgment," to cite a tradition attributed to the Prophet.[94] Many Sunni ulama go so far as to exclude from the community whoever does not perform this ritual, which is the main path to salvation.[95] Supported by the ideological authority of the religious establishment, hisba agents thus energetically act in the field in order to save the souls of their coreligionists.

No fewer than 2,840,662 arrests involving failure to respect ritual were recorded in the registers of the various committee offices and centers between 1991 and 2008. This "efficiency" is due to the multiple support networks that are available to the *mutawi'a* in urban neighborhoods throughout the kingdom. In order to force those who do not attend prayer at the mosque to do so, the ulama have adopted the method described by the voyager Amin al-Rihani in the early twentieth century: one must first of all send a trustworthy man to privately confer with anyone who refuses to attend collective prayers. Should he fail in his mission, a delegation of neighborhood worthies led by the imam must visit the offender at home to admonish him. In the event of yet another failure, a complaint against him must be lodged with the local committee, which will take the necessary legal measures to persuade him to observe ritual prayer.[96] This strategy generally bears fruit because, in the Saudi public sphere structured by representation, all individuals without exception are afraid of losing face and being singled out by the group.

In keeping with Hanbali-Wahhabi tradition, the ulama particularly insist on the importance of collective prayer (*salat al-jama'a*) as the cement that unifies the community around its mystical body. From a pragmatic and no doubt unconscious point of view, they believe that a large part of their ideological authority depends on the force of the believers' faith, the best stimulant of which is no doubt prayer. They therefore defend it with all their power. In 2010, the director of the Mecca hisba office, Ahmad Qasim al-Ghamidi (b. 1964), stated that collective prayer is not obligatory (*wajiba*) and that shops do not as a consequence have to close during prayer hours.[97] His remarks were reported in several "liberal" media outlets. With these remarks, al-Ghamidi called into question not only one of the pillars of Hanbali-Wahhabi doctrine, but also the main prerogative of the Committee for the Promotion of Virtue and the Prevention of Vice. This act also threatened to destroy the unanimity of the religious establishment on this subject. The ulama's response was not long in coming. The Permanent Commission issued a fatwa reiterating, scriptural evidence in hand, that collective prayer was an obligatory tradition inherited from the prophetic era. This legal judgment also defended the work of hisba agents, stating that they are heirs of a sacred duty formerly carried out by the pious ancestors (*al-salaf al-salih*). In order for Muslims to reach eternal salvation and acquire power in this world, the ulama underscored the fact that they must follow the path of their prestigious forebears.[98] This judgment was reiterated by several members of the corporation and their collaborators.[99] The president of the Committee for the Protection of Virtue and the Prevention of Vice even tried to dismiss this "lost sheep" but was rebuffed by the king, who was no doubt concerned to preserve his image as a "reformer" in the eyes of international opinion.[100]

On the basis of this example and the statistical data on *mutawi'a* actions, one can conclude that the religious establishment is not disposed to make concessions in the domain of prayer because it constitutes the very heart of its doctrinal system and one of the bulwarks of its ideological authority.

Twenty-two percent of the cases handled by hisba agents, or 865,404 arrests between 1991 and 2008, concern moral behavior in public places (*al-akhlaq, al-adab al-'amma*). This involves any act that undermines human—and particularly women's—dignity: prostitution, pimping, adultery, rape, kidnapping, homosexuality, cruising, moral and sexual harassment, nonrespect of the vestimentary code by men and women, failure to cover women's stores in order to render them invisible, gambling, hanging photographs of women in the public sphere, and so on. The *mutawiʿa* nevertheless devote most of their efforts to the fight against mixed-gender groups (*al-ikhtilat*).

Given their negative vision of human nature, the Hanbali-Wahhabi ulama see such mixing as a permanent danger for men and women, the natural outcome of which is *fitna*, or disorder leading to eternal damnation.[101] Everything possible must therefore be done in order to reduce interaction between the sexes to protect virtue (*hirasat al-fadila*)[102] and preserve the possibility of reaching salvation.[103] Following the meticulous strategy mapped out by Grand Mufti Muhammad ibn Ibrahim and thanks to energetic action on the part of the Committee for the Promotion of Virtue and the Prevention of Vice and support from the political authorities—several Royal Orders explicitly forbid mixing[104]—the religious establishment has been able to impose two nearly parallel societies on Saudi Arabia: an exclusively masculine one and an exclusively feminine one. There are of course pathways connecting these two worlds and small islands where they meet, but they remain very restricted and vulnerable, for they only exist thanks to the goodwill of an important prince or a faction of the royal house, who generally create them in order to make a good impression on Western partners. But outside of these princely redoubts, the ulama remain hostile to any attempt to upset the system of strict gender segregation. The debates that took place in Saudi Arabia in 2009 and 2010 on this subject bear witness to their intransigence. It all began when King Abd Allah announced the opening of a scientific university (the KAUST) that was to be named after him and, according to rumors, coeducational. Feeling that this project called one of their foremost ideas into question, the ulama rapidly stepped into the breach. Saʿd al-Shathri (b. 1967), a member of both the Committee of Grand Ulama and the Permanent Commission, was the first to publicly express himself. In the course of a television program devoted to fatawa, al-Shathri remarked—courteously, to be sure, and with many compliments for the king—that, as in any other academic establishment, coeducation at this university could lead only to corruption and vice (*mafasid*, sing. *mafsada*), moral and sexual harassment, rape, and serious problems for couples because of jealousy and suspicion. In short, it would distract students from their academic objectives. He thus respectfully called upon the king to prevent this sin.[105]

Rather than follow his advice, the Saudi sovereign dismissed al-Shathri from his duties a few days later.[106] But far from backing down, the corporation intensified its efforts to defend its spiritual and temporal interests, and this despite a ferocious media campaign conducted by the king's supporters, not only against the ideas of al-Shathri but also against the action of *mutawiʿa*.[107] While the members of the religious establishment, particularly Grand Mufti Abd al-Aziz Al al-Shaykh (b. 1943) and Salih al-Fawzan (b. 1935), issued fatawa in support of their colleague's opinions, their supporters conducted a media counteroffensive in the press, on television, through the Internet, and during Friday prayers and instruction in the mosques.[108]

Conscious that without the support of the coercive power of the state their protest would be in vain, the ulama realized they needed to find a protector within the royal house to strengthen their hand. As experts of the antagonisms that cut across the House of Saud, which governs horizontally,[109] they naturally sought out the support of Prince Nayif (d. 2012), the country's powerful minister of the interior and strongman. With close ties to the religious establishment, Prince Nayif for his part understood that giving aid to the trustees of ideological authority could only reflect positively on him and his faction. He thus hastened to extend his unconditional support to them. On the one hand, he took advantage of all public occasions for reiterating that sharia is the basis of Saudi society and that the Committee for the Promotion of Virtue and the Prevention of Vice was only one of this mystical body's manifestations.[110] On the other hand, he expressed his support by symbolic acts; for example, the prince forbade (officially, at least) all mixed-gender groups at the March 2010 Riyadh book fair.[111]

The minister of the interior's intervention on behalf of the establishment thus allowed the ulama to maintain the status quo. But the question of mixed-gender groups threatens to increasingly intrude into Saudi social space, less for ideological reasons than on account of practical considerations. Indeed, the rapid growth of the Saudi population coupled with high levels of unemployment, economic dependence on millions of foreign workers, and an inadequate redistribution of petroleum revenue—which will no doubt diminish in the future—will oblige the political power and the religious authority to revise their stance on this question. I would not be surprised to see the religious establishment adopt a new meaning for the notion of protecting virtue (*hirasat al-fadila*) in order to better adapt to social change and maintain the centrality of its discourse in the framework of the ethic of responsibility.[112]

Infractions of the rules regarding prayer and mixed-gender groups thus represent 98 percent of all interventions on the part of agents of the Committee for the Promotion of Virtue and the Prevention of Vice. In addition to their importance in the Hanbali-Wahhabi doctrinal system, the obligation of communal prayer and gender segregation are the two most demonstrative signs of the Islamic character of Saudi society. And in order to preserve this image in a public sphere that is precisely structured by representation, a strict behavioral code must, according to the ulama, be enforced.

Offenses relating to printed material (*al-matbu'at*)—that is, the sale or distribution of magazines, pornographic films, pirated electronic chips for watching satellite channels, and non-Wahhabi religious propaganda—represent 1 percent of the cases dealt with by the committee, or 48,241 cases between 1991 and 2008. This weak percentage can be explained by the relative number of hisba agents focusing on ritual and public morality and by the intervention in these cases of other state institutions, such as the ministries of the interior (police), culture (censorship service), trade (office of fraud repression), and so on. The same line of reasoning can be employed concerning cases of the consumption and sale of alcohol and drugs. Generally tied to prostitution and gambling, such cases represent only 1 percent and 0.7 percent of the committee's arrests, respectively.

Finally, it is astonishing to see that infractions of dogma—that is, the fact of having publicly contradicted one of the doctrinal principles of the Hanbali-Wahhabi tradition (insulting God, the religion, the Prophet and his companions; committing an act of sorcery; visiting mausoleums or what are considered holy places outside of the sanctuaries of Mecca and Medina; possessing talismans, etc.)—represent only 0.3 percent of the arrests carried out by the *mutawi'a*, or a total of 11,476 between 1991 and 2008. This is mainly due to the self-regulation exhibited by native Saudis, expatriates, and pilgrims who are not followers of the Hanbali-Wahhabi tradition. Indeed, the generally spectacular and widely covered interventions of hisba agents in this domain and the heavy penalties applied to certain offenders (up to and including capital punishment) are dissuasive. This is particularly true for the Saudi Sunni and Shiite minorities, who know very well that in order to continue to freely practice their rituals in private, they must behave discreetly in public. As a result, between 1994 and 2008,[113] only 18 percent of defendants in cases of dogma were Saudi. The majority of these actions were directed against foreign populations, particularly pilgrims.

The operations of hisba agents particularly target popular rituals (pious visits, Sufi and Shiite commemorations such as *mawlid*—the nativity of the Prophet or the death of Al-Husayn), which are seen as blameworthy innovations by the religious establishment and acts of sorcery, which they consider an impious effort to anticipate divine will, something that is in total contradiction with the dogma of predestination.[114]

The distribution of arrests carried out by agents of the Committee for the Promotion of Virtue and the Prevention of Vice on Saudi territory more or less corresponds to the distribution of their offices and centers (Figure 16). This is further evidence that the main preoccupation of the religious establishment is

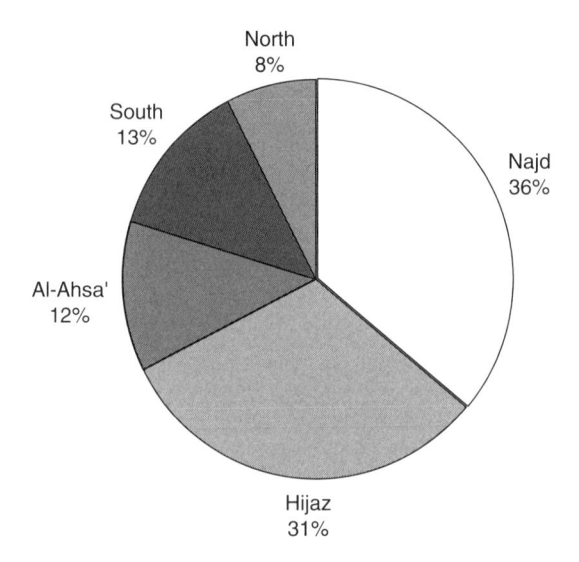

Figure 16. Distribution of the cases handled by the Committee for the Promotion of Virtue and the Prevention of Vice by region (1991–2008).

to preserve religious homogeneity and the invented conservative traditions of Najd in order to continue to dominate the other regions of Saudi Arabia and broadly display its power, particularly in the holy places of Islam.

All of the prerogatives of the committee that we have examined fall under the aegis of the prevention of vice (*al-nahy 'an al-munkar*). We now examine the efforts that these agents devote to promoting virtue (*al-amr bi al-ma'ruf*). It must first be said that the activities of the committee in this domain represent only a diminishingly small part of the efforts made by all bodies of the corporation taken together (the Committee of Grand Ulama, the Ministry of Islamic Affairs, the Ministry of Justice, the universities, foundations, etc.) in the framework of the duty of religious predication (*al-da'wa*). While the committee has a monopoly on the prevention of vice, a duty that can upset the political order if not properly managed, it shares the promotion of virtue with other bodies.

Between 1993 and 2008,[115] the various offices and centers distributed 62,349,991 texts (brochures, leaflets, and books) and 12,173,401 audio recordings (cassettes and CDs). They also organized no fewer than 133,980 collective and individual conferences across the provinces of the kingdom. The subjects discussed concerned the history of hisba (an effort is made to draw a connection between the Saudi system and the medieval institution), the rights and duties of its agents, and the socioreligious problems that this body seeks to resolve. In order to work more closely with the population, the various offices and centers organize advisory and orientation visits in schools, universities, government offices, and even private homes, with more than 220,917 visits organized between 1993 and 2008. Several agents even proselytize among foreign workers, an effort that sometimes results in conversions.[116]

The hisba apparatus is part of the long history of this institution, which has nearly always enjoyed many more prerogatives in the domain of preventing vice than in that of promoting virtue. This is entirely understandable given the fact that it participates in a process of state construction aiming to monopolize all royal attributes and coercive resources in order to preclude the emergence of poles of competition and opposition.

Having reviewed the principal prerogatives of the committee with the support of statistics, we now examine the procedure followed by hisba agents in dealing with recorded infractions. Following the example of the muhtasib of the classical period, the *mutawi'a* uniquely deal with established facts. If a case requires investigation, they have to call upon the competent state services (such as the police and the office of fraud repression). In the event that a committee office or center receives a complaint or denunciation, the agents must check the veracity of the information before intervening by interviewing the plaintiff and witnesses.[117]

Like any service endowed with police prerogatives, the committee has to respect all regulations in force concerning the manner in which defendants are detained and investigated.[118] The organic regulation (*al-la'iha al-tanfidhiyya*) governing the work of the *mutawi'a* particularly insists on the need to respect the rights of arrested women. In addition to the rules governing search and seizure, which must be carried out by a pious woman, female defendants can be interrogated only in the presence of a male member of their family (*mahram*).[119] In the event that a private residence is raided, female defendants must be given time to clothe themselves in accordance with the Law before withdrawing into a separate room before witnesses. It is only then that the *mutawi'a* can carry out their search. The complementary code precisely describes the approach the *mutawi'a* are to follow, how they are to handle evidence, conduct interrogations, and so on.[120] In order to conduct certain difficult arrests (drug traffickers, drinking binges, gambling circles, brothels), the *mutawi'a* can call upon the police forces for support, with several contingents permanently assigned to them.[121]

The Committee for the Promotion of Virtue and the Prevention of Vice disposes of genuine repressive power. In addition to the power of holding someone suspected of having committed an offense in custody without charges for up to seventy-two hours,[122] the directors of the offices and centers can, if the punishment is not explicitly set by sharia, directly inflict a punishment of their choice (*ta'zir*) on offenders. These are not to exceed three days in prison or fifteen lashes after approval from the governor of the province.[123] The complaints of Saudi citizens and expatriates relating to abuses on the part of hisba agents in this domain have led the political authorities to seek to deprive the committee of its repressive powers. In 1987, King Fahd issued a written instruction that withdrew these from them.[124] But the sociohistorical circumstances and malfunctions of the Saudi state relating to the horizontal distribution of power in the royal house prevented this instruction from taking effect. It was only after the September 11 attacks, with the committee an object of disapprobation abroad and also in some circles within the country, that this idea once again surfaced in the framework of efforts to improve the kingdom's image. Just a few weeks after the destruction of New York's Twin Towers, the new code of penal procedures officially withdrew all repressive powers from the committee. Henceforth, hisba agents were to immediately hand defendants over to the police after each accusation so that the police could begin classic legal proceedings as necessary.[125] Yet it must not be forgotten that less than 10 percent of the cases handled by the *mutawi'a* from 1991 to 2008 enter into this category: the others ended "on friendly terms" with a reprimand (*tawbikh*) or the signature by the offender of an honorary certificate (*ta'ahhud*) promising not to commit a second offense.[126]

This change marks a new step, not only in the long process of the Hanbali-Wahhabi doctrine's routinization and its adaptation to internal and external constraints, but also in a process of state construction driven by the desire to unify repressive power around a single pole. Yet it must be said that the process of routinization will remain very fragile as long as deep and innovative thought is not conjoined with a steadfast political will. In Saudi Arabia, these are rare things indeed.

9

AT THE CROSSROADS

The Religious Establishment Put to the Test of the Saudi Politico-Religious Space

Having examined how the clerical corps imposes and defends orthodoxy and orthopraxy in the public sphere, we now study how it defends the established order—in the Hanbali-Wahhabi view of things, an indispensable bulwark of any effort to achieve salvation. For purposes of illustration, I draw upon three important episodes from contemporary Saudi Arabian history: the seizure of the Grand Mosque of Mecca in 1979, the Islamist protest movement of the early 1990s, and the Jihadist threat following the September 11 terrorist attacks. My aim in the present chapter is not to study these events in their own right—something that has already been done elsewhere—but rather to analyze the manner in which the ulama responded to them. More particularly, I examine how they tailored this response with a view to enforcing the principles of the corporation (the foundation of their ideological authority) and defending the symbiotic relationship with the political power (the guarantor of their discursive hegemony).

In order to manage more or less violent crises, distinguish itself from protesters, and ensure that the order necessary for the observance of the prescriptions of sharia is maintained, the religious establishment has found itself obliged to adopt a clear position on certain political and theologico-juridical questions. Fearing *fitna* (destructive discord), which can only result in ruin, desolation, and damnation, the tradition's representatives applied an ethic of responsibility and forged ahead with the process of routinization. Indeed, the ongoing redefinition of certain important concepts and key words has contributed to the near total transformation of Hanbali-Wahhabism; having emerged as a counter-religion, it is now a religion in its own right. The need to confront three major crises in less than a half-century has allowed Hanbali-Wahhabism to carry out a sort of "aggiornamento" in regards to fundamental questions.

THE BREAK WITH MESSIANISM

As we saw in the preceding chapter, the Juhayman al-Utaybi group was born of a rejection of the changes that occurred in Saudi Arabia in the 1960s as a result of King Faysal's developmentalist policy, which was characterized by urbanization, the massive arrival of foreign workers, and changes in modes of consumption and communication.[1] During its first ten years of existence, al-Jama'a al-Salafiyya al-Muhtasiba (the Salafi company for the hisba) was merely a peripheral pietist and conservative group; its members wanted to preserve the socio-religious structures that had characterized the country before the petroleum boom and showed no particular interest in politics. The failure of this purely religious activity, however, combined with the disappointment and frustration they felt as a result of the absence of material and immaterial recompense, led a fringe of the Jama'a to engage in political action.

Starting in 1976, Juhayman, the ideologue and spokesman of this faction—which, it is worth noting, also called itself the Ikhwan, in nostalgic allusion to the tribal army destroyed by Abd al-Aziz—began to accuse the state of corruption and the religious establishment of dishonest compromise. This stance, which ran contrary to Hanbali-Wahhabi principles, led the members of the corporation who had supervised the activities of the Jama'a from a distance to break all ties with it several months later. At the same time, institutional (the unification of the Committees for the Promotion of Virtue and the Prevention of Vice under a single presidency and the launching of a new policy of field agent recruitment) and repressive (the arrest of Juhayman and several of his comrades) measures were taken by the Saudi political power and the religious authority.[2] These moves only served to radicalize the Ikhwan.

Between 1977 and 1979, Juhayman established a highly structured and disciplined little group. Thanks to an intense network of socialization and sustained community life requiring the total commitment of its members, the group was able to completely break with its environment. In line with most protest movements in the Muslim world since the seventh century, this small group adopted a messianic ideology: its members believed that one of them—Muhammad bin Abd Allah al-Qahtani (d. 1979)—was the Mahdi, the Muslim messiah, who would reestablish justice and prosperity in the world, thereby preparing the way for the last judgment.[3] Like many messianic movements throughout history, Islamic or otherwise, the Juhayman group was driven by a quest for collective salvation (to save the souls of all Muslims, not just those of the Saudis). This quest was total, terrestrial, immediate, and supported by the supernatural. With the help of an army of angels, the universal reign of the Mahdi would reestablish the state of perfection in the universe. In order to make way for this new world, the group thus sought to put an end to the established religious and political order.

According to certain traditions attributed to the Prophet, the Mahdi was to make his appearance in the Grand Mosque of Mecca (al-Haram al-makki), where his followers would pledge their allegiance before setting out to conquer the universe with the support of cohorts of angels.[4] Adopting an ethic of conviction—that is, the rigid application of the ideal in which one believes without concern for the consequences that may result—the Juhayman group decided to follow the prophetic tradition to the letter. Their conviction was no doubt strengthened by another tradition attributed to Muhammad according to which, at the beginning of each century, God sends the Muslim community a man whose mission is to renew the religion (*jaddada*, from whence derives the messianic title of *mujaddid*, or cyclical reformer).[5] What's more, 20 November 1979 corresponded to the first day of the year 1400 of the Hegira, that is, the turn of a new century. On that day, a group of between two hundred and three hundred men led by Juhayman and his Mahdi seized the Grand Mosque of Mecca. They took thousands of pilgrims hostage while awaiting the realization of the divine marvels that would allow them to conquer the world.[6]

The event immediately caused a stir around the world and commanded the full attention of the House of Saud, whose power and legitimacy were brutally shaken. In addition to the military measures required to dislodge the messianic group from the sanctuary, the monarchy needed unwavering ideological support to justify military intervention in one of Islam's holiest places, which religious prescription stated was inviolable. No one was better suited to this delicate operation than the representatives of the Hanbali-Wahhabi tradition, whose own spiritual and temporal interests were also at stake. King Khalid therefore called the leading figures of the religious establishment to Riyadh's al-Mu'adhdhar Palace to explain the situation to them and receive their juridico-religious opinion.[7] The division of labor between the two partners occurred naturally: while Saudi troops carried out a military encirclement of the rebels, the representatives of the Najdi tradition symbolically isolated them.

At the end of this meeting, the ulama immediately issued their first fatwa in response to this unprecedented situation.[8] This document above all insisted on the practical measures that could be taken to put an end to the rebellion while at the same time scrupulously respecting the prescriptions of sharia. In keeping with the most orthodox Hanbali tradition, they encouraged the king to call upon the rebels to put down their arms. If the rebels agreed to surrender, their lives would be spared until their cases could be judged before a court.[9] If they refused to surrender, however, the king, as legitimate authority (*waliyy al-amr*) and religious leader of the community (*al-imam*), could take all necessary measures up to and including the use of force to silence what the ulama saw as an unjust sect (*al-ta'ifa al-zalima*) that had dared threaten the order and security of Saudi Arabia.

What's more, several ulama issued individual fatawa to clarify and strengthen this collective fatwa.[10] These were widely reported in the Saudi media. The most important of these individual legal opinions was that of Abd al-Aziz ibn Baz. Drawing upon a large number of Qur'anic verses and prophetic traditions, Ibn Baz held that this attack against the sacred sanctuary was an unparalleled act of impiety (*ilhad*), the result of which could only be injustice, hardship, and corruption on a scale that was without precedent in Islamic history. There had of course been many precedents, the most famous of which was the seventh-century attack by Umayyad troops against the pretender Abd Allah ibn al-Zubayr (d. 692), who had entrenched himself in the holy city, and its sack by the Qarmatian Shiite sect in the tenth century. But Ibn Baz, who was aware of these facts, dramatized the 1979 event in order to better galvanize the Muslim imaginary, which is very attached to Mecca's sacred status, and thus destroy any potential sympathy for the Juhayman group.

Ibn Baz held that the oath of allegiance sworn to the supposed Mahdi—the main justification for the rebellion—had no religious validity (*fasid*) given that everything concerning the Messiah in Islam was a metaphysical matter (*masa'il ghaybiyya*). From this, he deduced that no Muslim could legitimately affirm that such a pretender was the true Mahdi as long as the physical (*'alamat*) and ecological (*sharat*) circumstances were not fully in keeping with the best-established prophetic traditions. Ibn Baz pursued this line of attack by asking how one could be sure that a given person was the true Mahdi solely on the basis of a single individual's vision (*ru'ya*)[11] when such a procedure is contrary to the precepts of sharia and the consensus of the ulama. According to the head of the corporation, this failure to respect the mystical body of the Muslim community was also reflected in the action of the supposed Mahdi and his followers, who had violated the sacred space of the Grand Mosque of Mecca by bringing weapons into it, rebelling against the legitimate head of the community, and seeking to destroy its unity. As a consequence, Ibn Baz authorized the political power to use all necessary resources, including force, to put an end to what he a considered seditious uprising.[12]

The individual and collective texts and statements of members of the religious establishment were formalized and made official by a fatwa on the part of the Committee of Grand Ulama.[13] Seen as a clique of lost souls (*fi'a dalla*), the Juhayman group was accused, with support from scriptural citations, of the following crimes:

1. Violating and profaning the sacred area, which was transformed into a battlefield despite the fact that doing so is categorically forbidden by the Qur'an.
2. Violating the sacred month of *muharram*, during which all acts of war are forbidden.
3. Disrupting various religious rites.
4. Executing dozens of innocent Muslims.
5. Recruiting innocent women and children into the service of a rash and hopeless cause.
6. Revolting against the community's legitimate leader (*waliyy al-amr*) and guide (*al-imam*), a transgression of the clearest and most performative religious texts.

Finally, the members of the Committee of Grand Ulama warned the population of the dangers contained in this group's publications, which included false interpretations and erroneous conclusions that reflected their authors' ignorance. These publications were thus only a source of *fitna*, the destructive discord that leads to eternal damnation.

The common theme running through these complementary fatawa is the preservation of the three O's: orthodoxy, orthopraxy, and the political order. In the latter domain, the ulama employed evocative imagery and key words to recall the legitimacy of the House of Saud, the only guarantor in their eyes of the Law's application. They forcefully underscored the fact that the Saudi population was tied to the monarchy by a juridico-religious contract, the *bay'a*. In keeping with this pledge of allegiance, the Saudis owed obedience and assistance to the king and his lieutenants as long as the latter observed sharia. Should the political power nevertheless transgress a few of its prescriptions, the population did not have the right to challenge this *bay'a*. Such a position is of course consistent with the long history of the Hanbali tradition in particular and that of Sunni Islam in general.

As they are used to designate the Saudi sovereign, the titles of *imam* and *waliyy al-amr* reinforce these claims. The first underscores the religious character of the Saudi monarchy: the king is the leader and guide of the community of believers; he sees to the application of sharia and protects the religion.[14] The second title refers to the legitimacy of the holder of power, who must be obeyed in all circumstances. Does not the Qur'an order believers "to obey Allah and obey the Messenger and those among you who hold command [*uli al-amr*]"?[15]

These terms appear frequently in the various fatawa, where their symbolic weight is employed to suggest uninterrupted filiation between the Saudi monarchy and the scriptural sources of Islam, the unique foundations of political legitimacy. In the eyes of the ulama, nothing justifies overthrowing the legitimate political order, especially not erroneous interpretations of the holy texts and dangerous phantasmagoric visions.

But in what respect were these interpretations erroneous and these visions so dangerous? Influenced by neo–Ahl al-Hadith ideas, Juhayman claimed to have directly drawn upon the Qur'an and the Sunna to deduce legal norms and religious teachings. He also claimed to have premonitory visions and dreams inspired by God. By asserting a direct tie with the sources of the Law, the founder of Jama'a al-Salafiyya al-Muhtasiba hoped not only to legitimate his undertaking, but also to break the Hanbali-Wahhabi corporation's monopoly over the Saudi market in the goods of salvation.[16]

Aware of the danger this presented, the ulama were obliged to forcefully reaffirm the special status of their corporation as the only organized body capable of mediating between God and the faithful. If they were to retain their monopoly on meaning, they had to discredit their adversary and his doctrine while simultaneously insisting on the centrality of sharia, the source of their ideological authority.

The classical terms with which the ulama referred to the Juhayman group— *al-khawarij, al-ta'ifa al-zalima,* and *al-fi'a al-dalla*—are revealing of their desire to discredit the group's doctrine and actions. The first of these terms is an attempt to identify the rebels with the medieval Khariji sect, associated in the Sunni imaginary with rigor, exclusivism (the Kharijis excommunicated all other Muslims in theory), and sedition (its various branches frequently revolted against the early Islamic caliphs). Their use of the second term had a twofold objective. *Ta'ifa* refers to the idea of a small, physically and ideologically isolated group—that is, a sect[17]—while *zalima* refers to the double injustice the group has committed. On this view, Juhayman and his followers had first of all showed injustice toward themselves by breaking all ties with the community. Their second injustice was toward others, fomenting a rebellion that provoked enormous human, material, and symbolic damage. In the Islamic imaginary and law, belonging to a seditious sect can only lead to hell. Finally, the expression *al-fi'a al-dalla* refers to an extremely small group whose ideas and actions have led it to stray from the righteous path. In this, the ulama were echoing the first sura of the Qur'an, which is recited by millions of Muslims five times a day.[18] The three main terms used by the ulama to designate the Juhayman group thus all evoked its sectarian, deviant, and numerically insignificant nature. In short, the group was ostracized and even located outside of the community.

In order to prove the group's deviant character, the representatives of the Hanbali-Wahhabi tradition put its project and actions to the test of sharia, declaring both illicit. It is worth noting that in keeping with classical Hanbalism, the ulama considered sharia to be the sole measure of all things and the only mechanism capable of producing order and salvation. They were further convinced that the representatives of sharia—that is to say, themselves—constituted the only body capable of mediating between God and the faithful. Indeed, according to the ulama, even the Mahdi (whose various portents, if one were to strictly follow tradition, are so difficult to bring together that his appearance would seem impossible) will not be sent by God as a substitute for the mystical body of the Muslim community. On the contrary, his main mission will be to reestablish orthodoxy, orthopraxy, and the political order. Like any dominant corporation claiming a monopoly on absolute truth, the Hanbali-Wahhabi tradition preaches a postmessianic eschatology: strict observance of sharia replaces extraordinary measures to prepare the universe for the final judgment.[19] All forms of extravagant messianism were thus almost completely ruled out.[20]

THE CONDEMNATION OF ISLAMISM[21]

One of the most important and lasting consequences of the policy of Islamic solidarity initiated by King Faysal (then prime minister) in the early 1960s was to make Saudi Arabia a land of refuge for Islamists, in general members of the Muslim Brotherhood. The latter were joined there by a number of ulama who adhered to the Hanbali-Wahhabi credo ('*aqida*) and had fallen afoul of the regimes in Cairo, Damascus, Baghdad, Alger, and so on. At a time when Saudi Arabia was desperately lacking personnel in all sectors, the arrival of these exiles, most of whom possessed significant educational capital, was seen by the authorities in Riyadh as a godsend. They provided an educated workforce that could be put to work constructing Saudi institutions, particularly in the educational and juridico-religious domains. Many Islamists reached positions of responsibility. In return, they had to forswear interfering in any way in Saudi political and religious affairs, the privileged terrain of the monarchy and the religious establishment.

While foreign Islamists respected the politico-religious ban, they nevertheless became discreetly but heavily involved in the cultural sphere in the broad sense of the term (educational systems and programs; extracurricular activities; religious, literary, historic, and "scientific" publications; conferences; salons and literary clubs, etc.). As Stéphane Lacroix has shown, their tireless efforts, particularly in high schools and universities, gradually resulted in the appearance of the first generation of Saudi Islamists toward the end of the 1970s and, above all, the early 1980s.[22] In contrast to other Arab countries, Saudi Islamism is not a reaction to the marginalization of Islam in the public sphere but rather a result of the strategy of national and international legitimation via Islam and Islamic solidarity that was adopted by the monarchy in the 1960s.

Like the versions of Islamism that emerged in other Arab countries, this nascent phenomenon, referred to as *al-sahwa al-islamiyya* (the Islamic Awakening), was plural and ideologically fragmented. Its ideas were the product of hybridization among the various tendencies of the Muslim Brotherhood, the Hanbali-Wahhabi creed, the nineteenth-century doctrine of *al-wala' wa al-bara'* (allegiance [toward Muslims] and rupture [with the infidels]), the doctrine of the neo–Ahl al-Hadith, and so on. Products of the educational system established by the Muslim Brotherhood and graduates of national and international universities, the personnel of the movement had various profiles: alongside graduates of the country's various Islamic universities, who were referred to as *al-du'at* (preachers), were to be found university professors, engineers, doctors, physicists, and so on. Despite their more or less significant ideological disagreements, the leading members of the various Islamist tendencies had two things in common: a desire to further Islamize society and an aspiration for upward social mobility.

The rise of the Islamists was favored by the 1979 Islamic Revolution in Iran and the Juhayman group's capture of the Grand Mosque of Mecca, which called into question the monarchy's legitimacy. The political power granted them a large margin for maneuver in the hope of demonstrating the Islamic nature of the Saudi state and putting the Islamists' sophisticated and "modern" discourse to use in countering Khomeinist propaganda in Sunni circles.

Following the example of their Muslim Brotherhood mentors, Saudi Islamists did not initially attack the prerogatives of the monarchy or the religious establishment. Rather, they contented themselves with reconquering the cultural space with the aim of eventually monopolizing it. They waged fierce intellectual battle against anything that struck them as non-Islamic and organized intense extracurricular activities with the blessing of the political power and the religious authority. This first period in the history of Saudi Islamism corresponds to what Gabriel Almond has described as the phase of synchronization proper to processes of political crisis. This phase is characterized by harmonious coordination among the various actors and respect for the prerogatives of each in keeping with the customary rules governing the social space.[23]

The second phase of this process is characterized by desynchronization, that is, a reduction in the performance of the traditional system as a result of ecological disturbances. In the 1980s, Saudi Arabia went through its worst economic crisis in recent history. As a result of collapsing oil prices, its gross national product diminished by more than 35 percent in the space of just a few years.[24] This ushered in a period of severe social stagnation, as the political power was no longer able to pursue its developmentalist policy or the generous redistribution of income with which it was associated. Thirsting for upward social mobility, graduates of the Saudi educational system found themselves obliged to accept positions that fell well short of their aspirations in an already bloated administration or to join the ranks of the unemployed. The service and industrial sectors, meanwhile, remained closed to them for reasons of cost and efficiency. The state, in other words, proved incapable of integrating the new generation into the administrative and private sector elites. It was in this context that the first ripples of protest made their appearance.

Not yet willing to attack the prerogatives of the monarchy and religious establishment, the Islamists sought to justify feelings of social unease by creating a scapegoat. After the example of nationalists and Arab Islamists elsewhere, they seized upon this classical mechanism of symbolic transfer to accuse Zionists and Americans of being responsible for all of the ills affecting the *umma*. Alarmed by this change of discourse, the political power began to take measures to avoid escalation. On 21 December 1988, a circular from the Ministry of Pilgrimage called upon preachers to end their attacks against the Jews and foreign governments.[25] Several weeks later, the authorities prohibited the posting of politico-religious tracts in the public sphere, and several stores selling Islamic cassettes (*al-tasjilat al-islamiyya*) were raided.[26] In the early 1990s, Prince Salman bin Abd al-Aziz (b. 1936), the governor of Riyadh, even held a meeting with high-ranking officials from the ministries of the Interior, Pilgrimage, and Information to develop a plan of action for keeping a better watch over preachers and Islamic cassette stores.[27] These measures were preventative and sought only to enforce the rules of the Saudi politico-religious game; the authorities did not seem to deeply fear the rise of the Islamists. However, an exceptional event of national scale was to hasten the arrival of what Gabriel Almond describes as the systemic crisis, that is, a break with the "normal" rules governing the social space and the onset of struggles to redefine the role of each individual or collective actor.

On 2 August 1990, the troops of Saddam Hussein (d. 2006) invaded Kuwait. Fearing that it would be the next victim of Iraqi expansionism, the Saudi monarchy called upon assistance from an international coalition led by the United States. On 7 August, the first American soldiers debarked in the province of Al-Ahsa'. It now only remained for the House of Saud to legitimate this development, for which purpose they once again turned to their faithful allies, the ulama. On 13 August 1990, the Committee of Grand Ulama issued an initial fatwa justifying the presence of foreign troops on Saudi soil.[28] Without the support of scriptural citation, the ulama claimed that the exceptional circumstances facing the Saudi government obliged it to "seek support from Arab and non-Arab countries" and "bring in well-trained and equipped troops capable of frightening anyone who wishes to invade our country."[29]

Dozens of individual and collective fatawa drawing on Qur'anic verses, prophetic traditions, and events from the first centuries of the Hegira (the epoch of the pious ancestors) were subsequently issued in confirmation of the Committee of Grand Ulama's opinion.[30] While the most detailed fatwa from a juridico-religious point of view was that of Muhammad al-Sbayyil,[31] imam of the Grand Mosque of Mecca and head of the administration responsible for managing the two holy places of Islam, those issued by Abd al-Aziz ibn Baz, the indisputable chief and principal spokesman of the religious establishment, were the most important, the most widely distributed, and above all the most revealing of what I have from the beginning of this book referred to as the routinization of the Hanbali-Wahhabi tradition. Indeed, on several occasions Ibn Baz claimed that calling upon non-Muslim troops to defend oneself against an external threat was permissible from the perspective of sharia, even though doing so could provoke *fitna*, with all of the unfortunate consequences on religious practices which that entailed.[32] This was the same man who, several decades earlier, had opposed the idea of allowing American technicians to reside on Saudi soil and who had forbidden Egyptian President Gamal Abdel Nasser from calling upon foreign troops.[33]

In this, Ibn Baz and his colleagues once again were only reflecting the religious establishment's capacity for adaptation. Faced with an extremely serious situation, the ulama chose what they saw as the solution most likely to preserve the three O's. Living in the midst of a hostile environment with little faith in the future and plagued by internal dissension, the Hanbali-Wahhabi ulama of the late nineteenth century forbade any alliance with foreign powers in the hope of preserving the independence of the Saudi Emirate. At the end of the twentieth century, by contrast, their successors, who had come of age in a more favorable environment, had profited from a stable political situation, and were sure of their identity, did not for a moment hesitate to support the political power's initiative in order to preserve all of the corporation's privileges. In all probability, they drew on the legal rule according to which the deduction of the legal norm depends on circumstances (*al-hukmu yaduru ma'a 'illatihi wujudan wa 'adaman*).

With much of their ideology based on a synthesis of the Hanbali-Wahhabi exclusivism of the nineteenth century, anti-imperialist positions, and the conspiracy theories of the Muslim Brotherhood, the Saudi Islamists were shocked by the initiatives of the political power and the religious authority. For reasons of conviction and ambition alike, some Islamist figures held that the moment had come to leave the narrow confines to which they had been assigned and interfere in affairs that had up until then been reserved for the monarchy and the religious establishment.

Beginning in late August 1990, the Islamists attacked the ideological authority of the ulama via enflamed sermons and forceful writings in which religious references, (pseudo)scientific analysis, and political demands were mixed. Their main grievance was the ulama's ignorance of the sociopolitical reality (*waqi'*) of the *umma*. They reproached them with restricting themselves to religious questions; in the Islamists' view, the clerics of Islam had to take an interest in all aspects of life, particularly its political ones. In keeping with a modern and highly politicized conception of Islam, they demanded that the members of the establishment transform themselves into political actors, an impossible prospect because foreign to the ulama's habitus and contrary to one of the corporation's foundations: observance of the symbiotic relationship with the House of Saud. The Islamists were well aware of this: in reality their aim was to demolish the corporation's ideological authority while promoting that of their own ulama, who they claimed were capable of reconciling religious knowledge with understanding of modern reality.

While continuing their incursions in the religious domain, the Islamists carefully prepared their intervention in the political space. In October 1990, a group of Islamist ulama, intellectuals, and technocrats set about drafting a petition to be submitted to the king in the framework of the discreet practice of *nasiha* (good advice); once the king had received the petition, they would release it to the public. In order to gather as many signatures as possible, a first draft was put into circulation in January 1991. In the hopes of legitimating their move, the Islamists approached Ibn Baz, who gave them his support after being informed that the *nasiha* would never be made public and that "liberals"[34] (regarded as contemptible secularists) had already presented a non-Islamic petition to the king.[35] Used by the Islamists as a sign of official approbation, the appearance of the head of the religious establishment's signature on the petition had an immediate effect. The leading Hanbali-Wahhabi figures signed it, sometimes without even having examined its content, so great was their confidence in Ibn Baz.

But the Islamists did not keep their promise to the head of the corporation: released under the title *The Letter of Demands* (*Khitab al-Matalib*), the petition was made public. Using carefully chosen politico-religious terms, the petition called upon the royal house to renounce its monopoly over the political space and adopt the following measures: the establishment of an independent advisory council, the creation of a unified and independent judicial system, the Islamization of all institutions and policies, and the instituting of a better distribution of wealth.[36] To all appearances paralyzed by the succession of grave events that had taken place since Iraqi troops first entered Kuwait, the political power responded only halfheartedly by way of the Committee of Grand Ulama.

Though they realized that they had been manipulated by the Islamists, the ulama were in no position to challenge the petition's content as doing so would risk diminishing their ideological authority. With the support of the monarchy, they therefore decided to criticize their rivals' method. In a fatwa issued by the Committee of Grand Ulama on 3 June 1991, they insisted upon the fact that the practice of *nasiha* had to obey precise conditions; above all, any advice proffered to the prince must be kept secret. The only possible aim of publicizing this advice was to sow ill-feeling, provoke hatred, and stir up the crowd—in short, to produce *fitna*. Without ever identifying them by name, the ulama warned the Islamists that they must no longer behave in this way if they hoped to "remain on the righteous path"—that of the pious ancestors.[37]

This fatwa marked the first sign of rupture between the ulama and the Islamists. Little by little, the members of the religious establishment realized that the interests of the corporation were genuinely threatened, particularly as the Islamist leadership included young ulama capable of producing religious discourse similar to their own on juridico-religious questions. In the second half of 1991, they therefore decided to launch a counterattack in the religious space. As a first step, the leading figures of the religious establishment stepped up their public interventions, loudly and clearly asserting their status as the only genuine representatives of the religious knowledge necessary for reaching truth and salvation. Any network of knowledge that did not pass through them was without juridico-religious value. They also reiterated that they were the heirs of the prophets (*warathat al-anbiya'*) to whom God had confided the task of protecting his Law. The faithful should thus trust them and follow their teachings to the exclusion of all other teaching. They were not to be criticized or misrepresented, for doing so was a grave offense.[38]

These statements reflect a desire on the part of the representatives of the Hanbali-Wahhabi tradition to defend the central place occupied by their discourse in the process of mediating between humanity and God. In contrast to most other Arab countries, they were not prepared to share the Saudi market of salvation goods with the new Islamist entrepreneurs. They understood that in order to neutralize their upwardly mobile young competitors, action was needed on the ground. In November 1991, the political power gave the ulama the green light to establish a five-member commission (al-Lajna al-khumasiyya) consisting of Abd al-Aziz ibn Baz (d. 1999), Salih al-Luhaydan (b. 1931), Abd al-Aziz Al al-Shaykh (b. 1943), Salih al-Fawzan (b. 1933), and Abd Allah al-Ghudayyan (d. 2010). Their mission was to examine the sermons and writings of all preachers (al-du'at) who had been accused of transgressing the prerogatives of the political power or the religious authority. If an accusation proved to be well-founded, the commission was authorized to apply a number of sanctions, including suspension, dismissal, and prison. Several preachers—the best known of whom was Abd al-Muhsin al-Ubaykan (b. 1956)—were thereby silenced.

The Hanbali-Wahhabi ulama's gradual reassertion of control over the religious space channeled the Islamist protest movement into what was its real space of action: politics. Up until then, the movement's leading spokesmen had been preachers. Henceforth, their place would increasingly be occupied by intellectuals, technicians, and technocrats. To maximize their material and symbolic advantages, these political actors sought to maintain pressure on the monarchy. In addition to distributing tracts and cassettes and holding veritable political meetings, they began to develop a program. As before, this took the form of a petition addressed to the king that was titled the *Memorandum of Advice* (*Mudhakkirat al-Nasiha*). This memorandum "provides a detailed summary, backed up by examples, of the claims put forward in the *Letter of Demands*.... The only fundamental difference with [the *Letter*] is to be found in the section titled 'The Role of the Ulama and the Preachers' [*Dawr al-'ulama' wa al-du'at*], where the actors seem inclined to promote Sahwist ulama over official ulama by favoring alternative religious institutions over those embodied by the latter."[39] The Islamists thus sought not only to take a share of political power for themselves, but also to seize religious authority. Their ideological condemnation was not long in coming.

On 16 September 1992, the Committee of Grand Ulama issued a fatwa unequivocally condemning the Islamists' memorandum, which they described as having been "written by teachers [*mudarrisun*] and several individuals claiming to have juridico-religious knowledge [*ba'd al-muntasibin ila al-'ilm*]."⁴⁰ By employing these two pejorative expressions to designate the memorandum's signatories, the ulama hoped to symbolically discredit them and thereby exclude them from the ranks of the elites who, in the classical Islamic conception, were alone fit to proffer advice to the prince. The representatives of the Hanbali-Wahhabi tradition held that this malicious piece of writing, which did not respect the legal procedure for transmitting *nasiha*, contained only religious error (*batil*) and falsehood and so could lead only to injustice (*al-jawr*) and rebellion (*al-baghy*).

For the first time, moreover, the ulama alluded to the protesters' ideological allegiance. This was meant to warn the population against the deviant ideas of their movement, which had adopted the principles of foreign groups and parties. As the *umma* was one and indivisible, the very existence of groups and parties entailed dissension, tumult, and the disruption of the three O's. Just a few months after this legal opinion was issued, the leading figures of the establishment issued fatawa of variable length and content to explain, with the support of scriptural citations, that Islam forbade membership in religious or political groups and parties, as their sectarian, heretical, and putschist character could only result in *fitna*. Movements as varied as the Muslim Brotherhood and the Tabligh thus found themselves included in the same category.⁴¹

While it reflects a clear and sincere religious position, the ulama's critique of faction also conceals quite worldly corporatist concerns. Accepting the Islamists would have meant opening the Saudi market in salvation goods to competition and therefore the possibility of a fragmentation of religious authority. The management of religious meaning would no longer have been the exclusive prerogative of the ulama, with all that this would have entailed for their spiritual and temporal privileges. It was, in short, an unacceptable scenario.

Several observers have claimed that some members of the Committee of Grand Ulama supported the Islamist petition. In support of this assertion, they note that seven of the committee's seventeen members, claiming to be ill, did not sign the fatwa condemning the Islamist memorandum and were pensioned off a month and a half later.⁴² The coincidence is at once troubling and seductive and can easily lead observers unfamiliar with the Hanbali-Wahhabi habitus and the real state of health of the seven ulama in question to draw false conclusions. Let's examine the matter. How likely is it that a group of mostly elderly ulama who never once strayed throughout their long careers should have chosen to act against a pillar of their faith—obedience? In addition to this very subjective but nevertheless important consideration, the following arguments can be advanced: if the monarchy had really pensioned off these ulama because of their supposed support for the Islamists, why did it not do the same with the four ulama, including Ibn Baz, who failed to sign the fatwa condemning the Islamists' first petition? What's more, the Hanbali-Wahhabi ulama are a collective actor. With few exceptions, the individual has no weight among them. Yet most of the ulama who were pensioned off were unknown to the broader public as well as to most observers. It thus appears evident that physical incapacity prevented the seven clerics from approving this condemnation. This supposition was borne out by all of my interviews in Saudi Arabia as well as the fact that most of the pensioned off ulama died just a few years after the events in question: Abd al-Razzaq Afifi and Abd al-Aziz bin Salih died in 1994 at the age of eighty-nine and eighty-three, respectively;[43] Abd Allah Khayyat and Sulayman ibn Ubayd died in 1995 at the age of eighty-seven; Salih ibn Ghusun and Abd al-Majid Hasan died in 1998 at the age of seventy-seven.[44] Only Ibrahim ibn Muhammad ibn Ibrahim Al al-Shaykh, though ill, was young at the time (fifty-two years old). But he was replaced by his younger brother Abd Allah, who is now president of the Advisory Council.[45]

Whatever the case, the Committee of Grand Ulama's fatwa triggered what Gabriel Almond refers to as a process of resynchronization—that is, the reestablishment of the rules traditionally governing the social space and the elimination of disruptive elements. Starting in late 1992, successive campaigns of repression came crashing down upon Islamist leaders (loss of employment, house arrest, imprisonment, etc.). Two years later, their protest movement was once and for all neutralized.[46] This campaign was not restricted to the domain of security but also targeted institutions. In order to restore some verticality within the religious establishment, the office of grand mufti was reestablished on 10 July 1993 and entrusted to Abd al-Aziz ibn Baz, who was already de facto head of the religious establishment. The same day, a ministry responsible for overseeing all Islamic affairs (such as preaching within the kingdom and abroad, mosques, religious personnel, mortmain goods) was created. At its head was the former president and founder of Al-Imam University Abd Allah al-Turki, who was known for his administrative talent and extensive familiarity with Islamist circles.[47] As we saw in the last chapter, the constitutionalization and professionalization of the Committee for the Promotion of Virtue and the Prevention of Vice was also part of this dynamic. Finally, private initiatives in the religious space were gradually prohibited. This included the closing of informal nongovernmental organizations, a relative ban on collecting donations outside of official channels, and so on.

DOCTRINAL READJUSTMENT IN RESPONSE TO AL-QAEDA

As Thomas Hegghammer has shown, Al-Qaeda "is a political movement based on the idea that the 'Muslim nation' is subjected to aggression on the part of outside forces and that all Muslims have a duty to come to the aid of their co-religionists in distress."[48] This pan-Islamic "nationalism" implies a global jihad against both Western powers and the Arab-Muslim regimes that support them. The ultimate aim is to expel non-Muslim powers from Muslim territories, overthrow what are considered apostate regimes, and reestablish the original unity of the *umma* in the framework of a well-governed caliphate. In the Saudi case, Al-Qaeda sought to expel U.S. troops from sacred land; politically and militarily combat the monarchy, which was seen as compromised by its dealings with the West; and cast discredit upon the religious establishment.

Like many Arab-Muslim countries, Saudi Arabia was obliged to confront this violent Islamism. Starting in the second half of the 1990s, various networks of the organization, which would later be baptized Al-Qaeda in the Arabian Peninsula, perpetrated attacks and organized media campaigns against the foreign presence on Saudi soil, the monarchy, and the corporation. This phenomenon became more pronounced after the terrorist attacks of 11 September 2001 and reached its height in the campaign of violence that took place across the various regions of the kingdom between 2003 and 2004.[49] The fact that the head of this terrorist movement and fourteen of the nineteen terrorists who destroyed New York's Twin Towers were of Saudi origin led the Western powers, particularly the United States, to exert unprecedented political and media pressure on the kingdom and to conflate the Hanbali-Wahhabi tradition with terrorism.

The political power and the religious authority divided the task of meeting this new challenge between themselves. While the House of Saud set about addressing this grave problem from a political and security point of view—an effort that, beginning in 2006, resulted in the weakening of Al-Qaeda in Saudi Arabia—the ulama for their part saw to the symbolic side of things, that is, "everything in the social world that is a matter of belief, credit or discredit, perception and valuation, knowledge and recognition."[50] Like all dominant groups and ideologies, the Hanbali-Wahhabi corporation worked toward social stability and the maintenance of political order. Without these two elements, it could neither dispose of its salvation goods nor control the religious market. In order to distinguish itself from these eminently political actors, most of whom adhered to only a miniscule portion of the Hanbali-Wahhabi corpus,[51] destroy the arguments with which they rallied their supporters, and discredit their project, the ulama once again drew upon their ethic of responsibility. On the one hand, they reiterated the corporation's position regarding certain important questions on which the public at large and many specialists were generally ignorant. On the other hand, they gradually redefined certain ambiguous or problematic concepts. This process of doctrinal readjustment is only at its beginnings and may take a long time, depending on the circumstances. Nevertheless, its outlines can be sketched here. Several important and generally interrelated questions are of particular note: the legitimacy of the political order, excommunication (*takfir*), relations with the Other as articulated by the concepts of *takfir* and *al-wala' wa al-bara'* (allegiance [toward Muslims] and rupture [with the infidels]), and finally, the question of the relationship between jihad and terrorism.

While the representatives of the Hanbali-Wahhabi tradition recommend close cooperation and solidarity among the various Muslim countries, they do not consider the caliphate to be a pillar of the religion. The political unity of the *umma*, in their view, is not a necessary condition for achieving salvation. Each local government is thus seen as the legitimate leader of its respective "national" community. This particularly holds for the Saudi monarchy, which has scrupulously applied sharia across its territory since coming to power.[52] Nothing, therefore, justifies insubordination and rebellion, whether discursive or military.

As Grand Mufti Abd al-Aziz Al al-Shaykh put it: "Disobedience is one of the aspects of *jahiliyya* (the pre-Islamic period characterized by ignorance of True Religion). Obedience to the prince is obligatory in all circumstances as long as it does not imply disobedience to a divine order. Our duty as ulama is to publicize the merits and virtues of the rulers. It is also our responsibility to show [the population] that the latter are a divine favor through which the unity of the *umma* is brought about. It is by obeying the prince that one avoids *fitna*."[53]

Whatever their motives or juridico-religious arguments, those who wish to overthrow the regime and sow discord by committing attacks thus stand accused of behaving in a way consistent with *jahiliyya*, which the Arab-Muslim imaginary represents as an era of unparalleled ignorance, impiety, and anarchy. The ulama thus threatened to exclude from the community of believers those who would trigger *fitna*, their principal fear. As was the case with the Juhayman group in 1979, the ulama employed the terms *al-khawarij*, *al-ta'ifa al-zalima*, and *al-fi'a al-dalla* to refer to the members of Al-Qaeda and emphasize the movement's small size and sectarian, heretical nature.[54]

In keeping with the realist vision of Ibn Taymiyya, the guardians of the Hanbali-Wahhabi tradition confirmed the break with the utopian and Pan-Islamic ideas of Al-Qaeda, in particular with regards to the question of the caliphate. For them, the form of the state is not important as long as it guarantees the security and stability required for the performance of religious duties. The state is thus a means for achieving salvation, not an end in itself. No firm dogmatic position can exist on this subject. The ulama confirmed that they are above all religious actors pursuing religious designs, even when responding to political problems. As a result, the latter must be left to the rulers, who are to act in accordance with the interests of the community and the needs of the moment. This is the very foundation of *al-siyasa al-shar'iyya*, illustrated by the symbiotic relationship between the House of Saud and the Hanbali-Wahhabi establishment.

This exclusively religious vision also applies to the very sensitive questions of *takfir* and *al-wala' wa al-bara'*, used by the ideologues of Al-Qaeda and Islamist movements more generally as political concepts and ideological props for legitimating their activity. Up until the turn of the twentieth century, the representatives of the Najdi tradition made political use of these two notions to forge an identity for themselves and justify the expansion of the Saudi Emirate. But the stabilization of the borders of this entity (renamed the Kingdom of Saudi Arabia in 1932) and the armed resistance of the Ikhwan at the end of the 1920s required them to gradually abandon this dimension of their thought. Henceforth, the two expressions were exclusively employed in the religious sphere. As it was never challenged by the most important actors of the Saudi social space, however, the ulama were not obliged to codify this major change of register. It was only with the rise of the radical Islamist movements of the 1990s, which made expert use of these notions, that the clerical corps realized that a corrective was necessary in order to avoid being confounded with them. Beginning in 1995, several fatawa were issued on this matter, and on 14 June 1998, the most representative and consensual of these—that of the Committee of Grand Ulama—was made public. This was no doubt in response to the creation several months earlier of Osama bin Laden's World Islamic Front for Jihad against Jews and Crusaders.

The text of the leading figures of the religious establishment reiterated that *takfir* was above all a juridico-religious issue (*hukm shar'i*) entailing grave consequences (annulment of marriage, prohibition of inheritance, confiscation of goods, capital punishment, etc.). Declaring a Muslim *kafir* (infidel, unbeliever) required a very strict procedure governed by the Qur'an and the Sunna. A sentence of this type was thus not to be hastily decided on the basis of presumptions alone. They further underscored the fact that no act of impiety, whether intentional or not, merits excommunication from the community or the denial of salvation (*kufr akbar mukhrij mina al-milla*). The procedure was even more demanding in the case of rulers: from the point of view of the Law, those who are unjust, consume alcohol or give themselves over to gambling or embezzlement are merely depraved and perverse (*fusuq*), neither of which leads to exclusion from the community and salvation. In the case of impiety, the ulama required it be given unambiguous expression in the public sphere. Moreover, the document stipulated that no man, whatever his authority, is entitled to excommunicate a Muslim in the absence of tangible evidence drawn from the Qur'an and Sunna.[55]

The desire to defuse this sensitive concept, which was as explosive as a powder keg in the hands of radical groups, led the representatives of the Hanbali-Wahhabi tradition to render *takfir* nearly impossible in practice. Specifically, the ulama took an interest in what may be called macro-*takfir*, that is, the excommunication of entire governments and populations rather than of individuals. Aware of the fact that terrorist groups depended on this concept to legitimate their activities—with military operations against "miscreant" governments and impious populations thereby converted into jihad—they placed particular emphasis on the impossibility of excommunicating the powers that be. This clearly reflected their main preoccupation: preserving the order necessary for the application of orthodoxy and orthopraxy, which of course went hand in hand with the interests of the corporation. But like any group that "uses psychological constraint by dispersion or refusal of the spiritual goods of salvation in order to guarantee its rules,"[56] the ulama conserved the right to engage in micro-*takfir*, that is, excommunication on an individual basis. Indeed, this practice is at the foundation of their ideological authority. In this way, they have been able to minimize the political reach of *takfir*, retaining only its religious dimension.

This also holds for the concept of allegiance and rupture, or *al-wala' wa al-bara'*. Jihadist ideologues have made "Huntingtonian" (after Samuel Huntington's theory of a clash of civilizations) use of this concept.[57] For them, the world is bipartite, and confrontation between Muslims and non-Muslims (whose civilization is thoroughly corrupt and oppressive) is imperative. Any physical or intellectual contact between these two worlds outside of the framework of this struggle is punishable by excommunication. In order to preserve and revive the Muslim world—which is, in their view, in the throes of an unprecedented existential crisis—these ideologues aspire to reproduce the model of *amixia* (exclusivism) described in chapter 3.

In the case at hand, the jihadists reproach the Saudi authorities for closely collaborating at all levels with "impious" forces. This cooperation has taken the form of military and political alliances, commercial and cultural exchanges, the presence of millions of foreign workers, and so on; in the eyes of the Islamists, all are flagrant violations of the duty of *al-wala' wa al-bara'*. In these circumstances, the ulama obviously had no choice but to put their own definition of this injunction into circulation.

Several ulama issued fatawa on this subject. Of these, the most important were those of Salih al-Fawzan, the establishment's specialist on the issue and a leading authority on the writings of Sulayman ibn Muhammad ibn Abd al-Wahhab (d. 1818).[58] Al-Fawzan claimed that false interpretations—generally the work of nonspecialists—were at the origin of the misuse of *al-wala' wa al-bara'*. These held, for example, that commercial relations and the exchange of gifts with non-Muslims fell under the purview of this concept. Not so, al-Fawzan argued. Drawing upon scriptural citations, al-Fawzan showed that commercial relations, the importation of foreign labor, and the signing of peace treaties and truces with non-Muslim countries were permissible to the degree that such cases of interaction were based on interest and not religious feeling. Indeed, such contacts in no way implied a belief in the truth of the Other's faith or a desire to imitate his way of life. Finally, al-Fawzan insisted on the need to locate the writings of Sulayman ibn Abd Allah and Hamad ibn Atiq—the main authorities cited by proponents of a political and exclusivist vision of the concept of *al-wala' wa al-bara'*—in their historical context, one that was characterized by grave crises (fratricidal struggle and foreign intervention).[59] According to al-Fawzan, their texts thus must be used with caution and care, something that only true ulama are capable of doing.[60]

In order to meet the jihadist challenge and adapt the Hanbali-Wahhabi tradition to its status as the official religion of a regional power that enjoyed influence throughout the Islamic world, the ulama were obliged to redefine *al-wala' wa al-bara'*. As with the question of macro-*takfir*, they completely evacuated the concept of the political import it had inherited from their nineteenth-century predecessors, retaining only its purely religious dimension (which only they were competent to judge). Henceforth, the ulama considered the concept of *al-wala' wa al-bara'* merely as a mark of identity and symbolic frontier separating Muslims from the Other.

As is the case of nearly all religious institutions of the contemporary Muslim world, the Hanbali-Wahhabi establishment has a very classical vision of jihad.[61] Indeed, it opposes all individual or collective undertakings that are unsupervised by the political power and the religious authority, seeing them as threats to the three O's.[62] We have seen how the ulama firmly condemned the Ikhwan's jihadist projects in the late 1920s. Similarly, they gave only very halfhearted support to the wars in Afghanistan and Bosnia.[63] What's more, at a time when "globalized" radical Islamism was only in its infancy, the religious establishment condemned any attempt to legitimate acts of terrorism by reference to an ideology of jihad.

On 25 August 1988, the Committee of Grand Ulama issued a fatwa stating that any act of terrorism (such as hijacking, destroying or seizing public or private goods in a Muslim or other country, and attacking the forces of order) was to be considered a form of rebellion against God (*hiraba*) and punished with death, as stipulated by the Qur'an: according to the ulama, nothing in the religion, which had been revealed to humanity in order to safeguard faith, life, honor, goods, and family, could justify such acts.[64] With the rise of violent Islamism during the 1990s and 2000s, particularly in Saudi Arabia, the religious establishment issued a growing number of individual and collective fatawa on this subject.[65] While reiterating Islam's ban on all forms of illegal violence, these juridico-religious documents emphasized three important points: the legal status of suicide attacks, the targets of attack, and terrorist financing.

Hanbali-Wahhabi ulama unanimously regard suicide attacks as illicit: the act of killing oneself—divine prerogative par excellence in monotheistic religions—is prohibited by Islam, no matter the circumstances.[66] As a consequence, the perpetrator of a suicide attack is not considered a martyr but rather a suicide condemned to eternal damnation.[67] Observing that most attacks target non-Muslim communities and security personnel, the ulama sought to clarify the situation and prohibit these operations. Indeed, they held that the assassination of nationals of non-Muslim countries with which peace and exchange agreements had been signed, particularly those who were temporarily or permanently residing in Islamic lands, was illicit. In keeping with the most incontrovertible religious prescriptions, foreign nationals are to benefit from the protection (*al-aman*) of the authorities.[68] Similarly, attacks against security personnel are also prohibited, as the latter are representatives of the legal authorities (or recognized as such) as well as Muslims.[69] Finally, recognizing that war is impossible without money, the Committee of Grand Ulama issued a fatwa on 13 April 2010 in which they held that all forms of terrorist financing are forbidden by law and subject to severe punishment.[70] Henceforth, Saudi courts can investigate cases of this type, with the Ministry of the Interior keeping a close watch over the finances of more than 580 charitable associations and 90 foundations.[71]

These doctrinal readjustments were accompanied, especially after 2001, by symbolic acts ushering in a new phase in the routinization of the Hanbali-Wahhabi tradition. In order to once and for all distinguish itself from violent Islamism and respond to the criticism of Western powers, the Saudi state set about revising the school programs that had been written by the Muslim Brotherhood. The authorities' objective here was to suppress all exclusivist passages while insisting on the moderate nature (*wasatiyya, i'tidal*) of Islam, an expression that recently entered the Hanbali-Wahhabi vocabulary. Led by a grandson of Grand Mufti Muhammad ibn Ibrahim, the Ministry of Islamic Affairs has tried to closely supervise the religious space (making imams employees of the state, surveilling sermons and informal instruction in the mosques, overseeing publication, etc.) in order to preclude ideological excess.

In the same spirit, on 12 August 2010 King Abd Allah decreed that only the Committee of Grand Ulama and members of the religious establishment who had been officially designated by the grand mufti would henceforth be authorized to publicly issue legal opinions by way of television programs, radio broadcasts, newspapers, sermons in mosques, and so on.[72] The aim of this effort was to ensure that a centralized and homogenous discourse reigns in the Saudi public sphere and that dissident, competing, or extremist voices are marginalized.[73] Though this monopolist process has only just gotten under way,[74] the authorities have already shown that they are determined to enforce the Royal Order. The following example illustrates this: while most Saudi Internet sites offering fatawa have withdrawn this service while awaiting official authorization, those that have failed to do so have been promptly shut down.

In 2003, moreover, the monarchy created a dialogue on values and national identity (*al-hiwar al-watani*) in which figures from the country's various religious traditions (Imamite Shiites and Isma'ilians as well as non–Hanbali-Wahhabi Sunni) participated alongside Hanbali-Wahhabi ulama:[75] the corporation thus extended de facto recognition to the kingdom's other traditions. The former president of this body, Salih al-Husayn (d. 2013), was an eminent member of the religious establishment. Among other things, he was president of the organization responsible for managing the holy places of Islam and, since 2009, a member of the Committee of Grand Ulama. To promote an image of the kingdom as tolerant and open to the Other, the monarchy also held several conferences for intrareligious and interreligious dialogue in 2008 at which the religious establishment played an important role.[76] While these initiatives are generally considered to be no more than branding operations—a traditional mode of legitimation in most patrimonial systems—they can sometimes produce genuine emergent effects. If this type of action becomes more common in Saudi Arabia in the coming years, it will no doubt have an effect on the evolution of the Hanbali-Wahhabi tradition.

Conclusion

Natura non facit saltus—nature does not make jumps. This adage, employed by philosophers and natural scientists since late antiquity, nicely captures the idea that all change proceeds from successive stages rather than abrupt transitions in space and time. The historical sociology of Hanbali-Wahhabism tends to confirm this premise. Reconstructing the genealogy of this tradition, retracing its historical trajectory, describing its origins and practices, determining its identity, grasping what is permanent and the changes that have cut across it—such were the ambitions of this work. Studying its *longue durée* has in effect allowed us to review the historical, social, and political variables that presided over the establishment of an *ethic of responsibility* that aims to preserve and transmit orthodoxy, orthopraxy, and the political order—what I have called the three O's. It has also made it possible to demonstrate that Hanbali-Wahhabism is not the monolithic entity described by others but is in fact a living tradition that interacts with social facts and responds to historical contingencies.

Identifying the main trends of medieval Hanbalism makes it clear that, despite its small number of followers, this tradition was at the heart of Sunnism. Its representatives above all struggled to impose sharia as the ideal center and norm for the Muslim community. Conscious of the fact that orthodoxy, orthopraxy, and the political order were integral parts of any effort to achieve salvation, medieval Hanbalis developed a coherent theory in the framework of a school of thought that was at once theological and juridical—a unique case in Arab-Muslim history. To complete this system, they also took an interest in a version of Sufism purified of its popular practices. As we have seen, contrary to a received idea, medieval Hanbalism was not hostile to mystical practices. Indeed, its main representatives—in particular, Ibn Taymiyya and Ibn Qayyim al-Jawziyya—were themselves believers.

As religious actors pursuing mainly religious projects, the Hanbali ulama saw politics as merely a tool—albeit an indispensable one—for maintaining the order necessary for the observance of juridico-religious duties. As a consequence, they required believers to show absolute fidelity toward their rulers as long as the latter did not publicly challenge the foundations of the religion. And while the Hanbalis forbade themselves direct interference in political affairs throughout the classical period, they nevertheless supported the powers that be in the framework of a symbiotic relationship. Yet despite the efforts of Abu Ya'la ibn al-Farra' and Ibn Taymiyya, whose writings on a sharia-based conception of politics are consulted to this day, it would not be until the eighteenth-century predication of the Najdi 'alim Muhammad ibn Abd al-Wahhab that the ulama's search for protection would find concrete expression.

A rereading of Ibn Abd al-Wahhab's career throws new light on the birth of Hanbali-Wahhabism. Contrary to a received idea, this was not a response to a chaotic situation on the Arabian Peninsula but rather the result of a personal initiative inspired by Ibn Abd al-Wahhab's belief that he was invested with a divine mission to reestablish orthodoxy and orthopraxy. To this end, he adopted a messianic attitude and an *ethic of conviction*, believing himself to be the reformer of the century (*al-mujaddid*). He gradually combined the purely theoretical condemnation of the contemporaneous practices of popular Islam (in, for example, *The Book of Divine Unity*) with what can only be described as religious activism. This led him to draw a rigorous distinction between true and false religion. Henceforth, only his interpretations and teachings, particularly in the theological domain (*al-'aqida*), represented true Islam: a total break with the recent history of the region and its religious traditions was the result. In this sense, the Najdi preacher established a counterreligion. This stance distinguished him from classic Hanbalism, which, while asserting its preeminence over all other traditions, never claimed to have a monopoly on the truth. This distinctive aspect of Ibn Abd al-Wahhab's mission was complemented by yet another: the condemnation of Sufism in all of its forms. But apart from these two important points, he only adapted and simplified classic Hanbali doctrines in the service of his religious ideal.

Ibn Abd al-Wahhab's approach was initially part of a purely religious dynamic in the sense that he did not seek to found a new political order to support it. It was only in reaction to a hostile environment that an embryonic state organization emerged to defend the predication and its followers in the framework of defensive jihad. The symbiotic relationship between the Najdi preacher and the House of Saud was therefore gradually established on a de facto basis. The Saudi Emirate was an emergent effect of the shaykh's action. Assured of increasingly powerful politico-military protection, the charismatic leader, whose ultimate concern was the victory of the True Religion, hoped to perpetuate and spread his teachings by establishing a tradition and constructing a corporation to defend and transmit it. To this end, he produced a coherent corpus, saw to the education of several disciples, and led campaigns of acculturation among the subjugated population. The work and action of Ibn Abd al-Wahhab therefore ultimately gave birth to a new politico-religious order: the Hanbali-Wahhabi tradition and the Saudi Emirate.

The defensive jihad conducted by the followers of the Najdi predication gradually transformed into an imperial effort. Between the end of the eighteenth century and the beginning of the nineteenth, they were able to subjugate the better part of the Arabian Peninsula, particularly the holy places of Islam. To come to terms with this rapid transformation, the heirs of Ibn Abd al-Wahhab adopted an ethic of responsibility and made a first attempt to routinize their doctrine to render themselves more broadly acceptable to local populations and Islamic opinion. But the Ottoman military intervention put a brutal end to this process. Worse yet, it led to political withdrawal and religious closure. Feeling under threat from a hostile environment, the representatives of Hanbali-Wahhabism developed the concept of *al-wala' wa al-bara'* (allegiance and rupture) in order to reduce to a strict minimum all contact with the external world as part of a policy of *amixia*. But this exclusivism in no way implied a clear and definite vision of the Other of the type that might have been supplied by a well-defined scholastic position. Following Ibn Abd al-Wahhab's lead, his heirs adopted affective and hesitant positions that evolved as dictated by circumstances, a stance reflected in the terminology they employed in their writings.

Yet this period of closure allowed the corporation to once and for all solidify its ties with the House of Saud: the symbiotic relationship became official and was implemented through a reinvention of the classical tradition, with the two partners clearly dividing prerogatives between themselves in the social space. Where the ulama legitimated the positions and actions of the emirs of Riyadh, the emirs supported the ulama in their efforts to impose orthodoxy and orthopraxy in the public sphere. In order to strengthen their grip over Najd, the ulama launched a true policy of homogenization, drawing its legitimacy from the Islamic duty to promote virtue and prevent vice.

This period of relative stability finally came to an end following the death of Emir Faysal in 1865. The war of succession among his descendants gave rise to an unbearable atmosphere of insecurity and uncertainty for the ulama, who saw all of their efforts to impose orthodoxy and orthopraxy reduced to nothing as a result of the lack of order. Their response was to blindly forge ahead, above all after the destruction of the Saudi Emirate in 1891. While dozens of ulama went abroad, particularly to India, in order to complete their education, others believed they had found salvation in messianic ideology and left to seek the Mahdi. As had been the case during the Ottoman invasion of 1818, the political crisis of the late nineteenth century allowed the corporation to enlarge its corpus and open up to other Sunni traditions, showing that the positions of its representatives changed with circumstances over time. Similarly, they did not ultimately give in to the messianic temptation, opting instead for strict observance of sharia (the unique source of salvation for them) and the restoration of the House of Saud (their only trustworthy partner).

The birth of the modern Saudi Kingdom in the twentieth century was accompanied by a renaissance of the Hanbali-Wahhabi tradition. Confirming the symbiotic relationship with King Abd al-Aziz, the ulama put all symbolic resources necessary for consolidating and extending his power at his disposal. They thus played a preeminent role in the sedentarization of the Bedouins and the creation of the Ikhwan army. But when the Ikhwan army attacked the prerogatives and interests of the corporation, the ulama did not hesitate, after vain attempts at reconciliation, to condemn their acts and authorize the king to cut them down to size. In addition to their clear transgressions of the tradition, the Ikhwan challenged the centrality of the corporation and the ideological authority of its members. In order to neutralize this effort, the ulama did not shy away from specifying the content of such key issues as jihad and its conditions, the limits of state expansion, the introduction of modern inventions, and so on. In other words, this internal crisis allowed Hanbali-Wahhabism to forge ahead with the process of routinization.

This process was also facilitated by the public relations campaign launched by the king with help from various contacts in India, the Levant, and above all Egypt. After several decades of unfavorable propaganda on the part of the Ottomans and their vassals, it was necessary to restore the prestige of the tradition in the Muslim world. The success of this campaign was such that Abd al-Aziz endeavored to dilute Hanbali-Wahhabi identity in a larger reformist movement that was widely supported by Muslim populations. Far from adapting to the situation, the clerical corps, which believed itself to be the exclusive keeper of religious truth, refused this undertaking on the grounds that it would destroy the tradition's identity and thwart all of their efforts. Nevertheless, contact with reformist circles led the ulama to realize that modern structures had to be established if the centrality of the corporation and the ideological authority of its representatives were to be preserved.

The birth of the Kingdom of Saudi Arabia offered extraordinary opportunities for expansion to the Najdi tradition. Apart from control over the public sphere across most of the Arabian Peninsula—in particular, the two holy places of Islam—the ulama were able to "convert" a significant part of the population. They took an interest in populations that had neither strong religious traditions nor a locally based religious elite. They particularly concentrated on the north and southwest of the kingdom, where most of the population adhered to Hanbali-Wahhabism after several years of thorough acculturation. This means that the corporation possessed a conversion strategy that was based both on rational calculation and on an ethic of responsibility. It sought to guarantee the best possible return on its investment while avoiding conflicts that might threaten the established order or, above all, harm its political partner.

In contrast to the clerical corps in nearly all other Arab countries, the Hanbali-Wahhabi corporation responded to the major structural challenges experienced by Saudi Arabia and the rest of the Muslim world in the 1950s and 1960s by taking the initiative to construct modern institutions. The ulama's main preoccupation was to maintain the centrality of their discourse in the social space. The struggle against Pan-Arabism favored their plans. The policy of Islamic solidarity inaugurated by the monarchy positively affected the tradition: on the one hand, it permitted the corporation to interact with other religious elites in the Muslim world and thereby profit from their competence and experience in many domains; on the other, it allowed the tradition to once and for all move beyond its status as a local phenomenon to become a global one. The time of *amixia* had come to an end, and the process of routinization resumed with renewed vigor.

The religious establishment would not have been able to maximize the benefits of this historic conjuncture were it not for the presence of a formidable strategist at its head: Grand Mufti Muhammad ibn Ibrahim, the founder of modern Hanbali-Wahhabism. Ibn Ibrahim worked methodically and patiently to establish a global, modern, centralized, and pyramidal organization. Indeed, the institutions he established still govern the Saudi juridico-religious space. Moreover, the institutionalization and routinization of the Najdi tradition are merely indicators of the process of state construction in the sense that the ruling class pursued a monopolist policy in all domains. But this process was not all smooth sailing. The ulama had to confront the monarchy's problems and growing appetite. After having decisively intervened in the issue of succession in order to preserve the political order, they defended the socioreligious interests of the corporation by opposing the large-scale introduction of positive laws. This, however, led to symbolic friction with the political power, which encouraged the monarchy to seriously consider decapitating the establishment and freeing itself from its legitimating discourse by establishing a differentiated legitimacy based on developmentalist rhetoric.

Profiting from the death of Grand Mufti Ibn Ibrahim, King Faysal tried to put an end to the establishment's centralized and monocephalic leadership and replace it with a fragmented and headless organization by creating a number of bodies, the most important of which was the Committee of Grand Ulama. But this attempt at fragmentation failed: the committee definitively established itself as the country's main legislative body and the regime's ideological shield. It thus became the heart of the corporation and the focus of the ulama's ideological authority as a collective actor.

The broad prerogatives enjoyed by the committee in the religious, social, and political domains justify the authorities' control over a part of its agenda. The aim of this oversight is to prevent the body from becoming a competing rostrum or hotbed of insubordination, particularly during periods of political transition and crisis. The political power aims less at absolute control of religious discourse itself than at the mastery of religious initiative. Proof of this is to be found in the near total independence of the Committee of Grand Ulama and its various components in what concerns the goods of salvation (in the framework of the Hanbali-Wahhabi school of thought, it goes without saying). Moreover, the grand ulama are not interested in achieving control over the political domain, as they fully identify themselves with the powers that be. Cooperation and obedience to the prince are at the very foundation of Hanbali doctrine as the Law cannot be applied, in their view, without the coercive force of the state. What's more, the spiritual and temporal interests of the Hanbali-Wahhabi establishment are intrinsically tied to those of the regime: if the regime is harmed, the corporation's dominance over Saudi territory and influence in Islamic space would be, too.

The wide-ranging prerogatives of this body encouraged the monarchy to seek not only to control a part of its agenda, but also to supervise access to it. For its part, the corporation aspired to protect its strength and identity by imposing an ever more rigorous process of socialization on future members. Enumerating the tacit conditions of access to the religious establishment thus gives us a faithful image of the evolution of the clerical habitus. Over the course of the second half of the twentieth century, the corporation adapted its goods of salvation to the social changes that occurred in Saudi Arabia and elsewhere in the Islamic space.

While the ulama's social origins, paths of initiation, and networks of socialization all favored the emergence of a closed elite devoted to promoting the corporation's social, religious, and political principles, regional '*asabiyya* (esprit de corps/solidarity) also played a large role. Like the country's other institutions, the Committee of Grand Ulama is monopolized by the Najdi element (more than 70 percent of members of the Saudi elite are from Najd). This region, after all, is the fief of Hanbali-Wahhabism and the ruling house. The prosopography of members of the Committee of Grand Ulama clearly shows that access to the summit of the Saudi religious establishment remains very restricted. Indeed, religious solidarity and identity have yet to supplant regional and tribal solidarity. This is an entirely normal phenomenon of patrimonial systems. As a consequence, we cannot speak of the routinization of Hanbali-Wahhabism in what specifically concerns the recruitment of the corporation's leaders.

The fundamental objective of any tradition claiming to possess the truth, whatever its origin, is to impose its vision of the world on the public sphere. The Hanbali-Wahhabi tradition is no exception to this rule. Since its emergence in the second half of the eighteenth century, its representatives have done everything in their power to realize this objective, making particular use of the duty to promote virtue and prevent vice. As a tool for dominating and homogenizing the population, this duty, in the hands of peripheral actors, can serve as a fierce weapon of protest. Throughout the twentieth century, the corporation, with support from the political power, sought to institutionalize and rationalize this duty in order to improve the system's efficiency and discourage excesses. But like any effort at centralization, this process was punctuated with politico-religious crises that produced emergent effects—in particular, a desire to transform the Committee for the Promotion of Virtue and the Prevention of Vice from a repressive apparatus into an apparatus for prevention and awareness-raising. This is obviously part of a larger dynamic: the routinization of Hanbali-Wahhabism.

The same phenomenon was reproduced in the politico-religious domain, where since 1979 the corporation has had to confront several antiestablishment religious groups (Messianism, Islamism, and Jihadism) that challenged its ideological authority and its symbiotic relationship with the House of Saud. As with the Ikhwan crisis, the ulama had to distance themselves from these groups by readjusting several aspects of their doctrine in the framework of the ethic of responsibility. They thus adopted clear positions on such key concepts as jihad, excommunication (*takfir*), *al-wala' wa al-bara'*, involvement with Islamist groups, and suicide attacks and thereby reduced their scope to the religious dimension alone. Though seemingly dictated by circumstances, these readjustments were in reality a reflection of a perception of politics inspired by medieval Hanbalism: politics is no more than a practical tool for ensuring the order necessary to implement orthodoxy and orthopraxy. In short, the ulama are religious actors and intend to remain such. Indeed, the corporation's strength is precisely due to the fact that it has confined itself to a well-determined space and role.

Today, the work of doctrinal reframing continues to be accompanied by action on the ground (intrareligious and interreligious dialogue, the purge of school textbooks, the institutionalization of the promotion of virtue and the prevention of vice, a monopoly on the promulgation of fatawa, etc.). This is contributing to the permanent transformation of Hanbali-Wahhabism from a counterreligion into a religion that interacts more openly with the Other. At the same time, the corporation has become a veritable church as Max Weber understood it. The question of routinization aside, we are thus now witnessing the birth of the first Sunni clergy in the strict sense of the term.

Appendix: House of Saud and Map of Saudi Arabia

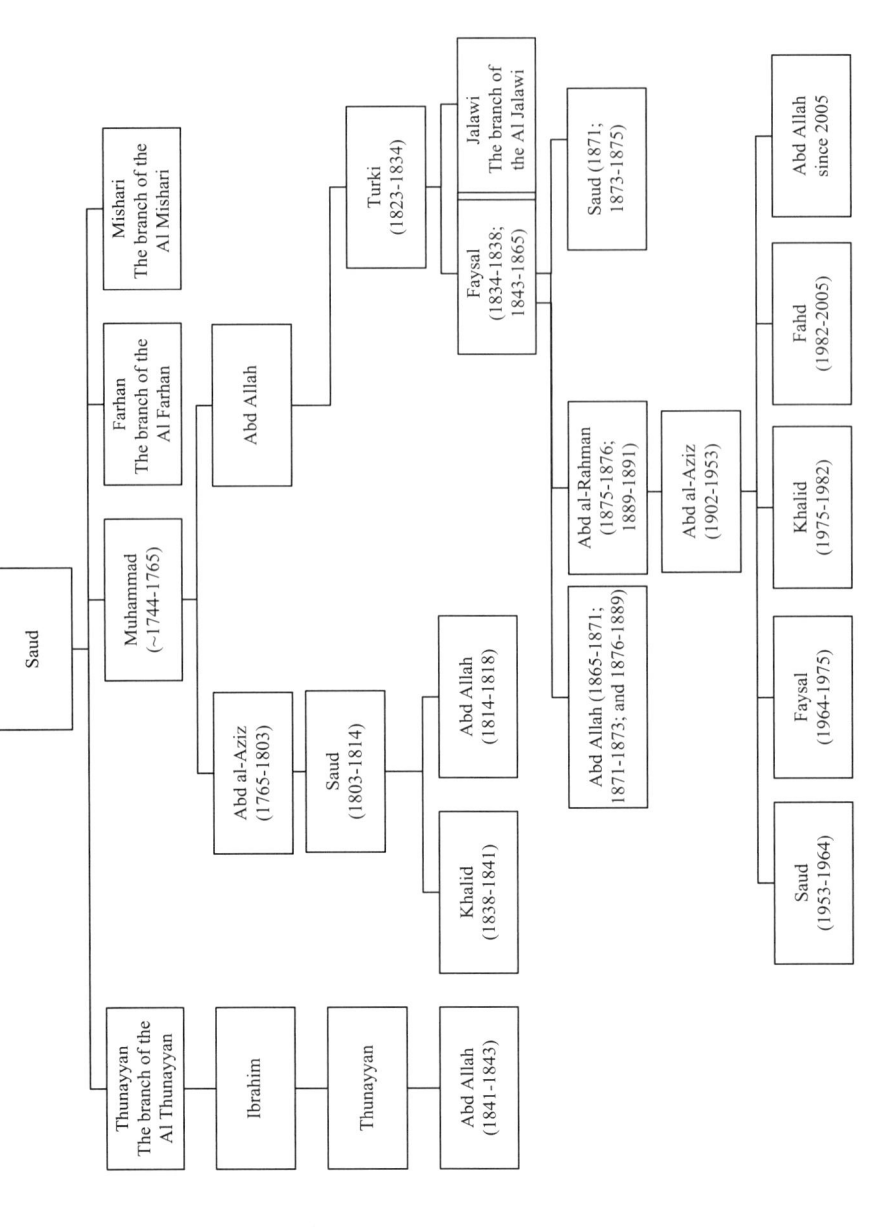

Figure 17. Genealogy of the House of Saud.

Map 3. Map of Saudi Arabia.

NOTES

INTRODUCTION

1. The full hadith is: "If anyone travels on a road in search of knowledge, God will cause him to travel on one of the roads of Paradise. The angels will lower their wings in their great pleasure with one who seeks knowledge. The inhabitants of the heavens and the Earth and even the fish in the deep waters will ask forgiveness for the learned man. The superiority of the learned over the devout is like that of the moon, on the night when it is full, over the rest of the stars. The learned [ulama] are the heirs of the Prophets, and the Prophets leave neither gold nor money, they leave only knowledge, and he who takes it takes an abundant portion." See Ibn Hanbal, *al-Musnad*, no. 20723; al-Darimi, *al-Sunan*, no. 346; al-Tirmidhi, *al-Sunan*, no. 2606; Ibn Majja, *al-Sunan*, no. 219.
2. Weber, *Économie et société*, vol. 1, p. 451.
3. Durkheim, *Les Formes élémentaires*, pp. 488, 494.
4. Abd al-Baqi, *al-Mu'jam*, pp. 469–480. On this notion, see Rosenthal, *Knowledge Triumphant*.
5. Dabashi, *Authority in Islam*; Zaman, *Religion and Politics*.
6. See the Qur'an, 4/83, 9/122, 17/107, 22/54, 28/14 and 80, 29/49, 35/28, 39/9, 58/11.
7. The term "ulama" mainly refers to traditionalists (*al-muhaddithun*) and legal specialists (*al-fuqaha'*). During the first centuries of Islamic history, several other names were also used, such as Qur'an scholars (*al-qurra'*); ascetics (*al-zuhhad*); collectors of religious, historical, literary, and philological information (*al-akhbariyyun*). Moreover, "ulama" may also be used to refer to specialists of grammar, history, exegesis, literature, and so on.
8. It is to be noted that, starting in the early ninth century, the ulama succeeded in once and for all sacralizing their function-vocation by devoting entire portions of the collections of prophetic traditions they assembled to praise of scholarship and scholars, in particular traditionalists (*al-muhaddithun*).
9. As regards "collective actor," it is interesting to note that the main European languages borrowed the plural term "ulama" (French, *ouléma*; English, ulama) to designate

both the individual and the group. This suggests that Europeans saw the clerics of Islam as a collective actor and not merely a collection of individuals.
10. Most of the pre–twentieth-century historical compilations, literary anthologies, and ethico-philosophical reflections available to us are the work of ulama.
11. On this aspect, see Ben Achour, *Aux Fondements de l'orthodoxie Sunnite*, pp. 2–9.
12. Duncan MacDonald, "ulama," in *Encyclopédie de l'islam*, 1st ed., vol. 4, pp. 1047–1048.
13. I here draw upon Aron, "Classe sociale" and "Structure sociale"; Mosca, *Ruling Class*; Pareto, *Traité de sociologie*; Busino, *Élites et bureaucratie*; Busino, *Élites et Élitisme*.
14. This meaning converges with one of the most enduring cultural schema of Islamic civilization: the division of society between *khassa* (the elite) and *amma* (the masses). Obedience is the sole duty of the masses, who are considered a rowdy and contemptible multitude.
15. Benveniste, *Vocabulaire*, vol. 2, p. 149.
16. Qur'an, 5/40, 9/116, and 7/54. Indeed, terms such as *sultan* (authoritative proof), *quwwa* (power), *amr* (commandment), *hukm* (judgment, decision), *mulk* (sovereignty, possession, power), and *qahr* (domination) denote this absolute sovereignty.
17. Qur'an, 2/30–34, 4/144, 11/96, and 55/1–27.
18. Crone and Hinds, *God's Caliph*; Goldziher, "Du sens propre."
19. Weber, *Économie et Société*, vol. 1, pp. 285–325.
20. Weber, *Le Savant*, p. 126.
21. Ibid.
22. Ibid., p. 127.
23. Willer, "Max Weber's."
24. Weber, *Économie et Société*, vol. 1, pp. 72, 55.
25. Willer, "Max Weber's," p. 235.
26. Satow, "Value-Rational Authority."
27. Chénu, *Introduction à l'étude*, p. 122. The ulama were conscious of this phenomenon and attempted to justify it by putting into circulation a saying attributed to the fourth caliph, Ali ibn Abi Talib (d. 661): "The Qur'an is only a mute book that men make speak [in order to defend their beliefs]." See al-Tabari, *Tarikh al-umam wa al-muluk*, vol. 5, p. 66.
28. Ibn Qasim, *al-Durar al-saniyya*, vol. 1, pp. 58–64, vol. 9, pp. 82–85; al-Bassam, *'Ulama' najd*, vol. 1, pp. 169–179.
29. Ibn Qasim, *al-Durar al-saniyya*, vol. 1, p. 5.
30. Ibid., vol. 1, p. 9; Abd al-Latif Al al-Shaykh, *'Uyun al-rasa'il*, vol. 1, p. 229; Abd al-Rahman ibn Hasan Al al-Shaykh, *al-Maqamat*, p. 73.
31. Ibn Qasim, *al-Durar al-saniyya*, vol. 11, p. 548.
32. Ibid., vol. 12, pp. 5–42.
33. Ibid., vol. 3, p. 49; al-Bassam, *'Ulama' najd*, vol. 2, pp. 176–181.
34. Ibn Qasim, *al-Durar al-saniyya*, vol. 1, pp. 15, 446, 564–577; vol. 4, pp. 52–59; vol. 10, pp. 248–249, 304; vol. 12, pp. 528–550; vol. 14, pp. 133–134; and vol. 16, pp. 237–313; al-Bassam, *'Ulama' najd*, vol. 1, pp. 169–179; vol. 2, p. 266; vol. 3, p. 501; and vol. 4, p. 511.

35. It was Ibn Abd al-Wahhab's own brother, Sulayman (d. ca. 1793–1794), who is said to have first used this term in a long epistle titled *The Refutation of Wahhabism in Arabic Sources*. See Sulayman ibn Abd al-Wahhab, *al-Sawa'iq al-ilahiyya*. Other detractors compared Ibn Abd al-Wahhab and his followers to *Khawarij*, a puritanical and extremist politico-religious current of the Islamic High Middle Ages.
36. Ibn Sahman, *al-Hadiyya al-saniyya* and *al-Sawa'iq al-mursala*.
37. Ibn Sahman, *al-Diya' al-shariq*, pp. 211–215, 243, 301; *Kashf ghayahib al-zalam*, pp. 10, 23, 93, 123.
38. Abd al-Rahman Al al-Shaykh, *Mashahir*, p. 297; Ahmad Dahlan (d. 1887) was the *shafi'ite* judge of Mecca and the author of several theological, legal, and historical works, in particular, a history of the holy city.
39. Ibn 'Isa, *al-Radd*; copy of the manuscript in possession of the author.
40. Ibn Qasim, *al-Durar al-saniyya*, vol. 1, p. 566.
41. See, for example, *Umm al-qura*, no. 24, 5 June 1925, p.2; no. 27, 26 June 1925, p. 4.
42. Rida, *al-Wahhabiyyun wa al-Hijaz*. See also Rida, "al-Wahhabiyya wa al-'aqida"; "al-Wahhabiyya wa da'wa al-Manar"; and "Rasa'il al-sunna wa al-shi'a."
43. Muhammad Hamid al-Fiqi, *Athar al-da'wa al-wahhabiyya*.
44. Al-Qasimi, *al-Thawra al-Wahhabiyya*.
45. *Umm al-qura*, no. 229, 16 May 1929, p. 1; Ibn Qasim, *al-Durar al-saniyya*, vol. 14, pp. 401–408. The letter dates from 1937.
46. Nevertheless, it must not be forgotten that the term *salafiyya* was also used by the ulama of Najd throughout the nineteenth century. See Ibn Qasim, *al-Durar al-saniyya*, vol. 1, pp. 446, 564–577, 595; vol. 3, pp. 54–55; vol. 12, pp. 528–550; vol. 16, pp. 11–17.
47. Gardet, *La Cité musulmane*, p. 24.
48. Hobsbawm and Ranger, eds., *Invention of Tradition*, p. 1.
49. Blondel, *Histoire et dogme*, p. 204.
50. Veyne, *Quand notre monde*, pp. 125–126.
51. Weber, *Économie et Société*, vol. 1, pp. 301–320; Eisenstadt, *Traditional Patrimonialism*; Médard, "L'État patrimonialisé" and "L'État néo-patrimonial."
52. Médard, "L'État néo-patrimonial."
53. Herb, *All in the Family*; Hertog, *Princes, Brokers*.
54. According to Lévi-Strauss, the house is a "moral person, the holder of a domain consisting of both material and immaterial goods, that perpetuates itself by transmitting its name, fortune, and titles in a real or fictive line that is taken for legitimate on the sole condition that this continuity be amenable to expression in the language of kingship, alliance or, most often, both at the same time." Lévi-Strauss, *Paroles données*, p. 190.
55. Radcliffe-Brown, *Structure and Function*, p. 52.
56. On this approach, see Marx, *Les Luttes de classes* and *Le 18 brumaire*; Wright, *L'élite du pouvoir*; Poulantzas, *Pouvoir politique*; Birnbaum et al., *La Classe dirigeante*; Pierre Bourdieu, "Le racisme de l'intelligence," in Bourdieu, *Questions de sociologie*, p. 188; Suleiman, *Les hauts Fonctionnaires* and *Les élites en France*.

57. On the rentier state, see Beblawi and Luciani, eds., *Rentier State*; Khaldun al-Naqib, *al-Mujtamaʿ wa al-dawla fi al-khalij wa al-jazira al-ʿarabiyya*, pp. 121–126; Beblawi, "al-Dawla," p. 281; Abd al-Fadil, *al-Tashkilat al-ijtimaʿiyya*.
58. Attention will also be given to other official bodies, including the Ministry of Islamic Affairs, the General Presidency of the Committee for the Promotion of Virtue and the Prevention of Vice, and the country's Islamic universities.
59. According to Assman, a counterreligion "excludes whatever precedes and is external to it by describing it as 'paganism'" (*Moïse l'Égyptien*, p. 20).
60. I would like to point out that, in regards to interviews with members of the establishment, my interlocutors wished to remain anonymous, less perhaps to avoid problems than to give the impression of speaking with a single voice.
61. Bourdieu, "L'illusion biographique."
62. E.g., Ibn Hanbal (d. 855), Ibn Qudama (d. 1223), Ibn Taymiyya (d. 1328), Ibn al-Jawziyya (d. 1350), al-Mardawi (d. 1480), al-Hajjawi (d. 1560), al-Karami (d. 1624), and al-Buhuti (d. 1641).

CHAPTER 1. THE BIRTH OF THE HANBALI TRADITION

1. Djaït, *La Grande discorde*; Madelung, *The Succession*.
2. Coulson, *A History*, pp. 24–26.
3. Al-Suyuti, *Tarikh al-khulafaʾ*, pp. 108–109.
4. Al-Tirmidhi, *al-Sunan*, no. 3619.
5. Crone and Hinds, *God's Caliph*, pp. 25–33, 102–103.
6. This idea is very close to Indo-European conceptions. See Dumézil, *Mythe et épopée*, vol. 2, p. 358; Daniel Dubuisson, "Le roi indo-européen"; Le Goff, "Les trois fonctions."
7. Qurʾan, 48/10.
8. Lambton, *State and Government*, p. 86.
9. Crone and Hinds, *God's Caliph*, p. 52; Zaman, "The Caliphs," p. 21; Zaman, *Religion and Politics*, pp. 137–138.
10. Dutton, *Origins of Islamic Law*, pp. 121–131.
11. Dabashi, *Authority in Islam*, pp. 92–93.
12. On these changes, see Kennedy, *Early ʿAbbassid Caliphate*; Sourdel, *L'état impérial*; Hawting, *First Dynasty*.
13. Juynboll, "Some Notes"; Motzki, *Origins*; Berg, ed., *Method and Theory*; Mourad, *Early Islam*.
14. Qurʾan, 33/21.
15. On the emergence, elaboration, and development of the hadith, see Goldziher, *Études*; Azami, *Studies in Hadith Methodology* and *Studies in Early Hadith Literature*; Juynboll, *Muslim Tradition*; Lucas, *Constructive Critics*.
16. Ibn al-Muqaffaʿ, *Risala fi al-Sahaba*, p. 354. On this author's political opinions, see Dov Goitein, "A Turning Point."
17. On this subject, see Jokisch, *Islamic Imperial Law*.

18. On the reign and religious policy of al-Ma'mum, see *Encyclopédie de l'islam*, 2nd ed. (hereafter cited as *EI²*), vol. 6, p. 315; Shaban, *Islamic History*, pp. 41–60; Hamdi, "Pro-Alid Policy"; Sourdel, "La politique religieuse."
19. *EI²*, vol. 7, p. 785; Ess, *Une lecture*; *Encyclopedia of Religion*, vol. 10, pp. 220–229; Urvoy, *Histoire*, pp. 172–191; Cruz Hernandez, *Histoire*, pp. 86–98.
20. *EI²*, vol. 7, p. 2; Wilfred Madelung, "The Origins"; Nawas, "A Reexamination" and "The Mihna of 218 A.H."; Hurvitz, "The Mihna."
21. Ahmad ibn Hanbal, *al-Musnad*, no. 20723; al-Darimi, *al-Sunan*, no. 346; al-Tirmidhi, *al-Sunan*, no. 2606; Ibn Majja, *al-Sunan*, no. 219.
22. Ibn Sa'd, *al-Tabaqat al-kubra*, vol. 3, p. 166, systematically reproduced by later compilers.
23. *EI²*, vol. 1, p. 272; Patton, *Ahmed ibn Hanbal*; Susan Spectorsky, "Ahmad Ibn Hanbal's fiqh," *Journal of the American Oriental Society*, no. 102, 1982, pp. 461–465; Aziz al-Azmeh, "Orthodoxy and Hanbalite Fideism," *Arabica*, no. 35, 1988, pp. 253–266; Cooperson, "Ibn Hanbal"; Nimrod Hurvitz, "Schools of Law and Historical Context: Re-Examining the Formation of the Hanbali Madhhab," *Islamic Law and Society*, vol. 7, no. 1, 2000, pp. 37–64; Hurvitz, *The Formation of Hanbalism*; Wesley Williams, "Aspects of the Creed of Imam Ahmad Ibn Hanbal: A Study of Anthropomorphism in Early Islamic Discourse," *International Journal of Middle East Studies*, no. 3, 2002, pp. 441–463; Christopher Melchert, "The Adversaries of Ahmad Ibn Hanbal," *Arabica*, no. 44, 1997, pp. 234–253; Melchert, *Ahmad ibn Hanbal*.
24. Patton, *Ahmed ibn Hanbal*, p. 2
25. Al-Khallal, *al-Musnad*, pp. 21–25; Ibn Ishaq, *Mihnat al-imam*, pp. 40–44, 81–88.
26. Ibn Hanbal, *Kitab al-Sunna*, p. 34.
27. Ibid., pp. 35–36.
28. Ibid., p. 35.
29. Ibid.
30. On Sufism, see Massignon, *Essai*; Molé, *Les Mystiques musulmans*; Anawati and Gardet, *Mystique musulmane*; Baldick, *Mystical Islam*; Popovic and Veinstein, eds., *Les Voies d'Allah*; Schimmel, *Le Soufisme*; Knysh, *Islamic Mysticism*.
31. For the eulogy, see Cooperson, "Ibn Hanbal."
32. Cook, *Commanding*, pp. 87–113.
33. Laoust, *Essai sur les doctrines sociales*, p. 2.
34. On the notion of personal example, see Weber, *Économie et société*, vol. 2, pp. 199–200.
35. Al-Tabari, *Tarikh al-umam wa al-muluk*, vol. 8, p. 522; Ibn al-Athir, *al-Kamil*, vol. 8, p. 551; al-Mas'udi, *Muruj al-dhahab*, vol. 4, p. 29; Miskawayh, *Tajarib al-umam*, vol. 6, p. 433; Ibn Kathir, *al-Bidaya wa al-nihaya*, vol. 10, p. 247; Anonymous, *al-'Uyun wa al-hada'iq*, vol. 3, p. 353.
36. For a chronological and bibliographical presentation of Hanbalism during this period, see Laoust, "Le hanbalisme sous le califat de Bagdad."
37. Ibn Abi Ya'la, *Tabaqat al-hanabila*, vol. 3, p. 73.
38. Ibn Khuzayma, *Kitab al-tawhid*; al-Tahawi, *Matn al-'aqida al-tahawiyya*.

39. This phenomenon is normal because the Malakites, Shafi'ites, Hanbalis, and a portion of the Hanafites belonged to the same group: the Ahl al-Hadith, the hardcore of Sunnism. See al-Khawarizmi, *Mafatih al-'ulum*, pp. 19–20.
40. Makdisi, "Ash'ari and Ash'arites" and *Ibn 'Aqil*, p. 407.
41. On the development of the Hanbali legal system in the tenth century, see Melchert, *Formation*, pp. 137–155.
42. Laoust, "Les premières professions."
43. Ibn Abi Ya'la, *Tabaqat al-hanabila*, vol. 3, pp. 36–80; Ibn al-Jawzi, *al-Muntazam*, vol. 6, p. 323; Ibn Kathir, *al-Bidaya wa al-nihaya*, vol. 11, p. 201; al-Dhahabi, *Siyar a'lam al-nubala'*, vol. 15, p. 90.
44. Al-Barbahari, *Sharh al-sunna*, pp. 51, 66, 74, 96, 112.
45. Laoust, *La profession*, p. xxiv.
46. Al-Maqdisi, *Ahsan al-taqasim*, p. 126; Ibn al-Jawzi, *al-Muntazam*, vol. 8, p. 312.
47. Cook, *Commanding*, pp. 114–144.
48. Translation of Ibn Batta by Laoust, *La profession*, p. 164.
49. Ibn al-Jawzi, *al-Muntazam*, vol. 7, p. 161.
50. Makdisi, *Ibn 'Aqil*, p. 209.
51. Ibid., pp. 238, 251, 256, 269; Swartz, "Rules of Popular Preaching."
52. Ibn Abi Ya'la, *Tabaqat al-hanabila*, vol. 1, pp. 24–27.
53. Ibid., vol. 2, p. 190.
54. *EI²*, vol. 3, p. 699; Makdisi, *Ibn 'Aqil*.
55. Ibn Abi Ya'la, *Tabaqat al-hanabila*, vol. 3, pp. 316–426.
56. Makdisi, "The Hanbali School."
57. Ibn Rajab, *Dhayl*.
58. Quoted in ibid., vol. 1, p. 68.
59. This was a popular handbook, typical of the Hanbali tradition, in which theology, law, morality, spiritual exercises, and heresiography are mixed. See al-Jilani, *al-Ghunya*.
60. Arberry, *Le soufisme*, pp. 98–99.
61. Ibn al-Jawzi, *al-Muntazam* and *Sifat al-safwa*.
62. See, for example, Ibn al-Jawzi, *Manaqib 'Umar b. al-Khattab*, *Manaqib 'Umar b. 'Abd al-'Aziz*, and *Manaqib al-imam Ahmad*.
63. Ibn al-Jawzi, *Talbis Iblis*.
64. Indeed, he wrote several historical and literary anthologies inspired by the "mirror for princes" genre (*al-adab al-sultaniyya*) that were intended to instruct the elite.
65. For a chronological and bio-bibliographical presentation of the Hanbalism of this period, see Laoust, "Le hanbalisme sous les Mamlouks."
66. Ibn Qudama also had close ties to Sufism. Indeed, his name is often associated with several other Hanbali figures in the chains of transmission of the 'Abd al-Qadir al-Jilani confraternity. See Makdisi, "L'isnad initiatique soufi" and *Ibn 'Aqil*, p. 427; Ibn Qudama, *Le livre des pénitents*, p. 275.
67. Ibn Rajab, *Dhayl*, vol. 2, pp. 13–23. On the practice of promoting virtue and preventing vice among the Hanbalis of Damascus, see Cook, *Commanding*, pp. 145–165.
68. *EI²*, vol. 3, p. 951; Laoust, *Essai sur les doctrines sociales*; Henri Laoust, "La biographie d'Ibn Taimiya d'après Ibn Kathir," *Bulletin d'études orientales*, no. 9, 1942, pp. 115–162;

Laoust, *Le traité de droit public d'Ibn Taimiya*; Laoust, "L'influence d'Ibn Taimiyya"; Henri Laoust, "Traité sur la Hisba [d'Ibn Taymiyya]," *Revue des études islamiques*, no. 52, 1984, pp. 19–114; Makdisi, "Ibn Taimiya"; Little, "The Historical and Historiographical Significance" and "Did Ibn Taymiyya Have a Screw Loose?"; Abdul Azim Islahi, "Ibn Taimiyah's Concept of Market Mechanism," *Journal of Research in Islamic Economics*, vol. 2, no. 2, 1985, pp. 55–66; Islahi, *Economic Concepts of Ibn Taimiyah*; Emil Homerin, "Ibn Taimiya's al-Sufiah wa-al-fuqara," *Arabica*, no. 32, 1985, pp. 219–244; Khaliq Ahmad Nizami, "The Impact of Ibn Taymiyya on South Asia," *Journal of Islamic Studies*, no. 1, 1990, pp. 120–149; Olesen, *Culte des saints*; Binyamin Abrahamov, "Ibn Taymiya and the Doctrine of 'ismah," *Bulletin of the Henry Martyn Institute of Islamic Studies*, vol. 12, no. 3, 1993, pp. 21–30; Sherman A. Jackson, "Ibn Taymiyya on Trial in Damascus," *Journal of Semitic Studies*, vol. 39, no. 1, 1994, pp. 41–85; Fons, "À propos des Mongols."
69. Little, "Historical and Historiographical."
70. Sultan al-Nasir first occupied the throne between 1293 and 1294 and then again from 1299 to 1309.
71. Ibn Taymiyya, *Dar' al-ta'arud bayna al-'aql wa naql*.
72. Ibn Taymiyya, *Naqd al-mantiq*.
73. Ibn Taymiyya, *Minhaj al-sunna*, vol. 2, p. 100, and *Tafsir surat al-ikhlas*, pp. 112–113.
74. One need only read his *Minhaj al-sunna* to see that there is nothing fanatical or exclusivist about his views according to the standards of the time.
75. Ibn Abd al-Hadi, *Bad' al-'Uqla bi-libs al-khirqa*, fol. 171–172; Makdisi, "Ibn Taimiya."
76. Laoust, *Essai*, pp. 22–32, 89–93.
77. Ibn Taymiyya, *Majmu' al-fatawa*, vol. 11, p. 18.
78. Ibn Taymiyya, *Iqtida' al-sirat*.
79. Little, "Did Ibn Taymiyya Have a Screw Loose?"
80. Ibn Taymiyya, *al-Amr bi al-ma'ruf*, p. 30.
81. Ibid., p. 32.
82. Ibid., pp. 13, 21, 28.
83. Ibid., p. 68; Ibn Taymiyya, *'Aqidat ahl al-sunna*, p. 59.
84. Ibn Taymiyya, *al-Siyasa al-shar'iyya*, p. 120.
85. Ibid., p. 118.
86. Ibn Taymiyya, *al-Khilafa wa al-mulk*, p. 41.
87. Ibn Taymiyya, *Qa'ida mukhtasara*.
88. Ibn Taymiyya, *al-Amr bi al-ma'ruf*, pp. 17, 21.
89. Ibn Qayyim al-Jawziyya, *al-Kafiyya*.
90. Al-Juhany, *Najd before*; Ibn 'Abd al-Hadi, *al-Jawhar*, pp. 15, 40, 112; Mubarak, "al-Wattha'iq al-shakhsiyya."
91. On this oasis and its role, see Al-Juhany, "Dawr 'Ulama'."
92. Cook, "On the Origins."
93. Ibn 'Isa, *'Aqd al-durar*.
94. Hobsbawm and Ranger, *Invention of Tradition*, p. 2.
95. Al-Bassam, *'Ulama' najd*, vol. 1, pp. 544–552 (Ahmad ibn Atwa); pp. 436–452 (Ahmad ibn Abi Humaydan); p. 433 (Abu Numayy al-Tamimi).

96. Ibid., vol. 2, pp. 558–561.
97. Abu Zayd, *'Ulama' al-hanabila*.
98. Steinberg, "Ecology."
99. For a list of religious works printed in the first half of the twentieth century, see Usaylan, "'Inayat al-malik."
100. *Majmu'at al-nuzum min 1345 [1926] ila 1357 [1938]*, section devoted to justice, rubric: the changes and amendments of 1928, pp. 11, 15, 39; Hamza, *al-Bilad*, p. 189. The latter book gives a list of six Hanbali works rather than four.

CHAPTER 2. SHEDDING NEW LIGHT ON THE LIFE OF MUHAMMAD IBN ABD AL-WAHHAB

1. Ibn Ghannam, *Rawdat*, vol. 1, pp. 5–12.
2. See, for example, Ibn Bishr, *'Unwan al-majd*, pp. 26–27, 33–34.
3. On the period before the emergence of Hanbali-Wahhabism, see al-Suwayda, *al-Alf sana al-ghamida*; al-Juhany, *Najd before the Salafi Reform*.
4. Al-Humaydan, "Imarat al-'Usfuriyyin" and "al-Tarikh al-siyasi"; al-Wuhbi, *Banu Khalid*.
5. Mouline, *Le califat*.
6. Ibn Ghannam, *Rawdat al-afkar*, vol. 1, pp. 113, 132.
7. Al-Manqur, *al-Fawakih*, vol. 1, p. 222; al-Bassam, *'Ulama' najd*, vol. 2, pp. 61, 182–183; *Majmu'at al-rasa'il wa al-masa'il al-najdiyya*, vol. 1, pp. 523–525.
8. Dallal, "The Origins."
9. Veyne, *Quand notre monde*, p. 83.
10. Weber, *Économie et société*, p. 83.
11. Ibn Humayd, *al-Suhub al-wabila*, vol. 2, pp. 413–415; Ibn Bishr, *'Unwan al-majd*, vol. 2, pp. 328–329; al-Bassam, *'Ulama' najd*, vol. 1, pp. 309–313, and vol. 3, pp. 669–670.
12. On this tradition, see Touati, *Islam et voyage*.
13. Abd al-Rahman bin Hasan Al al-Shaykh, *al-Maqamat*, p. 66. But Ibn Ghannam claims that he wrote it in the oasis of Huraymila' (*Rawdat al-afkar*, vol. 1, pp. 29–30).
14. Corancez, *Histoire des wahabis*, pp. 12–13.
15. Ibn Hisham, *al-Sira al-nabawiyya*, pp. 178, 185–186.
16. On the symbolism of purifying fire, see Bayard, *Le Feu*, pp. 50–60, 115; Leroi-Gourhan, *Evolution et technique*, pp. 60–68.
17. Ibn Ghannan, *Rawdat al-afkar*, vol. 1, pp. 15–25.
18. Ibn Bishr, *'Unwan al-majd*, vol. 1, p. 33.
19. On the intellectual milieu of Medina at the time, see Voll, "Muhammad Hayya al-Sindi."
20. For an analysis of the supposed movements of Ibn Abd al-Wahhab, see Cook, "On the Origins," pp. 191–197.
21. Ibn Ghannan, *Rawdat al-afkar*, vol. 1, pp. 27–28.
22. Ibn Hisham, *al-Sira al-nabawiyya*, pp. 421–424.

23. Ibid., pp. 478–480.
24. Ibn Ghannam, *Rawdat al-afkar*, vol. 1, pp. 107–113, p. 184; Ibn Abd al-Wahhab, *al-Rasa'il al-shakhsiyya*, in *Mu'allafat* [Complete Works], vol. 7, pp. 212–214.
25. Ibn Abd al-Wahhab, *al-Rasa'il al-shakhsiyya*, in *Mu'allafat* [Complete Works], vol. 7, p. 67.
26. The term "shaykh," which can be translated as "elder," designates a person who has acquired a status of special authority by virtue of his age, wisdom, or social position.
27. Ibn Abd al-Wahhab married the emir's paternal aunt, al-Jawhara bint 'Abd Allah b. Mu'ammar.
28. Ibn Ghannam, *Rawdat al-afkar*, vol. 1, p. 30; Ibn Bishr, *'Unwan al-majd*, vol. 1, p. 122.
29. Ibn Bishr, *'Unwan al-majd*, vol. 1, p. 43.
30. Ibn Ghannam, *Rawdat al-afkar*, vol. 1, pp. 29–31, 112, and vol. 2, p. 4.
31. Ibid., vol. 1, pp. 55, 140–141, and vol. 2, p. 2; Ibn Bishr, *'Unwan al-majd*, vol. 1, p. 23; Ibn Abd al-Wahhab, *al-Rasa'il al-shakhsiyya*, in *Mu'allafat* [Complete Works], vol. 7, pp. 67, 154.
32. Ibn Ghannam, *Rawdat al-afkar*, vol. 1, pp. 113–123, 138–145, 218; *Majmu'at al-tawhid al-najdiyya*, pp. 150–51; Ibn Abd al-Wahhab, *al-Rasa'il al-shakhsiyya*, in *Mu'allafat* [Complete Works], vol. 7, p. 148.
33. Ibn Ghannan, *Rawdat al-afkar*, vol. 1, p. 30.
34. Ibid., vol. 1, pp. 114, 140.
35. Weber, *Sociologies des religions*, p. 264.
36. Ibn Ghannam, *Rawdat al-afkar*, vol. 1, pp. 106–113.
37. Ibn Abd al-Wahhab, *al-Rasa'il al-shakhsiyya*, in *Mu'allafat* [Complete Works] vol. 7, p. 183; *Majmu'at al-rasa'il wa al-masa'il al-najdiyya*, vol. 4, p. 42; Ibn Qasim, *al-Durar al-saniyya*, vol. 10, pp. 5–10; Samer Traboulsi, "An Early Refutation of Muhammad ibn 'Abd al-Wahhab's Reformist Views," *Die Welt des Islams*, vol. 42, no. 3, 2002, pp. 381–382; R. Y. Ebied and M. J. L. Young, "An Unpublished Refutation of the Doctrine of the Wahhabis," *Revista degli Studi Orientali*, no. 3–4, 1976, pp. 377–397.
38. Ibn Abd al-Wahhab, *al-Rasa'il al-shakhsiyya*, in *Mu'allafat* [Complete Works], vol. 7, pp. 318–320.
39. Several other versions exist. See Amor ben Hamadi, "Autour du hadith."
40. Ibn Ghannam, *Rawdat al-afkar*, vol. 1, pp. 106–111.
41. Ibid., vol. 2, p. 3; Ibn Bishr, *'Unwan al-majd*, vol. 1, p. 23; Anonymous, *Lam' al-shihab*, p. 31.
42. Ibn Ghannam, *Rawdat al-afkar*, vol. 1, pp. 142, 150; Ibn Qasim, *al-Durar al-saniyya*, vol. 2, pp. 172–173; *Majmu'at al-rasa'il wa al-masa'il al-najdiyya*, vol. 4, pp. 9–10; Ibn Abd al-Wahhab, *al-Rasa'il al-shakhsiyya*, in *Mu'allafat* [Complete Works], vol. 7, pp. 48, 158.
43. Ibn Bishr, *'Unwan al-majd*, vol. 1, p. 23.
44. Ibn Ghannam, *Rawdat al-afkar*, vol. 1, pp. 31, 222.
45. For convenience, we here use the term "Saud" (Al Su'ud in Arabic), which took several decades to establish itself. At the time of Ibn Abd al-Wahhab's move to Al-Dir'iyya, the dominant lineage called itself Al Muqrin; the Saud were its main branch.

46. Ibn Ghannam, *Rawdat al-afkar*, vol. 2, p. 3; Ibn Bishr, *'Unwan al-majd*, vol. 1, pp. 23–25.
47. Ibn Ghannam, *Rawdat al-afkar*, vol. 2, pp. 3–4; Ibn Bishr, *'Unwan al-majd*, vol. 1, pp. 24–25; Anonymous, *Lam' al-shihab*, pp. 26–27.
48. Ibid.
49. Ibn Ghannan, *Rawdat al-afkar*, vol. 1, pp. 6–9; Ibn Bishr, *'Unwan al-majd*, vol. 1, pp. 28–33.
50. Ibn Ghannam, *Rawdat al-afkar*, vol. 1, p. 15, and vol. 2, p. 6.
51. Ibid., vol. 2, pp. 6–19, 45–53; Ibn Bishr, *'Unwan al-majd*, vol. 1, pp. 33–42.
52. All appearances suggest that the late intervention of the Banu Khalid was due to the fratricidal struggles that during this period opposed several members of the dominant line for a monopoly of power.
53. Ibn Ghannam, *Rawdat al-afkar*, vol. 2, pp. 54–67; Ibn Bishr, *'Unwan al-majd*, vol. 1, pp. 51–60; Niebuhr, *Voyage*, vol. 2, p. 140.
54. Ibn Ghannam, *Rawdat al-afkar*, vol. 2, pp. 80–81; Ibn Qasim, *al-Durar al-saniyya*, vol. 1, pp. 55–56.
55. Ibn Ghannam, *Rawdat al-afkar*, vol. 1, pp. 27, 77–88; Ibn Bishr, *'Unwan al-majd*, vol. 1, pp. 66–75; Anonymous, *Kayf kan zuhur shaykh al-islam*, p. 76.
56. Ibn Ghannam, *Rawdat al-afkar*, vol. 2, pp. 88–111, 126, 168; Ibn Bishr, *'Unwan al-majd*, vol. 1, pp. 67, 78–86, 92–100, 130–132.
57. Izzi, *Tarikh*, p. 207.
58. Kursun, *al-'Uthmaniyyun wa Al Su'ud fi al-arshif al-'Uthmani*, p. 48.
59. Ibn Yusuf, *Tarikh*, pp. 139–143; Ibn 'Abbad, *Tarikh*, pp. 85–88.
60. Ibn Qasim, *al-Durar al-saniyya*, vol. 2, p. 24.
61. The terminology used by Ibn Abd al-Wahhab, and in particular the terms *jahiliyya* and *taghut* (the idol), consists of commonplaces of Islamic politico-religious language. But it must be noted that the meaning of these terms as he employed them remained confined within the religious domain. It is thus useful to not confuse them with the political use to which they were put by, for example, Sayyid Qutb (d. 1966) and all of his direct and indirect disciples in the contemporary period.
62. Ibn Sahman, *al-Hadiyya al-saniyya*, p. 121.
63. Ibn Qasim, *al-Durar al-saniyya*, vol. 1, pp. 147–164.
64. Ibn Sahman, *al-Hadiyya al-saniyya*, p. 65.
65. Ibn Qasim, *al-Durar al-saniyya*, vol. 1, pp. 64–74, 147–164, and vol. 2, pp. 66–76.
66. Ibid., vol. 10, pp. 90–92.
67. Ibid., vol. 3, pp. 9–12.
68. Ibn Abd al-Wahhab, *al-Rasa'il al-shakhsiyya*, in *Mu'allafat* [Complete Works], vol. 7, pp. 7, 263–265; *Tafsir ayat min al-qur'an al-karim*, in *Mu'allafat* [Complete Works], vol. 5, p. 228; *Masa'il lakhkhasaha al-shaykh al-imam Muhammad b. 'Abd al-Wahhab min kalam shaykh al-islam Ibn Tamiyya*, in *Mu'allafat* [Complete Works], vol. 13, p. 73; *Majmu'at al-rasa'il wa al-masa'il al-najdiyya*, vol. 2, pp. 82–87, 174, 307–308, and vol. 3, p. 240.
69. Ibn Qasim, *al-Durar al-saniyya*, vol. 1, p. 144.

70. Ibid., vol. 1, pp. 58–64, 74–83.
71. Ibn Sahman, *al-Hadiyya al-saniyya*, p. 36.
72. Ibn Qasim, *al-Durar al-saniyya*, vol. 1, pp. 29–35.
73. Ibid., vol. 8, p. 51.
74. Ibid., vol. 1, pp. 99–101, 197–200.
75. Ibid., vol. 1, pp. 102–104, and vol. 2, pp. 5–26; Ibn Abd al-Wahhab, *al-Fatawa wa al-masa'il*, in *Mu'allafat* [Complete Works], vol. 4, pp. 9–11.
76. Ibn Ghannam, *Rawdat al-afkar*, vol. 1, pp. 109, 122, 145–148; *Majmu'at al-rasa'il wa al-masa'il al-najdiyya*, vol. 4, p. 42; Ibn Qasim, *al-Durar al-saniyya*, vol. 1, p. 54, and vol. 10, p. 9; Ibn Abd al-Wahhab, *al-Rasa'il al-shakhsiyya*, in *Mu'allafat* [Complete Works], vol. 7, pp. 58–71; Ibn Qasim, *al-Durar al-saniyya*, vol. 2, pp. 66–76, and vol. 8, p. 5.
77. Ibn Ghannam, *Rawdat al-afkar*, vol. 1, pp. 113–123, 138–145, 218.
78. *Majmu'at al-rasa'il wa al-masa'il al-najdiyaa*, vol. 3, pp. 5, 21, 35, 82, 306, and vol. 4, pp. 12–23, 43.
79. Ibn Qasim, *al-Durar al-saniyya*, vol. 13, p. 395.
80. Ibn Abd al-Wahhab, *al-Rasa'il al-shakhsiyya*, in *Mu'allafat* [Complete Works], vol. 7, p. 11.
81. Ibn Qasim, *al-Durar al-saniyya*, vol. 3, p. 24.
82. Ibid., pp. 18–19.
83. Ibid., vol. 1, pp. 35–55, 184, and vol. 2, p. 220.
84. Ibid., vol. 1, pp. 35–55, 222–241.
85. Ibn Abd al-Wahhab, *al-Fatawa wa al-masa'il*, in *Mu'allafat* [Complete Works], vol. 4, p. 67.
86. Ibid., vol. 1, p. 173, and vol. 2, p. 133; vol. 9, pp. 5–6.
87. Ibn Qasim, *al-Durar al-saniyya*, vol. 10, p. 128.
88. Ibn Abd al-Wahhab, *Mukhtasar zad al-ma'ad*, in *Mu'allafat* [Complete Works], vol. 6, pp. 158–179.
89. On Ibn Abd al-Wahhab's unclear vision of jihad, see Ibn Qasim, *al-Durar al-saniyya*, vol. 1, pp. 74–83, 183, and vol. 2, pp. 55–56.
90. Summaries of the main writings of Ibn Abd al-Wahhab are available in Abd Allah al-Uthaymin, *Muhammad ibn 'Abd al-Wahhab*, pp. 76–109.
91. These are found, respectively, in Ibn Abd al-Wahhab, *Mu'allafat* [Complete Works], vol. 1, pp. 7–151, 153–181, 183–196, 203–227, and 370–373.
92. Ibn Abd al-Wahhab, *al-Kaba'ir*, in *Mu'allafat* [Complete Works], vol. 1, part 2, pp. 1–63; *Ahadih fi al-fitan wa al-hawadith*, in *Mu'allafat* [Complete Works], vol. 7, pp. 15–273; for a compilation of Ibn Abd al-Wahhab's anthologies concerning other subjects, see the eleven volumes of his *Mu'allafat* [Complete Works].
93. Ibn Abd al-Wahhab, *Mukhtasar al-sira al-nabawiyya*, in *Mu'allafat* [Complete Works], vol. 4; *Mukhtasar zad al-ma'ad*, in *Mu'allafat* [Complete Works], vol. 6; *Mukhtasar al-insaf wa al-sharh al-kabir*, in *Mu'allafat* [Complete Works], vol. 2; *Masa'il lakhkhasaha al-shaykh al-imam Muhammad b. 'Abd al-Wahhab min kalam shaykh al-islam Ibn Taymiyya*, in *Mu'allafat* [Complete Works], vol. 3.

94. Ibn Abd al-Wahhab, *al-Fiqh*, in *Mu'allafat* [Complete Works], vol. 3.
95. Ibn Abd al-Wahhab, *al-Fatawa wa al-masa'il*, in *Mu'allafat* [Complete Works], vol. 4; and *al-Rasa'il al-shakhsiyya*, in *Mu'allafat* [Complete Works], vol. 7.
96. Ibn Ghannam, *Rawdat al-afkar*, vol. 2, p. 4; Ibn Bishr, *'Unwan al-majd*, vol. 1, pp. 25–27, 171, 302, and vol. 2, pp. 227–230.
97. Abd al-Rahman Al al-Shaykh, *Mashahir*, pp. 43–77.
98. In order to translate this charismatic heritage, the descendants of Ibn Abd al-Wahhab adopted the very significant patronymic Al al-Shaykh, the descendants of the shaykh, with a capital S.
99. Ibn Qasim, *al-Durar al-saniyya*, vol. 1, pp. 169–170.
100. Ibn Abd al-Wahhab, *Kashf al-shubuhat*, in *Mu'allafat* [Complete Works], vol. 1, pp. 153–181; Ibn Ghannam, *Rawdat al-afkar*, vol. 1, p. 63.
101. Ibn Abd al-Wahhab, *Talqin usul al-'aqida lil-'awamm*, in *Mu'allafat* [Complete Works], vol. 1, pp. 370–373; *al-Usul al-thalatha*, in *Mu'allafat* [Complete Works], vol. 1, pp. 183–196.
102. Ibn Abd al-Wahhab, *Fatawa wa masa'il*, in *Mu'allafat* [Complete Works], vol. 4, part 2, pp. 12–15, 44, 85–87, 100–102.
103. Ibn Ghannam, *Rawdat al-afkar*, vol. 2, pp. 133–135, 162; Ibn Bishr, *'Unwan al-majd*, vol. 1, pp. 103, 129; al-Bassam, *'Ulama' najd*, vol. 1, pp. 56, 294.
104. Ibn Ghannam, *Rawdat al-afkar*, vol. 1, pp. 31, 55, 140–141, and vol. 2, pp. 2–4; Ibn Bishr, *'Unwan al-majd*, vol. 1, pp. 31, 55, 140–141, and vol. 2, pp. 2–4; Ibn Bishr, *'Unwan al-majd*, vol. 1, pp. 23–27; Ibn Abd al-Wahhab, *al-Fatawa wa al-masa'il*, in *Mu'allafat* [Complete Works], vol. 4, p. 67; *al-Rasa'il al-shakhsiyya*, in *Mu'allafat* [Complete Works], vol. 7, p. 154.

CHAPTER 3. HANBALI-WAHHABISM IN THE NINETEENTH CENTURY

1. Abd al-Rahman Al al-Shaykh, *Mashahir*, pp. 48–71; al-Bassam, *'Ulama' najd*, vol. 1, pp. 169–179. On the subject of his religious ideas, which were very close to those of his father, see Ibn Qasim, *al-Durar al-saniyya*, vol. 1, p. 300; vol. 4, pp. 17–19, 31–35, 52–59; and vol. 7, pp. 164–165, 175–176, 230–236.
2. Ibn Qasim, *al-Durar al-saniyya*, vol. 10, pp. 248–249.
3. Ibn Ghannam, *Rawdat al-afkar*, vol. 2, pp. 120–167; Ibn Bishr, *'Unwan al-majd*, vol. 1, pp. 96–137.
4. Dahlan, *Khulasat al-kalam*, vol. 2, p. 263.
5. Ibn Ghannam, *Rawdat al-afkar*, vol. 2, pp. 173–174; Ibn Bishr, *'Unwan al-majd*, vol. 1, pp. 135–136.
6. The Saudi Emirate also organized occasional raids against some regions, in particular southern Iraq and southern Syria-Palestine, in order to demonstrate its power, make an impression, and above all refill the coffers of the treasury with plunder. The most famous raid was no doubt that which ended, in 1803, with the sack of the town of Karbala, the massacre of a large part of its population, and the pillage of its mausoleums. The main political consequence of this raid was the assassination of Emir Abd al-Aziz by a Shiite bent on revenge in the mosque of Al-Diriyah the same year.

7. Isa, *al-Hayat*, p. 73.
8. Ibn Ghannam, *Rawdat al-afkar*, vol. 2, pp. 200–201.
9. Ibid., vol. 2, pp. 186–187, 200–201, 232–235; Ibn Bishr, *'Unwan al-majd*, vol. 1, pp. 149–152; Dahlan, *Khulasat al-kalam*, vol. 2, p. 267.
10. Ibn bishr, *'Unwan al-majd*, vol. 1, p. 153; Dahlan, *Khulasat al-kalam*, vol. 2, p. 267.
11. Ibn Hisham, *al-Sira al-nabawiyya*, pp. 983–995.
12. Ibn Bishr, *'Unwan al-majd*, vol. 1, p. 162; Dahlan, *Khulasat al-kalam*, vol. 2, pp. 271–272.
13. Ibn Bishr, *'Unwan al-majd*, vol. 1, pp. 162–163, 182–185; Dahlan, *Khulasat al-kalam*, vol. 2, pp. 273, 280–287.
14. Al-Jabarti, *'Aja'ib al-athar*, vol. 3, p. 549; el-Abbassi, *Voyages d'Ali Bey*, vol. 2, pp. 320–324, 449–455.
15. El-Abbassi, *Voyages d'Ali Bey*, vol. 4, pp. 8–9, 84.
16. Ibn Qasim, *al-Durar al-saniyya*, vol. 1, pp. 222–241.
17. On this question, also see ibid., p. 245.
18. These are the collections of al-Bukhari (d. 870), Muslim (d. 875), Ibn Majja (d. 887), Abu Dawud (d. 888), al-Tirmidhi (d. 892), and al-Nasa'i (d. 915).
19. Al-Jazuli, *Dala'il al-khayrat*; al-Yafi'i, *Rawd al-Rayahin*.
20. On this question, see also Ibn Qasim, *al-Durar al-saniyya*, vol. 7, pp. 175–176.
21. Ibn Hisham, *al-Sira al-nabawiyya*, p. 1253.
22. Al-Jabarti, *'Aja'ib al-athar*, vol. 4, pp. 360–361.
23. See a "type" letter in Ibn Qasim, *al-Durar al-saniyya*, vol. 1, p. 307. For more on how these letters were received by the authorities of some Muslim countries, see Green, "A Tunisian Reply"; Commins, *Islamic Reform*, pp. 22–23; Muhammad al-Mansur, *al-Maghrib*, pp. 238–242.
24. Al-Nasiri, *al-Istiqsa*, vol. 8, pp. 119–124.
25. See the text of the letter in Husayn Khaz'al, *Hayat*, pp. 377–378.
26. Ibn Bishr, *'Unwan al-majd*, vol. 1, pp. 198–199.
27. Ibn Qasim, *al-Durar al-saniyya*, vol. 1, p. 307.
28. *Khatti Humayun* (Sultan's decree), 19698-A, 16 May 1819, manuscript at King Fahd National Library, Riyadh.
29. Abd al-Rahman Al al-Shaykh, *Mashahir*, pp. 206–215; al-Bassam, *'Ulama' najd*, vol. 3, pp. 319–323, 354–365.
30. Sadleir, *Diary*, pp. 65–67.
31. Ibn Qasim, *al-Durar al-saniyya*, vol. 11, p. 552.
32. Ibid., vol. 8, pp. 121–143.
33. *Majmu'at al-tawhid*, pp. 109–122.
34. Ibid., pp. 47–51.
35. It must be emphasized that this debate and these struggles were intra-Islamic and in no way concerned other religions, which were largely ignored by the Hanbali-Wahhabis up until the twentieth century. In *al-Durar al-saniyya*, for example, the largest collection of Hanbali-Wahhabi fatawa, Christians were mentioned only twice and Jews never.
36. Ibn Qasim, *al-Durar al-saniyya*, vol. 8, pp. 145, 161–164.

37. Abd al-Rahman, *al-Dawla al-Su'udiyya al-ula*, pp. 392–393. Italics added.
38. Kohlberg, "Some Zaydi Views," "Bara'a in Shi'i Doctrine," and "Some Imami Shi'i Views"; Bu'jila, *al-islam al-Khariji*; al-Bakkay, *Harakat al-khawarij*.
39. Ibn Abi Ya'la, *Tabaqat al-hanabila*, vol. 1, p. 72.
40. Ibn Taymiyya, *Iqtida' al-sirat*.
41. Derenbourg, *Essai*, p. 76. For more on *amixia*, see Berthelot, *Philanthrôpia*.
42. Douglas, *In the Wilderness*.
43. On Abd al-Rahman Ibn Hasan, see Abd al-Rahman Al al-Shaykh, *Mashahir*, pp. 78–92; al-Bassam, *'Ulama' najd*, vol. 1, pp. 180–201; on Abd al-Latif, see *Mashahir*, pp. 93–121, and *'Ulama' najd*, vol. 1, pp. 202–214; on Hamad ibn Atiq, see *Mashahir*, pp. 244–245, and *'Ulama' najd*, vol. 2, pp. 84–91.
44. Ibn Qasim, *al-Durar al-saniyya*, vol. 8, p. 179.
45. Ibid., vol. 1, p. 434.
46. Ibid., vol. 8, pp. 354, 371 (*al-ta'ifa al-kafira*); Hamad bin 'Atiq, *Bayan al-Najat wa ak-fakak min muwalat al-murtaddin wa ahl al-ishrak* and *Majmu'at al-tawhid*, p. 246 (*al-dawla al-kufriyya*).
47. Ibn Qasim, *al-Durar al-saniyya*, vol. 1, p. 434, and vol. 8, p. 317.
48. Ibid., vol. 8, pp. 329–340. Ottoman propaganda used a similar rhetoric to deform the beliefs of the Hanbali-Wahhabis and discredit their actions. See, for example, Ra'uf, *al-'Iraq*, pp. 18–20.
49. Ibn Qasim, *al-Durar al-saniyya*, vol. 8, pp. 364–371, 391–394; vol. 9, p. 24; and vol. 11, p. 512.
50. Ibid., vol. 9, pp. 47–54.
51. Ibid., vol. 8, p. 324.
52. Ibid., vol. 8, pp. 297–309 ("corrupts the faith"); pp. 312–314, 424 ("certain conditions"); p. 275 ("any Muslim who does not respect").
53. Ibid., vol. 8, pp. 238, 261, 273, 277–295, 354–359.
54. Ibn Bishr, *'Unwan al-Majd*, vol. 2, p. 73; Abd al-Rahman, *Muhammad 'Ali*, vol. 2, p. 296.
55. Ibn Qasim, *al-Durar al-saniyya*, vol. 12, pp. 177, 262.
56. Ibid., vol. 14, pp. 187–188.
57. His father, Abd al-Rahman ibn Hasan Al al-Shaykh, returned to Najd in 1826 to take over the leadership of the corporation.
58. See, for example, Abd al-Rahman ibn Hasan Al al-Shaykh, *Minhaj al-ta'sis wa al-taqdis fi al-radd 'ala Ibn Jirjis*.
59. Ibn Bishr, *'Unwan al-majd*, vol. 2, pp. 113, 235.
60. Emir Faysal first reigned from 1834 to 1838 before being chased from power by the troops of Muhammad Ali. He was replaced by his cousin, Khalid ibn Saud, who was seen as more accommodating by the Ottoman authorities.
61. Ibn Qasim, *al-Durar al-saniyya*, vol. 14, pp. 38, 46; vol. 8, p. 363.
62. Ibid., vol. 14, p. 54.
63. *Majmu'at al-rasa'il wa al-masa'il al-najdiyya*, vol. 2, p. 10.
64. Ibn Qasim, *al-Durar al-saniyya*, vol. 4, p. 200.

65. Ibid., vol. 4, p. 381.
66. Ibn Qasim, *al-Durar al-saniyya*, vol. 10, p. 428.
67. Palgrave, *Narrative*, vol. 1, pp. 409–410.
68. Ibn Qasim, *al-Durar al-saniyya*, vol. 14, pp. 67–75, 173–186; *Majmu'at al-rasa'il wa al-masa'il al-najdiyya*, vol. 4, p. 343.
69. Ibn Qasim, *al-Durar al-saniyya*, vol. 14, pp. 67–75, 86–90, 173–186.
70. Pelly, *Report*, p. 70.
71. Ibn Qasim, *al-Durar al-saniyya*, vol. 14, pp. 133–134.
72. On teaching during this period, see al-Bassam, *'Ulama' najd*, vol. 2, pp. 112, 250, 263; vol. 3, p. 509; vol. 6, p. 195; and vol. 9, p. 230; *Majmu'at al-rasa'il wa al-masa'il al-najdiyya*, vol. 4, p. 463.
73. On the relationship between commerce and the preservation of traditional Hanbalism, see Steinberg, "Ecology," pp. 83–98; Ibrahim, *Najdiyyun*.
74. Al-Bassam, *'Ulama' najd*, vol. 4, pp. 370–377; Ibn Humayd, *al-Suhub al-wabila*, vol. 2, pp. 641–644; Ibn Hamdan, *Tarajim*, pp. 94–95.
75. Weismann, *Taste of Modernity*, pp. 65–67.
76. Al-Bassam, *'Ulama' najd*, vol. 2, pp. 373–380.
77. Ibid., vol. 5, pp. 86–106; al-Qadi, *Rawdat al-Nazirin*, vol. 2, pp. 104–108.
78. Al-Bassam, *'Ulama' najd*, vol. 5, p. 92; Abd al-Rahman bin Hasan Al al-Shaykh, *al-Maqamat*; Abd al-Latif bin Abd al-Rahman Al al-Shaykh, *Misbah al-zalam*.
79. Al-Bassam, *'Ulama' najd*, vol. 5, pp. 95–97.
80. Ibn Qasim, *al-Durar al-saniyya*, vol. 4, p. 425.
81. Ibid., vol. 14, pp. 133–134.
82. Al-Bassam, *'Ulama' najd*, vol. 1, pp. 449–456, 494–497, 528–532; vol. 2, pp. 402–404, 482, 528; vol. 4, pp. 426–430; and vol. 6, pp. 236–245, 292–302; Ibn Humayd, *al-Suhub*, vol. 3, pp. 969–980; Husayn, *Lamha*; al-Juhany, *Najd before*, pp. 125–126.
83. The same argument can be made for the Saud. Without the ideological support of the ulama, they would have had only a derisory claim to traditional authority, like other local chiefs.
84. Ibn Qasim, *al-Durar al-saniyya*, vol. 9, pp. 11–14, 29; *Majmu'at al-rasa'il*, vol. 22, pp. 3–13, and vol. 3, pp. 62–63, 40, 38.
85. Ibn Qasim, *al-Durar al-saniyya*, vol. 14, pp. 77, 84–85.
86. Ibid., vol. 8, p. 9, and vol. 14, pp. 95, 103, 107, 160, 167.
87. Ibn Isa, *'Aqd al-durar*, pp. 52–57; al-Fakhiri, *al-Akhbar al-najdiyya*, pp. 188–189; Ibn Qasim, *al-Durar al-saniyya*, vol. 9, pp. 15–54.
88. al-Rasheed, *Politics in an Arabian Oasis*.
89. Ibn Isa, *'Aqd al-durar*, pp. 77–101; al-Fakhiri, *al-Akhbar al-najdiyya*, pp. 188–189; Ibn Qasim, *al-Durar al-saniyya*, vol. 9, p. 44; al-Rashid, *Nubdha tarikhiyya 'an Najd*, pp. 105–108.
90. Ibn Qasim, *al-Durar al-saniyya*, vol. 9, pp. 11–14, 29.
91. Ibid., vol. 8, p. 324, and vol. 9, p. 18.
92. Ibid., vol. 8, pp. 319–327, 385–393, and vol. 9, pp. 17–22.
93. Ibid., vol. 8, pp. 18–19.

94. For more details on the attitude of Abd al-Latif during this period of crisis, see Crawford, "Civil War."
95. Ibn Qasim, *al-Durar al-saniyya*, vol. 8, pp. 323–325, 335–343, 353–355, 383.
96. Ibid., vol. 8, p. 361; *Majmu'at al-rasa'il*, vol. 4, p. 383.
97. Al-Bassam, *'Ulama' najd*, vol. 1, pp. 215–230.
98. Wallin, *Travels in Arabia*, pp. 183–189; al-Rasheed, *Politics in an Arabian Oasis*, pp. 91–94.
99. Ibn Ubayd, *Tadhkirat*, vol. 2, p. 279; al-Bassam, *'Ulama' najd*, vol. 1, pp. 273–293, and vol. 4, pp. 324–334; al-Zahiri, "Dunya al-Watha'iq."
100. Al-Bassam, *'Ulama' najd*, vol. 4, pp. 324–334.
101. Ibn Qasim, *al-Durar al-saniyya*, vol. 8, pp. 85–88.
102. His maternal grandfather, 'Abd Allah Muhammad bin 'Abd al-Wahhab, head of the corporation before the destruction of the emirate, introduced him to the Hanbali-Wahhabite corpus and passed on the works of the founder.
103. EI^2, vol. 1, p. 267; Metcalf, *Islamic Revival*, pp. 139–153.
104. Al-Bassam, *'Ulama' najd*, vol. 3, pp. 330–335; vol. 4, pp. 138–149, 216–217, 265–279, 398–409, 457; vol. 5, pp. 305–307, 378–382, 567; and vol. 6, pp. 335–336.
105. In this connection, one may cite the names of Ishaq ibn Abd al-Rahman Al al-Shaykh (d. 1901), Abd Allah ibn Blihid (d. 1940), Abd Allah al-Anqari (d. 1954), and Abd Allah al-Qar'awi (d. 1969), all of whom were among the era's most famous Hanbali-Wahhabi ulama.
106. Al-Bassam, *'Ulama' najd*, vol. 2, pp. 220–227.
107. Ibid., vol. 4, p. 457.
108. Abu Dawud, *al-Sunan*, vol. 4, p. 156. On the notion of *mujaddid*, see Landau-Tasseron, "'Cyclical Reform.'"
109. Ibn Abd al-Wahhab, *Ahadith fi al-fitan wa al-hawadith*, in *Mu'allafat* [Complete Works], vol. 7.
110. Al-Bassam, *'Ulama' najd*, vol. 5, pp. 305–307.
111. Al-Bukhari, *al-Sahih*, nos. 3517, 7117, 7139; Muslim, *al-Sahih*, no. 2910. For more information on the enigmatic figure of al-Qahtani, see Nu'aym ibn Hammad, *Kitab al-fitan*, vol. 1, p. 431, and vol. 2, pp. 63, 67, 236–238, 245–251.
112. While the figure of the Mahdi is the most famous, the Sunni vision of the Messiah is confused, to say the least. The traditions attributed to the Prophet mention five other providential figures who are to emerge before the end of the world in order to establish order and justice: al-Yamani, al-Qahtani, al-Mansur, al-Sufyani, and Jesus.
113. Ibn Qasim, *al-Durar al-saniyya*, vol. 1, pp. 558–563.

CHAPTER 4. THE BIRTH OF A KINGDOM AND
THE RENAISSANCE OF A TRADITION

1. Abd al-Aziz officially adopted the title "king" in 1926, but for the sake of convenience, I will here use the term here. His successive titles nicely reflect the evolution of his

career, pretensions, and alliances. Between 1902 and 1932, he thus adopted, one after the other, the titles of imam, emir and Great Leader (*al-shuyukh*), governor (*qa'im maqam*, *wali*, *pasha*), sultan, and then finally king.

2. Vassiliev, *History*, pp. 210–221, 221—223.
3. Al-Bassam, *'Ulama' najd*, vol. 4, pp. 265–279; Abd al-Rahman Al al-Shaykh, *Mashahir*, pp. 381–383.
4. Ibn Qasim, *al-Durar al-saniyya*, vol. 8, p. 47.
5. Ibid., vol. 11, pp. 67–82.
6. Ibid., vol. 10, pp. 429.
7. Ibid., vol. 11, pp. 289–296.
8. Ibid., vol. 8, p. 422, and vol. 11, pp. 82–85.
9. Ibid., vol. 9, pp. 67–82.
10. Weber, *Économie et société*, vol. 1, p. 97.
11. Al-Bassam, *'Ulama' najd*, vol. 1, pp. 273–293, 404–410, 436–452, and vol. 22, pp. 89, 220–222, 383–385; Abd al-Rahman Al al-Shaykh, *Mashahir*, pp. 260–264.
12. Al-Bassam, *'Ulama' najd*, vol. 1, pp. 436–452; Abd al-Rahman Al al-Shaykh, *Mashahir*, pp. 260–264.
13. Al-Umari, *'Ulama' al Silim*.
14. Al-Bassam, *'Ulama' najd*, vol. 9, p. 263.
15. Ibn Qasim, *al-Durar al-saniyya*, vol. 14, pp. 373–376.
16. Al-Rihani, *Najd wa mulhaqatuha*, pp. 194–196.
17. Décobert, *Le mendiant*, pp. 167–173; Djaït, *La vie de Muhammad*, pp. 177–182.
18. Al-Bassam, *'Ulama' najd*, vol. 9, p. 263; ibid., vol. 1, pp. 231–241, vol. 3, pp. 81–82, vol. 5, p. 347, and vol. 6, p. 277.
19. Ibn Sahman, *al-Hadiyya al-saniyya*.
20. From a copy of an untitled private manuscript in the author's possession.
21. Several factors presided over the creation of this army. By creating the Ikhwan, the ulama were able to profit from the zeal and enthusiasm of the new converts, channel tensions among the various tribal confederations, direct their strength as warriors against an external enemy, and provide for the economic needs of these groups, which before sedentarization had relied heavily on the practice of raiding.
22. See, for example, Habib, *Ibn Saud's Warriors*; Joseph Kostiner, "On Instruments and Their Designers: The Ikhwan of Najd and the Emergence of the Saudi State," *Middle Eastern Studies*, no. 21, 1985, pp. 298–323; Kishk, *al-Su'udiyyun*, pp. 549–693; Vassiliev, *History*, pp. 227–231, 272–281; al-Rasheed, *History*, pp. 62–71.
23. On these tensions, see Fahad, "The Imama."
24. Ibn Qasim, *al-Durar al-saniyya*, vol. 8, pp. 421–422.
25. Ibid., vol. 14, pp. 345–347.
26. Ibid., vol. 8, pp. 82–84.
27. Ibid., vol. 8, pp. 80–82, 454–455.
28. Ibid., vol. 9, pp. 127–139.
29. Ibid., vol. 7, pp. 474–475.
30. Al-Bassam, *'Ulama' najd*, vol. 2, pp. 28–32.

31. Ibn Qasim, *al-Durar al-saniyya*, vol. 8, pp. 474–483.
32. Al-Bassam, *'Ulama' najd*, vol. 2, pp. 32.
33. Ibn Qasim, *al-Durar al-saniyya*, vol. 8, pp. 82–84; vol. 9, pp. 94–96.
34. Ibid., vol. 14, pp. 373–376.
35. Ibid., vol. 14, pp. 377–380.
36. Abd al-Rahman Al al-Shaykh, *Mashahir*, p. 382; al-Qadi, *Rawdat al-Nazirin*, vol. 1, p. 409.
37. Ibn Qasim, *al-Durar al-saniyya*, vol. 9, pp. 194–198.
38. Ibid., vol. 9, pp. 348–352.
39. These figures were leaders of the most important factions of Mutayr, Utayba, and al-Ajman, respectively.
40. Ibn Qasim, *al-Durar al-saniyya*, vol. 14, pp. 299–300.
41. Al-Bassam, *'Ulama' najd*, vol. 3, pp. 105–109; vol. 5, p. 32; and vol. 6, pp. 173–174.
42. Al-Zirikli, *Shibh al-jazira*, vol. 2, p. 472.
43. Ibn Hadhlul, *Tarikh muluk al Su'ud*, p. 185–186; Hafiz Wahba, *Jazirat al-'arab*, p. 221.
44. In order to symbolize their participation in the annual pilgrimage to Mecca and display their power, the rulers of Egypt had since the thirteenth century sent a camel lavishly festooned with embroidered quilts and decorated bedding to accompany the head of their official delegation (*amir al-hajj*). On the *mahmal*, see EI^2, vol. 6, p. 43; Jomier, *Le mahmal*; Gaudefroy-Demombyne, *Le pèlerinage*, pp. 155–161.
45. Ibn Qasim, *al-Durar al-saniyya*, vol. 9, pp. 179–180; Wahba, *Jazirat al-'arab*, pp. 292–293.
46. *Umm al-qura*, no. 121, 8 April 1927, p. 1.
47. Ibn Qasim, *al-Durar al-saniyya*, vol. 8, pp. 31–37, and vol. 9, pp. 175–179.
48. *Umm al-qura*, no. 208, 18 December 1928, pp. 1–5.
49. *Umm al-qura*, no. 406, 23 September 1932, pp. 2–3.
50. Ibn Qasim, *al-Durar al-saniyya*, vol. 5, p. 244, vol. 9, pp. 88–94, 103–106, 106–194, 200–211, 345–348, and vol. 14, p. 304.
51. Ibid., vol. 9, pp. 156–166.
52. Easton, *Analyse du système politique*, p. 20.
53. For a complete list of Hanbali-Wahhabi works published in India, see al-Dubayyib, "Harakat Ihya'"
54. Al-Ajami, *al-Rasa'il*; Commins, *Islamic Reform*; Weismann, "Naqshbandiyya-khalidiyya" and *Taste of Modernity*.
55. Al-Nadawi, *Muhammad b. Abd al-Wahhab*.
56. In Iraq, the members of the al-Alusi family and their disciples. In Syria, Jamal al-Din al-Qasimi (d. 1913), 'Abd al-Razzaq al-Baytar (d. 1916), and Muhammad Kamal al-Qassab (d. 1918). In Egypt, Muhammad Rashid Rida (d. 1935), Muhibb al-Din al-Khatib (d. 1969), and Muhammad Hamid al-Fiqi (d. 1959), etc. See al-Ajami, *al-Rasa'il*; Commins, *Islamic Reform*; Weismann, "Naqshbandiyya-khalidiyya" and *Taste of Modernity*.
57. Al-Juhaymi, *al-Malik 'Abd al-'Aziz*.

58. Al-Alusi, *Tarikh najd*; al-Fiqi, *Athar al-da'wa al-wahhabiyya*; Muhibb al-Din al-Khatib, the owner of the al-Salafiyya printing house in Cairo, played an important role in the publication and spread of the ideas of the Hanbali-Wahhabi corporation.
59. On Muhammad Rashid Rida's relations with King Abd al-Aziz, see Kramer, *Islam Assembled*, pp. 108–117.
60. Most of these articles were brought together in a collection titled *al-Wahhabiyyun wa al-Hijaz* and published by Al-Manar Press in 1925.
61. Rida, *al-Wahhabiyyun wa al-Hijaz*, pp. 87, 98.
62. Mérad, *Le réformisme musulman*, pp. 653–689.
63. Amin, *Zu'ama' al-islah*, pp. 10–25.
64. Al-Zirikli, *al-A'lam*, vol. 6, p. 257.
65. *Umm al-qura*, no. 229, 16 May 1929, p. 3.
66. Qazzaz, *Ahl al-Hijaz*, p. 205; Ali, *Dhikrayat*, pp. 71–76. The establishment reopened its doors in 1928 after renaming itself the Saudi Scientific Institute (al-Ma'had al-'ilmi al-su'udi), with the more modest aim of training instructors. As before, the teachers consisted of reformists recruited from Egypt, Syria, Morocco, and India.
67. Among the Egyptian professors who taught in this institute are to be found the names of ulama who were to later become famous, including Muhammad Abu Zahra, Muhammad al-Dhahabi, Muhammad Mutawalli al-Sha'rawi, Muhammad Abu Shubha, and 'Abd al-Razzaq 'Afifi. See Abd al-Aziz al al-Shaykh, *Lamahat*, p. 47; *Al-Manhal*, vol. 7, 1946, p. 584.
68. Al-Bassam, *'Ulama' najd*, vol. 1, pp. 81–116.
69. *Umm al-qura*, no. 1118, 3 August 1946, p. 2, and no. 1221, 30 July 1948.
70. Al-Marik, *Min shiyam*, vol. 3, pp. 331–334; al-Huqayl, *'Abd al-'Aziz fi al-tarikh*, p. 37.
71. Al-Marik, *Min shiyam*, vol. 3, p. 335.
72. Steinberg, "The Shiites.
73. Ibn Qasim, *al-Durar al-saniyya*, vol. 8, pp. 439–454.
74. Ibid., vol. 14, pp. 299–300.
75. Ibid., vol. 9, pp. 316–317.
76. Wahba, *Jazirat al-'arab*, pp. 266–267.
77. Ibn Qasim, *al-Durar al-saniyya*, vol. 14, pp. 518, 531, 533–539.
78. Al-Bassam, *'Ulama' najd*, vol. 6, p. 193; Wahba, *Jazirat al-'arab*, p. 30.
79. *Umm al-qura*, no. 91, 3 September 1926, p. 2.
80. Mark, "Saudis Sufis."
81. Ende, "The Nakhawila."
82. Al-Bassam, *'Ulama' najd*, vol. 6, pp. 56, 277.
83. Wahba, *Jazirat al-'arab*, p. 37.
84. Abd al-Rahman Al al-Shaykh, *Mashahir*, pp. 146–147.
85. Ibn Qasim, *al-Durar al-saniyya*, vol. 1, pp. 564–577.
86. Ibid., vol. 14, pp. 524–528.
87. Al-Bassam, *'Ulama' najd*, vol. 4, pp. 398–409; Abd al-Rahman Al ash-Shaykh, *Mashahir*, pp. 320–325; *Al-Manhal*, vol. 8, May 1948, pp. 185–190; author interviews with various figures from the provinces of Asir and Jazan, June 2006 and May 2007.

88. Al-Bassam, *'Ulama' najd*, vol. 1, pp. 231–241, and vol. 4, p. 302; Abd al-Rahman Al ash-Shaykh, *Mashahir*, pp. 152–163.
89. Ibn Qasim, *al-Durar al-saniyya*, vol. 9, pp. 348–352.
90. Ibid., vol. 9, pp. 310–316; Ibn Hadhlul, *Tarikh muluk al Su'ud*, pp. 185–186.
91. Ibn Qasim, *al-Durar al-saniyya*, vol. 5, pp. 62–64.
92. Wahba, *Jazirat al-'arab*, p. 280.
93. Ibid., pp. 281–284.
94. Ibid., pp. 126–128.
95. Ibn Qasim, *al-Durar al-saniyya*, vol. 9, pp. 333–334.
96. This consisted of a delegation of American engineers and technicians who had come to supervise the modernization of local agricultural production.
97. Rashid, *Saudi Arabia Enters the World*, vol. 1, pp. 201–203.

CHAPTER 5. ROUTINIZATION AND INSTITUTIONALIZATION OF HANBALI-WAHHABISM

1. Mouline, "Pouvoir et transition."
2. In order to express this exclusion, Abd al-Aziz established a hierarchical system of titles based on the model of European monarchies: royal highness (*sahib al-sumuww al-maliki*), highness (*sahib al-sumuww*), and emir (*amir*). Only those who held the first title—that is, his own descendants—had a claim to the throne.
3. Troeller, *Birth of Saudi Arabia*, pp. 60–61; Jacob Goldberg, "The 1914 Saudi-Ottoman Treaty"; Sinan Ughlu, *Najd wa al-hijaz fi al-wata'iq al-'Uthmaniyya*, Beirut, 2002, p. 127.
4. On the treaty, see Aydarus, "Ittifaqiyyat Darin"; Troeller, *Birth of Saudi Arabia*, pp. 85–86.
5. *Umm al-qura*, no. 405, 16 September 1932, pp. 2–3.
6. Ibid., no. 406, 23 September 1932, pp. 2–3.
7. Abir, *Saudi Arabia and the Oil Era*, pp. 34–36; Amin, *al-Haraka al-adabiyya*, pp. 106–109, 149–151; Teitelbaum, *Rise and Fall*, pp. 208–213.
8. Saud was thus crown prince and governor of Najd; Faysal was minister of foreign affairs and viceroy of the Hijaz; Fahd was minister of education; Sultan was head of the Royal Guard; Mish'al was minister of defense, and so on. On the posts held by the sons of Abd al-Aziz, see al-Zirikli, *al-Wajiz fi sirat al-malik 'Abd al-'Aziz*, pp. 346–351.
9. At his death in 1953, King Abd al-Aziz left thirty-four sons.
10. Shamiyya, *Al Su'ud*, pp. 244–245.
11. However, the economic, social, and diplomatic dimensions of this crisis must not be neglected: the chaotic management of power, particularly of the kingdom's financial affairs; the emergence of more or less structured opposition movements with ties to socialist-leaning Pan-Arabism; the instability of the regional situation and the rivalry with Egypt, etc.
12. Kepel, *Fitna*, pp. 335–336.
13. The author consulted a collection of twenty nearly identical letters in June 2006 at a private collector's home in Riyadh.

14. Author interviews with various participants in Riyadh and Mecca, June 2006, May 2007, and April 2008.
15. *Area Handbook for Saudi Arabia*, p. 155.
16. They were Muhammad ibn Ibrahim Al al-Shaykh, Abd al-Latif ibn Ibrahim Al al-Shaykh, Umar ibn Hasan Al al-Shaykh, Abd al-Malik ibn Ibrahim Al al-Shaykh, Abd al-Aziz al-Shathri, Abd Allah ibn Humayd, Abd al-Aziz ibn Baz, Abd al-Aziz ibn Salih, Muhammad al-Harkan, Sulayman ibn Ubayd, Abd al-Aziz ibn Rashid, and Abd al-Rahman ibn Faris.
17. *Umm al-qura*, no. 2015, 3 April 1964, p. 1.
18. The ulama uses the term "king" instead of "prince" because both Khalid and Fahd later acceded to the throne. The former ruled from 1975 to 1982 and the latter from 1982 to 2005.
19. Gaury, *Faisal*, pp. 30–133.
20. For the different variants of this maxim, see al-Bayhaqi, *al-Sunan al-kubra*; Ibn Qutayba, *'Uyun al-akhbar*, vol. 1, p. 273; al-Jahiz, *al-bukhala'*, p. 31; Ibn 'Abd Rabbih, *al-'Iqd al-farid*, vol. 2, p. 306; and Ibn 'Abd al-Barr, *Bahjat al-majalis*, vol. 2, p. 345.
21. *Umm al-qura*, no. 2045, 6 November 1964, p. 1.
22. Abir, *Saudi Arabia and the Oil Era*, pp. 36, 72–80; Vassiliev, *History of Saudi Arabia*, pp. 336–340; al-Mudayris, *al-Ba'thiyyun*, pp. 51–60; Holden and Johns, *House of Saud*, pp. 195–276; Lackner, *House Built on Sand*, pp. 96–97; Robert Vitalis, "Black Gold."
23. Kramer, *Islam Assembled*, pp. 1–85.
24. For more on this struggle, see Salamé, *al-Siyasa al-kharijiyya*, pp. 617–640.
25. Ibn Baz, *Naqd al-qawmiyya al-'arabiyya 'ala daw' al-islam wa al-waqi'*, in *Majmu'at fatawa wa maqalat mutanawwi'a*, vol. 1, pp. 280–318.
26. Ibn Ibrahim Al al-Shaykh, *Fatawa wa rasa'il*, no. 4507.
27. Ibn Baz, *Naqd al-qawmiyya al-'arabiyya*, p. 282.
28. Ibid., pp. 300–301.
29. Weber, *Économie et Société*, vol. 1, p. 97.
30. Ibn Qasim, *al-Durar al-saniyya*, vol. 3, pp. 18–19 (al-Ghazali), vol. 5, p. 76 (al-Zamakhshari), vol. 7, p. 239 (Ibn Rushd), and vol. 10, pp. 475–491 (al-Razi).
31. On this congress, see Kramer, *Islam Assembled*, pp. 106–191; Sékaly, *Le congrès du khalifat*, pp. 11–25, 125–219.
32. This Hanbali-Wahhabi association was founded in 1926 by Muhammad Hamid al-Fiqi (d. 1959). See al-Tahir, ed., *Jama'at ansar al-sunna al-Mohammediyya*.
33. *Umm al-qura*, no. 1527, 20 August 1954, p. 6.
34. Ibn Ibrahim Al al-Shaykh, *Fatawa wa rasa'il*, nos. 17, 4059, 4425, 4510.
35. The members of the Constituent Assembly of the World Islamic League in 1962 were Muhammad ibn Ibrahim Al al-Shaykh (Saudi Arabia), Abd al-Aziz ibn Baz (Saudi Arabia), Muhammad al-Harkan (Saudi Arabia), Ahmadu Bello (Nigeria), Allal al-Fasi (Morocco), Abu al-Hasan al-Nadawi (India), Abu al-A'la al-Maududi (Pakistan), Ibrahim Inas (Senegal), Amin al-Husayni (Palestine), Husayn Muhammad Makhluf (Egypt), Abd al-Rahman al-Iryani (Yemen), Muhammad al-Kattani (Syria), Muhammad al-Ibrahimi (Algeria), Muhammad al-Mujaddidi (Afghanistan), Muhammad Fal

ibn al-Bannani (Mauretania), Sa'id Ramadan (Egypt), Ibrahim al-Saqqaf (Singapore), Muhammad al-Sawwaf (Iraq), Ahmad al-Wuntu (Philippines), Muhammad hanifa Muhammad (Sri Lanka), Muhammad al-Qalqili (Jordan), Kamil al-Sharif (Jordan), Ahmad al-Bashir al-Tayyib (Sudan), Sa'di Yasin (Syria-Lebanon), Salih Uzjan (Turkey), Sin Shwan Wo (China), and Mansur al-Mahjub (Libya).

36. Ibn Ibrahim Al al-Shaykh, *Fatawa wa rasa'il*, nos. 120, 123, 148, 529, 609, 685, 808, 3902, 4477, and 4484.
37. Rida, *al-Khilafa*, pp. 128–135.
38. Ibn Ibrahim Al al-Shaykh, *Fatawa wa rasa'il*, no. 4539.
39. Ibid., no. 4512.
40. *Umm al-qura*, no. 1885, 8 September 1961, p. 1.
41. Ibid., no. 1871, 2 June 1961, p. 4.
42. *Al-Da'wa*, no. 964, 1985, p. 18.
43. Zeghal, *Gardiens de l'islam*, pp. 95–103.
44. On the Egyptian personnel (particularly members of the Muslim Brotherhood) who settled in Saudi Arabia, see Lacroix, *Les islamistes saoudiens*, pp. 48–64.
45. Ibn Qasim, *al-Durar al-saniyya*, vol. 1, pp. 13, 46; al-Bassam, *'Ulama' najd*, vol. 1, pp. 170, 205, 252, 271; vol. 2, p. 215; and vol. 3, p. 397.
46. The modernization of religious spaces and institutions in other Arab-Muslim countries had been carried out by the political authorities, who hoped to radically control the elite and religious discourse. This was particularly the case in countries such as Egypt, Morocco, and Tunisia, where the religious elites wielded much influence in the social space. See Zeghal, *Gardiens de l'islam*; Tozy, *Monarchie et islam politique au Maroc*; Hajji, *Burqiba wa al-islam: al-za'ama wa al-imama*.
47. Abd al-Rahman Al al-Shaykh, *Mashahir*, pp. 169–184; al-Bassam, *'Ulama' najd*, vol. 1, pp. 242–263.
48. Abd al-Rahman Al al-Shaykh, *Mashahir*, pp. 125–126; al-Bassam, *'Ulama' najd*, vol. 1, pp. 340–349.
49. See, for example, Ibn Qasim, *al-Durar al-saniyya*, vol. 9, pp. 106–123, 175–179, and vol. 15, pp. 413–417.
50. Contrary to an idea that is frequently encountered in traditional biographies, because of his young age, Ibn Ibrahim did not succeed his uncle Abd Allah ibn Abd al-Latif (d. 1920). It was another member of the Al al-Shaykh lineage, Abd Allah ibn Hasan, who became unofficial head of the establishment in order to look after the tradition.
51. Ibn Ibrahim Al al-Shaykh, *Fatawa wa rasa'il*, nos. 4547, 4558, 4559.
52. Wahba, *Jazirat al-'arab*, pp. 124–128 (modern educational system); al-Jawwad, *al-Tatawwur*, pp. 44–50 (judicial system).
53. Berger, *Sacred Canopy*, p. 107.
54. Ibn Qasim, *al-Durar al-saniyya*, vol. 5, pp. 79–80; Wahba, *Jazirat al-'arab*, pp. 129–131, 280–284.
55. Author interview with a grand ulama and former collaborator of Grand Mufti Ibn Ibrahim, April 2009.
56. Author interview with a grand ulama, April 2008.

57. *Umm al-qura*, no. 1489, 13 November 1953, p. 5. It is nevertheless to be noted that, in the 1950s, Ibn Ibrahim had to justify the choice of this title, which some of his followers considered too pretentious, by claiming that it had been conferred upon him by others. See Ibn Ibrahim Al ash-Shaykh, *Fatawa wa rasa'il*, no. 239.
58. *Al-Da'wa*, no. 659, 1978, p. 7.
59. Al-Mu'ayqil, *al-Ma'ahid al-'ilmiyya bayna al-Madi wa al-hadir*, p. 21.
60. Jami'a al-imam, *al-Kitab al-sanawi li-'am 1394*, pp. 43, 65.
61. *Umm al-qura*, no. 2079, 16 June 1965, pp. 1, 4; *Risalat al-ma'ahid al-'ilmiyya*, no. 7, 1391–1392, pp. 56–59. The period of study at the Higher Institute of the Magistracy was subsequently reduced from three to two years.
62. Jami 'at al-Imam, *al-Kitab al-sanawi li-'am 1394*, pp. 23–30.
63. *Umm al-qura*, no. 1565, 13 May 1955, p. 2.
64. The collection of Ibn Ibrahim's fatawa contains hundreds of examples addressing the most recurrent problems and questions.
65. Ibn Ibrahim Al al-Shaykh, *Fatawa wa rasa'il*, nos. 4418, 4421, 4423, 4424.
66. Abd al-Rahman Al al-Shaykh, *Mashahir*, pp. 152–163; al-Bassam, *'Ulama' najd*, vol. 1, pp. 231–241.
67. On the Saudi judicial system, see Vogel, *Islamic Law*; Layish, "Saudi Arabian Legal Reform."
68. Ibn Ibrahim Al al-Shaykh, *Fatawa wa rasa'il*, no. 4475.
69. Ibn Qasim, *al-Durar al-saniyya*, vol. 16, pp. 46–48, 100–101. Other members of the religious establishment did the same. See ibid., vol. 16, pp. 46–48, 163–165; Uthaymin, *Fitan al-majallat*.
70. Abd al-Rahman Al al-Shaykh, *Mashahir*, pp. 164–168; al-Bassam, *'Ulama' najd*, vol. 3, pp. 553–554.
71. Author interview with a former manager of *Rayat al-islam* magazine, May 2007.
72. Ibn Ibrahim Al al-Shaykh, *Fatawa wa rasa'il*, nos. 4530, 4533; no. 4531.
73. *Al-Da'wa* later became a monthly review, which it remains to this day.
74. *Al-Da'wa*, no. 959, 1985, pp. 10–13, 24–25.
75. Author interview with one of the publishing house's founding members, June 2006.
76. Letter from Abd al-Aziz ibn Baz to King Saud, 11 May 1961, unnumbered document, King Fahd National Library, Riyadh.
77. The name of this enterprise was Dar al-thaqafa al-islamiyya li at-tiba'a wa al-tarjama wa al-tawjih wa al-nashr (The Islamic House for Publishing, Translation, Orientation, and Diffusion).
78. Author interview with a former collaborator and disciple of Ibn Ibrahim, May 2007.
79. *Al-Da'wa*, no. 863, 1982, pp. 18–19.
80. Hertog, *Princes, Brokers*, p. 37. For more on the emergence of the Saudi bureaucracy, see ibid., pp. 37–83.
81. Ibn Ibrahim Al al-Shaykh, *Fatawa wa rasa'il*, nos. 4037, 4039, 4040, 4041.
82. Ibid., nos. 4033, 4038.
83. Ibn Qasim, *al-Durar al-saniyya*, vol. 16, pp. 206–218.
84. Ibid., p. 218.

85. To justify his relatively complacent position vis-à-vis the political partner, the grand mufti claimed that there were two sorts of *kufr* (impiety): (1) disbelief by conviction (*kufr i'tiqad*) consists in denying the truth of revelation, holding that positive laws are superior to sharia or continuing to apply customary or tribal law; (2) disbelief by action (*kufr al-'amal*) consists of applying positive laws in particular domains while holding that sharia is superior to them. While the rulers of this latter category are still considered Muslim if they show remorse, those of the former are definitively excluded from the community and deprived of eternal salvation.
86. Ibn Ibrahim Al al-Shaykh, *Fatawa wa rasa'il*, nos. 4037, 4039, 4040, 4043, 4048; Ibn Qasim, *al-Durar al-saniyya*, vol. 16, pp. 204–219.
87. Ibn Ibrahim Al al-Shaykh, *Fatawa wa rasa'il*, nos. 4049, 4050, 4051, 4053.
88. Ibid., nos. 4035, 4041.
89. Ibn Qasim, *al-Durar al-saniyya*, vol. 16, pp. 28–30, 46–48, 219–226.
90. Ibid., vol. 16, pp. 177, 191–195.
91. Author interviews with several of Ibn Humayd's disciples, June 2006 and May 2007.
92. Ibn Qasim, *al-Durar al-saniyya*, vol. 16, pp. 233–237, 237–313.
93. Ibn Ibrahim Al al-Shaykh, *Fatawa wa rasa'il*, nos. 4042, 4043, 4045, 4046, 4047, 4048.
94. It is interesting to note that the grand mufti, while condemning the civil servant code, used it to defend the interests of religious personnel who joined the civil service. See ibid., nos. 421, 1194.
95. Ibid., no. 4044.
96. Vogel, *Islamic Law*, pp. 302–303; al-Jawwad, *al-Tatawwur*, pp. 119–122.
97. Salih al-Luhaydan, *Mafhum tatbiq al-shari'a*, audio cassette, side 1. The new labor code was thus promulgated on 8 July 1969. See *Umm al-qura*, no. 2299, 28 November 1969.
98. al-Amr, *Lamahat*, p. 4; Baghdadi, *al-Intilaqa*, vol. 1, p. 271.
99. *Al-Kitab al-ihsa'i li-'am 1386*, p. 60. The two schools in Riyadh were Mabarrat al-karimat (The Daughters of King Saud's Foundation), created in 1956, and Mabarrat al-malik Abd al-Aziz (The King Abd al-Aziz Foundation), created in 1958. See *Al-Manhal*, no. 5, 1956, pp. 485–486; *al-Nasiriyya*, no. 4, 1959, p. 77.
100. Ibn Ibrahim Al al-Shaykh, *Fatawa wa rasa'il*, no. 4570.
101. Ibn Qasim, *al-Durar al-saniyya*, vol. 16, pp. 71–84, 92–98.
102. *Umm al-qura*, no. 1827, 15 July 1960, p. 1. The General Chancellor of Girls' Schools was later renamed the General Chancellery for Girls' Education (al-Ri'asa al-'amma li-ta'lim al-banat).
103. On the position of the ulama in regards to the introduction of radio, television, and cinema and its evolution, see Ibn Qasim, *al-Durar al-saniyya*, vol. 15, pp. 27–33, 230–249; Ibn Ibrahim Al al-Shaykh, *Fatawa wa rasa'il*, nos. 2851–2874. On their position in regards to the teaching of Copernican theories, foreign languages, and the dispatch of student delegations abroad, see Ibn Ibrahim Al al-Shaykh, *Fatawa wa rasa'il*, nos. 4450–4462, 4557, 4558, 4567; Ibn Baz, *al-Adilla al-naqliyya wa al-hissiyya 'ala imkan al-su'ud ila al-kawakib wa 'ala jarayan al-shams wa al-qamar wa sukun al-ard*; Ibn Baz, *Majmu'at fatawa wa maqalat mutanawwi'a*, vol. 1, pp. 330–335, vol. 3, pp. 342–346, vol. 4, pp. 192–194, vol. 5, p. 405. On the adoption of European clothing

styles, particularly in the military domain, see Ibn Qasim, *al-Durar al-saniyya*, vol. 15, pp. 363–395.

CHAPTER 6. THE COMMITTEE OF GRAND ULAMA

1. Indeed, Jihadists and the Saudi Islamist opposition used the fatawa and writings of Muhammad bin Ibrahim—taken out of context, of course—for polemical ends as part of their effort to delegitimize the regime and excommunicate the monarchy. See, for example, al-Maqdisi, *al-Kawashif*; al-Mas'ari, *al-Adilla*.
2. Zeghal, *Gardiens de l'Islam*, pp. 91–130.
3. *Umm al-qura*, no. 1944, 9 November 1962, p. 1.
4. On these components, see ibid., p. 6.
5. The grand mufti was the first cousin of Faysal's mother and was thus considered his uncle; his advanced age, genealogy, and religious knowledge made him, in a patriarchal society that respects elders, a father (*walid*), not only to the sons of King Abd al-Aziz, but also to all believers.
6. *Al-Kitab al-ihsa'i al-sanawi 1970*, Table 10/4.
7. al-Rasheed, *Contesting the Saudi State*, p. 28.
8. Ibn Bishr, *'Unwan al-majd*, vol. 1, p. 174.
9. Al-Yassini, *Religion and State*, pp. 67–79; Kechichian, "Role of the Ulama."
10. Indeed, between 1972 and 1974, five meetings took place between Saudi ulama and representatives of the Christian world. Following an initial interreligious meeting in Riyadh on 22 March 1972, the ulama toured Europe, including stops in Paris (23 October 1974), the Vatican (25 October 1974), Geneva (30 October 1974), and Strasbourg (4 November 1974).
11. Kepel, *Fitna*, pp. 208–212; Lacroix, *Les islamistes saoudiens*, pp. 48–52.
12. A not insignificant number of the ulama of the religious establishment had received their doctorates from Al-Azhar. For the statistics, see chapter 7.
13. These events included the sudden death of King Faysal in 1975, the messianic revolt in Mecca in 1979, the Islamic Revolution in Iran and the Shiite revolt in the province of Al-Asha the same year, the drop in the price of petroleum in 1982, and the "immoral" behavior of several influential members of the ruling house.
14. Al-Jundi, "Hay'at kibar."
15. Abd al-Muta'al al-Sa'idi, "Ra'yun fi al-shart."
16. Al-Mat'ani, "Majma' al-buhuth"; al-Lajna al-'Ulya lil-ihtifal bi al-'id al-alfi lil-Azhar, *Majama' al-buhuth*. In 2012, this body once again assumed its original name, Hay'at Kibar al-'Ulama'.
17. *Umm al-qura*, no. 2387, 3 September 1971, p. 1. Royal Order A/88 of 29 May 2001 stipulates that the number of members of the Committee of Grand Ulama cannot be fewer than twelve nor greater than twenty-two.
18. It should be noted that, contrary to a widespread rumor among observers and scholars, the *'alim* Abd Allah ibn Jibrin (d. 2009) was replaced by a member of the *ifta'* as a civil servant of the Ri'asa al-'amma without having for all that been a member of the Committee of Grand Ulama.

19. Al-Duwayyish, ed., *Fatawa al-lajna*; http://www.islamspirit.com/islamspirit_program_004.php; http://www.aleman.com/islamlib/viewchp.asp?bid=262&cid=1; http://www.almeshkat.net/books/open.php?book=128&cat=15.
20. A private secretary and a research assistant (a graduate of one of the country's Islamic universities) assist members of the Permanent Commission.
21. It must not be forgotten that, constantly solicited by the population, the members of the Permanent Commission and other members of the Committee of Grand Ulama every day issue dozens and even hundreds of fatawa before or after daily prayers, during special meetings held in a mosque or at home, and in written responses to the most representative questions in the country's largest papers and magazines, on television and radio programs, at their Internet sites, and via online podcasts, etc.
22. Direct observation at the headquarters of the Permanent Commission in Dar al-Ifta', April 2005.
23. The post of mufti had been vacant since the death of Ibn Ibrahim in 1969.
24. The members of the Permanent Commission are also members of the Council of the Committee of Grand Ulama.
25. http://www.alifta.com/bayan.aspx; http://www.alriyadh.com/2009/01/01/article399204.html.
26. Author interview with the presidency's director of public relations, April 2005.
27. The works most widely published by the presidency are those of Ibn Taymiyya, Ibn Qayyim al-Jawziyya, Ibn Abd al-Wahhab and his descendants, and those of members of the Committee of Grand Ulama.
28. All numbers of the *Islamic Research Review* are available at http://www.almeshkat.net/books/open.php?cat=49&book=3029; the URL for the website is http://www.alifta.net/. On this subject, see http://www.aawsat.com/details.asp?section=4&article=440249&issueno=10540; http://www.alarabiya.net/articles/2007/10/06/40011.html.
29. Author interviews with eleven officials of the presidency, April 2005 and June 2006.
30. Abd al-Aziz ibn Baz was the presidency's leader from 1975 to 1993.
31. *Majallat al-Tadamun al-islami*, October 1988, pp. 77–89 (penal law); *Abhat hay'at kibar al-'Ulama'*, vol. 2, pp. 529–553, 489–494, and vol. 4, pp. 307–315, 427–431 (civil law).
32. *Majallat al-Buhuth al-Islamiyya*, no. 58, 1421, pp. 379–380 (medical domain); *Al-Da'wa*, no. 1972, 1426, pp. 28–30 (economic domain).
33. *Al-Da'wa*, no. 1133, 1408, pp. 4–9 (Khomeini); *Majallat al-Buhuth al-Islamiyya*, no. 29, 1411, pp. 349–350 (Saddam Hussein).
34. *Majallat al-Buhuth al-Islamiyya*, no. 69, 1424, pp. 367–380.
35. *Al-Da'wa*, no. 1156, 1989, pp. 12–13; *Majallat al-Buhuth al-Islamiyya*, no. 47, 1995, pp. 367–370; no. 56, 1998, pp. 357–362 (suicide attacks); "La jihad fi al-'iraq bal huwa makan li al-tahluka wa tadmir al-shabab," available at http://www.alwatan.com.sa/news/newsdetail.asp?issueno=2437&id=7835; http://www.aawsat.com/details.asp?section=17&article=162676&issueno=8887 (fighting in Iraq).
36. *Al-Sharq al-awsat*, no. 9633.
37. *Al-Da'wa*, no. 731, 1400, pp. 8–9 (capture of Mecca); *Al-Da'wa*, no. 1104, 1407, pp. 34–35; no. 1105, 1409, pp. 22–25; no. 1110, 1408, pp. 4–5; no. 1133, 1408, pp. 4–9; no. 1139, 1408, pp. 4–5, 10 (pilgrim riots).

38. Since its creation in 1971, the Committee of Grand Ulama has had five general secretaries: Muhammad ibn Awda, Ibrahim al-Dabbasi, Abd al-Aziz al-Falih, Abd al-Aziz Abd al-Mun'im, and Fahd al-Majid.
39. Author interviews with members of the Committee of Grand Ulama, April 2005, June 2006, and May 2007. See also *Al-Da'wa*, no. 623, 1397, p. 6.
40. After deliberation, a member of the Council of the Committee of Grand Ulama proposes an initial version of the fatawa and circulates it among the members, who take turns correcting it. The definitive version must satisfy the majority: if it nevertheless remains unsatisfied, they can indicate this at the end of the text that is issued. It goes without saying that political fatawa must be unanimous.
41. The hills of al-Safa and al-Marwa are separated from one another by a distance of 394 meters, referred to as *al-mas'a*, where the pilgrims carry out a ritual race (*sa'y*).
42. Fatwa no. 227, 22 March 2006. Document in the author's possession.
43. http://www.aawsat.com/details.asp?section=1&article=468485&issueno=10742; http://www.aawsat.com/details.asp?section=1&article=469695&issueno=10753.
44. Though it must not be forgotten that parallel and/or complementary legal and judicial systems exist—in particular, various local customs (*a'raf*, sing. *'Urf*) and the regulatory power of sovereigns (*qawanim*, sing. *qanun*).
45. It goes without saying that each legal school has its own corpus, which is based on a set of references that is broadly shared by all currents of Islam, in particular, the four schools of Sunni Islam.
46. *Umm al-qura*, no. 141, 26 August 1927, p. 1.
47. *Majmu'at al-nuzum min 1345 [1926] ila 1357 [1938]*, section devoted to justice, heading: The changes and amendments of 1928, pp. 11, 15, and 39.
48. Fu'ad Hamza (d. 1961), one of King Abd al-Aziz's Lebanese collaborators, cites a list of six works: (1) *al-Iqna'*, by al-Hajjawi; (2) *Kashshaf al-qina' 'an matn al-iqna,'* by al-Buhuti; (3) *Muntaha al-irada*, by al-Futuhi; (4) *Sharh muntaha al-iradat*, by al-Buhuti; (5) *al-Mughni*, by Shams al-din ibn Qudama; and (6) *al-Sharh al-kabir*, by 'Abd al-Rahman ibn Qudama. See Hamza, *al-Bilad*, p. 189.
49. Ibn Qasim, *al-Durar al-saniyya*, vol. 9, pp. 179–180, 310–316.
50. It must be noted, however, that the refusal of this initiative was in all likelihood also motivated by corporatist and regionalist considerations. Al-Qari' was from Mecca and also did not belong to the Hanbali-Wahhabi corporation. We will return to these questions in chapter 7.
51. Al-Bassam, *Taqnin al-shari'a adraruhu wa mafasiduhu*, pp. 5–7; pp. 7–8; pp. 8–10; and pp. 8, 10–11.
52. Author interviews with several members of the Committee of Grand Ulama and two religious personnel who participated in preparing the study, April 2005, June 2006, May 2007, and April 2008.
53. Al-Lajna al-da'ima, "Tadwin al-rajih min aqwal al-fuqaha' fi al-mu'amalat wa ilzam al-qudat bihi," *Majallat al-Buhuth al-Islamiyya*, no. 31, 1991, pp. 16–57; no. 32, 1991, pp. 18–65; and no. 33, 1991, pp. 20–25.
54. *Majallat al-Buhuth al-Islamiyya*, no. 31, 1991, pp. 58–65.
55. Ibid., pp. 60–62.
56. Ibid., pp. 63–64.

57. They were Abd al-Majid Hasan, Rashid ibn Khunayn, Salih ibn Ghusun, Abd Allah Khayyat, Abd Allah ibn Mani', and Muhammad ibn Jubayr.
58. *Majallat al-Buhuth al-Islamiyya*, no. 31, 1991, pp. 26–52.
59. Ibid., pp. 26–27.
60. Schacht, *Introduction*, p. 64.
61. For a review of the various positions on this question, see Abd al-Rahman al-Jar'i, *Taqnin al-ahkam al-shar'iyya bayna al-mani'in wa al-mujizin*, available at http://www.almeshkat.net/books/open.php?cat=50&book=3533 and http://islamtoday.net/bohooth/artshow-86-5987.htm.
62. Author interviews with several ulama and specialists of the Saudi judicial system, April 2005, June 2006, May 2007, April 2009, and March 2010.
63. http://www.elaph.com/ElaphWeb/Politics/2007/12/290570.htm.
64. http://www.alriyadh.com/2008/01/21/article310908.html;http://www.okaz.com.sa/okaz/osf/20090104/Con20090104250035.htm; http://www.alriyadh.com/2008/12/04/article392421.html.
65. The Ministry of Justice has discussed creating a body specializing in the centralization, preparation, and publication of judgments handed down by the courts.
66. The three editions are available at the Saudi Ministry of Justice website, http://www.moj.gov.sa/mdona_moj/default.aspx.
67. http://www.aawsat.com/details.asp?section=43&article=508495&issueno=11047; http://www.aawsat.com/details.asp?section=1&issueno=11113&article=517549.
68. http://www.alriyadh.com/2009/07/26/article447767.html; http://islamtoday.net/albasheer/artshow-17-116590.htm; http://www.albiladdaily.com/news.php?action=show&id=33666.
69. Author interviews with figures close to certain members of the Committee of Grand Ulama and the officials of Dar al-ifta',March 2010.
70. http://www.alriyadh.com/2010/01/26/article493052.html.
71. http://www.alriyadh.com/2010/02/03/article495198.html.
72. http://www.al-jazirah.com.sa/20100408/ln11d.htm; http://www.al-madina.com/node/244789.

CHAPTER 7. RAISING THE VEIL ON THE CONDITIONS OF ACCESS TO THE RELIGIOUS ESTABLISHMENT

1. Al-Isa, *al-Hayat*; al-Bassam, *al-Hayat*.
2. On this notion, see Bourdieu, *Le sens pratique*, pp. 200–204.
3. Al-Zamil, ed., *'Abd Allah b. Humayd*; al-Bassam, *'Ulama' najd*, vol. 4, pp. 431–445; al Qadi, *Rawdat al Nazirin*, vol. 2, p. 55; Ibn Qasim, *al-Durar al-saniyya*, vol. 16, pp. 476–477.
4. Ibn Humayd also held a large number of other juridico-religious posts, particularly in the World Islamic League (member of the Constitutive Council, president of the Council of Islamic Jurisprudence, etc.).
5. Two of Abd Allah ibn Humayd's other sons, Ahmad and Ibrahim, are also actors in the religious space as professors of Muslim law and the prophetic tradition.

6. Four of Ibn Humayd's six children pursued religious studies.
7. This alliance was of course expressed in the language of kinship. Several marriages between the two lineages took place across this period, with the most famous being that between King Abd al-Aziz and the daughter of Abd Allah ibn Abd al-Latif, head of the religious establishment. Faysal, king of Saudi Arabia between 1964 and 1975, was born of this union.
8. Indeed, Grand Mufti Muhammad ibn Ibrahim was accompanied by his brothers, Abd al-Latif, Abd Allah, and Abd al-Malik, and his sons, Abd al-Aziz and Ibrahim. The last member of the delegation was Muhammad ibn Faris. See *Umm al-qura*, no. 1489, 13 November 1953, p. 5.
9. *Umm al-qura*, no. 2015, 3 April 1962, p. 1.
10. See the decree appointing him at the website of King Saud, http://www.kingsaud.net/ara/alarshef/almrasem_almlkeah/1377_h/almrswm_almlke_alkhass_btaeen_alshekh_eebrahem_bn_mhmd_bn_eebrahem_naba_lsmahah_almftaa_alakbr_fe_aleeftaa.
11. See the decree appointing him at the website of King Saud, http://www.kingsaud.net/ara/alarshef/almrasem_almlkeah/1377_h/almrswm_almlke_alkhass_balshekh_mhmd_bn_eebrahem_bwjwb_taeen_naba_lsmahth_fe_rasah_alqdhaa.
12. Abd al-Rahman Al al-Shaykh, *Mashahir*, pp. 164–168.
13. Ibid., pp. 152–163; 148–151.
14. On the phenomenon of social reproduction, see Bourdieu and Passeron, *Les héritiers* and *La reproduction*; Boudon, *L'inégalité des chances*; Petitat, "Le paradigme"; Berthelot, "Reflexions"; Duru-Bellat, *L'inflation scolaire*.
15. Pierre Bourdieu and Jean-Claude Passeron, *The Inheritors: French Students and Their Relations to Culture*, Chicago, 1979, p. 36.
16. Among the members of the lineage who occupied posts in other domains, one can cite Muhammad ibn Abd al-Rahman Al al-Shaykh, former director of Royal Protocol; Abd Allah ibn Abd al-Rahman Al al-Shaykh, former director of National Safety; Hasan ibn Abd al-Aziz Al al-Shaykh and Muhammad ibn Abd al-Aziz Al al-Shaykh, former ministers of Municipal and Rural Affairs; Abd al-Rahman ibn Sulayman Al al-Shaykh, former minister of agriculture; Abd al-Aziz ibn Abd Allah Al al-Shaykh, former minister of national education, Abd Allah ibn Ibrahim Al al-Shaykh, former secretary general of the King Abd al-Aziz Foundation (al-Dara); and Umar ibn Abd al-Aziz Al al-Shaykh, former head of the department of dermatology at King Saud University.
17. Other members of the Al al-Shaykh lineage of course held juridico-religious offices. But these were generally of secondary importance and under the benevolent control of the political authorities. For example, Abd al-Muhsin ibn Abd Allah Al al-Shaykh was head of the Direction of Religious Affairs at the Ministry of Defense. His work consisted entirely of distributing religious guidance brochures and managing logistics for the ministry's mosques. See *Al-Da'wa*, no. 1022, 1986, pp. 28–31.
18. *Majallat al-'adl*, no. 34, 2007, pp. 251–258.
19. *Asbar al-'Ulama'*, vol. 2, p. 596; *Akhbar al-hisba*, no. 0, 1993, p. 5; *Majallat al-'adl*, no. 27, 2005, pp. 233–244.
20. In what follows, I use the term "tribe" by default, for the "genealogical reality" of the Najd and the Arab Peninsula is very complex (Bedouin tribal confederations based

on an eponymous imaginary ancestor, tribal confederations based on political and military alliance, sedentary lineages that claim to descend from medieval Arab tribes, etc.). Unfortunately, this important question has yet to be the object of serious study.
21. On this subject, see Fahad, "'Imama vs. the 'Iqal."
22. While most of the Shammar supported the Ha'il Emirate, led by the al-Rashid, factions of the Utayba and the Mutayr supported the Ikhwan rebellion at the end of the 1920s. The Ajman rejected the authority of King Abd al-Aziz in the early twentieth century and rallied behind several of his rivals.
23. Ibn Sunaytan, al-Nukhab al-su'udiyya, pp. 70–73 (Council of Ministers); pp. 93–96 (Advisory Council); pp. 177–178 (high-ranking civil servants).
24. Ibid., pp. 177–178.
25. With the exception of Abd al-Razzaq Afifi (d. 1994), who was Hanbali-Wahhabi in dogma and law, the other foreign ulama continue to issue fatawa in keeping with their legal schools of origin. For example, Muhammad al-Amin al-Shanqiti (d. 1974) was Maliki and Abd al-Majid Hasan al-Jabarti (d. 1998) was Shafi'i.
26. Ibn Sunaytan, al-Nukhab al-su'udiyya, pp. 71, 94.
27. On this subject, see Makdisi, "Law and Traditionalism."
28. Abd al-Rahman Al al-Shaykh, Mashahir, pp. 170–172; author interviews with five former disciples of Muhammad ibn Ibrahim, April 2005, June 2006, and May 2007.
29. Al-Bassam, 'Ulama' najd, vol. 3, pp. 467–483.
30. Several children follow informal courses in public or private Qur'anic schools (kuttab, dar tahfiz al-qur'an).
31. Document no. 5/3/23/1648, 12 May 1955, Institute of Public Administration, Riyadh.
32. On the history and doctrine of these two movements, see Lacroix, Les islamistes saoudiens, pp. 47–97.
33. Al-Da'wa, no. 821, 1982, pp. 27–42, and no. 964, 1405, p. 18; http://www.imamu.edu.sa/colleg_instt/colleg/Pages/default.aspx; http://www.imamu.edu.sa/colleg_instt/institute/Pages/default.aspx.
34. The two national satellite campuses are located in Al-Kharj and Al-Ahsa; the three international satellites are located in Japan, Indonesia, and Djibouti.
35. Their work tends to be directed against other currents of Islam rather than against other religions.
36. See, for example, Vincent et al., Les nouveaux clercs.
37. Several other classic titles, such as 'alim (scholar), al-'allama (the knowledgeable one), al-faqih (jurist), al-muhaddith (traditionalist), and al-imam (guide) are frequently used to reinforce this dimension.
38. Abu Zayd, "Taghrib al-alqab al-'ilmiyya," in al-Majmu'a al-'ilmiyya, pp. 301–334.
39. Several ulama continue to maintain their own circles for transmitting religious knowledge (halaqat 'ilmiyya, sing. halqa 'ilmiyya). These are held at their homes or in a mosque (generally both) several times a week on fixed days and times.
40. Uthaymin, Kitab al-'ilm, pp. 240–241; Abu Zayd, "Hilyat Talib al-'ilm," in, al-Majmu'a al-'ilmiyya, pp. 158–161.
41. Al-Bassam, 'Ulama' najd, vol. 6, p. 124.
42. Lacroix, "L'apport de Nasir" and "Between Revolution and Apoliticism."

43. Bourdieu, *Langage et pouvoir*, pp. 175–186.
44. Al-Bassam,'*Ulama' najd*, vol. 3, pp. 275–279; http://www.afifyy.com/.
45. From 14 February 2009, the Minister of Justice has been Muhammad ibn Abd al-Karim Al-Isa.
46. A brief period in the Muslim Brotherhood in the 1960s allowed him to acquire a good understanding of the Islamic space as well as significant organizational experience that he was to put to the service of the corporation.
47. For a complete list of his publications, see *Asbar al-'ulama'*, vol. 2, pp. 717–718; http://www.themwl.org/Profile/default.aspx?l=AR&pl=1&mid=42; http://www.alriyadh.com/2007/12/20/article302969.html.
48. Collective, *Inhiyar suq al-ashum al-su'udiyya wa ta'thiruhu 'ala al-thiqa bi-mustaqbal al-suq*, cited by Collectif, *Tadayyun al-su'udiyyin*, vol. 1, pp. 35–37.
49. See the decree nominating Ibrahim ibn Muhammad ibn Ibrahim at the website devoted to King Saud, http://www.kingsaud.net/ara/alarshef/almrasem_almlkeah/1377_h/almrswm_almlke_alkhass_btaeen_alshekh_eebrahem_bn_mhmd_bn_eebrahem_naba_lsmahah_almftaa_alakbr_fe_aleeftaa.
50. Al-Shathri, *Ithaf al-labib*; al-Bassam, '*Ulama' najd*, vol. 3, pp. 287–288.
51. Ibn Sunaytan, *al-Nukhab al-su'udiyya*, pp. 59–62.
52. Saluting the flag: http://www.alarabiya.net/programs/2005/07/14/14931.html#003; engaging in jihad: http://www.aawsat.com/leader.asp?section=3&article=263861&issueno=9473; http://www.alriyadh.com/2004/10/06/article13063.html.
53. Interview with the author, Mecca, April 2005.
54. Interview with the author, Burayda, April 2005.
55. Interview with the author, Riyadh, April 2005.

CHAPTER 8. RELIGIOUS AUTHORITY IN PRACTICE

1. Habermas, *Structural Transformation*, p. 8.
2. *EI²*, vol. 3, p. 503; Tyan, *Histoire de l'organisation*, pp. 617–650; Foster, "Agoranomos and Muhtasib"; Floor, "The Office of Muhtasib"; Buckley, "The Muhtasib"; Hoexter, Eisenstadt, and Levtzion, eds., *Public Sphere*; Cook, *Commanding*.
3. *Hisba* refers to the duty of every Muslim to promote virtue and prevent vice. In towns, the *muhtasib* sees to it that hisba is observed in moral behavior and, more particularly, the markets. I use it here as a synonym of *al-amr bi al-ma'ruf wa al-nahy 'an al-munkar*.
4. Cook, *Commanding*, pp. 165–170.
5. Ibn Abd al-Wahhab, *al-Rasa'il al-shakhsiyya*, in *Mu'allafat* [Complete Works], vol. 7, pp. 11, 114, 276, 296, and *Mabhat fi al-ijtihad wa al-ikhtilaf*, in *Mu'allafat* [Complete Works], vol. 3, p. 17; Ibn Qasim, *al-Durar al-saniyya*, vol. 1, pp. 29–35.
6. Ibn Qasim, *al-Durar al-saniyya*, vol. 1, pp. 222–241.
7. Palgrave, *Narrative*, pp. 243–250, 316–318.
8. Abd al-Rahman Al al-Shaykh, *Mashahir*, pp. 381–383; al-Bassam, '*Ulama' najd*, vol. 4, p. 302.
9. Al-Rihani, *Muluk al-'arab*, pp. 556–564. Contemporaneous Western reports confirm this information. See Harrison, "Al Riyadh," p. 418; Philby, *Heart of Arabia*, vol. 1, p. 97.

10. *Umm al-qura*, no. 34, August 1925, p. 4, and no. 68, April 1926, p. 4.
11. On the *mahmal*, see *EI²*, vol. 6, p. 44; Jomier, *Le mahmal*; Gaudefroy-Demombyne, *Le pèlerinage*, pp. 155–161.
12. *Umm al-qura*, no. 78, June 1926, p. 1; Armstrong, *Lord of Arabia*, pp. 245–250.
13. Abd al-Rahman Al al-Shaykh, *Mashahir*, pp. 344–351; al-Bassam, *'Ulama' najd*, vol. 4, pp. 138–149.
14. Hafiz Wahba (d. 1967), Egyptian collaborator of King Abd al-Aziz, affirms that the idea originated with him. But it must be noted that he boasts throughout his book of being the daemon responsible for passing on all good ideas to the king and other leading figures in the kingdom. On this account, he was the true inspiration for the modern Saudi Kingdom. See Wahba, *Jazirat al-'arab*, p. 315.
15. *Umm al-qura*, no. 91, 10 September 1926, p. 2.
16. From Mecca: Muhammad Aqil, Muhammad Shirwani, Abd Allah al-Shibi, Abd al-Rahman Bushnaq, Umar Jan, Abbas Abd al-Jabbar, Umar Fiqi, Abd al-Rahman al-Zwawi, Husayn Baslama, and Husayn, Steward of the Harem. From Nadj: Muhammad ibn Muddayan, Ali al-Mansur al Hadyan, Ahmad ibn Rakban, and Abd Allah al-Sulayman al Muhanna.
17. Mazhar, *Dalil al-hajj,*, pp. 47–50.
18. *Umm al-qura*, no. 111, January 1927, p. 1; no. 113, February 1927, p. 1; no. 114, February 1927, pp. 1–2; no. 115, February 1927, p. 1; no. 116, March 1927, p. 2; no. 117, March 1927, p. 2; no. 118, March 1927, p. 1.
19. Ibn Qasim, *al-Durar al-saniyya*, vol. 8, pp. 82–84, and vol. 9, pp. 106–123.
20. Royal Order no. 546, 6 July 1928, Regulations of the Committee for the Promotion of Virtue and the Prevention of Vice for the year 1347, Institute of Public Administration, Riyadh.
21. Ibid.
22. On al-Samh, see al-Tahir, *Ansar al-sunna al-muhammadiyya*, pp. 222–228; al-Jabbar, *Siyar wa tarajim*, p. 257.
23. *Umm al-qura*, no. 241, August 1929, p. 1.
24. Regulation no. 546, 6 July 1928, Regulations of the Committee for the Promotion of Virtue and the Prevention of Vice for the year 1939, Institute of Public Administration, Riyadh.
25. *Akhbar al-hisba*, no. 0, 1414, p. 6.
26. *Lamahat 'an al-ri'asa al-'amma lil-amr bi al-ma'ruf wa al-nahy 'an al-munkar*, p. 13; http://www.okaz.com.sa/new/Issues/20100325/Con20100325340393.htm.
27. Ibn Ibrahim Al al-Shaykh, *Fatawa wa rasa'il*, no. 4551.
28. *Al-Kitab al-ihsa'i al-sanawi*, Riyadh, 1967.
29. Ibid.
30. Ibn Qasim, *al-Durar al-saniyya*, vol. 15, pp. 15–21, vol. 14, pp. 414–419, 43–44; Ibn Ibrahim Al ash-Shaykh, *Fatawa wa rasa'il*, nos. 1434, 1435.
31. *Umm al-qura*, no. 1944, 9 November 1962, p. 6.
32. Ibn Qasim, *al-Durar al-saniyya*, vol. 14, p. 501.
33. Ibid., vol. 15, pp. 8–14.

34. Ibid., vol. 15, pp. 34–41; Ibn Ibrahim Al al-Shaykh, *Fatawa wa rasa'il*, nos. 1442, 1444, 1447.
35. Ibn Qasim, *al-Durar al-saniyya*, vol. 14, pp. 507–517; vol. 15, pp. 27–33, 78–200, 201–205, 206–230, 230–249.
36. Ibid., vol. 15, pp. 76–77.
37. Ibid., vol. 15, pp. 27–33.
38. Lacroix, *Les islamistes saoudiens*, pp. 104–109.
39. Author interviews with several eyewitnesses, April 2005, June 2006, May 2007, April 2009, and March 2010.
40. *Umm al-qura*, no. 2641, 3 September 1976, p. 1.
41. Ibid.
42. Lacroix, *Les islamistes saoudiens*, pp. 109–121; Trofimov, *Siege of Mecca*; Hegghammer and Lacroix, "Rejectionist Islamism"; Kechichian, "Islamic Revivalism."
43. Jones, "Rebellion."
44. This regulation was signed by the king on 6 September 1980 and published in *Umm al-qura*, no. 2853, on 24 January 1981. See also *Nizam hay'at al-amr bi al-ma'ruf wa al-nahy 'an al-munkar*.
45. On this crisis, see Abir, *Saudi Arabia: Government*, pp. 99–100, and *Saudi Arabia and the Oil Era*, p. 179; al-Rasheed, *A History*, p. 149.
46. For an idea of the sums allocated to several juridico-religious bodies, see Hertog, *Princes, Brokers*, p. 126.
47. This comeback was part of a more general religious effervescence, later called al-Sahwa al-islamiyya (the Islamic Awakening), that was attendant upon the coming of age of the first generations of Saudis who had gone through the educational system that had been established in collaboration with the exiled Muslim Brotherhood. See Lacroix, *Les islamistes saoudiens*, pp. 53–64.
48. Author interviews with observers of the Saudi media and artistic scenes, May 2007 and April 2008.
49. On Saudi Islamism, see al-Rasheed, *Contesting the Saudi State*, pp. 59–101; Fandy, *Saudi Arabia*; Teitelbaum, *Holier Than Thou: Saudi Arabia's Islamic Opposition*; Lacroix, *Les islamistes saoudiens*.
50. Certain protest figures, in particular Abd al-Muhsin al-Ubaykan (b. 1956), even recommended establishing volunteer *mutawi'a* committees to support official agents. Moreover, several groups of young al-Qasim took action by attacking video and cassette stores, women's clothing boutiques, etc. Author interviews with several actors, May 2007, April 2008, and April 2009.
51. *Akhbar al-hisba*, no. 6, 1415, p. 7, no. 8, 1416, p. 7; *al-Hisba*, no. 28, 1420, p. 12, no. 29, 1420, p. 14.
52. http://www.mofa.gov.sa/detail.asp?InNewsItemID=24887&InTemplateKey=print.
53. *Al-Da'wa*, no. 1467, 1415, p. 5; no. 1462, 1415, p. 10; and no. 1463, 1415, p. 10.
54. *Akhbar al-hisba*, no. 7, 1416, pp. 1–2; *al-Hisba*, no. 19, 1418, p. 1.
55. *Al-Hisba*, no. 16, 1417, p. 1, and no. 18, 1418, pp. 1–4.
56. *Akhbar al-hisba*, no. 3, 1415, p. 4.

57. *Al-Hisba*, no. 21, 1418, p. 3.
58. *Akhbar al-hisba*, no. 2, 1415, p. 3.
59. All issues of the review are now available at the website of the Committee for the Promotion of Virtue and the Prevention of Vice. See http://www.pv.gov.sa/books/pages/default.aspx?PageNo=1&View=Tree&NodeID=1&BookID=5&lang=ar.
60. *Al-Da'wa*, no. 1435, 1414, p. 3.
61. *Akhbar al-hisba*, no. 2, 1415, p. 3.
62. Ibid., no. 9, 1416, p. 2.
63. Ibid., no. 1, 1415, p. 5.
64. *Al-Hisba*, no. 15, 1417, p. 16; no. 16, 1417, p. 7; and no. 25, 1419, p. 4.
65. For the figures of these activities in certain provinces of the kingdom, see for example *Akhbar al-hisba*, no. 1, 1415, p. 2, and no. 5, 1415, p. 2.
66. Ibid., no. 6, 1415, pp. 1–2.
67. Ibid., no. 0, 1414, p. 6. Several articles of this supplement are available on the website for the Committee for the Promotion of Virtue and the Prevention of Vice. See http://www.pv.gov.sa/letter/Pages/Default.aspx.
68. http://www.pv.gov.sa/.
69. These were the King Abd Allah Chair for Hisba and the Application of Its Precepts in the Contemporary Era (King Saud University in Riyadh), the Prince Sultan ibn Abd al-Aziz Chair for Research on Youth and Hisba Affairs (King Abd al-Aziz University in Jeddah), the Prince Nayif ibn Abd al-Aziz Chair in Promoting Virtue and Preventing Vice Studies (Islamic University of Medina), and the Prince Salman ibn Abd al-Aziz Chair for the Training of Muhtasib (Al-Imam University of Riyadh). See http://www.alarabiya.net/articles/2009/11/03/90071.html, http://www.al-jazirah.com/20100331/ln18d.htm, http://www.aawsat.com/details.asp?section=4&article=555245&issueno=11388, and http://ksa.daralhayat.com/ksaarticle/39550.
70. http://uqu.edu.sa/page/ar/1.
71. The directors of this project have established an Internet site and an official bulletin. See http://www.hisba.gov.sa/.
72. http://www.spa.gov.sa/details.php?id=674565; http://www.al-jazirah.com.sa/249885/plid.htm; http://www.aawsat.com/details.asp?section=4&article=523088&issueno=11154; http://www.al-madina.com/node/175326.
73. http://www.aawsat.com/details.asp?section=43&article=29722&issueno=11202.
74. http://www.aawsat.com/details.asp?section=17&issueno=11200&article=529385.
75. http://www.alriyadh.com/2010/04/04/article513000.html; http://www.aawsat.com/details.asp?section=43&article=530644&issueno=11209.
76. Moreover, this project for the first time presented a long-term vision, which implies a new change in the Hanbali-Wahhabi mentality. Up until then, the guardians of this tradition refused to imagine themselves in the future, for in keeping with the doctrine of predestination (*al-qada' wa al-qadar*), that amounted to anticipating divine will, something that was a sin in their eyes. Up until the early 1990s, for example, the ulama were opposed to subscribing to any form of insurance.
77. The logo was officially adopted on 27 December 1992.
78. Muslim, *al-Sahih*, no. 70.

79. Al-Bukhari, *al-Sahih*, no. 2313.
80. http://www.mofa.gov.sa/detail.asp?InNewsItemID=24887&InTemplateKey=print.
81. *Nizam hay'at al-amr bi al-ma'ruf wa al-nahy 'an al-munkar*, p. 12.
82. *Al-Hisba*, no. 39, 1422, p. 18; http://aawsat.com/details.asp?section=43&article=472927&issueno=10777; http://www.aldaawah.com/?p=1775.
83. *Nizam hay'at al-amr bi al-ma'ruf wa al-nahy 'an al-munkar*, p. 11.
84. *Al-Taqrir al-sanawi 1427–1428*, p. 23.
85. *Akhbar al-hisba*, no. 3, 1415, p. 4.
86. Al-Tabari, *Tarikh al-umam wa al-muluk*, vol. 8, p. 522; Ibn al-Athir, *al-Kamil fi a-tarikh*, vol. 8, p. 551; al-Mas'udi, *Muruj al-dhahab*, vol. 4, p. 29; Miskawayh, *Tajarib al-umam*, vol. 6, p. 433; Ibn Kathir, *al-Bidaya wa al-nihaya*, vol. 10, p. 247; Anonymous, *al-'Uyun wa al-hada'iq*, vol. 3, p. 353.
87. Author interviews with several retired hisba agents, June 2006, May 2007, and April 2009.
88. Ibn Ibrahim Al al-Shaykh, *Fatawa wa rasa'il*, nos. 1435, 1438, 1441; http://www.alarabiya.net/articles/2008/03/16/47009.html; http://www.saaid.net/alsafinh/h14.htm; http://www.cib.gov.sa/art_uot59.htm; http://www.al-madina.com/node/145902; http://www.saaid.net/alsafinh/h10.htm; http://www.alriyadh.com/2008/05/03/article339412.html; http://www.aawsat.com/details.asp?section=43&article=564425&issueno=11455.
89. *Al-Da'wa*, no. 1435, 1414, p. 3 ("preventative medicine"); http://www.daralhayat.com/portalarticlendah/124893 ("safety valve"); *Akhbar al-hisba*, no. 0, 1414, pp. 3–4, and no. 1, 1415, p. 5 ("carry out the duty").
90. Braud, *L'émotion en politique* and *Petit traité des émotions*.
91. Balandier, *Le détour*, p. 88.
92. *Nizam hay'at al-amr bi al-ma'ruf wa al-nahy 'an al-munkar*, p. 13.
93. *Al-La'iha al-tanfidhiyya li-nizam hay'at al-amr bi al-ma'ruf wa al-nahy 'an al-munkar*, pp. 21–22.
94. Al-Tirmidhi, *al-Sunan*, no. 378; al-Nasa'i, *al-Sunan*, no. 461
95. Al-Duwayyish, ed., *Fatawa al-lajna al-da'ima*, nos. 4321, 6396.
96. Author interviews with several imams and neighborhood notables in the towns of Riyadh, Burayda, Unayza, Jeddah, Mecca, Medina, and Abha, June 2006, May 2007, April 2008, April 2009, and March 2010. Also see *al-Hisba*, no. 29, 1420, pp. 12–13.
97. http://www.okaz.com.sa/new/Issues/20100417/Con20100417344908.htm; http://www.al-madina.com/node/240958; http://www.aleqt.com/2010/04/24/article_383553.html; http://www.aawsat.com/details.asp?section=43&article=564425&issueno=11455; http://www.alwatan.com.sa/news/writerdetail.asp?issueno=3500&id=19112&Rname=51.
98. http://www.alifta.net/BayanNew.aspx?NewsID=2.
99. Many of the polemical articles against al-Ghamidi have been gathered together on "Ibn Qasim's Blog": http://ibnqasim.blogspot.com/.
100. http://www.aleqt.com/2010/04/25/article_384165.html; http://ksa.daralhayat.com/ksa article/134656; http://www.lematin.ch/flash-info/monde/arabie-confusion-autour-limogeage-chef-police-religieuse.
101. Several fatawa by members of the establishment and opinion pieces by their collaborators are available at http://www.saaid.net/female/k.htm.

102. Abu Zayd, *Hirasat al-fadila*; *Al-Hisba*, no. 37, 1421, p. 22; http://www.pv.gov.sa/news/Pages/n1-17830.aspx; http://www.saaid.net/Doat/khalid/12.htm.
103. http://www.alifta.net/BayanNew.aspx?NewsID=4.
104. These consisted, in particular, of Royal Orders no. 11651 (1 March 1983), no. 2966 (19 June 1984), and no. 759/8 (31 December 2000).
105. http://www.youtube.com/watch?v=vmEUc5fxy9w. Al-Shathri also specified the establishment of juridico-religious commissions (*lijan shar'iyya*) to verify the propriety of areas of scientific study, particularly the theory of evolution.
106. http://www.alwatan.com.sa/news/newsdetail.asp?issueno=3293&id=120058&groupID=0; http://www.okaz.com.sa/new/Issues/20091005/Con20091005307886.htm; http://www.al-madina.com/node/184564. Abd Allah dismissed this ulama from his duties because he was in breach of Hanbali-Wahhabi tradition. On the one hand, he publicly offered advice (*nasiha*) to the sovereign, something that tradition stipulates must take place in private. On the other hand, he intervened in a domain that is reserved to the king to the degree that the university can be considered a fief and a "deterritorialized" island where the king has full liberty to act in the interest of advancing his political affairs.
107. See, for example, http://www.okaz.com.sa/new/Issues/20091209/Con20091209319589.htm; http://www.alwatan.com.sa/news/writerdetail.asp?issueno=3500&id=19112&Rname=51; http://www.alarabiya.net/articles/2009/12/12/93988.html.
108. http://www.saaid.net/Minute/291.htm; http://www.youtube.com/watch?v=XnPbzHfzuAo; http://www.mashahd.net/view_video.php?viewkey=19ab1995838afb3d7b92.
109. On the divisions within the royal house and the question of succession, see Mouline, "Pouvoir et transition."
110. http://www.youtube.com/watch?v=97UGk5QdNfg&NR=1; http://www.youtube.com/watch?v=2dsW9848jW8&feature=related; http://www.youtube.com/watch?v=dXgZB_kX15I&feature=related; http://www.youtube.com/watch?v=OlDSFUoc69A&NR=1; http://www.al-jazirah.com/20100618/fn1d.htm; http://www.alwatan.com.sa/Local/News_Detail.aspx?ArticleID=7521&CategoryID=5; http://aawsat.com/details.asp?section=1&issueno=11525&article=574514&feature=; http://www.saaid.net/alsafinh/h43.htm; http://www.alshameh1.com/news-action-show-id-1802.htm.
111. http://www.alrassedu.gov.sa/index/news/news-action-show-id-1378.htm.
112. Isolated and still peripheral voices within the corporation—in particular, the director of the Mecca office of the Committee for the Promotion of Virtue and the Prevention of Vice, Ahmad al-Ghamidi—profited from the debate occasioned by al-Shathri's dismissal to express themselves in favor of a form of gender mixing that is consistent with the precepts of sharia. See http://www.youtube.com/watch?v=oPYw2PueDX4&feature=player_embedded; http://www.alriyadh.com/2010/05/01/article521378.html; http://www.alarabiya.net/articles/2010/01/10/96895.html; http://www.alarabiya.net/articles/2010/05/14/108594.html; http://www.alwatan.com.sa/news/writerdetail.asp?issueno=3395&id=17084&Rname=396; http://www.youtube.com/watch?v=KGxeEcdOE00.
113. Statistics are available beginning in 1994.

114. Al-Duwayyish, ed., *Fatawa al-lajna al-da'ima*, nos. 220, 2017, 9336, 2871, 3321, 4141, 5476, 4335, 6773 (popular rituals); nos. 837, 845, 4228, 6285, 6289, 9295 (acts of sorcery).
115. Statistics are available from 1993.
116. *Akhbar al-hisba*, no. 8, 1416, p. 5.
117. *Al-La'iha al-tanfidhiyya li-nizam hay'at al-amr bi al-ma'ruf wa al-nahy 'an al-munkar*, p. 23.
118. Ibid., p. 24.
119. Ibid., p. 37
120. Ibid., pp. 25–31.
121. Ibid., p. 39.
122. Ibid., p. 34.
123. When it is a matter of cases in which the punishment is set by the Law (alcohol, adultery, drug trafficking, etc.), they must transfer the file to the police and from there to the courts.
124. Letter from the President of the Council of Ministers, no. 4/b/2008, 30 September 1987, Institute of Public Administration, Riyadh.
125. http://www.moj.gov.sa/Systems/Nezam.tmp.html.
126. *Al-La'iha al-tanfidhiyya li-nizam hay'at al-amr bi al-ma'ruf wa al-nahy 'an al-munkar*, p. 33.

CHAPTER 9. AT THE CROSSROADS

1. On the history and sociology of this movement, see Lacroix, *Les islamistes saoudiens*, pp. 109–121; Trofimov, *Siege of Mecca*; Hegghammer and Lacroix, "Rejectionist Islamism"; and Kechichian, "Islamic Revivalism."
2. Juhayman and his associates were freed with the help of Abd al-Aziz ibn Baz, who did not believe that the group was political in nature.
3. Al-Qahtani was chosen because his physical appearance and name corresponded to the descriptions of the Mahdi given by the traditions attributed to the Prophet of Islam. On the figure of the Mahdi, see Ei^2, vol. 7, p. 1221; Margoliouth, "On Mahdis and Mahdiism"; Sachedina, *Islamic Messianism*; Madelung, "The Sufyani"; Cook, *Contemporary Muslim*; Garcia-Arenal, *Messianism*; Filiu, *L'Apocalypse*.
4. For an overview of the traditions attributed to the Prophet concerning the Mahdi and criticism of same, see Ibn Khaldun, *al-Muaqddima*, pp. 245–259.
5. On the figure of the *mujaddid*, see Ei^2, vol. 7, p. 292; Landau-Tasseron, "The 'Cyclical Reform.'"
6. These marvels did not come to pass. After two weeks of intermittent fighting, the insurgents, diminished by their losses and a lack of ammunition, had to surrender to Saudi troops, who were supported by the special forces of several countries, including France.
7. Author interviews with three ulama present on this occasion, April 2005, June 2006, and April 2009.

8. *Al-Da'wa*, no. 725, 1400, pp. 2–3.
9. Al-Farra', *al-Ahkam al-sultaniyya*, pp. 54–60; Ibn Taymiyya, *al-Siyasa al-shar'iyya*, pp. 68–84.
10. For a summary of all interventions, see *Al-Da'wa*, no. 732, 1400.
11. Juhayman claimed to have had a vision in which the Prophet Muhammad told him that Muhammad ibn Abd Allah al-Qahtani was the Mahdi. See *Al-Da'wa*, no. 722, 1400, pp. 10–13.
12. *Majallat al-Buhuth al-Islamiyya*, no. 5, 1400, pp. 309–311.
13. Ibid., pp. 322–324; *Al-Da'wa*, no. 731, 1400, pp. 8–9.
14. It must be noted that the Saudi sovereigns had officially held the title of imam since the nineteenth century.
15. Qur'an 4/59.
16. Juhayman thus followed the strategy adopted by most representatives of messianic ideologies, who break all intellectual ties with their milieu, particularly those linking them with the religious authorities of their time.
17. In certain Qur'anic verses and prophetic traditions, *ta'ifa* refers to the positive notion of the group of the elected.
18. In the name of Allah, the Beneficent, the Merciful. Praise be to Allah, Lord of the Worlds, the Beneficent, the Merciful. Master of the Day of Judgment, Thee (alone) we worship; Thee (alone) we ask for help. Show us the straight path, the path of those whom Thou hast favored; not the (path) of those who earn Thine anger nor of those who go astray.
19. Hanbalism, it must be noted, has generally been more nomocentric than other Muslim traditions and further removed from messianic ideas. Indeed, it possesses fewer writings on these questions than any other tradition. And we have seen above how Hanbali-Wahhabi ulama reacted to the messianic ideas circulating in Najd in the late nineteenth century.
20. Several Hanbali-Wahhabi ulama went so far as to reject the idea of the Mahdi, arguing that most traditions attributed to the Prophet are apocryphal. See *Majallat al-Buhuth al-Islamiyya*, no. 13, 1405, pp. 101–113.
21. On Saudi Islamism, see al-Rasheed, *Contesting the Saudi State*, pp. 59–101; Fandy, *Saudi Arabia and the Politics of Dissent*; Teitelbaum, *Holier Than Thou*; Lacroix, *Les islamistes saoudiens*.
22. Lacroix, *Les islamistes saoudiens*, pp. 48–97.
23. Almond, *Crisis, Choice, and Change*.
24. Al-Rasheed, *History of Saudi Arabia*, p. 149.
25. Circular no. 3719/1409, 21 December 1988, Institute of Public Administration, Riyadh.
26. Author interviews with former owners of Islamic cassette stores and officials from the Ministry of the Interior, May 2007, April 2009, and March 2010.
27. Author interviews with witnesses of this meeting, June 2006, May 2007, and April 2008.
28. *Majallat al-Buhuth al-Islamiyya*, no. 29, 1411, pp. 349–350.
29. Ibid., pp. 349, 350.

30. Ibid., no. 30, 1411, pp. 273–279; *Al-Da'wa*, no. 1253, 1411, pp. 36–39, no. 1258, 1411, pp. 19–23, and no. 1280, 1411, p. 27; *Majallat al-majma' al-fiqhi*, no. 5, 1411.
31. Al-Sbayyil, "Hukm al-isti'ana bi-ghayr al-muslimin fi al-jihad."
32. http://www.binbaz.org.sa/mat/8341; *Al-Da'wa*, no. 1257, 1411, pp. 14–17, no. 1280, 1411, pp. 13–18, 19–20.
33. al-Rashid, ed., *Saudi Arabia Enters the World*, vol. 1, pp. 201–203 (American technicians); Abd al-Aziz ibn Baz, *Naqd al-qawmiyya al-'arabiyya 'ala daw' al-islam wa al-waqi'*, *Majmu'at fatawa wa maqalat mutanawwi'a*, vol. 1, pp. 300–301 (foreign troops).
34. Dekmejian, "The Liberal Impulse."
35. Author interview with one of the protagonists in this encounter, April 2009.
36. For an analysis and translation of this petition, see Lacroix, *Les islamistes saoudiens*, pp. 214–218, 346–347.
37. *Majallat al-Buhuth al-Islamiyya*, no. 32, 1411–1412, pp. 341–343.
38. http://www.binbaz.org.sa/mat/8201; http://www.binbaz.org.sa/mat/8360; http://www.binbaz.org.sa/mat/8372; http://www.ibnothaimeen.com/all/noor/article_3136.shtml; *Al-Da'wa*, no. 1323, 1412, pp. 8–9, and no. 1328, 1412, pp. 24–25; *Majallat al-Buhuth al-Islamiyya*, no. 32, 1411–1412, pp. 6–7, 116–121, no. 33, 1412, pp. 338–345, and no. 35, 1412–1413, pp. 6–12.
39. Lacroix, *Les islamistes saoudiens*, pp. 219–220.
40. *Bayan Hay'at kibar al-'Ulama' hawla mudhakkirat al-nasiha*, 39th session, 16 September 1992. Copy in the author's possession.
41. Al-Duwayyish, ed., *Fatawa al-lajna al-da'ima*, no. 1674; Bakr Abu Zayd, *Hukm al-intima' ila al-firaq wa al-ahzab wa al-jama'at al-islamiyya*, in *al-Majmu'a al-'ilmiyya*; Fawzan, *al-Ijtima' wa nabdh al-furqa*; *Al-Da'wa*, no. 1293, 1411, pp. 3–9, no. 1621, 1418, p. 41, no. 1620, 1418, pp. 22–25; *Majallat al-Buhuth al-Islamiyya*, no. 33, 1412, pp. 96–100; http://www.binbaz.org.sa/mat/46; http://www.binbaz.org.sa/mat/1759; http://www.binbaz.org.sa/mat/21342; http://www.fatwa1.com/anti-erhab/hezbeh/ftawa_jamaat.html#.
42. Dekmejian, "Rise of Political Islamism"; Teitelbaum, *Holier Than Thou*, pp. 9–40.
43. In addition to being paralyzed, Abd al-Razzaq Afifi suffered from hypertension and severe diabetes.
44. In 1992, Ibn Ghusun spent several months in the United States, where he underwent several surgeries, including a liver transplant.
45. It must be noted that for both psychological and ideological reasons, several lower-ranking Hanbali-Wahhabi ulama did indeed support the Islamists' demands. Believing that they did not occupy the rank they deserved in the religious establishment, these ulama were very resentful toward their seniors on the Committee of Grand Ulama. They had also refused to accept the process of routinization of the tradition, particularly in what concerned the call for assistance from non-Muslim troops.
46. *Al-Da'wa*, no. 1392, 1413, p. 15, and no. 1460, 1415, pp. 8–9.
47. In order to monitor the operation of this strategic ministry from a distance, in October 1994 the ruling house revived the High Council of Islamic Affairs, which is officially responsible for supervising preaching at the international level. See *Al-Da'wa*, no. 1503, 1416, pp. 20–22.

48. Hegghammer, "Violence politique."
49. On this phenomenon, see Hegghammer, *Jihad in Saudi Arabia*; Filiu, *Les Neuf*, pp. 137–154; Riedel and Saad, "Al Qaeda's Third Front"; al-Rasheed, *Contesting the Saudi State*, pp. 134–174; Cordesman and Obaid, "Al-Qaeda in Saudi Arabia"; Thomas, *Les Hommes d'al-Qaida*, pp. 39–58.
50. Bourdieu, *La distinction*, p. 281.
51. Apart from adopting a few elements of the Hanbali-Wahhabi creed and the nineteenth-century ideology of *al-wala' wa al-bara'*, Al-Qaeda and its offshoots did not favor a particular school in the legal domain and in the political domain followed the ideology of the Muslim Brotherhood, particularly its Qutbist current. Osama bin Laden (d. 2011) was almost exclusively socialized among the Muslim Brotherhood in Saudi Arabia and later in Afghanistan.
52. Al-Husayn, ed., *al-Fatawa al-shar'iyya*, pp. 71–109.
53. Abd al-Aziz Al al-Shaykh, *Kulluna 'Ulama' sultan*, available at http://www.sohari.com/nawader_v/fatawe/almufti.html.
54. Al-Husayn, ed., *al-Fatawa al-shar'iyya*, pp. 19–59.
55. *Majallat al-Buhuth al-Islamiyya*, no. 56, 1419, pp. 357–362.
56. Weber, *Économie et Société*, vol. 1, p. 97.
57. See, for example, Wagemakers, "Transformation of a Radical Concept." The historical portion of this article, however, must be read with caution as it contains many mistranslations and misleading turns of phrase. Huntington, *Clash of Civilizations*.
58. As we have already seen, the Jihadists drew heavily upon this ulama's writings on the question of *al-wala' wa al-bara'*.
59. Muhammad ibn Abd al-Latif Al al-Shaykh had used the same arguments to persuade the Ikhwan in the early twentieth century.
60. *Al-Da'wa*, no. 1135, 1408, p. 32, and no. 1136, 1408, pp. 12–13; *Fatawa al-'Ulama' fi al-takfir wa al-muwalat*, CD-ROM in the author's possession; al-Fawzan, *Sharh risalat*.
61. On the history of jihad in Islam, see Ei^2, vol. 2, p. 551; Cook, *Understanding Jihad*; Bonner, *Le Jihad*; Morabia, *Le Gihad*.
62. The religious establishment's most important fatawa concerning jihad have been collected in a single volume. See al-Husayn, ed., *Tadhkir al-'ibad*.
63. *Al-Da'wa*, no. 1043, 1406, p. 5, no. 1100, 1407, pp. 5, 26–27, and no. 1431, 1414, p. 26. Most Saudis who traveled to these countries went by way of Muslim Brotherhood networks and their offshoots. Saudi financing for these various adventures had more to do with political considerations than with religious feeling.
64. *Majallat al-Buhuth al-Islamiyya*, no. 24, 1409, pp. 384–387.
65. Al-Husayn, ed., *al-Fatawa al-shar'iyya*, pp. 23–59.
66. Al-Husayn, ed., *Tadhkir al-'ibad*, pp. 87–107.
67. For example, the Permanent Commission of *ifta'* received the following question: When a female Muslim resistance fighter believes that infidel soldiers will rape her and force information from her concerning the *mujahidun*, can she commit suicide? The response was as short as it was performative: "the religion forbids suicide even if this woman is subjected to what she describes. In the case of nonconsensual rape, she

will be pardoned"; ibid., p. 87. The ulama also condemned the suicide attacks carried out by Palestinian activists; ibid., pp. 88, 96–97.
68. Al-Husayn, ed., *al-Fatawa al-shar'iyya*, pp. 111–129.
69. Ibid., pp. 132–139.
70. http://www.alifta.net/BayanNew.aspx?NewsID=5.
71. http://www.alarabiya.net/articles/2010/06/05/110510.html; http://international.daralhayat.com/ksaarticle/147713.
72. The Royal Order is available at http://www.alriyadh.com/2010/08/12/article551239.html.
73. Only fatawa of a personal nature, particularly concerning questions of ritual, are excluded from this measure. But they must be issued in private while avoiding questions relating to dogma and excommunication.
74. At this writing, the Saudi religious authorities have yet to establish any system to regulate the domain of fatawa.
75. http://www.kacnd.org/.
76. http://www.alriyadh.com/2009/10/19/article 467394.html; http://www.alarabiya.net/articles/2008/06/04/50949.html; http://web.alquds.com/node/85843; http://www.aljazeera.net/News/archive/archive?ArchiveId=1161310; http://www.albiladdaily.com/news.php?action=show&id=593.

BIBLIOGRAPHY

ARABIC AND EUROPEAN LANGUAGE SOURCES

Abbassi, Ali Bey el-, *Voyages d'Ali Bey en Afrique et en Asie*, Paris, 1814.
Abd Allah, Anwar, *al-'ulama' wa al-'arsh*, Paris, 2004.
Abd al-Jabbar, Umar, *Siyar wa tarajim ba'd 'ulama'ina fi al-qarn al-rabi' 'ashar*, Jeddah, 1982.
Abd al-Rahman, Abd al-Rahim, *al-Dawla al-Su'udiyya al-ula*, Cairo, 1975.
———, *Muhammad 'Ali wa shibh al-jazira al-'arabiyya*, Cairo, 1981.
Abda, Muhammad al-, *Khawatir fi al-da'wa*, London/Riyadh, 1997.
———, *Ta'ammulat fi al-fikr wa al-da'wa*, Amman, 2000.
Abhat hay'at kibar al-'ulama', Riyadh, 2001–2004.
Abu As'ad, Muhammad, *al-Su'udiyya wa al-ikhwan al-muslimun*, Cairo, 1995.
Abu Dawud, *al-Sunan*, Beirut, 1988.
Abu Dharr, *Thawra fi rihab Makka*, Beirut, 1980.
Abu Kulayla, Hani, *al-Ta'lim al-'ali fi al-mamlaka al-'arabiyya al-su'udiyya*, Alexandria, 2001.
Abu Zayd, Bakr, *al-Majmu'a al-'ilmiyya*, Riyadh, 1996.
———, *Hirasat al-fadila*, Cairo, 2006.
———, *Tasnif al-nas bayna al-zann wa al-yaqin*, Riyadh, 1994.
———, *'Ulama' al-hanabila min al-imam Ahmad al-mutawaffa sanat 241 ila wafayat 'am 1420*, Riyadh, 2001.
Ahmad, Rif'at Sayyid, *Rasa'il Juhayman al-'Utaybi: qa'id al-muqtahimin li al-masjid al-haram bi-Makka*, Cairo, 2004.
Ahmad, Salah al-Din Maqbul, *Da'wat shaykh al-islam Ibn Taymiyya wa atharuha fi al-harakat al-islamiyya al-mu'asira*, New Delhi, 1992.
Ajalani, Munir al-, *Tarikh al-bilad al-'arabiyya al-su'udiyya*, Beirut, n.d.
Ajami, Muhammad al-, *al-Rasa'il al-mutabadala bayna Jamal al-din al-Qasimi wa Mahmud Shukri al-Alusi*, Beirut, 2001.
Al al-Shaykh, Abd al-Aziz, *Lamahat 'an al-ta'lim wa bidayatuh fi al-mamlaka al-'arabiyya al-su'udiyya*, Riyadh, 1992.

Al al-Shaykh, Abd al-Latif ibn Abd al-Rahman, *Misbah al-zalam fi al-radd 'ala man kadhaba 'ala al-shaykh al-imam*, Riyadh, n.d.

Al al-Shaykh, Abd al-Latif ibn Hasan, *'Uyun al-rasa'il wa al-ajwiba 'ala al-rasa'il*, Riyadh, n.d.

Al al-Shaykh, Abd al-Rahman, *Da'wat al-shaykh wa munasiruh*, Cairo, 1964.

——, *Mashahir 'ulama' Najd*, Riyadh, 1972.

Al al-Shaykh, Abd al-Rahman ibn Hasan, *al-Maqamat*, Riyadh, 2005.

——-, *Minhaj al-ta'sis wa al-taqdis fi al-radd 'ala Ibn Jirjis*, Riyadh, 1987.

Al-Shaykh, Muhammad ibn Ibrahim, *Fatawa wa rasa'il*, Mecca, 1978.

Ali, Ahmad, *Al Su'ud*, Beirut, 1993.

——, *Dhikrayat*, Al-Ta'if, 1977.

Ali, Ibrahim Muhammad al-, *Muhammad Nasir al-Din al-Albani: muhaddith al-'asr wa nasir al-sunna*, Damascus, 2001.

Al-La'iha al-tanfidhiyya li-nizam hay'at al-amr bi al-ma'ruf wa al-nahy 'an al-munkar, Riyadh, 1987.

Alusi, al-, *Tarikh Najd*, Cairo, 1924.

Amin, Ahmad, *Zu'ama' al-islah fi al-'asr al-hadith*, Beirut, n.d.

Amir, Abd al-Latif al-, *al-Haraka al-islamiyya fi al-jazira al-'arabiyya*, n.p., 1987.

Amr, Ali al-, *Lamahat 'an ta'lim al-banat fi al-mamlaka bayna al-madi wa al-hadir*, Unayza, 1985.

Anonymous, *al-'Uyun wa al-hada'iq*, Damascus, 1973.

Anonymous, *Kayf kan zuhur shaykh al-islam Muhammad b. 'Abd al-Wahhab*, Riyadh, 1983.

Anonymous, *Lam' al-shihab fi sirat al-shaykh Muhammad ibn Abd al-Wahhab*, Beirut, 1967.

Anonymous, *Lam' al-Shihab fi sirat Muhammad b. 'Abd al-Wahhab*, Riyadh, n.d.

Aqil, Abd Allah al-, *Min a'lam al-haraka wa al-da'wa al-islamiyya al-mu'asira*, Kuwait, 2001.

Aql, Nasir al-, *al-'ulama' hum al-du'at*, Riyadh, 1992.

Aqqad, Salah al-, *Jazirat al-'arab fi al-'asr al-hadith*, Cairo, 1969.

Arfaj, Abd Allah al-, *al-Madhahib al-arba'a fi al-Ahsa'*, n.p., 2004.

Armstrong, H. C., *Lord of Arabia Ibn Saud: The Intimate Study of a King*, Riyadh, 2005.

Asbar al-'ulama' wa al-mutakhassisin fi shari'a al-islamiyya fi al-mamlaka al-'arabiyya al-su'udiyya, Riyadh, n.d.

Awda, Salman al-, *Man yamlik haqq al-ijtihad*, Riyadh, 2003.

——, *Nahwa fiqh al-hiwar*, Riyadh, 2003.

Baghdadi, Abd Allah, *al-Intilaqa al-ta'limiyya fi al-mamlaka 'arabiyya al-su'udiyya*, Jeddah, 1948.

Baghdadi, al-, *'Unwam al-majd fi bayan ahwal Baghdad wa al-Basra wa Najd*, Baghdad, n.d.

Barbahari, al-, *Sharh al-sunna*, Riyadh, 1998.

Bassam, al-, *Taqnin al-shari'a adraruhu wa mafasiduhu*, Mecca, 1960.

——, *'Ulama' Najd khilal thamaniyyat qurun*, Riyadh, 1997.

Bibliography

Bayhaqi, al-, *al-Sunan al-kubra*, no. 4744, Beirut, 1968.
Buhuti, al-, *al-Rawd al-Mubi' sharh zad al-mustaqni'*, Riyadh, 1988.
——, *Kashshaf al-qina' 'an al-iqna'*, Riyadh, 2003–2008.
——, *Sharh muntaha al-iradat*, Riyadh, 2000.
Bukhari, al-, *al-Sahih*, Damascus, 1994.
Burckhardt, John Lewis, *Notes on the Bedouins and Wahábys: Collected during His Travels in the East*, London, 1831.
Corancez, Louis de, *Histoire des wahabis: depuis leur origine jusqu'à la fin de 1809*, Paris, 2008.
Dabbagh, Mustafa al-, *al-Jazira al-'arabiyya*, Beirut, 1965.
Dahlan, *Khulasat al-kalam fi bayan umara' al-balad al-haram*, Cairo, 1887.
Darimi, al-, *al-Sunan*, Riyadh, 2000.
Dawud, Abd al-Aziz al-, *'An al-shaykh Muhammad ibn Ibrahim Al al-shaykh rahimahu Allah–sirat 'alim . . . wa masirat imam*, Riyadh, 2004.
Dhahabi, al-, *Siyar a'lam al-nubala'*, Beirut, 1996.
Duwayyish, Ahmad al-, ed., *Fatawa al-lajna al-da'ima lil-buhuth al-'ilmiyya wa al-ifta'*, Riyadh, 2005.
Fakhiri, al-, *al-Akhbar al-najdiyya*, Riyadh, 1970.
Farra', Abu Ya'la al-, *al-Ahkam al-sultaniyya*, Beirut, 2000.
Fawzan, Salih al-, *al-Ijtima' wa nabdh al-furqa*, Riyadh, 2004.
——, *Sharh risalat al-dala'il fi hukm muwalat ahl al-ishrak*, Riyadh, 2007.
Fiqi, Muhammad Hamid al-, *Athar al-da'wa al-wahhabiyya fi al-islah al-dini wa al-'umrani fi jazirat al-'arab wa ghayriha*, Cairo, 1935.
Fuhayd, Abd al-Aziz al-, *Mihnat al-qada' al-su'udi: tawthiq asbab istiqalat amir Makka wa sijn wakilihi*, London, 2002.
Furayh, Ahmad al-, *al-Shaykh Ibn Baz wa mawaqifuhu al-thabita*, Kuwait, 2000.
Ghamidi, Sa'id Falih al-, *al-Bina' al-qabali wa al-tahaddur fi-l-mamlaka al-'arabiyya al-su'udiyya*, Alexandria, 1990.
Hajlawi, Nur al-Din al-, *Ta'thir al-fikr al-nasiri 'ala-l-khalij al-'arabi 1952–1971*, Beirut, 2003.
Hamza, Fu'ad, *al-Bilad al-'arabiyya al-su'udiyya*, Riyadh, 1968.
——, *Qalb al-jazira al-'arabiyya*, Riyadh, 1968.
Hanbal ibn Ishaq, *Mihnat al-imam Ahmad ibn Muhammad ibn Hanbal*, Cairo, 1987.
Haraka al-islamiyya lil-islah, al-, *al-Qadiyya al-su'udiyya bayna al-sa'il wa al-mujib*, n.p., n.d.
Harbi, Ubayyid al-, *Dawr al-'ulama' wa al-du'at fi 'amaliyyat rad' al-ghuzat*, Riyadh, 1993.
Harras, Muhammad Khalil, *al-Haraka al-wahhabiyya*, Beirut, n.d.
Harrison, Paul, "Al Riyadh, the Capital of Nejd," *Moslem World*, vol. 8, 1918, pp. 412–419.
Hawali, Safar al-, *Kashf al-ghumma 'an 'ulama' al-umma*, London, 1991.
Huber, Charles, *Journal d'un voyage en Arabie*, Paris, 1891.
Huqayl, Hamad al-, *'Abd al-'Aziz fi al-tarikh*, Beirut, 1968.
Husayn, Ali Aba, *Lamha min tarikh madinat al-Zubayr*, Riyadh, 2009.

Husayn, Muhammad al-, ed., *al-Fatawa al-shar'iyya fi al-qadaya al-'asriyya*, Riyadh, 2004.
——, *Tadhkir al-'ibad bi-fatawa ahl al-'ilm fi al-jihad*, Riyadh, 2006.
Husayn, Sa'd al-, *Tasawwur islami li al-ta'lim al-thanawi*, Mecca, 1983.
Huzaymi, Nasir al-, *Ayyam ma'a Juhayman*, n.p., n.d.
Ibn 'Abbad, *Tarikh*, Riyadh, 1999.
Ibn 'Abd al-Barr, *Bahjat al-majalis*, Cairo, 1967.
Ibn Abd al-Hadi, *al-Jawhar al-Munaddad fi Tabaqat muta'akhkhiri Ashab Ahmad*, Cairo, 1987.
Ibn Abd al-Hadi, Yusuf, *Bad' al-'Uqla bi-libs al-khirqa*, manuscript in the Yahuda collection at Princeton University, Princeton, NJ.
Ibn Abd al-Wahhab, Muhammad, *Mu'allafat al-shaykh Muhammad b. 'Abd al-Wahhab* [Complete Works of Muhammad b. 'Abd al-Wahhab], Riyadh, 1978.
Ibn Abd al-Wahhab, Sulayman, *al-Sawa'iq al-ilahiyya fi al-radd 'ala al-wahhabiyya*, Cairo, 1987.
Ibn 'Abd Rabbih, *al-'Iqd al-farid*, Beirut, 1951.
Ibn Abi Ya'la, *Tabaqat al-hanabila*, Riyadh, 1999.
Ibn Ajrum, *al-Ajrumiyya*, Riyadh, 1992.
Ibn al-Athir, *al-Kamil fi al-tarikh*, Beirut, 1965.
Ibn al-Jawzi, *al-Muntazam fi akhbar al-muluk wa al-umam*, Beirut, 1992.
——, *Manaqib al-imam Ahmad*, Riyadh, 1979.
——, *Manaqib Umar b. Abd al-Aziz*, Alexandria, 1996.
——, *Manaqib Umar b. al-Khattab*, Beirut, 1985.
——, *Sifat al-safwa*, Haidarabad, 1969.
——, *Talbis Iblis*, Riyadh, 2002.
Ibn al-Muqaffa', *Risala fi al-Sahaba, al-Mu'allafat al-kamila*, Beirut, n.d.
Ibn Aqil, *Sharh Ibn 'Aqil 'ala alfiyyat Ibn Malik*, Beirut, 1997.
Ibn Batta, *al-Ibana al-sughra*, Medina/Damascus, 2002; translation Henri Laoust, *La profession de foi d'Ibn Batta*, Damascus, 1958.
Ibn Baz, Abd al-Aziz, *al-Adilla al-naqliyya wa al-hissiyya 'ala imkan al-su'ud ila al-kawakib wa 'ala jarayan al-shams wa al-qamar wa sukun al-ard*, Riyadh, 1982.
——, *Majmu'at fatawa wa maqalat mutanawwi'a*, Riyadh, 1999.
Ibn Bishr, *'Unwan al-majd fi tarikh najd*, Riyadh, 1971.
Ibn Dhish, Abd al-Latif, *al-Ta'lim al-hukumi al-munazzam fi 'ahd al-malik 'Abd al-'Aziz: nash'atuhu wa tatawwuruhu*, Mecca, 1987.
Ibn Ghannam, *Rawdat al-afkar wa al-afham li-murtad hal al-imam wa ti'dad ghazawat dhawi al-islam*, Cairo, 1949.
Ibn Hadhlul, *Tarikh muluk Al Su'ud*, Riyadh, 1960.
Ibn Hamdan, *Tarajim muta'khkhiri al-hanabila*, Dammam, 2000.
Ibn Hammad, Nu'aym, *Kitab al-fitan*, Damascus, 1993.
Ibn Hanbal, Abd Allah ibn Ahmad, *Kitab al-Sunna*, Cairo, 1930.
Ibn Hanbal, Ahmad, *al-Musnad*, Beirut, 1993.
——, *Kitab al-Wara'*, Cairo, 1922; partial translation in *Hespéris*, 1952, pp. 97–112.
Ibn Hisham, *al-Sira al-nabawiyya*, Riyadh, 1999.

Ibn Hisham, *Sharh qutr al-nada wa ball al-sada*, Beirut, 1998.
Ibn Humayd, *al-Suhub al-wahabila fi dara'ih al-hanabila*, Beirut, 1996.
Ibn Isa, *al-Radd 'ala ma ja' fi khulasat al-kalam min al-ta'n 'ala al-wahhabiyya wa al-iftira'*, copy of manuscript in possession of the author.
——, *'Aqd al-durar fima waqa'a min al-hawadith fi al-qarn al-thalith 'ashar wa awwal al-rabi' 'ashar*, Riyadh, 1966.
Ibn Kathir, *al-Bidaya wa al-nihaya*, Cairo, 2002.
——, *Tafsir al-qur'an al-'azim*, Beirut, 2000.
Ibn Khaldun, *al-Muqaddima*, Beirut, 1993.
Ibn Khuzayma, *Kitab al-tawhid*, Cairo, 1983.
Ibn Majja, *al-Sunan*, Cairo, 1998.
Ibn Malik, *al-Alfiyya fi al-nahw wa al-sarf*, Beirut, 2003.
Ibn Qasim, *al-Durar al-saniyya fi al-ajwiba al-najdiyya*, Riyadh, 2004.
Ibn Qayyim al-Jawziyya, *al-Kafiyya al-shafiyya fi al-intisar lil-firqa al-najiyya*, Beirut, 1993.
——, *al-Turuq al-hukmiyya fi al-siyasa al-shar'iyya*, Cairo, s.d.
——, *I'lam al-muwaqqi'in 'an rabb al-'alamin*, Beirut, 1973.
——, *Madarij al-salikin*, Beirut, 1973.
——, *Zad al-ma'ad fi sirat khayr al-'ibad*, Beirut, 1986.
Ibn Qudama, *Le livre des pénitents, Kitab al-tawwabin*, Damascus, 1961.
Ibn Qutayba, *'Uyun al-akhbar*, Cairo, 1964.
Ibn Rajab, *Dhayl Tabaqat al-hanabila*, Damascus, 1951.
Ibn Sa'd, *al-Tabaqat al-kubra*, Beirut, 1969.
Ibn Sahman, *al-Diya' al-shariq fi radd shubuhat al-madhiq al-Mariq*, Riyadh, 1992.
——, *al-Hadiyya al-saniyya wa al-tuhfa al-wahhabiyya al-najdiyya*, Cairo, 1924.
——, *al-Sawa'iq al-mursala al-wahhabiyya 'ala al-shubah al-dahida al-shamiyya*, Riyadh, n.d.
——, *Kashf ghayahib al-zalam 'an awham jala' al-afham*, Riyadh, n.d.
Ibn Sunaytan, Muhammad, *al-Nukhab al-su'udiyya: dirasa fi-l-tahawwulat wa ikhfaqat*, Beirut, 2004.
Ibn Taymiyya, *al-Amr bi al-ma'ruf wa al-nahy 'an al-munkar*, Beirut, 1984.
——, *al-Hisba fi al-islam*, Damascus, 1967.
——, *al-Khilafa wa al-mulk*, al-Zarqa', 1994.
——, *al-Sarim al-Maslul 'ala shatim al-rasul*, Dammam, 1997.
——, *al-Siyasa al-shar'iyya fi islah al-ra'i wa al-ra'iyya*, Beirut, 1983; Riyadh, 2003.
——, *'Aqidat ahl al-sunna wa al-firaq al-najiyya*, Cairo, 1939.
——, *Dar' al-ta'arud bayna al-'aql wa naql*, Beirut, 1997.
——, *Iqtida' al-sirat al-mustaqim li-mukhalafat ashab al-jahim*, Beirut, 1999.
——, *Majmu' al-fatawa*, Cairo, 1984.
——, *Minhaj al-sunna*, Riyadh, 1986.
——, *Naqd al-mantiq*, Cairo, 1951.
——, *Qa'ida mukhtasara fi wujub ta'at Allah wa rasulih wa wulat al-umur*, Riyadh, 1997.
——, *Tafsir surat al-ikhlas*, Cairo, 1905.

Ibn Ubayd, *Tadhkirat uli al-nuha wa al-'irfan bi ayyam al-wahid al-dayyam wa dhikr hawadith al-zaman*, Riyadh, n.d.

Ibn Yusuf, *Tarikh*, Riyadh, 1999.

Ikri, Abd al-Nabi al-, *al-Tanzimat al-yasariyya fi al-jazira wa al-khalij al-'arabi*, Beirut, 2003.

Izzi, Sulayman, *Tarikh*, Istanbul, 1784.

Jabarti, al-, *'Aja'ib al-athar fi al-tarajim wa al-akhbar*, Cairo, 1999.

Jabbar, Abd Allah Abd al-, *al-Tayyarat al-adabiyya al-haditha fi qalb al-jazira al-'arabiyya*, Cairo, 1959.

Jahiz, al-, *al-bukhala'*, Cairo, 1939.

Jami'a al-imam, Muhammad ibn Su'ud, *al-Kitab al-sanawi li-'am 1394*, Riyadh, 1975.

Jasir, Hamad al-, *al-Mu'jam al-jughrafi lil-bilad al-'arabiyya al-su'udiyya*, Riyadh, 1977.

Jazuli, al-, *Dala'il al-khayrat wa shawariq al-anwar fi dhikr al-salat 'ala al-nabiyy al-mukhtar*, Beirut 2000.

Jilani, Abd al-Qadir al-, *al-Ghunya li-talib tariq al-haqq*, Beirut, 1996.

Juhaymi, Nasir al-, *al-Malik 'Abd al-'Aziz fi al-sahafa al-'arabiyya*, Riyadh, 1999.

Jumu'a, Muhammad Kamal, *Intishar da'wat al-shaykh Muhammad b. 'Abd al-Wahhab kharij al-jazira al-'arabiyya*, Riyadh, 1977.

Kamil, Umar, *al-Mutatarrifun khawarij al-'asr*, Beirut, 2002.

Karami, al-, *Dalil al-Talib li-nayl al-matalib*, Damascus, 1961.

Katib, Ahmad al-, *al-Fikr al-siyasi al-wahhabi*, n.p., 2004.

Khallal, al-, *al-Musnad min masa'il Abi Abd Allah Ahmad b. Muhammad b. Hanbal*, Dhaka, 1975, pp. 21–25.

Khashuqji, Jamal, *'Alaqat harija: al-su'udiyya ba'da 11 sibtambar*, Beirut, 2002.

Khawarizmi, al-, *Mafatih al-'ulum*, Cairo, 1930.

Kishk, Muhammad Jalal, *al-Su'udiyyun wa al-hall al-islami*, West Hanover, MA, 1981.

Kitab al-ihsa'i lil-'am 1386, al-, Riyadh, 1967.

Laoust, Henri, *La profession de foi d'Ibn Batta*, Damascus, 1958.

——, *Essai sur les doctrines sociales et politiques de Taki-d-din Ahmad b. Taymiya*, Cairo, 1939.

Madani, Muhammad al-, *Firqat al-ikhwan al-islamiyya bi-Najd*, Cairo, 1955.

Mahzuz, Muhammad, *al-Hiwar wa al-wahda al-wataniyya fi al-mamlaka al-'arabiyya al-su'udiyya*, London, 2004.

Majdhub, Muhammad al-, *Ma'a al-mujahidin wa al-muhajirin fi Bakistan*, Medina, 1984.

——, *'Ulama' wa mufakkirun 'ariftuhum*, Cairo, 1986.

Majmu'at al-nuzum min 1345 [1926] ila 1357 [1938], Riyadh, n.d.

Majmu'at al-rasa'il wa al-masa'il al-najdiyya, Cairo, 1928.

Majmu'at al-tawhid al-najdiyya, Riyadh, 1999.

Majmu'at rasa'il wa fatawa fi masa'il muhimma tamussu ilayha hajat al-'asr li-'ulama' Najd al-a'lam, Cairo, 1928.

Manqur, al-, *al-Fawakih al-'adida fi al-masa'il al-mufida*, Damascus, 1963.

——, *Tarikh*, Riyadh, 1999.

Maqdisi, Abu Muhammad al-, *al-Kawashif al-jaliyya fi kufr al-dawla al-su'udiyya*, n.d., available at http://www.almaqdese.net.
Maqdisi, al-, *Ahsan al-Taqasim fi ma'rifat al-aqalim*, Leiden, 1906.
Marik, Fahd al-, *al-Tatawwur al-fikri fi al-jazira al-'arabiyya*, Damascus, 1962.
——, *Min shiyam al-malik 'Abd al-'Aziz*, Riyadh, 1980.
Mas'ari, Muhammad al-, *al-Adilla al-qat'iyya 'ala 'adam shar'iyyat al-dawla al-su'udiyya*, London, 1997, available at http://www.alhramain.com.
Mas'udi, al-, *Muruj al-dhahab wa ma'adin al-jawhar*, Beirut, 1989.
Mazhar, Abd al-Wahhab, *Dalil al-hajj*, Cairo, 1928.
Milad, Zaki al-, *Min al-turath ila al-ijtihad: al-fikr al-islami wa qadaya al-islah wa al-tajdid*, Beirut, 2004.
——, *Tajdid al-tafkir al-dini fi mas'alat al-mar'a*, Beirut, 2001.
Miskawayh, *Tajarib al-umam*, Cairo, 1914.
Mu'ayqil, Abd Allah al-, *al-Ma'ahid al-'ilmiyya bayna al-Madi wa al-hadir*, Riyadh, n.d.
Mudayris, Falah Abd Allah al-, *al-Ba'thiyyun fi al-khalij wa al-jazira al-'arabiyya*, Kuwait, 2002.
Mudhakkirat al-nasiha, n.p., 1992.
Muhammad, Muhammad Abd al-Jawwad, *al-Tatawwur al-tashri'i fi al-mamlaka al-'arabiyya al-su'udiyya*, Alexandria, 1977.
Mumayyiz, Amin al-, *al-Mamlaka al-'arabiyya al-su'udiyya kama 'ariftuha*, Baghdad, 1966.
Munajjid, Salah al-Din al-, *Faysal ibn 'Abd al-'Aziz*, Beirut, 1972.
Muntada al-islami al-, *al-Madaris wa al-katatib al-qur'aniyya-waqafat tarbawiyya wa idariyya*, London/Riyadh, 1997.
Muqrin, Abd al-Karim al-, *14 'aman ma'a samahat al-'allama al-shaykh Muhammad ibn Salih al-Uthaymin*, Riyadh, 2001.
Murri, Isam Abd al-Mun'im al-, *al-Qawl al-mufid fi hukm al-anashid*, Ajman, 2000.
Musil, Alois, *Northern Negd: A Topographical Itinerary*, New York, 1928.
Muslim, *al-Sahih*, Cairo, 1983.
Nahwa ada' mutamayyiz li-halaqat al-qur'an al-karim, London/Riyadh, 2002.
Namla, Ali al-, *al-Jihad wa al-mujahidun fi Afghanistan: waqfat taqyim*, Riyadh, 1994.
Nasa'i, al-, *al-Sunan*, Beirut, 1997.
Nasiri, al-, *al-Istiqsa li-akhbar al-maghrib al-aqsa*, Casablanca, 1997.
Niebuhr, M. Carsten, *Voyage de M. Niebuhr en Arabie et en d'autres pays de l'Orient*, Geneva, 1780.
Nizam hay'at al-amr bil-ma'ruf wa al-nahy 'an al-munkar, Riyadh, 2000.
Olesen, Niels Henrik, *Culte des saints et pèlerinages chez ibn Taymiyya*, Paris, 1991.
Palgrave, William G., *Narrative of a Year's Journey through Central and Eastern Arabia*, London, 1865 (French: *Une année de voyage dans l'Arabie central*, Paris, 1866).
Pelly, Lewis, *Report on a Journey to Riyadh in Central Arabia*, Bombay, 1866.
Philby, Harry, *The Heart of Arabia*, London, 1922.
Qadi, al-, *Rawdat al-Nazirin 'an ma'athir 'ulama' najd wa hawadith al-sinin*, Riyadh, 1989.

Qarni, Awad al-, *al-Hadatha fi mizan al-islam*, Jeddah, 2002.
Qasimi, Abd al-Allah al-, *al-Thawra al-wahhabiyya*, Cairo, 1936.
Qawaqji, Fawzi al-, *Mudhakkirat Fawzi al-Qawaqji*, Beirut, 1975.
Qazzaz, Hasan, *Ahl al-Hijaz bi-'abaqihim al-tarikhi*, Jeddah, 1994.
Qur'an, translation of Muhammad Hamidullah, Medina, 1990.
Rashid, Dari al-, *Nubdha tarikhiyya 'an Najd*, Riyadh, 1966.
Rashid, Ibrahim (al-), ed., *Saudi Arabia Enters the World: Secret U.S. Documents on the Emergence of the Kingdom of Saudi Arabia as a World Power, 1936–1949*, Salisbury, NC, 1980.
Ra'uf, Imad Abd al-Salam, *al-'Iraq fi watha'iq Muhammad 'Ali*, Baghdad, 1999.
Raymond, Jean, *L'origine des Wahabys: sur la naissance de leur puissance et sur l'influence dont ils jouissent comme nation*, Cairo, 1925.
Rida, Muhammad Rashid, *al-Khilafa*, Algier, 1983.
——, "al-Wahhabiyya wa al-'aqida al-diniyya li al-najdiyyin," *al-Manar*, vol. 27, 1926, pp. 275–278.
——, "al-Wahhabiyya wa da'wat al-Manar ila madhhab al-salaf," *al-Manar*, vol. 28, 1927, pp. 3–5.
——, *al-Wahhabiyyun wa al-Hijaz*, Cairo, 1925–1926.
——, "Rasa'il al-sunna wa al-shi'a," *al-Manar*, vol. 29, 1928, p. 683.
Rifa'i, Muhammad al-, *al-Mashru' al-islahi fi al-su'udiyya: qissat al-hawali wa al-'awda*, n.p., 1995.
Rihani, Amin al-, *Muluk al-'arab*, Beirut, 1987.
——, *Najd wa mulhaqatuha*, Beirut/Riyadh, 1981.
Rousseau, Jean-Baptiste, *Mémoire sur les Wahabis, les Nosaïris et les Ismaëlis*, Paris, 1818.
Sadleir, George, *Diary of a Journey across Arabia*, Bombay, 1866.
Sa'id, Amin, *Faysal al-'azim*, Beirut, 1965.
——, *Tharikh al-dawla al-su'udiyya*, Beirut/Riyadh, 1972.
Sa'id, Nasir al-, *Tarikh Al Su'ud*, n.p., n.d.
Salih, Abd al-Rahman, *al-Minhaj al-dirasi*, Riyadh, 1986.
Saqqaf, Hasan al-, *al-Salafiyya al-wahhabiyya: afkaruha al-asasiyya wa judhuruha al-tarikhiyya*, Beirut, 2005.
Sayf, Mahmud Muhammad, *Jughrafiyyat al-mamlaka al-'arabiyya al-su'udiyya*, al-Minya, 2006.
Sbayyil, Muhammad al-, "Hukm al-isti'ana bi-ghayr al-muslimin fi al-jihad," *Majallat al-majma' al-fiqhi*, no. 5, 1411, pp. 205–222.
Shamiyya, Jubran, *Al Su'ud: madihum wa mustaqbaluhum*, n.p., 1989.
Shathri, Muhammad al-, *Ithaf al-Labib fi sirat al-shaykh abu habib*, Riyadh, 1990.
Sulayman, Muhammad al-, "Athar al-da'wa al-salafiyya fi al-'alam al-islami," *Majallat kulliyat al-'ulum al-ijtima'iyya*, no. 1, 1977, pp. 449–491.
Suyuti, al-, *Tarikh al-khulafa'*, Beirut, n.d.
Tabari, al-, *Tarikh al-umam wa al-muluk*, Cairo, 1967.
Tahawi, Abd al-Hakim al-, *al-Malik Faysal wa al-'alaqat al-kharijiyya al-su'udiyya*, Cairo, 2002.

Tahawi, al-, *Matn al-'aqida al-tahawiyya*, Beirut, 1995.
Tahir, Ahmad Muhammad al-, ed., *Ansar al-sunna al-Muhammadiyya*, al-Mansura, 2004.
Tirmidhi, al-, *al-Sunan*, Beirut, 1996.
Turki, Abd Allah al-, *Usul madhhab al-imam Ahmad: dirasa usuliyya muqarana*, Beirut, 1998.
Tuwayjiri, Hammud al-, *al-Qawl al-baligh fi al-tahdhir min jama'at al-tabligh*, Riyadh, 1997.
Umar, Nasir al-, *Luhum al-'ulama' masmuma*, Riyadh, 1991.
Uthaymin, Muhammad ibn Salih al-, *al-Sahwa al-islamiyya–dawabit wa tawjihat*, Riyadh, 2003.
——, *Fitan al-majallat*, Riyadh, 1987.
——, *Kitab al-'ilm*, Riyadh, 2002.
——, *Majmu' fatawa wa rasa'il*, Riyadh, 1993.
Wadi'i, Muqbil al-, *Mushahadati fi-l-mamlaka al-'arabiyya al-su'udiyya*, Sanaa, 2005.
Wahba, Hafiz, *Jazirat al-'arab fi al-qarn al-'ishrin*, Cairo, 1956, 1961 (for the section concerning the creation of the Committee for the Promotion of Virtue and the Prevention of Vice).
——, *Khamsun 'aman fi jazirat al-'arab*, Cairo, 2001.
Wallin, Georg August, *Travels in Arabia*, Cambridge, 1979.
Wardani, Salih al-, *Ibn Baz faqih Al Su'ud*, Cairo, 1998.
Wuhaym, Talib Muhammad, *Mamlakat al-Hijaz 1916–1925: dirasat al-awda' al-siyasiyya*, Bassora, 1982.
Yafi'i, al-, *Rawd al-Rayahin fi hikayat al-salihin*, Beirut, 2000.
Zahiri, Abu 'Abd al-Rahman al-, "Dunya al-Watha'iq," *Majallat al-Dir'iyya*, no. 2, 1998, pp. 264–326.
Zahran, Sayyid, *Muluk wa umara'. Al-Dawla wa al-din fi al-su'udiyya*, Cairo, n.d.
Zamil, Salah al-, ed., *'Abd Allah b. Humayd fi 'uyun muhibbih wa talamidhatih wa ba'd rasa'ilih wa atharih al-'ilmiyya*, Riyadh, 2008.
Zirikli, Khayr al-Din al-, *al-A'lam*, Beirut, 1980.
——, *al-Wajiz fi sirat al-malik 'Abd al-'Aziz*, Beirut, 1999.
——, *Shibh al-jazira fi 'ahd al-malik 'Abd al-'Aziz*, Beirut, 1997.

CONTEMPORARY SCHOLARSHIP

Aarts, Paul, and Gerd Nonneman, eds., *Saudi Arabia in the Balance: Political Economy, Society, Foreign Relations*, London, 2005.
Abd al-Baqi, Muhammad Fu'ad, *al-Mu'jam al-mufahras li-alfaz al-qur'an al-karim*, Beirut, n.d.
Abd al-Fadil, Mahmud, *al-Tashkilat al-ijtima'iyya wa al-takwinat al-tabaqiyya fi al-watan al-'arabi: dirasa tahliliyya li-ahamm al-tatawwurat wa al-ittijahat khilal al-fatra 1945–1985*, Beirut, 1989.
Abd al-Jawwad, Muhammad, *al-Tatawwur al-tashri'i fi al-mamlaka al-'arabiyya al-Su'udiyya*, Cairo, 1977.

Abir, Mordechai, *Saudi Arabia and the Oil Era: Regime and Elites; Conflict and Collaboration*, London, 1988.
——, *Saudi Arabia: Government, Society and the Gulf Crisis*, London, 1993.
Albers, Henry H., *Saudi Arabia: Technocrats in a Traditional Society*, New York, 1989.
Almond, Gabriel, *Crisis, Choice, and Change: Historical Studies of Political Development*, Boston, 1973.
Amin, Bakri Shaykh, *al-Haraka al-adabiyya fi al-mamlaka al-'arabiyya al-su'udiyya*, Beirut, 2005.
Anawati, Georges C., and Louis Gardet, *Mystique musulmane: aspects et tendances, expériences et techniques*, Paris, 1986.
Anderson, Lisa, "Absolutism and the Resilience of Monarchy in the Middle East," *Political Science Quarterly*, no. 106, 1991, pp. 1–15.
——, "The State in the Middle East and North Africa," *Comparative Politics*, no. 1, 1987, pp. 1–18.
Arberry, Arthur John, *Le Soufisme*, Paris, 1952.
Area Handbook for Saudi Arabia, Washington, DC, 1966.
Aron, Raymond, "Classe sociale, classe politique, classe dirigeante," *Archives européennes de sociologie*, vol. 1, no. 2, 1960, pp. 260–281.
——, "Structure sociale et structure de l'élite," *Etudes sociologiques*, Paris, 1988, pp. 111–142.
Assman, Jan, *Moïse l'Égyptien. Un essai d'histoire de la mémoire*, Paris, 2001.
Aydarus, Muhammad Hasan, "Ittifaqiyyat Darin bayna Ibn Su'ud wa Britanya: dirasa watha'iqiyya," *Majallat jami'at Dimashq*, no. 1–2, 2005, pp. 93–124.
Ayubi, Nazih N., *Over-stating the Arab State: Politics and Society in the Middle East*, London, 1995.
Azami, Muhammad Mustafa, *Studies in Early Hadith Literature: With a Critical Edition of Some Early Texts*, Indianapolis, IN, 1978.
——, *Studies in Hadith Methodology and Literature: With a Critical Edition of Some Early Texts*, Indianapolis, IN, 1977.
Badie, Bertrand, *Les deux états: pouvoir et société en occident et en terre d'islam*, Paris, 1997.
Badie, Bertrand, and Pierre Birnbaum, *Sociologie de l'état*, Paris, 2004.
Bakkay, Latifa al-, *Harakat al-khawarij: nash'atuha wa tatawwuruha ila nihayat al-'asr al-umawi*, Beirut, 2001.
Balandier, Georges, *Le détour. Pouvoir et modernité*, Paris, 1985.
Baldick, Julian, *Mystical Islam: An Introduction to Sufism*, London, 1989.
Bassam, Ahmad al-, *al-Hayat al-'ilmiyya fi Najd fi al-qarnayn al-hadi al-'ashar wa al-thani 'ashar*, Riyadh, 2005.
Bayard, Jean-Pierre, *Le feu*, Paris, 1958.
Beblawi, Hazem, "al-Dawla al-ri'iyya fi al-'alam al-'aradi," in Ghassan Salamé, ed., *al-Umma wa al-dawla wa al-indimaj fi al-watan al-'arabi*, vol. 2, Beirut, 1989.
Beblawi, Hazem, and Giacomo Luciani, eds., *The Rentier State*, Peckenham, 1987.
Belaid, Sadok, "Role of Religious Institutions in Support of the State," Adeed Dawisha, ed., *Beyond Coercion: The Durability of the Arab State*, London, 1988, pp. 147–163.

Bibliography

Beling, Willard A., ed., *King Faisal and the Modernization of Saudi Arabia*, London, 1980.
Ben Achour, Yadh, *Aux Fondements de l'orthodoxie Sunnite*, Paris, 2008.
Benveniste, Émile, *Vocabulaire des institutions indo-européennes*, Paris, 1969.
Berg, Herbert, ed., *Method and Theory in the Study of Islamic Origins*, Leiden, 2003.
Bergen, Peter L., *Holy War Inc.: Inside the Secret World of Osama bin Laden*, New York, 2002.
——, *The Osama bin Laden I Know*, New York, 2006.
Berger, Peter L., *The Sacred Canopy: Elements of a Sociological Theory of Religion*, New York, 1967.
Berthelot, Jean Michel, "Réflexions sur les théories de la scolarisation," *Revue française de sociologie*, no. 4, 1982, pp. 585–604.
Berthelot, Katell, *Philanthrôpia judaica. Le débat sur la "misanthropie" des lois juives dans l'antiquité*, Leiden, 2003.
Birnbaum, Pierre, Charles Barucq, Michel Bellaïche, and Alain Marié, *La classe dirigeante française. Dissociation, interpénétration, intégration*, Paris, 1978.
Bligh, Alexander, *From Prince to King: Royal Succession in the House of Saud in the Twentieth Century*, New York, 1984.
——, "The Saudi Religious Elite (Ulama) as Participant in the Political System," *International Journal of Middle East Studies*, no. 17, 1985, pp. 37–50.
Blondel, Maurice, *Histoire et dogme: les lacunes philosophiques de l'exégèse moderne*, La Chapelle-Montligeon, 1904.
Bonner, Michael, *Le Jihad. Origines, interprétations et combats*, Paris, 2004.
Boudon, Raymond, *L'inégalité des chances. La mobilité sociale dans les sociétés industrielles*, Paris, 1973.
Bourdieu, Pierre, *La distinction*, Paris, 1979.
——, *Langage et pouvoir symbolique*, Paris, 2001.
——, *Le sens pratique*, Paris, 1980.
——, "L'illusion biographique," *Actes de la recherche en sciences sociales*, no. 62–63, 1986, pp. 69–72.
——, *Questions de sociologie*, Paris, 1980.
Bourdieu, Pierre, and Jean-Claude Passeron, *La reproduction. Éléments pour une théorie du système d'enseignement*, Paris, 1970.
——, *Les héritiers: les étudiants et la culture*, Paris, 1964.
Braud, Philippe, *L'émotion en politique: problèmes d'analyse*, Paris, 1996.
——, *Penser l'état*, Paris, 2004.
——, *Petit traité des émotions, sentiments et passions politiques*, Paris, 2007.
Briquet, Jean-Louis, and Frédéric Sawicki, eds., *Le clientélisme politique dans les sociétés contemporaines*, Paris, 1998.
Bronson, Rachel, *Thicker than Oil: America's Uneasy Partnership with Saudi Arabia*, Oxford, 2006.
Buckley, R. P., "The Muhtasib," *Arabica*, vol. 39, 1992, pp. 59–117.
Buʿjila, Najiyya al-Warimi, *Al-islam al-khariji*, Beirut, 2006.
Burke, Jason, *Al-Qaeda: Casting a Shadow of Terror*, London, 2003.

Busino, Giovanni, *Élites et bureaucratie. Une analyse critique des théories contemporaines*, Geneva, 1988.
——, *Élites et élitisme*, Paris, 1992.
Carré, Olivier, *L'utopie islamique dans l'orient arabe*, Paris, 1991.
——, *Mystique et politique: lecture révolutionnaire du Coran par Sayyid Qutb, frère musulman radical*, Paris, 1984.
Carré, Olivier, and Gérard Michaud, *Les frères musulmans: Égypte et Syrie (1928–1982)*, Paris, 1983.
Champion, Daryl, *The Paradoxical Kingdom: Saudi Arabia and the Momentum of Reform*, London, 2003.
Chenu, M. D., *Introduction à l'étude de Saint Thomas d'Aquin*, Paris, 1950.
Collectif (multiple editors/contributors), *Tadayyun al-su'udiyyin*, Riyadh, 2009.
Commins, David, *Islamic Reform: Politics and Social Change in Late Ottoman Syria*, Oxford, 1990.
——, *The Wahhabi Mission and Saudi Arabia*, London, 2006.
Cook, David, *Contemporary Muslim Apocalyptic Literature*, Syracuse, NY, 2005.
——, *Understanding Jihad*, Berkeley, 2005.
Cook, Michael, *Commanding Right and Forbidding Wrong in Islamic Thought*, Cambridge, 2001.
——, "On the Origins of Wahhabism," *Journal of the Royal Asiatic Society*, vol. 2, 1992, pp. 191–202.
Cooperson, Michael, "Ibn Hanbal and Bishr al-Hafi: A Case Study in Biographical Traditions," *Studia Islamica*, no. 86, 1997, pp. 71–101.
Cordesman, Anthony H., *Saudi Arabia Enters the Twenty-First Century: The Political, Foreign Policy, Economic, and Energy Dimensions*, Westport, CT, 2003.
——, *Saudi Arabia: Guarding the Desert Kingdom*, Boulder, CO, 1997.
Cordesman, Anthony H., and Nawaf E. Obaid, "Al-Qaeda in Saudi Arabia: Asymmetric Threats and Islamic Extremists," Washington, DC, 2005.
——, *National Security in Saudi Arabia: Threats, Responses, and Challenges*, Washington, DC, 2005.
Coulson, Noel, *A History of Islamic Law*, Edinburgh, 1960.
Crawford, Michael, "Civil War, Foreign Intervention and the Question of Political Legitimacy: A Nineteenth-Century Sa'udi Qadi's Dilemma," *International Journal of Middle East Studies*, no. 14, 1982, pp. 227–248.
Crone, Patricia, and Martin Hinds, *God's Caliph: Religious Authority in the First Centuries of Islam*, Cambridge, 1986.
Cruz Hernandez, Miguel, *Histoire de la pensée en terre d'islam*, Paris, 2005.
Dabashi, Hamid, *Authority in Islam: From the Rise of Muhammad to the Establishment of the Umayyads*, New Brunswick, 1989.
Dahl, Robert A., *Polyarchy: Participation and Opposition*, New Haven, CT, 1971.
Dallal, Ahmad, "The Origins and Objectives of Islamic Revivalist Thought, 1750–1850," *Journal of the American Oriental Society*, vol. 113, no. 3, 1993, pp. 341–359.
Dazi-Heni, Fatiha, *Monarchies et sociétés d'Arabie: le temps de la confrontation*, Paris, 2006.

Bibliography

Décobert, Christian, "L'autorité religieuse aux premiers siècles de l'islam," *Archives des sciences sociales des religions*, no. 125, 2004, pp. 23–44.

———, *Le mendiant et le combattant. L'institution de l'islam*, Paris, 1991.

Dekmejian, Hrair, "The Liberal Impulse in Saudi Arabia," *Middle East Journal*, no. 3, 2003, pp. 400–413.

———, "The Rise of Political Islamism in Saudi Arabia," *Middle East Journal*, no. 4, 1994, pp. 627–643.

———, "Saudi Arabia's Consultative Council," *Middle East Journal*, no. 2, 1998, pp. 204–218.

Delong-Bas, Natana, *Wahhabi Islam: From Revival and Reform to Global Jihad*, Oxford, 2004.

Derenbourg, Joseph, *Essai sur l'histoire et la géographie de la Palestine d'après le Thalmuds et les autres sources rabbiniques*, Paris, 1867.

Djaït, Hichem, *La grande discorde: Religion et politique dans l'islam des origines*, Paris, 1989.

———, *La vie de Muhammad: la prédication prophétique à la Mecque*, Paris, 2008.

Douglas, Mary, *In the Wilderness: The Doctrine of Defilement in the Book of Numbers*, Oxford, 2001.

Doumato, Eleanor A., "Gender, Monarchy and National Identity in Saudi Arabia," *British Journal of Middle Eastern Studies*, no. 1, 1992, pp. 31–47.

Dov Goitein, Shelomo, "A Turning Point in the History of the Islamic State," *Islamic Culture*, no. 23, 1949, pp. 120–135.

Dresch, Paul, and James Piscatori, eds., *Monarchies and Nations: Globalization and Identity in the Arab States of the Gulf*, London, 2005.

Dubayyib, Ahmad Muhammad al-, "Harakat Ihya' al-thurath qabla tawhid al-jazira," *al-Dara*, no. 1, 1975, pp. 42–61.

Dubuisson, Daniel, "Le roi indo-européen et la synthèse des trois fonctions," *Annales ESC*, no. 33, 1978, pp. 21–34.

Dumézil, Georges, *Mythe et épopée*, Paris, 1986.

Durkheim, Émile, *Les formes élémentaires de la vie religieuse: le système totémique en Australie*, Paris, 1960.

Duru-Bellat, Marie, *L'inflation scolaire. Les désillusions de la méritocratie*, Paris, 2006.

Dutton, Yasin, *Origins of Islamic Law: The Qur'an, the Muwatta' and Madinan 'Amal*, New York, 1999.

Easton, David, *Analyse du système politique*, Paris, 1974 (English: A Systems Analysis of Political Life, New York, 1965).

Eickelman, Dale, and James P. Piscatori, eds., *Muslim Politics*, Princeton, NJ, 2004.

Eisenstadt, Shmuel N., *Traditional Patrimonialism and Modern Neopatrimonialism*, Beverly Hills, CA, 1973.

Encyclopaedia of the Qur'an, Leiden, 2001–2006.

Encyclopédie de l'islam, 2nd ed., Leiden, 1960–2007.

Ende, Werner, "The Nakhawila: A Shiite Community in Median Past and Present," *Die Welt des Islams*, no. 3, 1997, pp. 263–348.

Esposito, John L., ed., *Political Islam: Revolution, Radicalism or Reform?*, Boulder, CO, 1997.

Ess, Joseph van, *Une Lecture à rebours de l'histoire du mu'tazilisme*, Paris, 1984.

Fahad, Abdulaziz al-, "From Exclusivism to Accommodation: Doctrinal and Legal Evolution of Wahhabism," *New York University Law Review*, no. 2, 2004, pp. 485–519.

——, "The 'Imama vs. the 'Iqal: Hadari Bedouin Conflict and the Formation of the Saudi State," Madawi Al-Rasheed and Robert Vitalis, eds., *Counter-Narratives: History, Contemporary Society, and Politics in Saudi Arabia and Yemen*, New York, 2004, pp. 35–75.

Fandy, Mamoun, *Saudi Arabia and The Politics of Dissent*, Basingstoke, 1999.

Filiu, Jean-Pierre, *L'Apocalypse dans l'islam*, Paris, 2008.

——, *Les frontières du jihad*, Paris, 2006.

——, *Les neuf vies d'al-Qaida*, Paris, 2009.

Floor, Willem, "The Office of Muhtasib in Iran," *Iranian Studies*, no. 1, 1985, pp. 53–74.

Fons, Emmanuel, "À propos des Mongols: une lettre d'Ibn Taymiyya au sultan al-Malik al-Nasir Muhammad b. Qalawun," *Annales islamologiques*, no. 43, 2010, pp. 31–73.

Foster, Benjamin R., "Agoranomos and Muhtasib," *Journal of the Economic and Social History of the Orient*, no. 2, 1970, pp. 128–144.

Garcia-Arenal, Mercedes, *Messianism and Puritanical Reform: Mahdis of the Muslim West*, Leiden, 2006.

Gardet, Louis, *La cité musulmane, vie sociale et politique*, Paris, 1976.

Gaudefroy-Demombynes, Maurice, *Le pèlerinage à la Mekke: une étude d'histoire religieuse*, Paris, 1923.

Gaury, Gerald de, *Faisal, King of Saudi Arabia*, London, 1966.

Gause, Gregory, III, *Oil Monarchies: Domestic and Security Challenges in the Arab Gulf States*, New York, 1994.

——, "The Persistence of Monarchy in the Arabian Peninsula: A Comparative Analysis," in Joseph Kostiner, ed., *Middle East Monarchies: The Challenge of Modernity*, Boulder, CO, 2000, pp. 167–186.

Goldberg, Jacob, "The 1914 Saudi-Ottoman Treaty: Myth or Reality?," *Journal of Contemporary History*, vol. 19, 1984, pp. 289–314.

Goldziher, Ignace, "Du sens propre 'd'ombre de Dieu et de khalife de Dieu' pour désigner les chefs dans l'islam," in *Sur l'islam. Origines de la théologie musulmane*, Paris, 2003, pp. 279–287.

——, *Études sur la tradition islamique*, Paris, 1952.

Green, Arnold, "A Tunisian Reply to a Wahhabi Declaration: Texts and Contexts," in Arnold Green, ed., *In Quest of an Islamic Humanism*, Cairo, 1984, pp. 155–177.

Habermas, Jürgen, *The Structural Transformation of the Public Sphere: An Inquiry into a Category of Bourgeois Society*, Cambridge, MA, 1991.

Habib, John S., *Ibn Sa'ud's Warriors of Islam: The Ikhwan of Najd and Their Role in the Creation of the Sa'udi Kingdom, 1910–1930*, Leiden, 1978.

Hajji, Lutfi, *Burqiba wa al-islam: al-za'ama wa al-imama*, Tunis, 2004.

Hallaq, Wael Ben, *The Origins and Evolutions of Islamic Law*, Cambridge, 2005.

Bibliography

Hamadi, Amor ben, "Autour du hadith relatif à la division de la communauté en plus de 70 sectes," *Cahiers de Tunisie*, no. 115–116, 1981, pp. 287–358.

Hamdi, Sidqi, "The Pro-alid Policy of Ma'mun," *Bulletin of the College of Arts and Science (Baghdad)*, no. 1, 1956, pp. 96–105.

Hawting, Gerald, *The First Dynasty of Islam: The Umayyad Caliphate, AD 661–750*, London, 2000.

Haykel, Bernard, *Revival and Reform in Islam: The Legacy of Muhammad al-Shawkani*, Cambridge, 2003.

Hegghammer, Thomas, *Jihad in Saudi Arabia: Violence and Pan-Islamism since 1979*, Cambridge, 2010.

———, "Violence politique en Arabie Saoudite: grandeur et décadence d' 'Al-Qaida dans la péninsule arabique,'" in Bernard Rougier, ed., *Qu'est-ce que le salafisme?*, Paris, 2008, p. 105–121.

Hegghammer, Thomas, and Stéphane, Lacroix, "Rejectionist Islamism in Saudi Arabia: The Story of Juhayman al-'Utaybi Revisited," *International Journal of Middle East Studies*, no. 37, 2007, pp. 103–122.

Helms, Christine Moss, *The Cohesion of Saudi Arabia*, London, 1981.

Herb, Michael, *All in the Family: Absolutism, Revolution and Democracy in the Middle Eastern Monarchies*, New York, 1999.

Hertog, Steffen, *Princes, Brokers, and Bureaucrats: Oil and the State in Saudi Arabia*, Ithaca, NY, 2010.

Hobsbawm, Eric, and Terence Ranger, *The Invention of Tradition*, Cambridge, 1983.

Hoexter, Miriam, Shmuel N. Eisenstadt, and Nehemia Levtzion, eds., *The Public Sphere in Muslim Societies*, Albany, NY, 2002.

Holden, David, and Richard Johns, *The House of Saud*, New York, 1982 (French: *La Maison des Saoud*, Paris, 1982).

Hudson, Michael, *Arab Politics: The Search for Legitimacy*, New Haven, CT, 1977.

Humaydan, Abd al-Latif al-, "al-Tarikh al-siyasi li-imarat al-jubur fi Najd wa sharq al-jazira al-'arabiyya," *Majallat Kulliyyat al-Adab, jami'at al-Basra*, no. 16, 1979, pp. 31–109.

———, "Imarat al-'usfuriyyin wa dawruha al-siyasi fi tarikh sharq al-jazira al-'arabiyya," *Majallat Kulliyyat al-Adab, jami'at al-Basra*, no. 15, 1979, pp. 69–140.

Huntington, Samuel, *The Clash of Civilizations and the Remaking of World Order*, New York, 1996.

Hurvitz, Nimrod, *The Formation of Hanbalism: Piety into Power*, London, 2002.

———, "The Mihna and the Public Space," in Shmuel Eisenstadt, ed., *The Public Sphere in Muslim Societies*, Albany, NY, 2012, pp. 17–30.

Ibrahim, Abd al-Aziz, *Najdiyyun wara' al-hudud*, Beirut, 1991.

Ibrahim, Fouad, *The Shi'is of Saudi Arabia*, London, 2007.

Isa, Mayy al-, *al-Hayat al-'ilmiyya fi Najd mundh qiyam al-shaykh Muhammad b. 'Abd al-Wahhab hatta suqut al-dawla al-su'udiyya al-ula*, Riyadh, 1996.

Islahi, Abdul Azim, *Economic Concepts of Ibn Taimiyah*, Leicester, 1988.

Jokisch, Benjamin, *Islamic Imperial Law: Harun-Al-Rashid's Codification Project*, Berlin, 2007.

Jomier, Jacques, *Le mahmal et la caravane égyptienne des pèlerins de La Mecque, XIII*ᵉ*–XX*ᵉ *siècles*, Cairo, 1953.

Jones, Toby Craig, "Rebellion on the Saudi Periphery: Modernity, Marginalization, and the Shi'a Uprising of 1979," *International Journal of Middle East Studies*, no. 2, 2006, pp. 213–233.

Juhany, Uwaidah al-, "Dawr 'ulama' ushayqir fi intishar al-haraka al-'ilmiyya fi Najd wa zuhur al-da'wa al-islahiyya al-salafiyya fi al-'Arid," *Majallat al-'usur*, vol. 8, no. 2, 1993, pp. 397–429.

———, *Najd before the Salafi Reform: Social, Religious, and Political Conditions during the Three Centuries Preceding the Rise of the Saudi State*, Ithaca, NY, 2002.

Jundi, Mujahid Tawfiq al-, "Hay'at kibar al-'ulama', safahatun matwiyya min tarikh al-Azhar," *al-Azhar*, vol. 11, 1983, pp. 1621–1633.

Juynboll, G. H. A., *Muslim Tradition*, Cambridge 1983.

———, "Some Notes on Islam's First Fuqaha' Distilled from Early Hadith Literature," *Arabica*, vol. 39, 1992, pp. 287–314.

Kechichian, Joseph A., "Islamic Revivalism and Change in Saudi Arabia: Juhayman al-Utaybi's 'Letters' to the Saudi People," *Muslim World*, no. 1, 1990, pp. 1–16.

———, "The Role of the Ulama in the Politics of an Islamic State: The Case of Saudi Arabia," *International Journal of Middle East Studies*, no. 1, pp. 53–71.

Kennedy, Hugh, *The Early 'Abbassid Caliphate: A Political History*, London, 1981.

Kepel, Gilles, *Fitna: guerre au cœur de l'islam*, Paris, 2004.

———, *Jihad: expansion et déclin de l'islamisme*, Paris, 2003.

———, *Le Prophète et le Pharaon*, Paris, 1993.

———, "Les oulémas, l'intelligentsia et les islamistes en Egypte," *Revue Française de Science Politique*, no. 3, 1985, pp. 424–445.

Kepel, Gilles, and Jean-Pierre Milelli, eds., *Al-Qaïda dans le texte*, Paris, 2005.

Khaz'al, Husayn, *Hayat al-shaykh Muhammad b. 'Abd al-Wahhab*, Beirut, 1968.

Kishk, Muhammad Jalal, *al-Su'udiyyun wa al-hall al-islami*, West Hanover, 1982.

Knysh, Alexander, *Islamic Mysticism: A Short History*, Leiden, 2000.

Kohlberg, Etan, "Bara'a in Shi'i Doctrine," *Jerusalem Studies in Arabic and Islam*, vol. 7, 1986, pp. 139–175.

———, "Some Imami Shi'i Views on the Companions of the Prophet," *Jerusalem Studies in Arabic and Islam*, vol. 5, 1994, pp. 145–175.

———, "Some Zaydi Views on the Companions of the Prophet," *Bulletin of the School of Oriental and African Studies*, no. 1, 1976, pp. 91–98.

Kostiner, Joseph, *The Making of Saudi Arabia: 1916–1936*, New York, 1993.

———, "State, Islam and Opposition in Saudi Arabia: The Post–Desert Storm Phase," *Terrorism and Political Violence*, no. 2, 1996, pp. 75–89.

———, "Transforming Dualities: Tribe and State Formation in Saudi Arabia," in Joseph Kostiner and Philip S. Khoury, eds., *Tribes and State Formation in the Middle East*, London, 1991, pp. 226–251.

Kostiner, Joseph, and Joshua Teitelbaum, *State-Formation and the Saudi Monarchy*, in Joseph Kostiner, ed., *Middle East Monarchies: The Challenge of Modernity*, Boulder, CO, 2000, pp. 131–150.

Kramer, Martin, *Islam Assembled: The Advent of Muslim Congresses*, New York, 1986.
Kursun, Zakariyya, *al-'Uthmaniyyun wa Al Su'ud fi al-arshif al-'uthmani*, Beirut, 2005.
Lacey, Robert, *The Kingdom: Arabia and the House of Saud*, New York, 1981.
Lackner, Helen, *A House Built on Sand: A Political Economy of Saudi Arabia*, London, 1978.
Lacroix, Stéphane, "Between Islamists and Liberals: Saudi Arabia's New Islamo-Liberal Reformists," *Middle East Journal*, no. 3, 2004, pp. 345–365.
——, "Between Revolution and Apoliticism: Nasir al-Din al-Albani and His Impact on the Shaping of Contemporary Salafism," in Roel Meijer, ed., *Global Salafism: Islam's New Religious Movement*, London, 2009, pp. 58–80.
——, "L'apport de Nasir al-Din al-albani au salafisme contemporain," in Bernard Rougier, ed., *Qu'est-ce que le salafisme*, Paris, 2008, pp. 45–64.
——, *Les Islamistes saoudiens: une insurrection manquée*, Paris, 2010.
Lajna al-'ulya lil-ihtifal bi al-'id al-alfi lil-Azhar, al-, *Majama' al-buhuth al-islamiyya Tarikhuhu wa tatawwuruhu*, Cairo, 1983.
Lambton, Ann, *State and Government in Medieval Islam*, Oxford, 1981.
Landau-Tasseron, Ella, "The 'Cyclical Reform': A Study of the Mujaddid Tradition," *Studia Islamica*, no. 70, 1989, pp. 79–117.
Laoust, Henri, *Essai sur les doctrines sociales et politiques de Taki-d-din Ahmad b. Taymiya*, Cairo, 1939.
——, "Le hanbalisme sous le califat de Bagdad," *Revue des Études Islamiques*, vol. 27, 1959, pp. 67–128.
——, "Le hanbalisme sous les Mamlouks Bahrides," *Revue des Études Islamiques*, vol. 27, 1960, pp. 1–71.
——, "Le réformisme orthodoxe des 'salafiyya' et les caractères généraux de son orientation actuelle," *Pluralismes dans l'Islam*, Paris, 1983.
——, "Les premières professions de foi hanbalites," in *Mélanges Louis Massignon*, Damascus, 1957, pp. 7–35.
——, *Le traité de droit public d'Ibn Taimiya* (annotated translation of *Siyasa al-shar'iyya*), Damas, 1950.
——, "L'influence d'Ibn Taimiyya," in Alford T. Welch and Pierre Cachia, eds., *Islam: Past Influence and Present Challenge*, Albany, 1979, pp. 15–33.
Layish, Aharon, "Saudi Arabian Legal Reform as a Mechanism to Moderate Wahhabi Doctrine," *Journal of the American Oriental Society*, no. 2, 1987, pp. 279–292.
Leca, Jean, "À propos de l'état: la leçon des 'États non-occidentaux,'" in *Études dédiées à Madeleine Grawitz: liber amicorum*, Paris, 1982, pp. 201–225.
Leca, Jean, and Madeleine Grawitz, eds., *Traité de science politique*, Paris, 1985.
Leca, Jean, and Yves Schemeil, "Clientélisme et patrimonialisme dans le monde arabe," *International Political Science Review*, no. 4, 1983, pp. 455–494.
Le Goff, Jacques, "Les trois fonctions indo-européennes, l'historien et l'Europe féodale," *Annales ESC*, no. 34, 1979, pp. 1187–1215.
Leroi-Gourhan, André, *Évolution et technique I: Homme et matière*, Paris, 1943.
Lévi-Strauss, Claude, *Paroles données*, Paris, 1984.

Little, Donald P., "Did Ibn Taymiyya Have a Screw Loose?," *Studia Islamica*, vol. 41, 1975, pp. 93–111.

———, "The Historical and Historiographical Significance of the Detention of Ibn Taymiyya," *International Journal of Middle East Studies*, vol. 4, 1973, pp. 311–327.

Lucas, Scott C., *Constructive Critics, Hadith Literature, and the Articulation of Sunni Islam*, Leiden, 2004.

Madeleine Grawitz: liber amicorum, Paris, 1982, pp. 201–225.

Madelung, Wilferd, "The Origins of the Controversy Concerning the Creation of the Koran," in J. M. Barral, ed., *Orientalia hispanica*, Leiden, 1974, pp. 504–525.

———, *The Succession to Muhammad*, Cambridge, 1997.

———, "The Sufyani between Tradition and History," *Studia Islamica*, no. 63, 1986, pp. 5–48.

Makdisi, George, "Ash'ari and Ash'arites in Islamic Religious History," *Studia Islamica*, nos. 17 and 18, 1962 and 1963, pp. 37–80 and 19–39.

———, "The Hanbali School and Sufism," *Actes du 4ᵉ congrès d'études arabes et islamiques*, Leiden, 1974, pp. 61–72.

———, *Ibn 'Aqil et la résurgence de l'islam traditionaliste au XIᵉ siècle*, Damascus, 1963.

———, "Ibn Taimiya: A Sufi of the Qadiriya Order," *American Journal of Arabic Studies*, no. 1, 1973, pp. 118–129.

———, "Law and Traditionalism in the Institutions of Learning of Medieval Islam," in G. E. von Grunebaum, ed., *Theology and Law in Islam*, Wiesbaden, 1971, pp. 79–80.

———, "L'isnad initiatique soufi de Muwaffaq al-din Ibn Qudama," in Jean-Francois, ed., *Louis Massignon*, Paris, 1970, pp. 88–99.

Mansur, Muhammad al-, *al-Maghrib qabl al-isti'mar: al-mujtama' wa al-dawla wa al-din (1792–1822)*, Casablanca, 2006.

Margoliouth, David Samuel, "On Mahdis and Mahdiism," *Proceedings of the British Academy*, 1915–1916, pp. 213–223.

Mark, J. R., "Saudis Sufis: Compromise in the Hijaz, 1925–1940," *Die Welt des Islams*, no. 3, 1997, pp. 349–368.

Marx, Karl, *Le 18 brumaire de Louis Bonaparte*, Paris, 1984.

———, *Les luttes de classes en France, 1848–1850*, Paris, 1984.

Massignon, Louis, *Essai sur les origines du lexique technique de la mystique musulmane*, Paris, 1954.

Mat'ani, Abd al-Azim al-, "Majma' al-buhuth al-islamiyya wa al-maham al-manuta bihi," *Majallat al-da'wa*, no. 13, 1977, pp. 36–37.

Médard, Jean-François, "L'État néo-patrimonial en Afrique noire," in Jean-François Médard ed., *États d'Afrique noire: formation, mécanisme et crise*, Paris, 1991, pp. 323–353.

———, "L'État patrimonialisé," *Politique africaine*, vol. 39, September 1990, pp. 25–36.

Melchert, Christopher, *Ahmad ibn Hanbal*, Oxford, 2006.

———, *The Formation of the Sunni Schools of Law, 9th–10th Centuries C.E.*, Leiden, 1997.

Mérad, Ali, *Le réformisme musulman en Algérie*, Paris–La Haye, 1967.

Metcalf, Barbara D., *Islamic Revival in British India: Deoband, 1860–1900*, Princeton, NJ, 1982.

Migdal, Joel S., *Strong Societies and Weak States: State-Society Relations and State Capabilities in the Third World*, Princeton, NJ, 1988.
Molé, Marijan, *Les mystiques musulmans*, Paris, 1965.
Morabia, Alfred, *Le Gihad dans l'islam médiéval*, Paris, 1993.
Mosca, Gaetano, *The Ruling Class*, New York, 1939.
Motzki, Harald, *The Origins of Islamic Jurisprudence: Meccan Fiqh before the Classical Schools*, Leiden, 2002.
Mouline, Nabil, *Le Califat imaginaire d'Ahmad al-Mansur: pouvoir et diplomatie au Maroc au XVIe siècle*, Paris, 2009.
——, "Pouvoir et transition générationnelle en Arabie Saoudite," *Critique internationale*, no. 46, 2010, pp. 125–146.
Mourad, Suleiman Ali, *Early Islam between Myth and History: Al-Hasan al-Basri (d. 728) and the Formation of His Legacy in Classical Islamic Scholarship*, Leiden, 2006.
Mousnier, Roland, *Les XVIe et XVIIe siècles*, Paris, 1993.
Mubarak, Abd al-Aziz al-, "al-Wattha'iq al-shakhsiyya," *Majallat al-'arab*, no. 1, 1967, pp. 51–59.
Nadawi, Mas'ud al-, *Muhammad b. 'Abd al-Wahhab: muslih mazlum wa muftara 'alayh*, translated into Arabic by 'Abd al-'Alim al-Bustawi, Riyadh, 2000.
Naqib, Khaldun al-, *al-Mujtama' wa al-dawla fi al-khalij wa al-jazira al-'arabiyya*, Beirut, 1987.
Nawas, John A., "The Mihna of 218 A.H./833 A.D. Revisited: An Empirical Study Author," *Journal of the American Oriental Society*, no. 4, 1996, pp. 698–708.
——, "A Reexamination of Three Current Explanations for al- Ma'mun's Introduction of the Mihna," *International Journal of Middle East Studies*, no. 26, 1994, pp. 615–629.
Niblock, Tim, *Saudi Arabia: Power, Legitimacy and Survival*, London, 2006.
——, ed., *State, Society and Economy in Saudi Arabia*, London, 1981.
Nonneman, Gerd, and Paul Aarts, eds., *Saudi Arabia in the Balance: Political Economy, Society, Foreign Relations*, London, 2005.
Ochsenwald, William, "Saudi Arabia," in Shireen T. Hunter, ed., *The Politics of Islamic Revivalism: Diversity and Unity*, Bloomington, IN, 1988.
——, "Saudi Arabia and the Islamic Revival," *International Journal of Middle Eastern Studies*, no. 3, 1981, pp. 271–286.
Olesen, Niels Henrik, *Culte des saints et pèlerinages chez ibn Taymiyya*, Paris, 1991.
Owen, Roger, *State, Power and Politics in the Making of the Modern Middle East*, London, 1992.
Pareto, Vilfredo, *Traité de sociologie générale, Oeuvres complètes*, vol. 12, Geneva, 1968.
Patton, W. M., *Ahmed ibn Hanbal and the Mihna: A Biography of the Imam Including An Account of the Muhammadan Inquisition Called the Mihna*, Leiden, 1897.
Petitat, André, "Le paradigme de la reproduction et ses limites," *Revue européenne des sciences sociales*, no. 63, 1982, pp. 5–27.
Picard, Elizabeth, ed., *La politique dans le monde arabe*, Paris, 2006.
Popovic, Alexandre, and Gilles Veinstein, eds., *Les voies d'Allah. Les ordres mystiques dans le monde musulman des origines à aujourd'hui*, Paris, 1996.
Poulantzas, Nicos, *Pouvoir politique et classes sociales*, Paris, 1971.

Radcliffe-Brown, Alfred, *Structure and Function in Primitive Society*, Glencoe, IL, 1952.
Rasheed, Madawi al-, "Circles of Power: Royals and Society in Saudi Arabia," in Gerd Nonneman and Paul Aarts, eds., *Saudi Arabia in the Balance: Political Economy, Society, Foreign Relations*, London, 2005, pp. 185–213.
———, *Contesting the Saudi State: Islamic Voices from a New Generation*, London, 2007.
———, "Deux prédécesseurs saoudiens de Ben Laden," *Critique Internationale*, no. 17, 2002, pp. 35–43.
———, "Dynasties durables et dynasties non durables: les Rachid et les Sa'ud en Arabie centrale," *Monde Arabe Maghreb Machrek*, January–March 1996, no. 147, 1996, pp. 13–25.
———, "God, the King and the Nation: Political Rhetoric in Saudi Arabia in the 1990s," *Middle East Journal*, no. 3, 1996, pp. 360–371.
———, *A History of Saudi Arabia*, New York, 2002.
———, *Politics in an Arabian Oasis: The Rashidi Tribal Dynasty*, London, 1991.
———, "The Shi'a of Saudi Arabia: A Minority in Search of Cultural Authenticity," *British Journal of Middle Eastern Studies*, February 1998, no. 1, 1998, pp. 121–138.
———, ed., *Transnational Connections and the Arab Gulf*, London, 2005.
Rasheed, Madawi al-, and Robert Vitalis, eds., *Counter-Narratives: History, Contemporary Society, and Politics in Saudi Arabia and Yemen*, New York, 2004.
Riedel, Bruce, and Bilal Y. Saad, "Al Qaeda's Third Front: Saudi Arabia," *Washington Quarterly*, no. 2, 2008, pp. 33–46.
Rosenthal, Franz, *Knowledge Triumphant: The Concept of Knowledge in Medieval Islam*, Leiden, 1970.
Roy, Olivier, *L'échec de l'islam politique*, Paris, 1992.
———, *L'islam mondialisé*, Paris, 2002.
Rugh, William A., "Education in Saudi Arabia: Choices and Constraints," *Middle East Policy*, no. 2, 2002, pp. 40–55.
———, "Emergence of a New Middle Class in Saudi Arabia," *Middle East Journal*, no. 1, 1973, pp. 7–20.
Sachedina, Abdulaziz Abdulhussein, *Islamic Messianism: The Idea of the* Mahdi *in Twelver Shi'ism*, Albany, NY, 1981.
Sa'idi, Abd al-Muta'al al-, "Ra'yun fi al-shart al-rabi' fi 'udw hay'at kibar al-'ulama'," *al-Risala*, no. 635, 1945, pp. 2–3.
Salamé, Ghassan, *al-Siyasa al-kharijiyya lil-mamlaka al-'arabiyya al-Su'udiyya mundhu 1945*, Beirut, 1980.
———, "Islam and Politics in Saudi Arabia," *Arab Studies Quarterly*, no. 3, 1987, pp. 306–325.
———, "Political Power and the Saudi State," *MERIP Reports*, October 1980, pp. 5–22.
———, ed., *Démocraties sans démocrates: politiques d'ouverture dans le monde arabe et islamique*, Paris, 1994.
———, ed., *The Foundations of the Arab State*, London, 1987.
Satow, Roberta Lynn, "Value-Rational Authority and Professional Organizations: Weber Missing Type," *Administrative Science Quarterly*, vol. 20, 1975, pp. 526–531.

Schacht, Joseph, *Introduction au droit musulman*, Paris, 1999.
Schimmel, Anne Marie, *Le Soufisme ou les dimensions mystiques de l'islam*, Paris, 1997.
Schmitter, Philippe, "Still the Century of Corporatism?," *Review of Politics*, no. 1, 1974, pp. 85–131.
Schulze, Reinhard, *Islamischer Internationalismus im 20, Jahrhundert: Untersuchungen zur Geschichte der Islamischen Weltliga*, Leiden, 1990.
——, "La da'wa saoudienne en Afrique de l'Ouest," in René Otayek, ed., *Le Radicalisme islamique en Afrique subsaharienne, da'wa, arabisation et critique de l'Occident*, Paris, 1993, pp. 25–38.
——, *A Modern History of the Islamic World*, New York, 2002.
Sékaly, Achille, *Le congrès du khalifat et le congrès du monde musulman*, Paris, 1926.
Shaban, M. A., *Islamic History: A New Interpretation*, Cambridge, 1978.
Sirriyeh, Elizabeth, "Wahhabis, Unbelievers and the Problems of Exclusivism," *British Society for Middle Eastern Studies Bulletin*, no. 2, 1989, pp. 123–132.
Sourdel, Dominique, "La politique religieuse du calife 'abbaside al-Ma'mun," *Revue des études islamiques*, no. 33, 1962, pp. 26–48.
——, *L'État impérial des califes Abbassides*, Paris, 1999.
Steinberg, Guido, "Ecology, Knowledge and Trade in Central Arabia during the 19th and Early 20th Centuries," in Madawi Al-Rasheed and Robert Vitalis, eds., *Counter-Narratives: History, Contemporary Society, and Politics in Saudi Arabia and Yemen*, pp. 77–102.
——, "Material Conditions, Knowledge and Trade in Central Arabia during the 19th and Early 20th Century," presentation at the Second Mediterranean Social and Political Research Meeting in Montecatini Terme, Italy, 21–25 March 2001, available at http://cadmus.iue.it/dspace/bitstream/1814/1774/1/02_16.pdf.
——, "The Shiites in the Eastern Province of Saudi Arabia (al-Ahsa'), 1913–1953," in Rainer Brunner and Werner Ende, eds., *The Twelver Shia in Modern Times: Religious Culture and Political History*, Leiden, 2002, pp. 245–254.
——, "The Wahhabi Ulama and the Saudi State: 1745 to the Present," in Gerd Nonneman and Paul Aarts, eds., *Saudi Arabia in the Balance: Political Economy, Society, Foreign Relations*, London, 2005, pp. 11–34.
Suleiman, Ezra N., *Les élites en France*, Paris, 1979.
——, *Les hauts fonctionnaires et la politique*, Paris, 1976.
Suwayda, Abd al-Rahman b. Zayd al-, *al-Alf sana al-ghamida min tarikh Najd*, Riyadh, 1988.
Swartz, Merlin, "The Rules of Popular Preaching in 12th Century Baghdad, according to Ibn Jawzi," in George Makdisi, ed., *Prédication et propagande au Moyen Age: Islam, Byzance et Occident*, Paris, 1983, pp. 223–240.
Teitelbaum, Joshua, *Holier Than Thou: Saudi Arabia's Islamic Opposition*, Washington, DC, 2000.
——, *The Rise and Fall of the Hashimite Kingdom of Arabia*, London, 2001.
Thomas, Dominique, *Les Hommes d'al-Qaïda: discours et stratégies*, Paris, 2005.
Touati, Houari, *Islam et voyage au Moyen Age*, Paris, 2000.

Tozy, Mohammed, *Monarchie et islam politique au Maroc*, Paris, 1999.
Troeller, Gary, *The Birth of Saudi Arabia: Britain and the Rise of the House of Saʻud*, London, 1976.
Trofimov, Yaroslav, *The Siege of Mecca*, New York, 2007.
Tyan, Émile, *Histoire de l'organisation judiciaire en pays d'islam*, Leiden, 1960.
Umari, Salih al-Sulayman al-, *'ulama' Al Silim wa talamidhatuhum wa 'ulama' al-qasim*, Riyadh, 1985.
Urvoy, Dominique, *Histoire de la pensée arabe et islamique*, Paris, 2006.
Usaylan, Abd Allah, "'Inayat al-malik 'Abd al-'Aziz bi al-kutub ittilaʻan wa nashran," *al-Daʻwa fi 'ahd al-malik 'Abd al-'Aziz*, available at http://www.al-islam.com/arb/NawaInfo.asp?f=nadwa.htm.
Uthaymin, Abd Allah al-, *Muhammad ibn 'Abd al-Wahhab: The Man and His Works*, London, 2009.
——, *Nash'at imarat al Rashid*, Riyadh, 1991.
Vassiliev, Alexei, *The History of Saudi Arabia*, London, 2000.
Veyne, Paul, *Quand notre monde est devenu chrétien*, Paris, 2007.
Vincent, Gilbert, et al., *Les nouveaux clercs, prêtres, pasteurs et spécialistes des relations humaines*, Geneva, 1985.
Vitalis, Robert, *America's Kingdom: Mythmaking on the Saudi Oil Frontier*, Stanford, CA, 2007.
——, "Black Gold, White Gold: An Essay on American Exceptionalism, Hierarchy and Hegemony in the Gulf," *Diplomatic History*, no. 2, 2002, pp. 185–213.
Vogel, Frank E., *Islamic Law and Legal System: Studies of Saudi Arabia*, Leiden, 2000.
——, "The Public and Private in Saudi Arabia: Restrictions on the Powers of Committees for Ordering the Good and Forbidding the Evil," *Social Research*, no. 2, 2003, pp. 749–768.
Voll, John, "Muhammad Hayya al-Sindi and Muhammad ibn 'Abd al-Wahhab: An Analysis of an Intellectual Group in Eighteenth-Century Madina," *Bulletin of the School of Oriental and African Studies, University of London*, vol. 38, no. 1, 1975, pp. 32–39.
Wagemakers, Joas, "The Transformation of a Radical Concept: al-wala' wa al-bara' in the Ideology of Abu Muhammad al-Maqdisi," in Roel Meijer, ed., *Global Salafism: Islam's New Religious Movement*, London, 2009, pp. 81–106.
Weber, Max, *Économie et société*, Paris, 1995 (English: *Economy and Society*, Berkeley, 1978).
——, *Le savant et le politique*, Paris, 1963.
——, *Sociologie des religions*, Paris, 1995.
Weismann, Itzchak, "The Naqshbandiyya-khalidiyya and Salafi Challenge in Iraq," *Journal of the History of Sufism*, vol. 4, 2004, pp. 229–240.
——, *Taste of Modernity: Sufism, Salafiya, and Arabism in Late Ottoman Damascus*, Leiden, 2001.
Willer, David E., "Max Weber's Missing Authority Type," *Sociological Inquiry*, vol. 37, 1967, pp. 231–239.
Wright, C. W., *L'élite du pouvoir*, Paris, 1969.

Wuhbi, 'Abd al-Karim al-, *Banu Khalid wa 'alaqatuhum bi Najd (1669–1794)*, Riyadh, 1989.

Yamani, Mai, *Changed Identities: The Challenge of the New Generation in Saudi Arabia*, London, 2000.

——, *Cradle of Islam: The Hijaz and the Quest for an Arabian Identity*, London, 2004.

Yassini, Ayman al-, *Religion and State in the Kingdom of Saudi Arabia*, Boulder, CO, 1985.

Yizraeli, Sarah, *The Remaking of Saudi Arabia: The Struggle between King Sa'ud and Crown Prince Faysal, 1953–1962*, Tel Aviv, 1997.

Zaman, Muhammad Qasim, "The Caliphs, the 'ulama', and the Law: Defining the Role and Functions of the Caliph in the Early 'Abbassid Period," *Islamic Law and Society*, no. 1, 1997, pp. 1–36.

——, *Religion and Politics under the Early Abbasids: The Emergence of the Proto-Sunni Elite*, Leiden, 1997.

Zaydi, Mufid al-, *al-Tayyarat al-fikriyya fi al-khalij al-'arabi 1938–1971*, Beirut, 2000.

Zeghal, Malika, *Gardiens de l'islam: les oulémas d'al-Azhar dans l'Egypte contemporaine*, Paris, 1996.

Zubaida, Sami, *Islam, the People and the State: Essays on Political Ideas and Movements in the Middle East*, London, 1993.